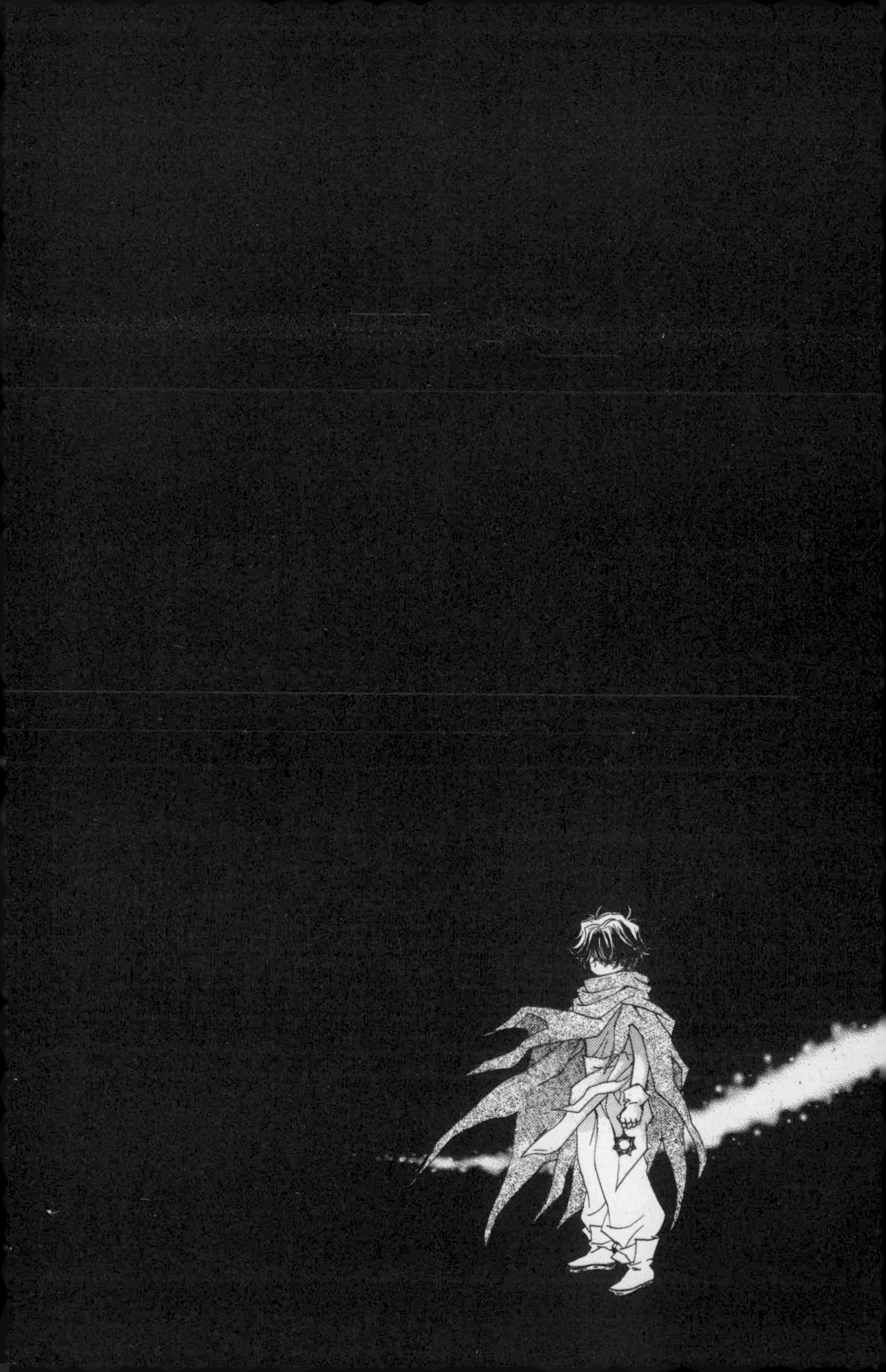

Shojo Beat

Märchen ✦ Prince

Volume 1

Story & Art by Matsuri Hino

Contents

MeruPuri: Märchen Prince

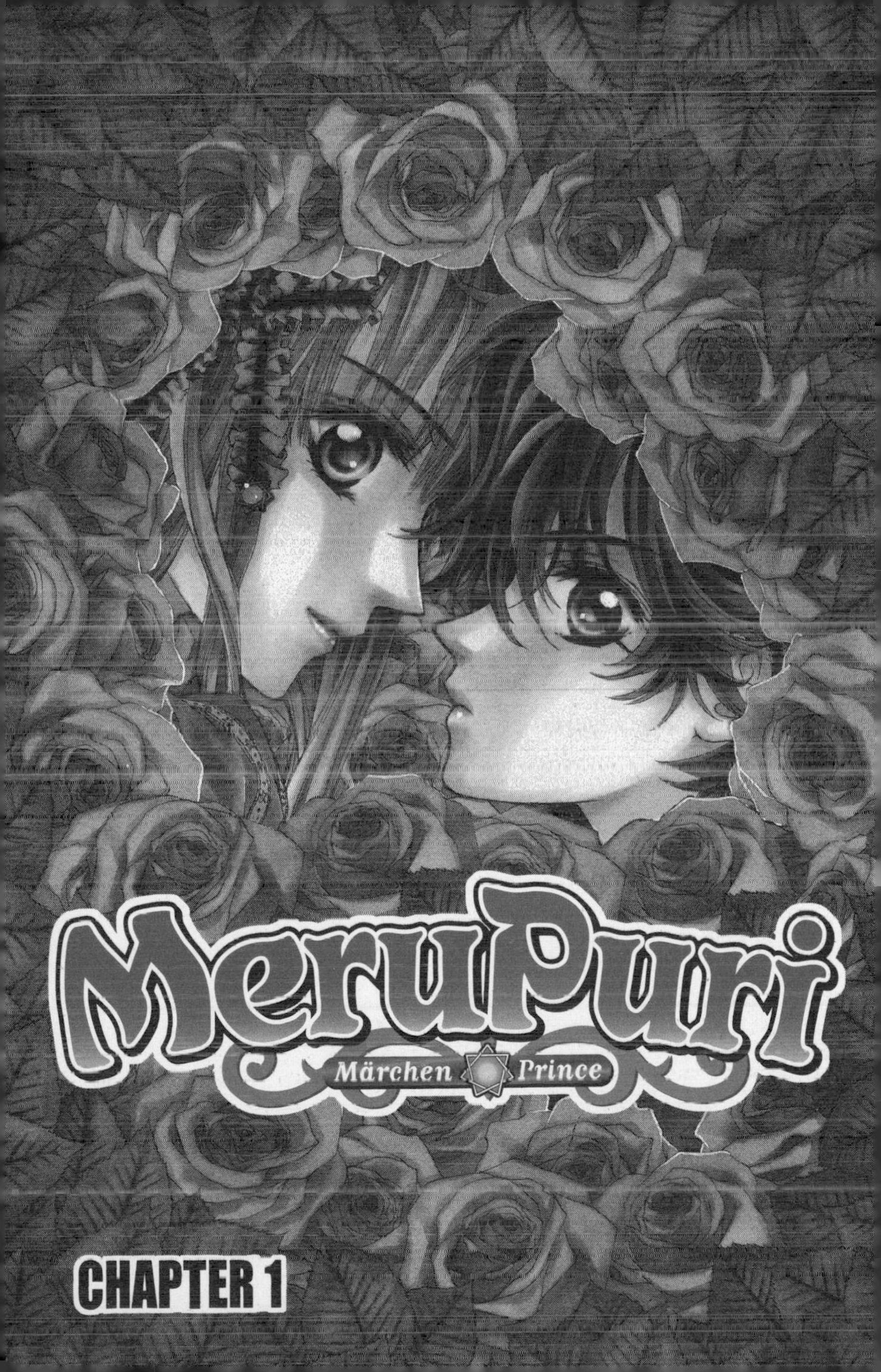
MeruPuri
Märchen Prince
CHAPTER 1

Hello, readers! This is Hino Matsuri, welcoming those of you who will be getting to know me for the first time with **MeruPuri**, and especially those kind readers who have been watching over me since **Toraware no Minoue**. (If you read **Toraware**, you may find some aspects of **MeruPuri** familiar...Heh heh. Actually, my editor and I have both mixed up "curse" and "spell" a number of times because of it. However, this story is headed in a totally different direction, so don't worry.)

In December of 2001, my editor traveled all the way to Sapporo to talk about a new serial, and all I had to say was, "I want to draw a 'magical boy.'" The publishing world was booming in that arena, thanks to the popularity of **Harry Potter** and **Lord of the Rings**, and my interest in drawing a "witch story" went back to when I'd first become a shôjo artist. I was just hoping that the timing was right and I could borrow a bit of strength from the boom...(ha!).

It was February of 2002 before our tale began to take shape. In the seven hours between lunch and the last flight out that day, I had several heated meetings with my editor, who was adamant that there should be multiple boys in our story. I wasn't so sure, but I went with it. (I figured that as long as I got to draw magical boys, I didn't care too much about the specifics. At that stage, I was all about blithe enthusiasm.)

We decided at last to make our main boy a prince from a magical land. He'd have luscious eyelashes and wear his curly hair flipped out; he'd sport pumpkin pants and frilly shirts; he'd carry a magical staff; and...he'd be an idiot.

That concept was eventually divided between two princes and, from our original list, only the pumpkin pants were rejected. (No surprise!) Over the course of those seven hours, we created almost all the main characters, decided on their relationships, and developed our "set." It was very exciting, let me tell you!! I think the working title was something like "4 Idiots." (I know, right?) We wracked our brains over that one. When it came time to make the final decision, I put a list of key-words on a sheet of A4 paper. "Märchen" and "prince" popped out at me, so I stuck them together—"Märchen Prince." There was a pregnant pause. For one thing, "märchen" is German and "prince" is English. I considered spelling it out in Hiragana as "meruhen purinsu." That would get rid of the nationality issue, and I love hiragana— it's so cute! (Thank you, ladies of the Heian period!) But in the end, I wasn't crazy about the effect. Maybe there were too many characters...?

(Continued on p.187)

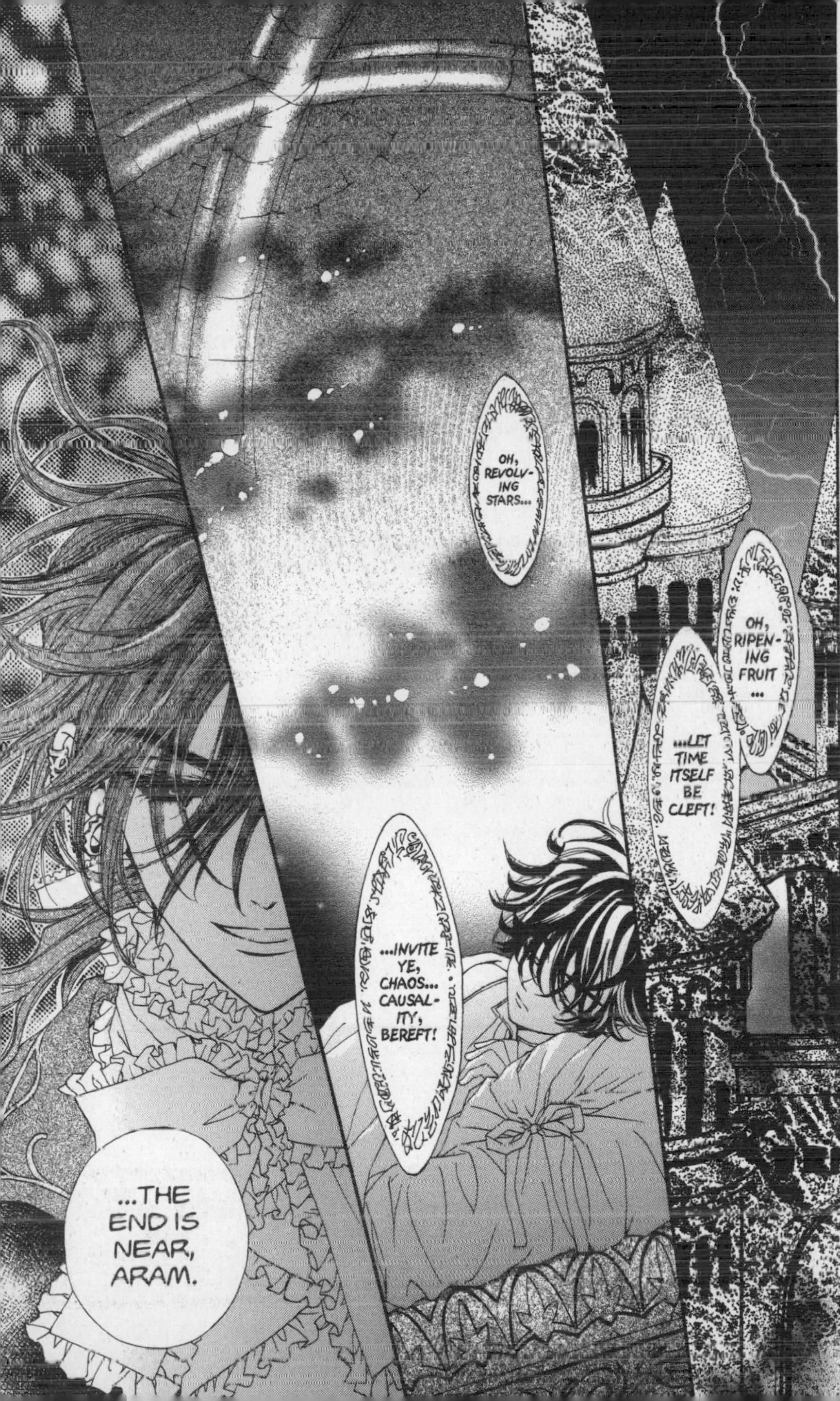
OH, RIPEN-ING FRUIT...
...LET TIME ITSELF BE CLEFT!
OH, REVOLV-ING STARS...
...INVITE YE, CHAOS... CAUSAL-ITY, BEREFT!
...THE END IS NEAR, ARAM.

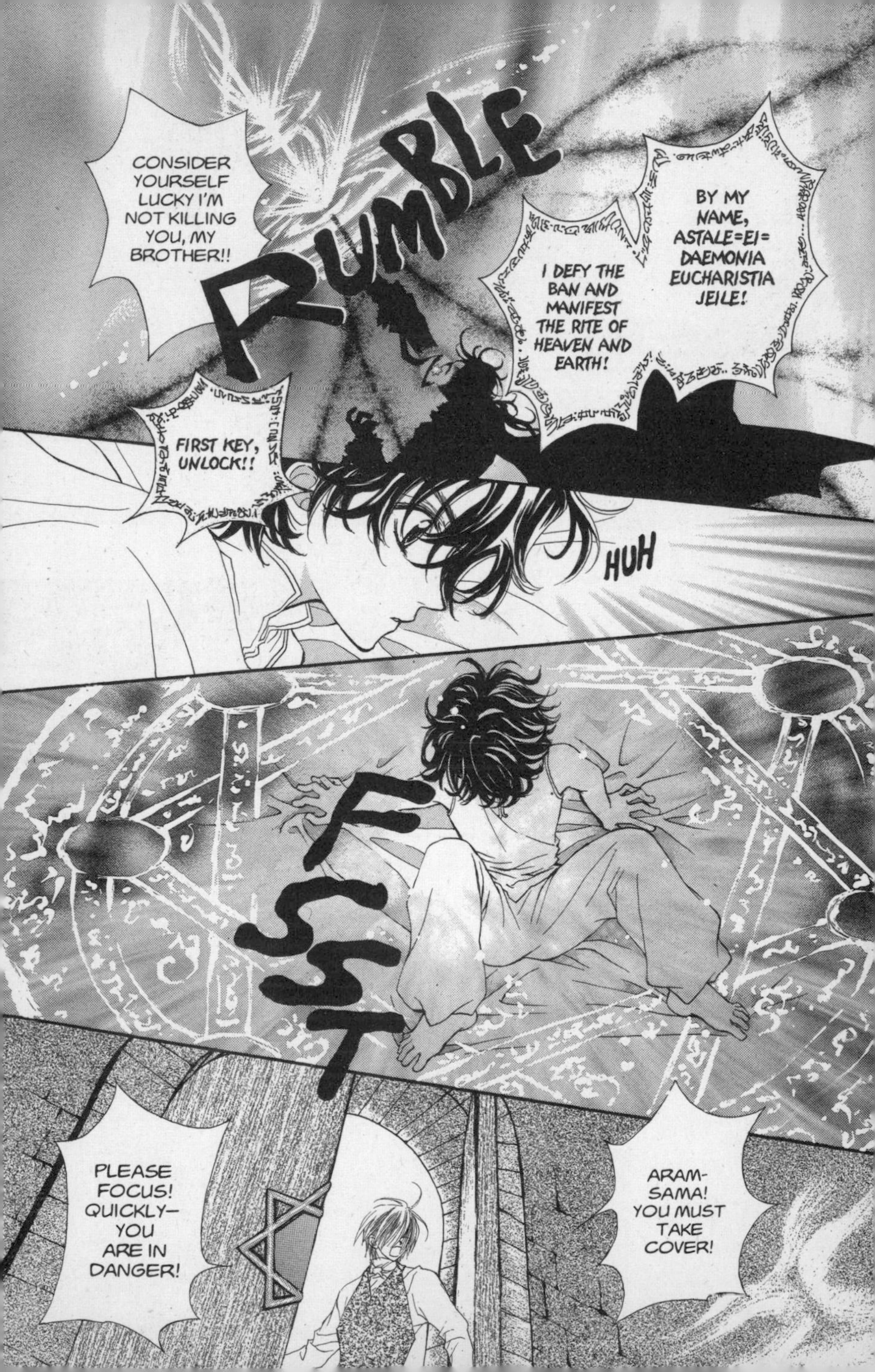
BY MY NAME, ASTALE=EI=DAEMONIA EUCHARISTIA JEILE!
I DEFY THE BAN AND MANIFEST THE RITE OF HEAVEN AND EARTH!
RUMBLE
CONSIDER YOURSELF LUCKY I'M NOT KILLING YOU, MY BROTHER!!
FIRST KEY, UNLOCK!!
HUH
FSST
ARAM-SAMA! YOU MUST TAKE COVER!
PLEASE FOCUS! QUICKLY— YOU ARE IN DANGER!

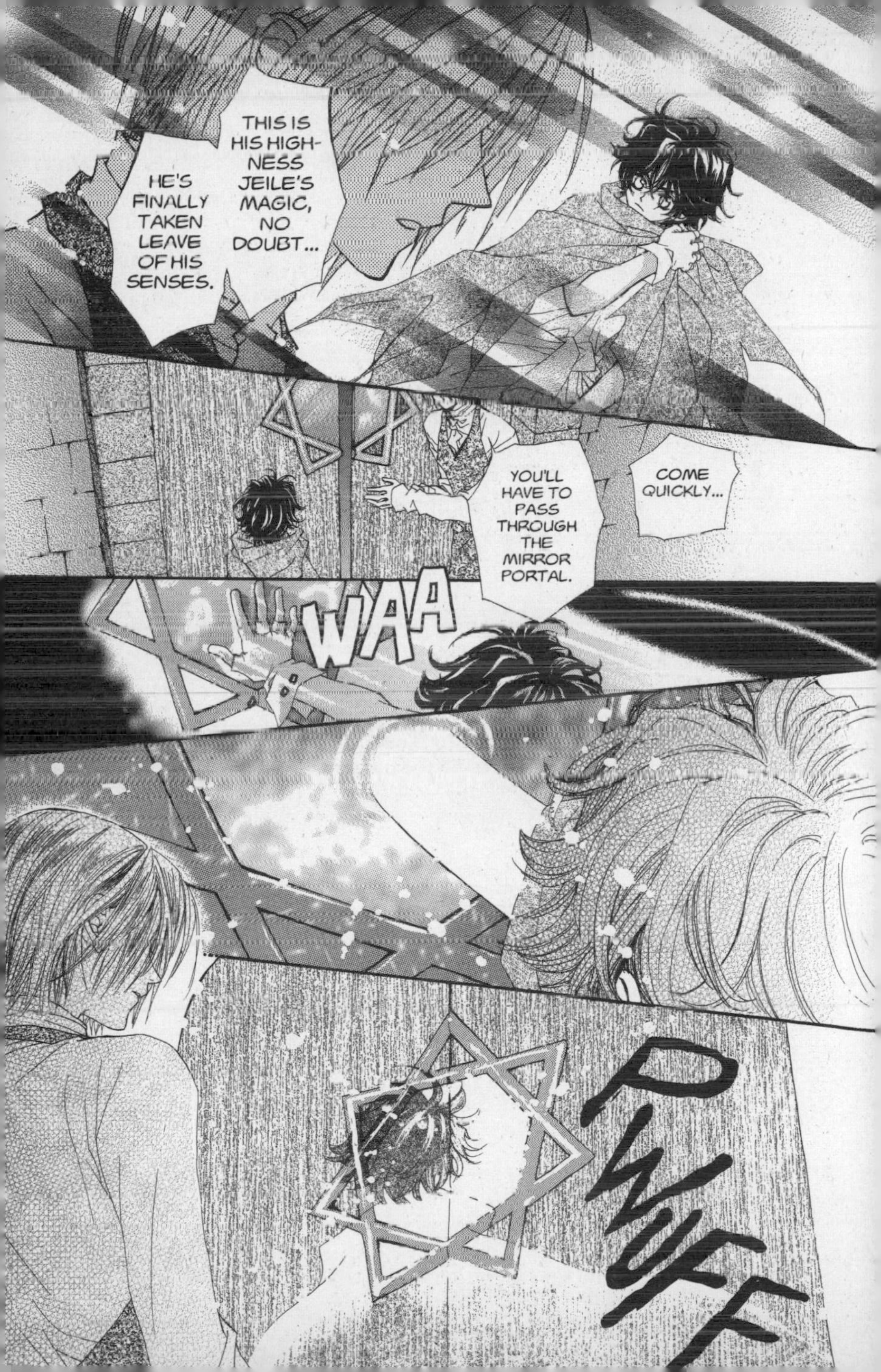
THIS IS HIS HIGHNESS JEILE'S MAGIC, NO DOUBT...
HE'S FINALLY TAKEN LEAVE OF HIS SENSES.
COME QUICKLY...
YOU'LL HAVE TO PASS THROUGH THE MIRROR PORTAL.
WAA
PWUFF

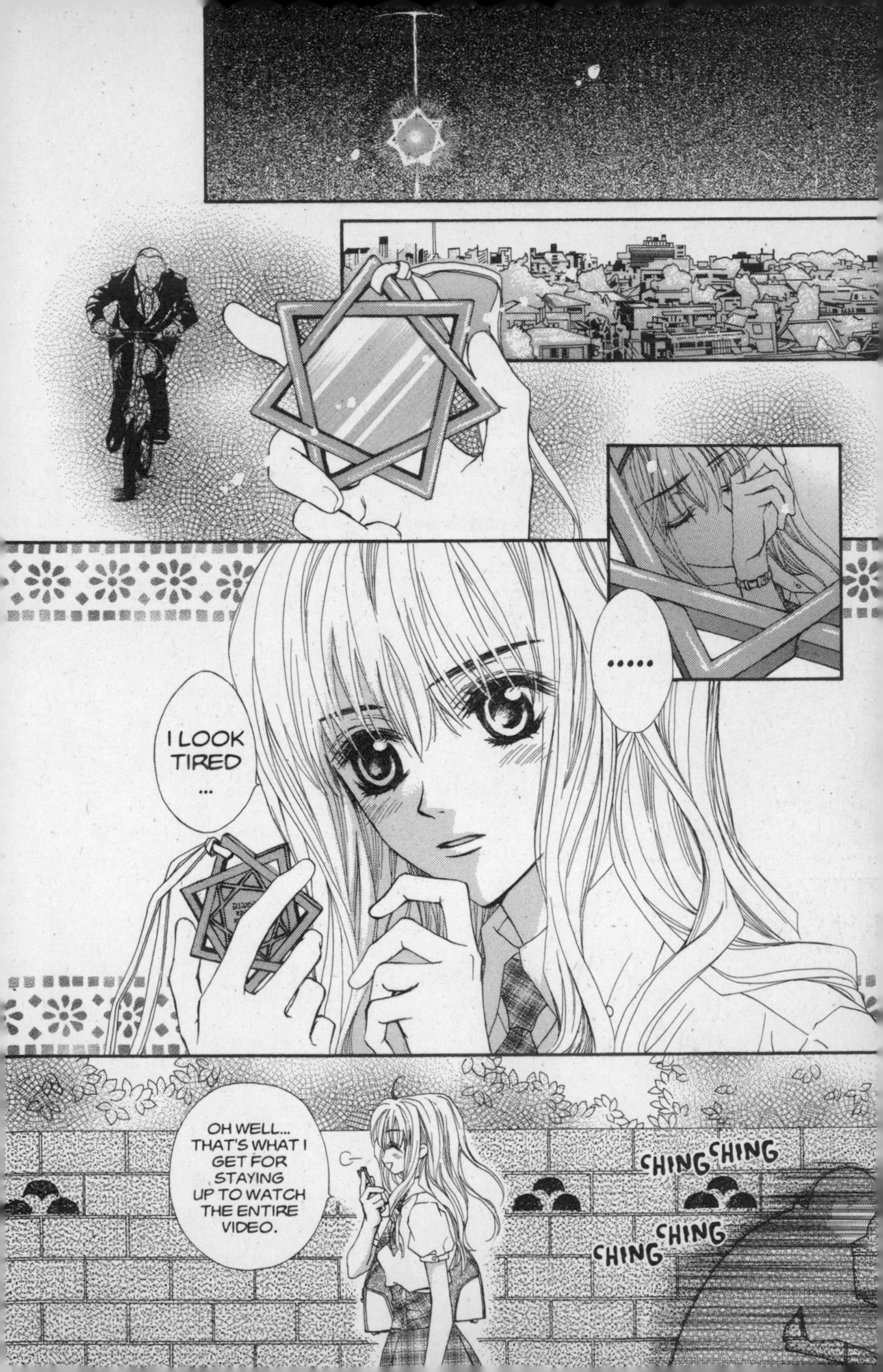
.....
I LOOK TIRED ...
OH WELL... THAT'S WHAT I GET FOR STAYING UP TO WATCH THE ENTIRE VIDEO.
CHING CHING
CHING CHING

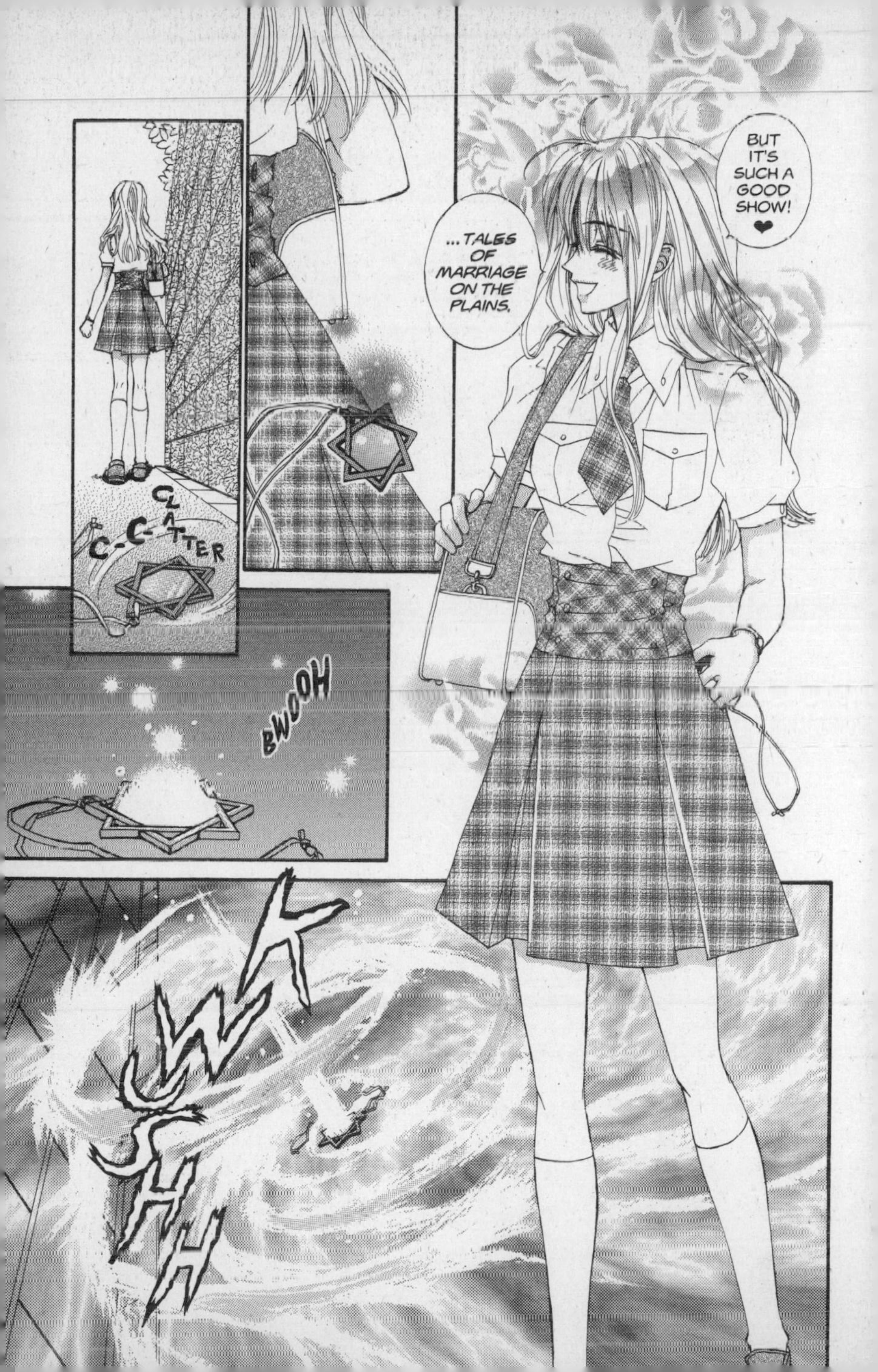

BUT IT'S SUCH A GOOD SHOW! ❤
...TALES OF MARRIAGE ON THE PLAINS.
C-C-CLATTER
BWOOH
SWISHH

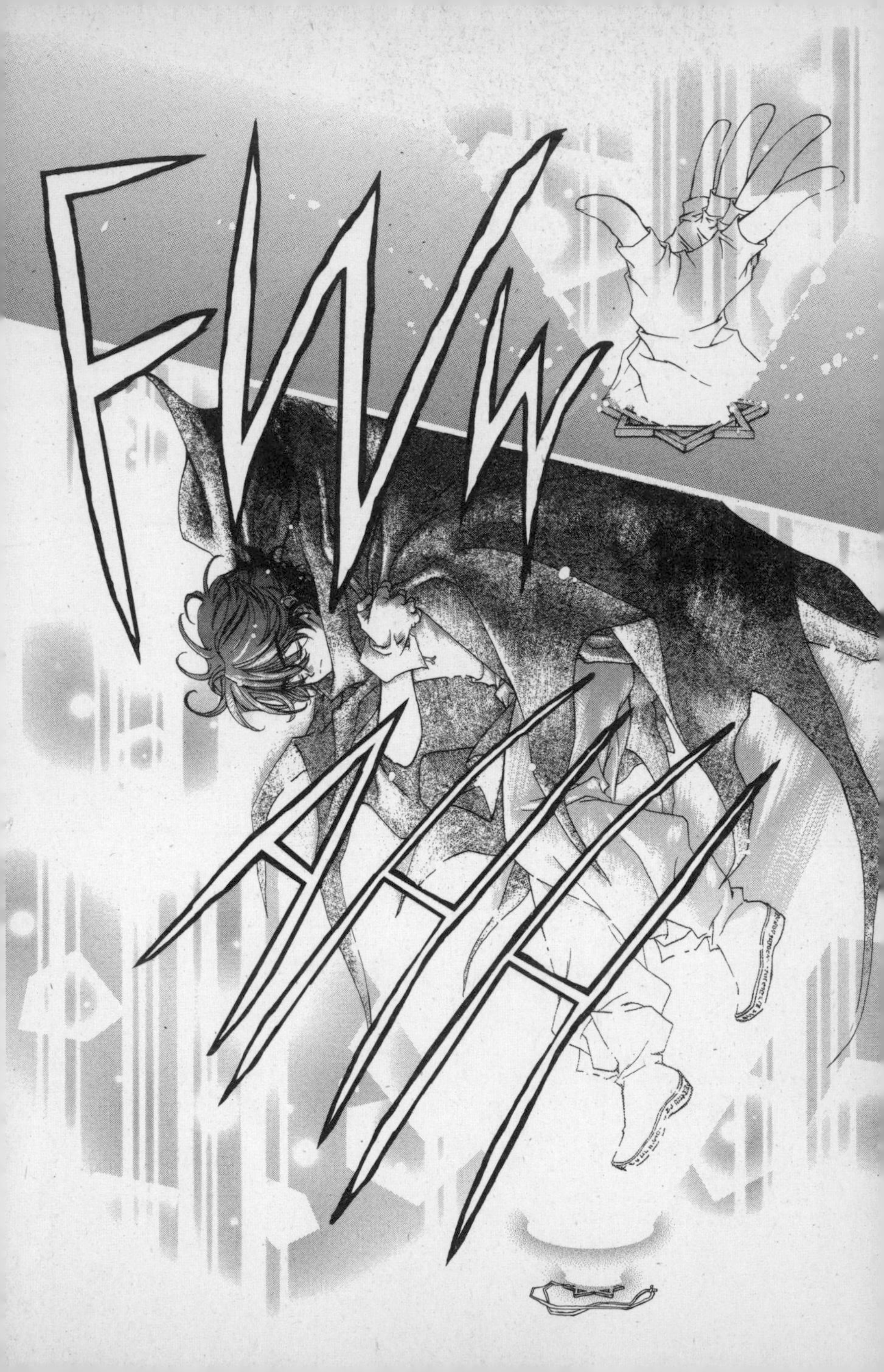
FWW
AHH

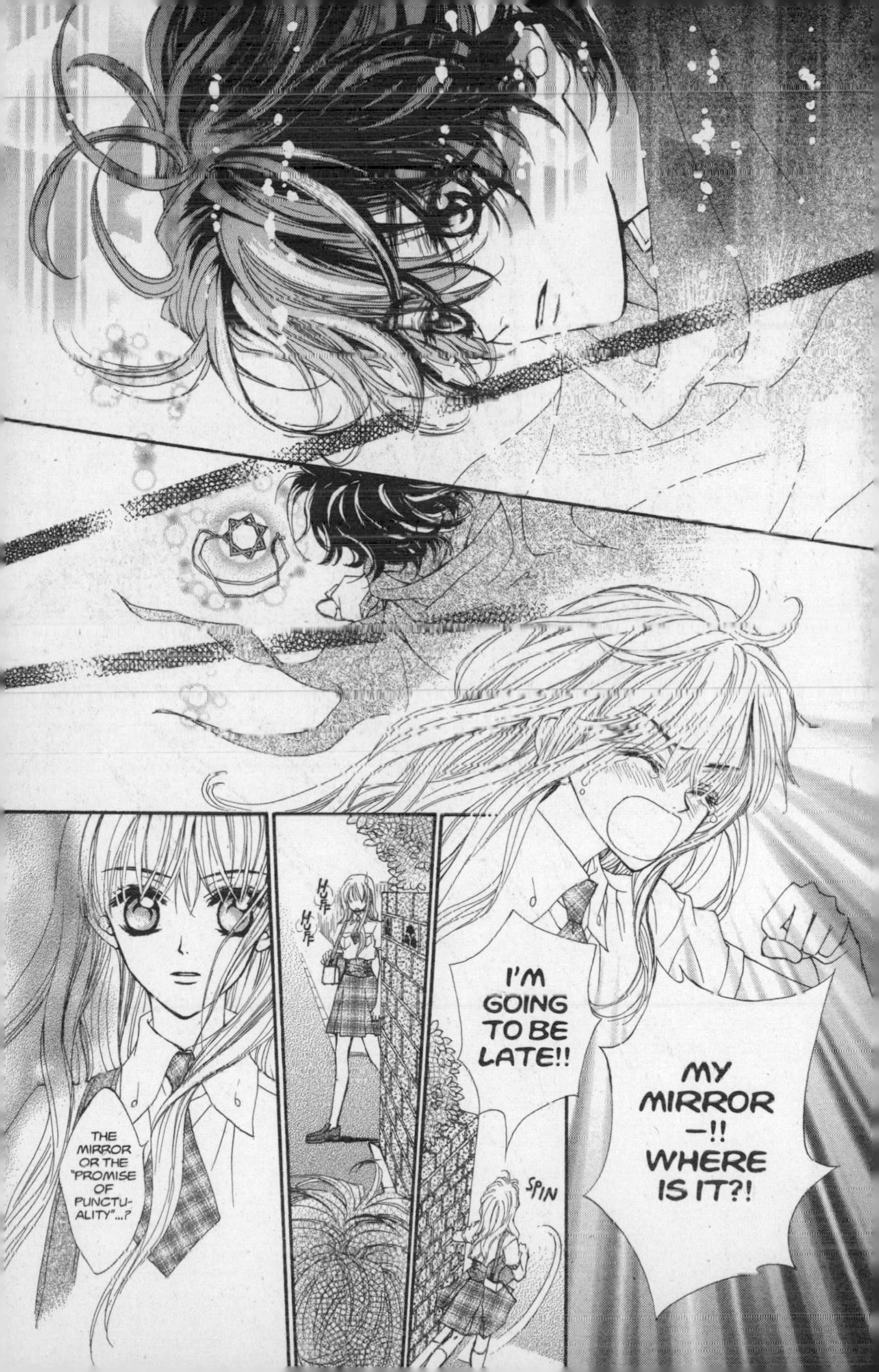
MY MIRROR —!! WHERE IS IT?!
I'M GOING TO BE LATE!!
SPIN
HUFF HUFF
THE MIRROR OR THE "PROMISE OF PUNCTU-ALITY"...?

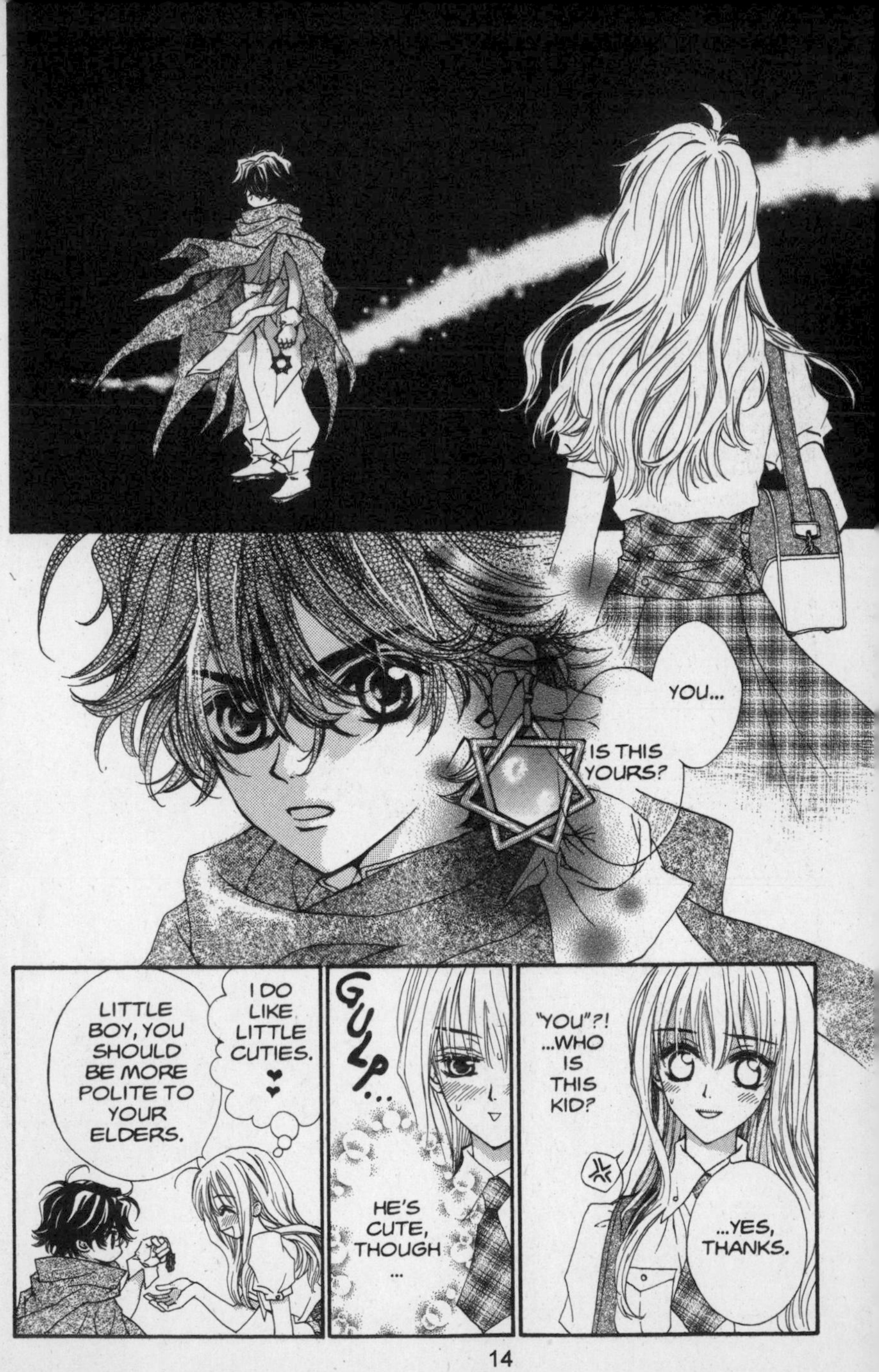
YOU...
IS THIS YOURS?
"YOU"?! ...WHO IS THIS KID?
...YES, THANKS.
GULP...
HE'S CUTE, THOUGH ...
I DO LIKE LITTLE CUTIES. ❤❤
LITTLE BOY, YOU SHOULD BE MORE POLITE TO YOUR ELDERS.

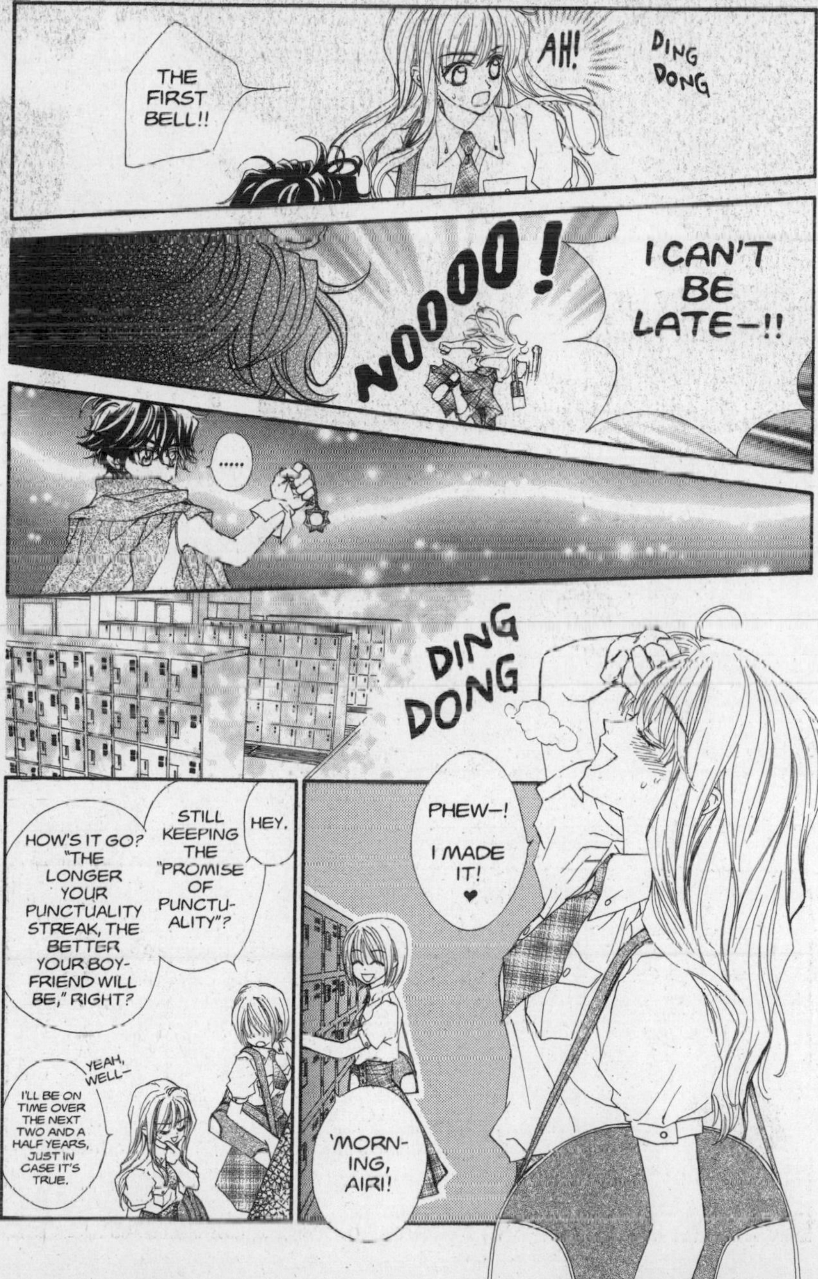
DING DONG
AH!
THE FIRST BELL!!
I CAN'T BE LATE—!!
NOOOOO!
......
DING DONG
PHEW—! I MADE IT! ♥
'MORNING, AIRI!
HEY.
STILL KEEPING THE "PROMISE OF PUNCTUALITY"?
HOW'S IT GO? "THE LONGER YOUR PUNCTUALITY STREAK, THE BETTER YOUR BOYFRIEND WILL BE," RIGHT?
YEAH, WELL—
I'LL BE ON TIME OVER THE NEXT TWO AND A HALF YEARS, JUST IN CASE IT'S TRUE.

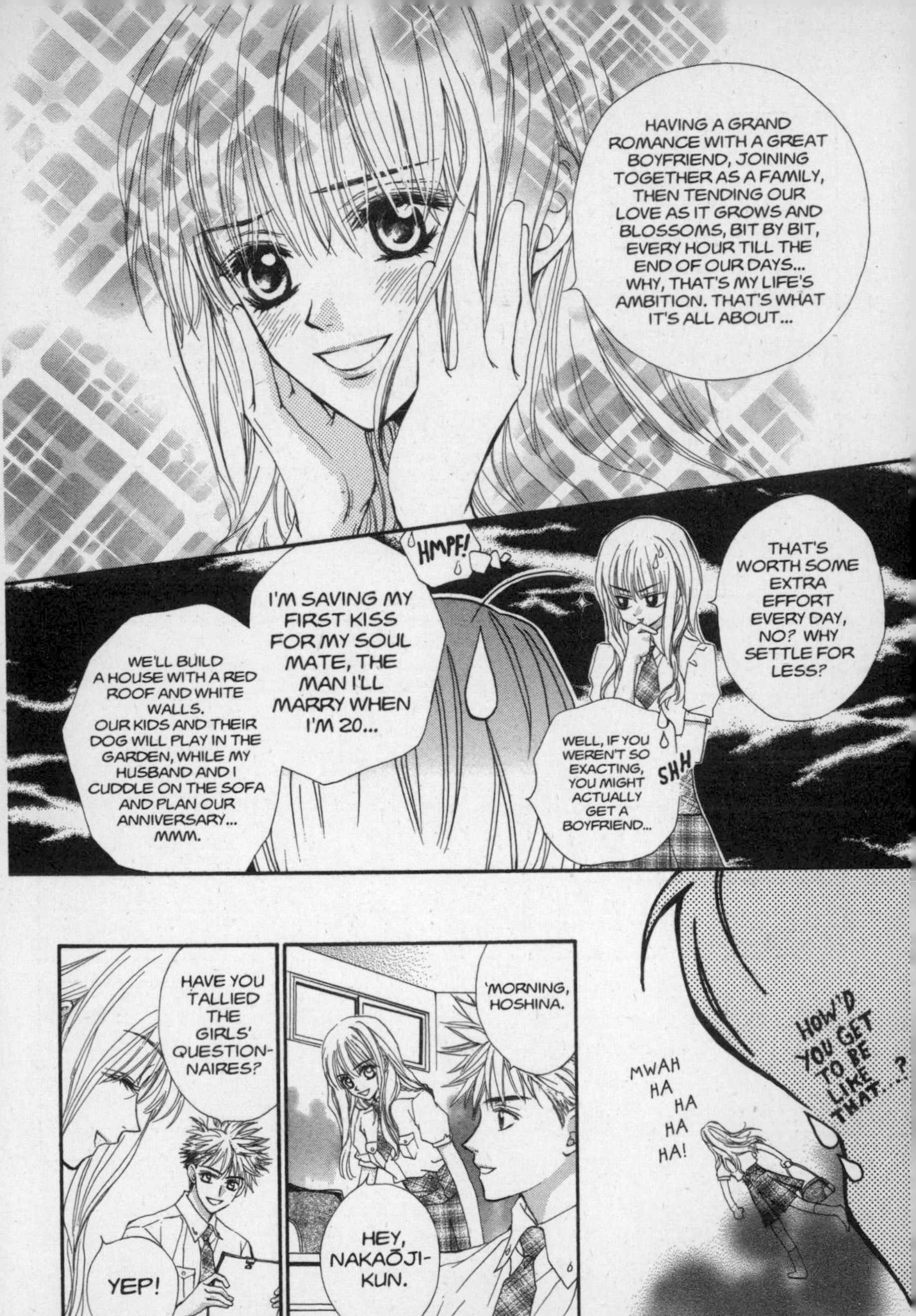
HAVING A GRAND ROMANCE WITH A GREAT BOYFRIEND, JOINING TOGETHER AS A FAMILY, THEN TENDING OUR LOVE AS IT GROWS AND BLOSSOMS, BIT BY BIT, EVERY HOUR TILL THE END OF OUR DAYS... WHY, THAT'S MY LIFE'S AMBITION. THAT'S WHAT IT'S ALL ABOUT...
THAT'S WORTH SOME EXTRA EFFORT EVERY DAY, NO? WHY SETTLE FOR LESS?
HMPF!
I'M SAVING MY FIRST KISS FOR MY SOUL MATE, THE MAN I'LL MARRY WHEN I'M 20...
WELL, IF YOU WEREN'T SO EXACTING, YOU MIGHT ACTUALLY GET A BOYFRIEND...
SHH
WE'LL BUILD A HOUSE WITH A RED ROOF AND WHITE WALLS. OUR KIDS AND THEIR DOG WILL PLAY IN THE GARDEN, WHILE MY HUSBAND AND I CUDDLE ON THE SOFA AND PLAN OUR ANNIVERSARY... MMM.
HOW'D YOU GET TO BE LIKE THAT...?
MWAH HA HA HA HA!
'MORNING, HOSHINA.
HEY, NAKAŌJI-KUN.
HAVE YOU TALLIED THE GIRLS' QUESTION-NAIRES?
YEP!

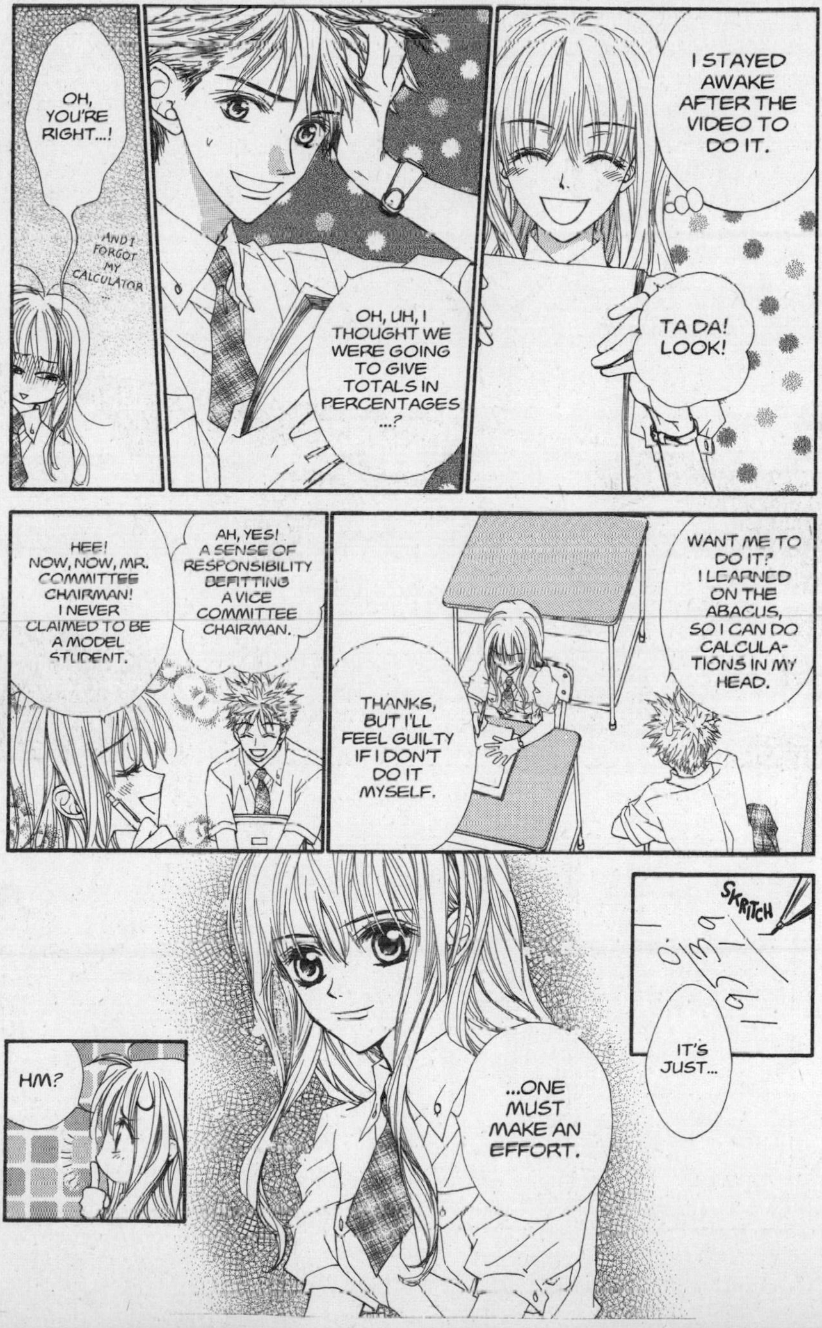
I STAYED AWAKE AFTER THE VIDEO TO DO IT.
TA DA! LOOK!
OH, UH, I THOUGHT WE WERE GOING TO GIVE TOTALS IN PERCENTAGES ...?
OH, YOU'RE RIGHT...!
AND I FORGOT MY CALCULATOR ...
WANT ME TO DO IT? I LEARNED ON THE ABACUS, SO I CAN DO CALCULATIONS IN MY HEAD.
THANKS, BUT I'LL FEEL GUILTY IF I DON'T DO IT MYSELF.
AH, YES! A SENSE OF RESPONSIBILITY BEFITTING A VICE COMMITTEE CHAIRMAN.
HEE! NOW, NOW, MR. COMMITTEE CHAIRMAN! I NEVER CLAIMED TO BE A MODEL STUDENT.
SKRITCH
IT'S JUST...
...ONE MUST MAKE AN EFFORT.
HM?

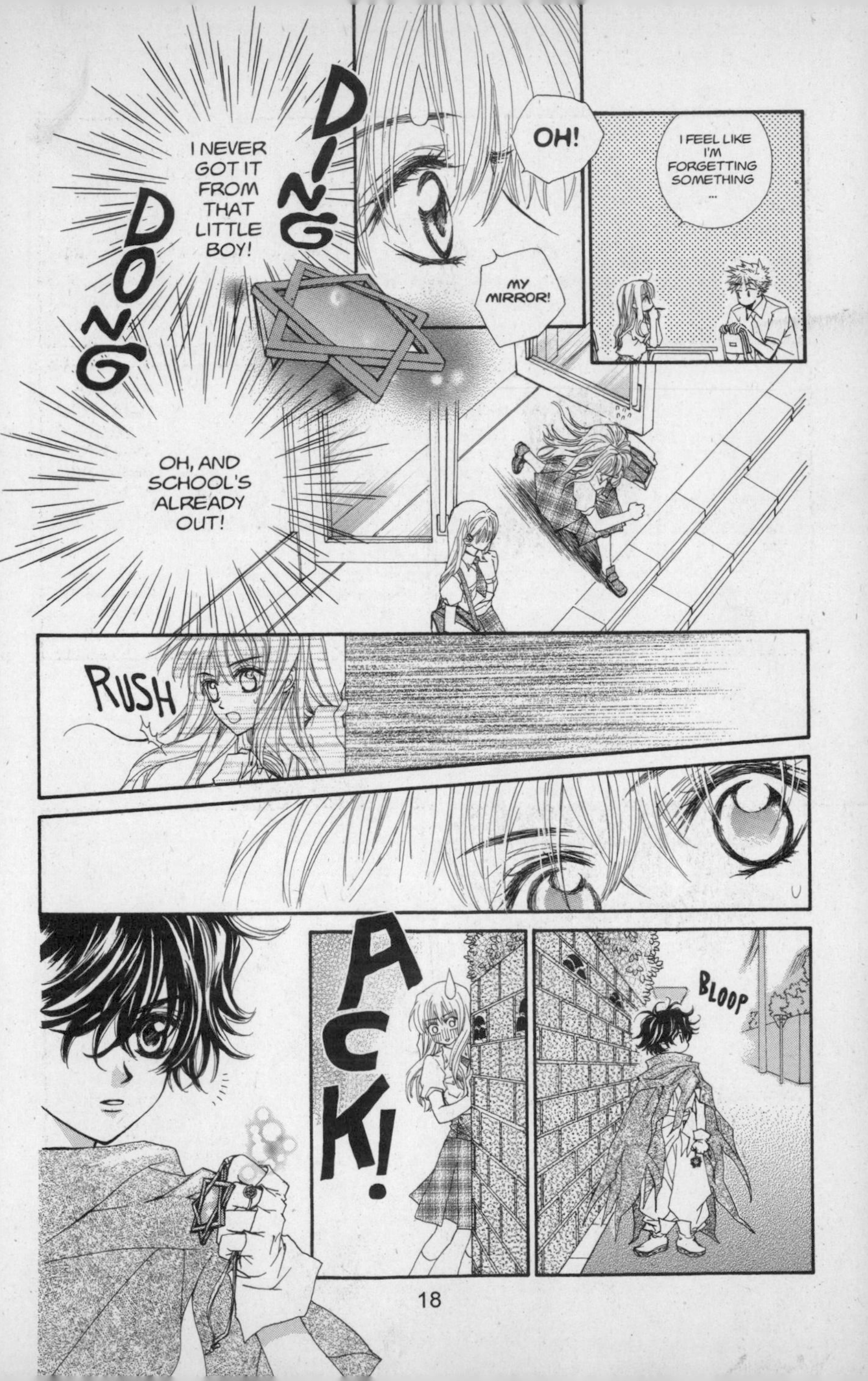
I FEEL LIKE I'M FORGETTING SOMETHING ...
OH!
MY MIRROR!
DING
DONG
I NEVER GOT IT FROM THAT LITTLE BOY!
OH, AND SCHOOL'S ALREADY OUT!
RUSH
BLOOP
ACK!

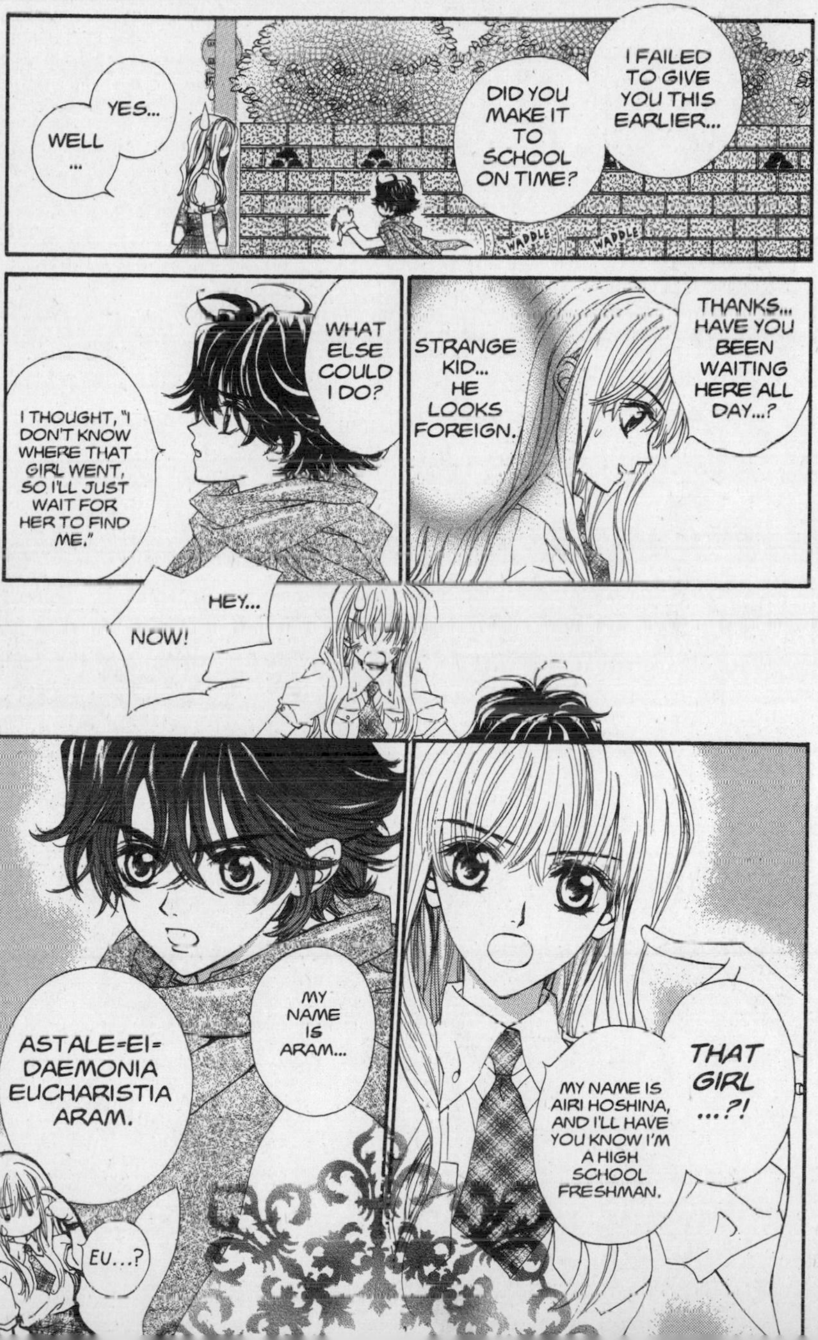
I FAILED TO GIVE YOU THIS EARLIER...
DID YOU MAKE IT TO SCHOOL ON TIME?
WADDLE
WADDLE
YES... WELL ...
THANKS... HAVE YOU BEEN WAITING HERE ALL DAY...?
STRANGE KID... HE LOOKS FOREIGN.
WHAT ELSE COULD I DO?
I THOUGHT, "I DON'T KNOW WHERE THAT GIRL WENT, SO I'LL JUST WAIT FOR HER TO FIND ME."
HEY... NOW!
THAT GIRL ...?!
MY NAME IS AIRI HOSHINA, AND I'LL HAVE YOU KNOW I'M A HIGH SCHOOL FRESHMAN.
MY NAME IS ARAM...
ASTALE=EI=DAEMONIA EUCHARISTIA ARAM.
EU...?

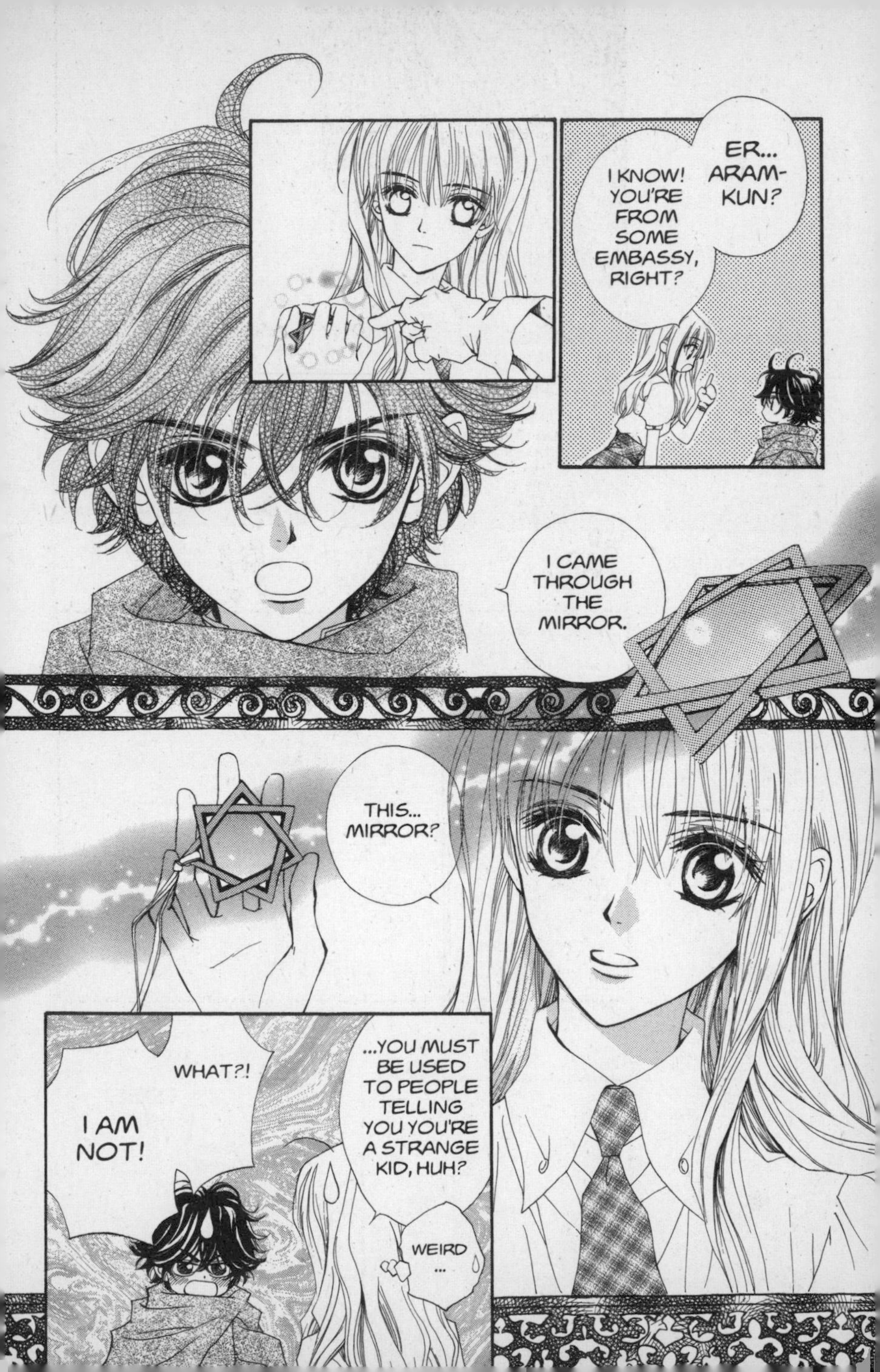
ER... ARAM-KUN?
I KNOW! YOU'RE FROM SOME EMBASSY, RIGHT?
I CAME THROUGH THE MIRROR.
THIS... MIRROR?
...YOU MUST BE USED TO PEOPLE TELLING YOU YOU'RE A STRANGE KID, HUH?
WEIRD ...
WHAT?!
I AM NOT!

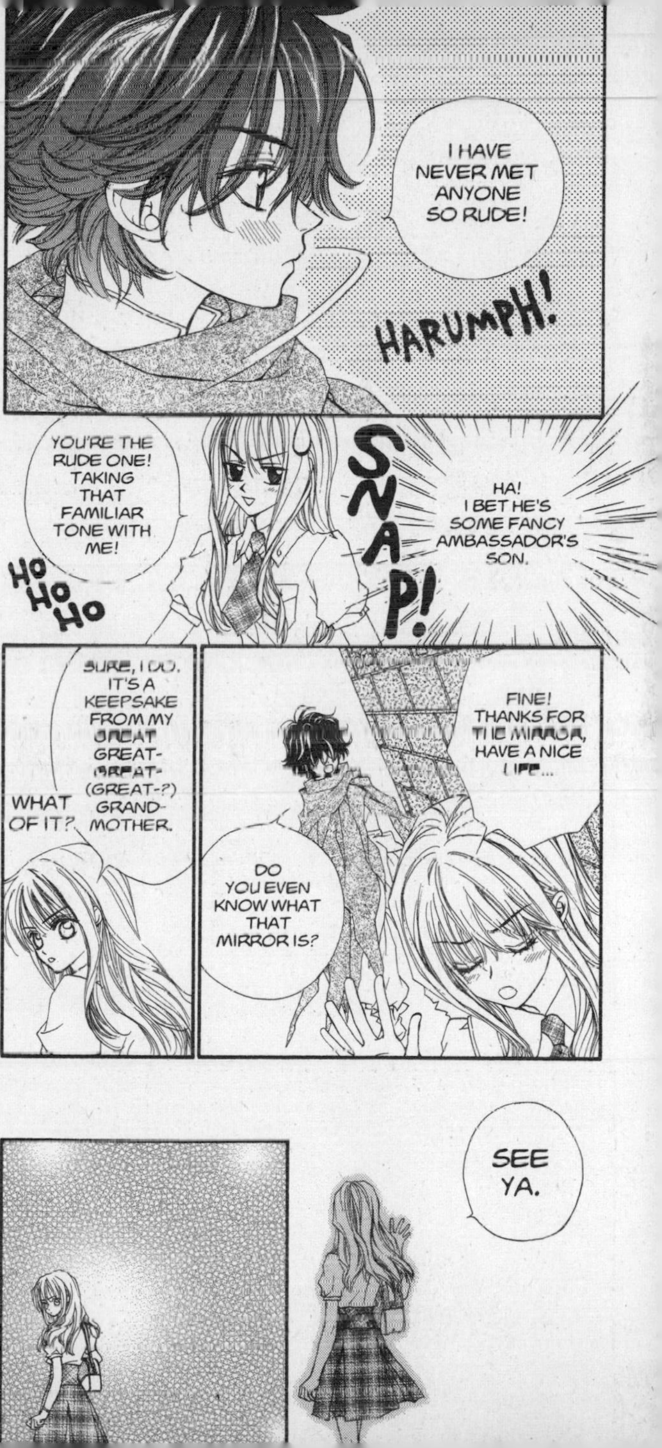
I HAVE NEVER MET ANYONE SO RUDE!
HARUMPH!
HA! I BET HE'S SOME FANCY AMBASSADOR'S SON.
SNAP!
YOU'RE THE RUDE ONE! TAKING THAT FAMILIAR TONE WITH ME!
HO HO HO
FINE! THANKS FOR THE MIRROR, HAVE A NICE LIFE...
DO YOU EVEN KNOW WHAT THAT MIRROR IS?
SURE, I DO. IT'S A KEEPSAKE FROM MY GREAT GREAT-GREAT-(GREAT-?) GRANDMOTHER.
WHAT OF IT?
SEE YA.

AIRI HOSHINA

"Hoshina" is an unusual family name, I know, but I wanted something "fairytale-like," and that seemed right to me.

I like Airi. She's there to be the "delusional maiden" (though she is turning into a babysitter, too!) and she was definitely the one I had the most difficulty creating. My editor and I had discussions about her that ran late into the evening. What troubled me was figuring out her insides. Her looks were easy—what do you think of when you hear the word "maiden"? We went with the stereotypical long wavy hair, and that was that. But she's our heroine, right? So I did some work on her eyes, trying to suggest a strong personality...suffice it to say, I meditated long and hard on Airi Hoshina.

Maruru, on other hand? Her character established itself at the speed of a synapse firing in the brain. She's earnest. That one word sums her up.

From here on out, things are going to get tough for Airi. She is the heroine, after all. First she'll set her sights on becoming a witch...

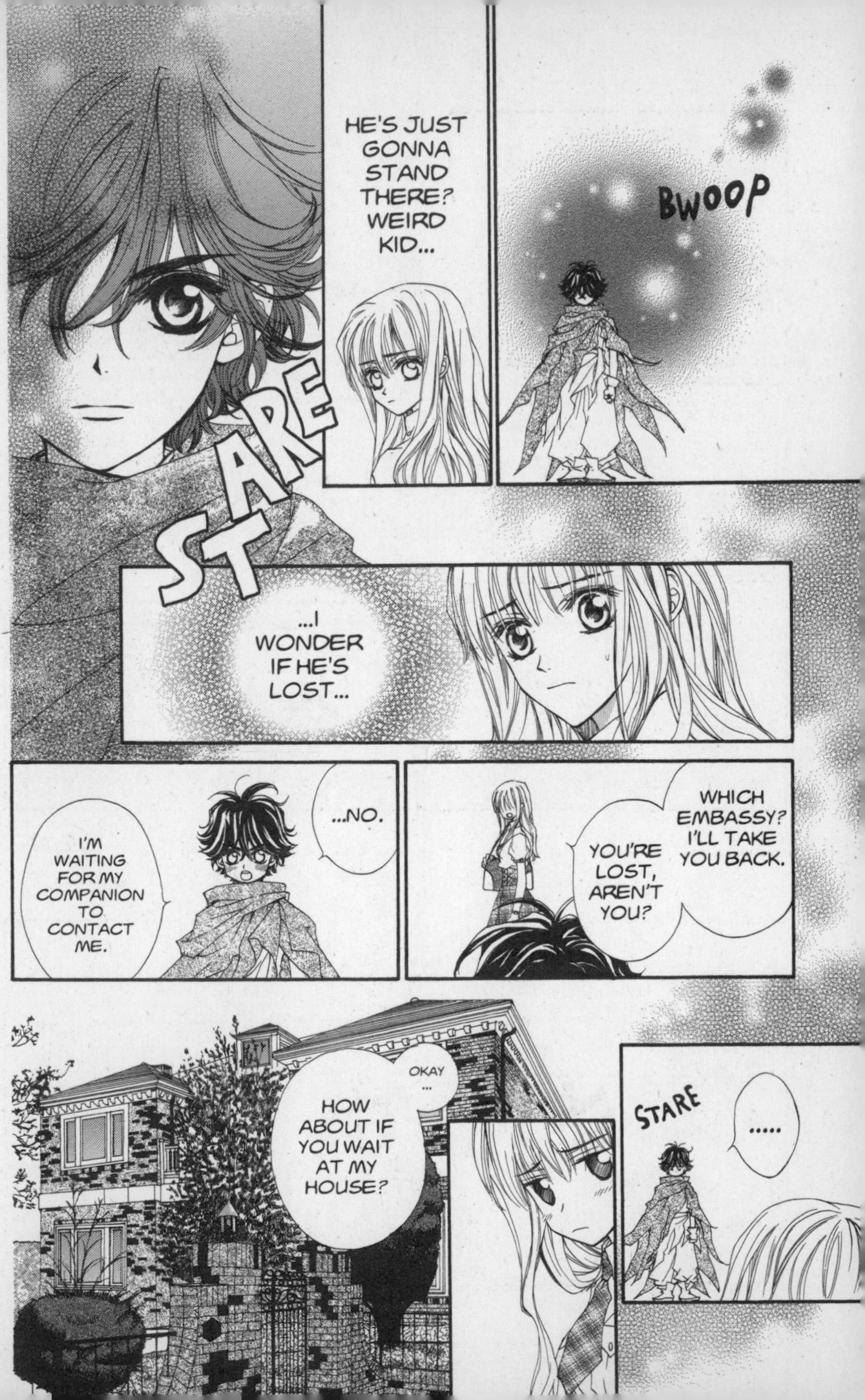
BWOOP
HE'S JUST GONNA STAND THERE? WEIRD KID...
STARE
...I WONDER IF HE'S LOST...
WHICH EMBASSY? I'LL TAKE YOU BACK.
YOU'RE LOST, AREN'T YOU?
...NO.
I'M WAITING FOR MY COMPANION TO CONTACT ME.
STARE
.....
OKAY...
HOW ABOUT IF YOU WAIT AT MY HOUSE?

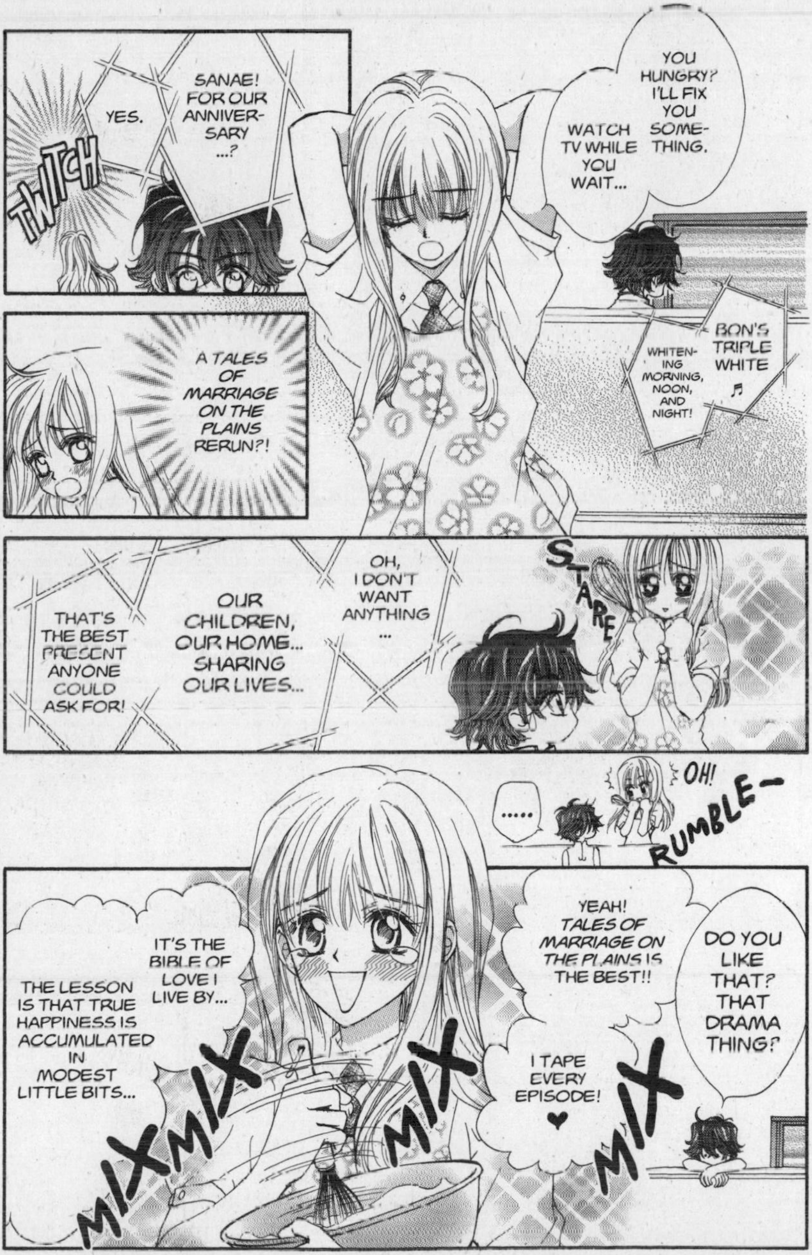
YOU HUNGRY? I'LL FIX YOU SOMETHING.
WATCH TV WHILE YOU WAIT...
BON'S TRIPLE WHITE ♪
WHITENING MORNING, NOON, AND NIGHT!
SANAE! FOR OUR ANNIVERSARY ...?
YES.
TWITCH
A TALES OF MARRIAGE ON THE PLAINS RERUN?!
STARE
OH, I DON'T WANT ANYTHING ...
OUR CHILDREN, OUR HOME... SHARING OUR LIVES...
THAT'S THE BEST PRESENT ANYONE COULD ASK FOR!
OH!
RUMBLE–
......
DO YOU LIKE THAT? THAT DRAMA THING?
MIX
YEAH! TALES OF MARRIAGE ON THE PLAINS IS THE BEST!!
I TAPE EVERY EPISODE! ♥
MIX
IT'S THE BIBLE OF LOVE I LIVE BY...
MIX MIX
THE LESSON IS THAT TRUE HAPPINESS IS ACCUMULATED IN MODEST LITTLE BITS...

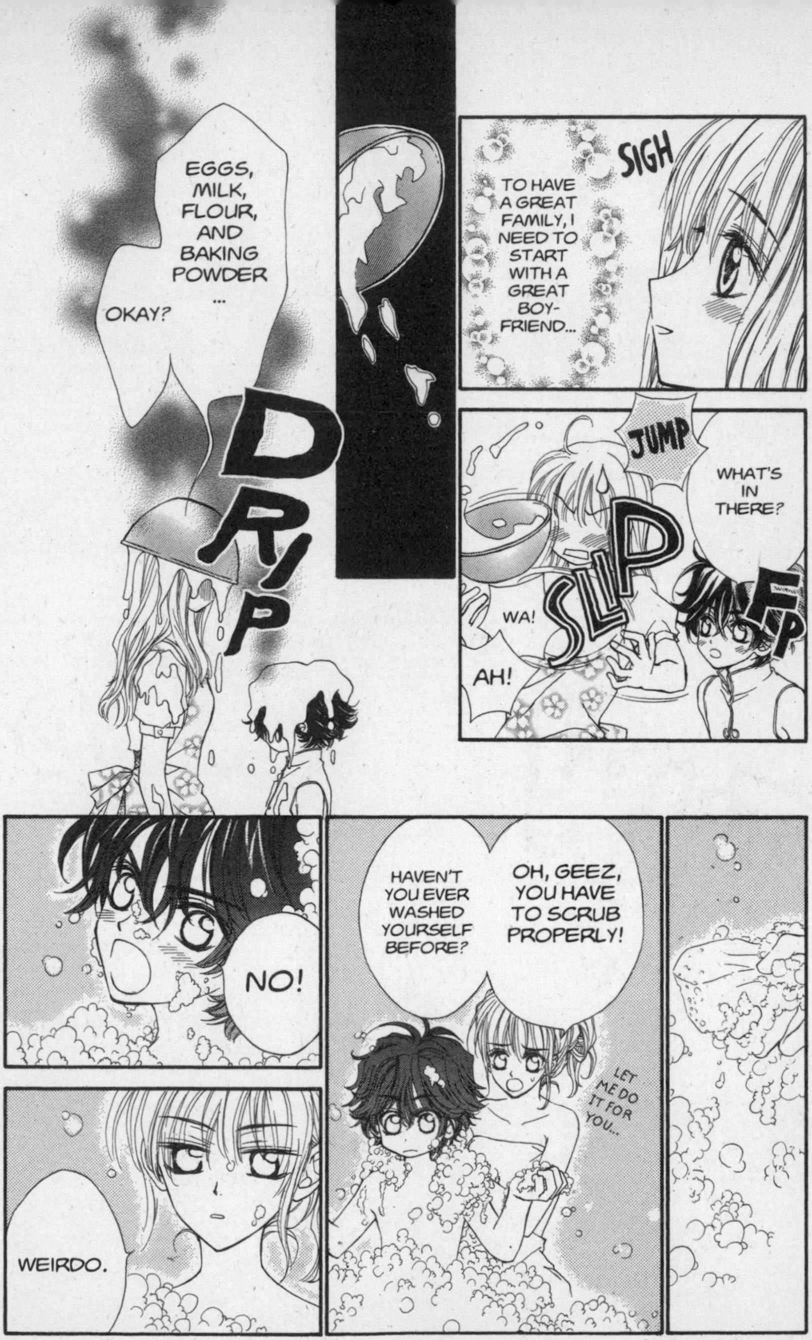
SIGH
TO HAVE A GREAT FAMILY, I NEED TO START WITH A GREAT BOY-FRIEND...
JUMP
WHAT'S IN THERE?
SLIP
WA!
AH!
EGGS, MILK, FLOUR, AND BAKING POWDER ... OKAY?
DRIP
OH, GEEZ, YOU HAVE TO SCRUB PROPERLY!
HAVEN'T YOU EVER WASHED YOURSELF BEFORE?
LET ME DO IT FOR YOU...
NO!
WEIRDO.

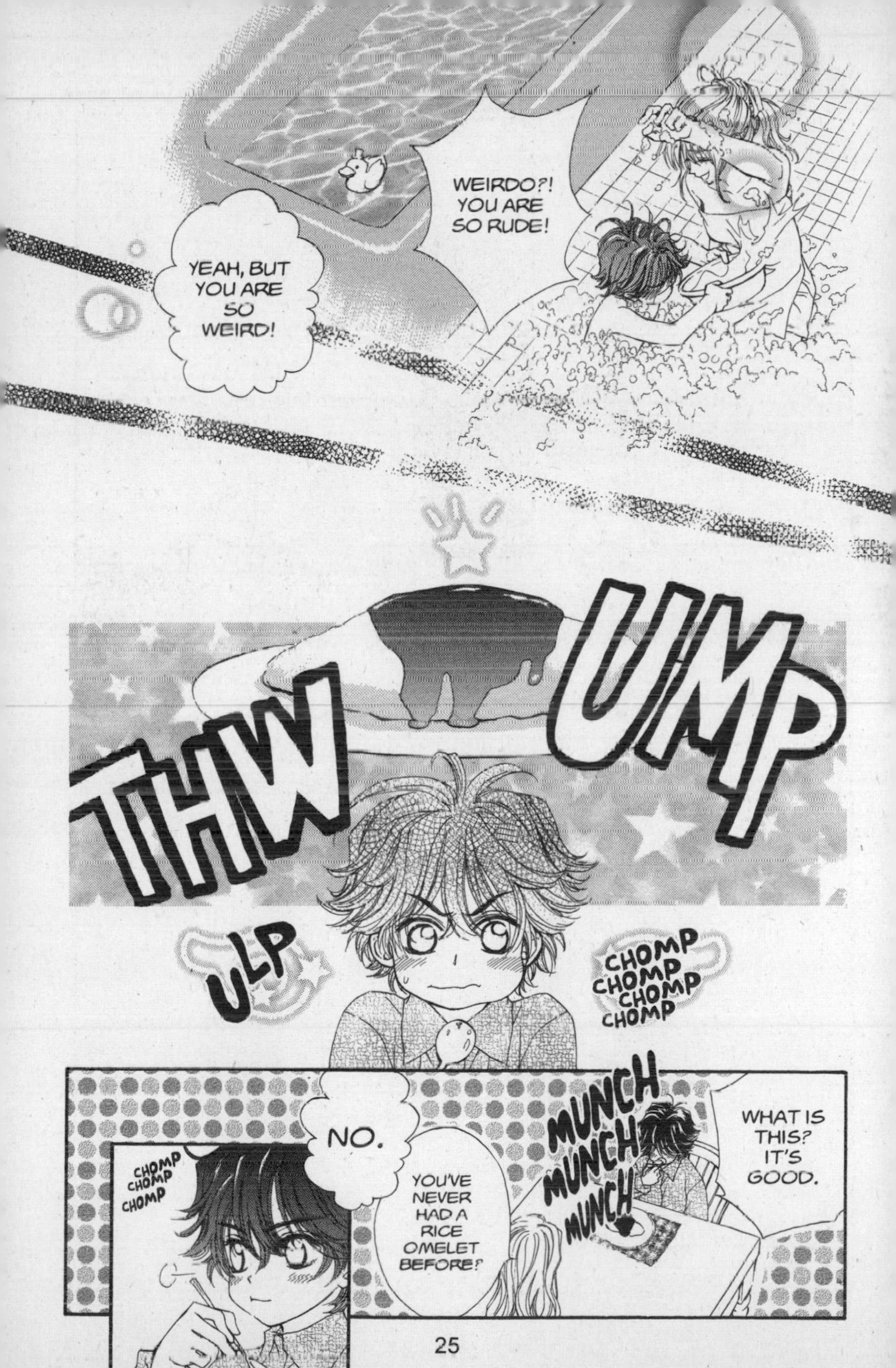
WEIRDO?! YOU ARE SO RUDE!
YEAH, BUT YOU ARE SO WEIRD!
THWUMP
CHOMP CHOMP CHOMP CHOMP
ULP
WHAT IS THIS? IT'S GOOD.
MUNCH MUNCH MUNCH
YOU'VE NEVER HAD A RICE OMELET BEFORE?
NO.
CHOMP CHOMP CHOMP

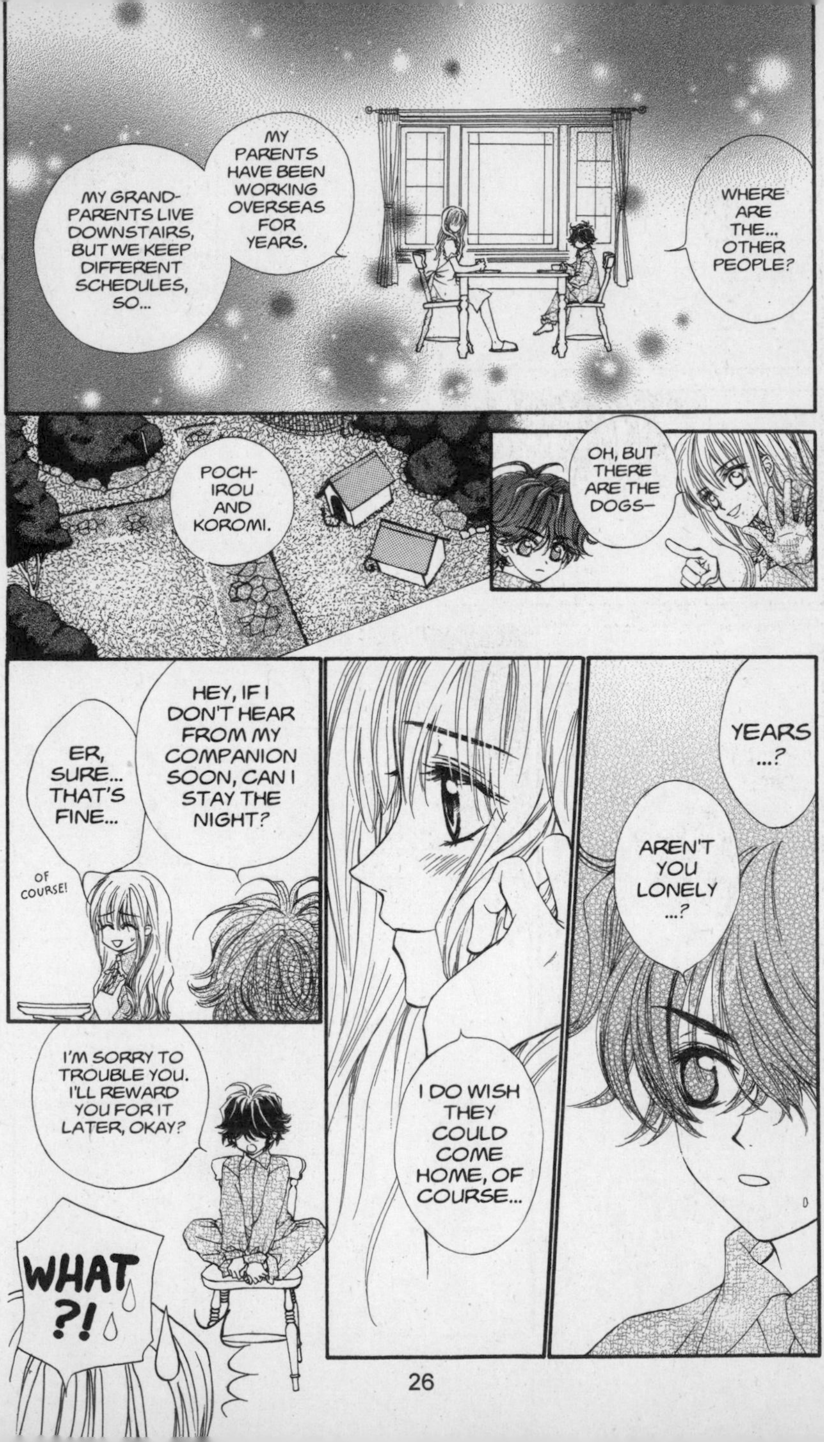
WHERE ARE THE... OTHER PEOPLE?
MY PARENTS HAVE BEEN WORKING OVERSEAS FOR YEARS.
MY GRAND-PARENTS LIVE DOWNSTAIRS, BUT WE KEEP DIFFERENT SCHEDULES, SO...
OH, BUT THERE ARE THE DOGS–
POCH-IROU AND KOROMI.
YEARS ...?
AREN'T YOU LONELY ...?
I DO WISH THEY COULD COME HOME, OF COURSE...
HEY, IF I DON'T HEAR FROM MY COMPANION SOON, CAN I STAY THE NIGHT?
ER, SURE... THAT'S FINE...
OF COURSE!
I'M SORRY TO TROUBLE YOU. I'LL REWARD YOU FOR IT LATER, OKAY?
WHAT ?!

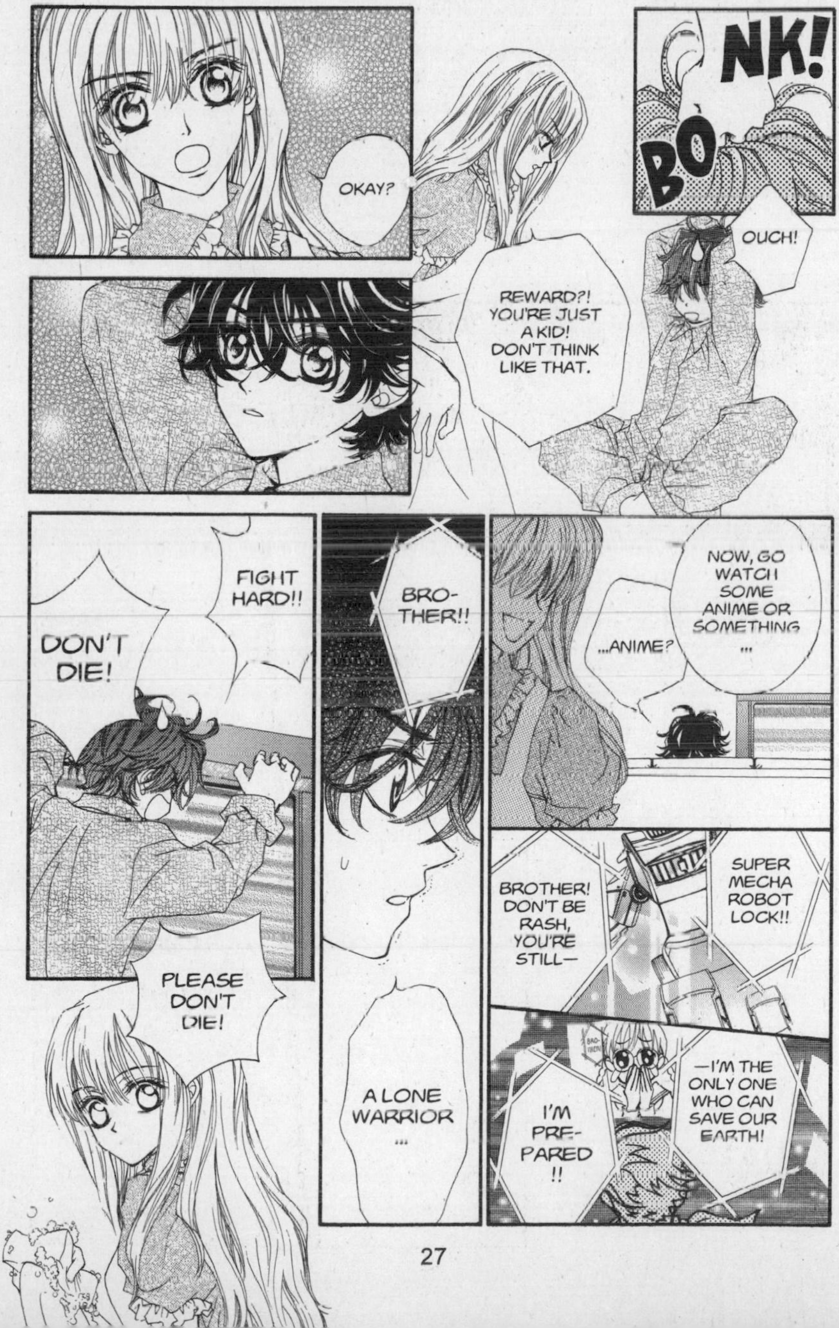
BONK!
OUCH!
OKAY?
REWARD?! YOU'RE JUST A KID! DON'T THINK LIKE THAT.
NOW, GO WATCH SOME ANIME OR SOMETHING ...
...ANIME?
SUPER MECHA ROBOT LOCK!!
BROTHER! DON'T BE RASH, YOU'RE STILL—
—I'M THE ONLY ONE WHO CAN SAVE OUR EARTH!
I'M PRE-PARED !!
BRO-THER!!
A LONE WARRIOR ...
FIGHT HARD!!
DON'T DIE!
PLEASE DON'T DIE!

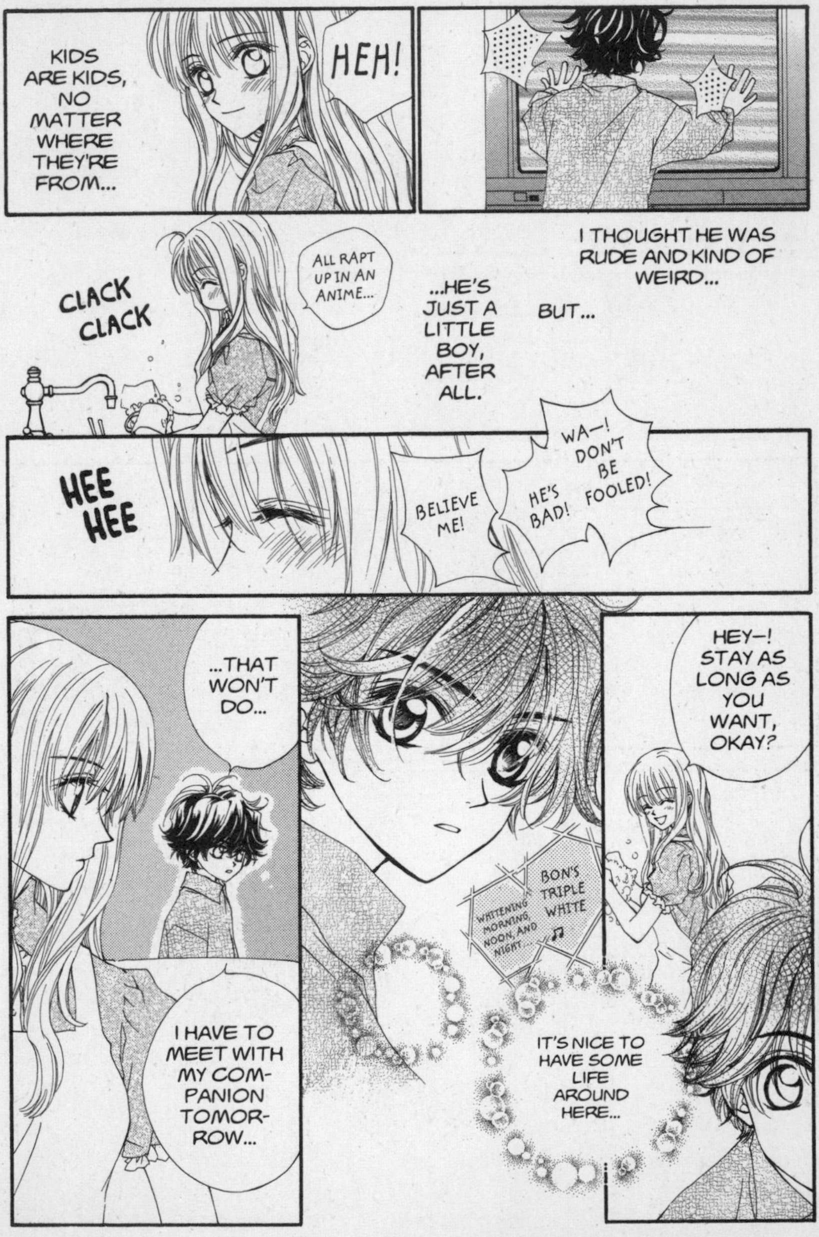
HEH!
KIDS ARE KIDS, NO MATTER WHERE THEY'RE FROM...
I THOUGHT HE WAS RUDE AND KIND OF WEIRD...
BUT...
...HE'S JUST A LITTLE BOY, AFTER ALL.
ALL RAPT UP IN AN ANIME...
CLACK CLACK
WA—! DON'T BE FOOLED!
HE'S BAD!
BELIEVE ME!
HEE HEE
HEY—! STAY AS LONG AS YOU WANT, OKAY?
BON'S TRIPLE WHITE ♪
WHITENING MORNING, NOON, AND NIGHT...
IT'S NICE TO HAVE SOME LIFE AROUND HERE...
...THAT WON'T DO...
I HAVE TO MEET WITH MY COMPANION TOMORROW...

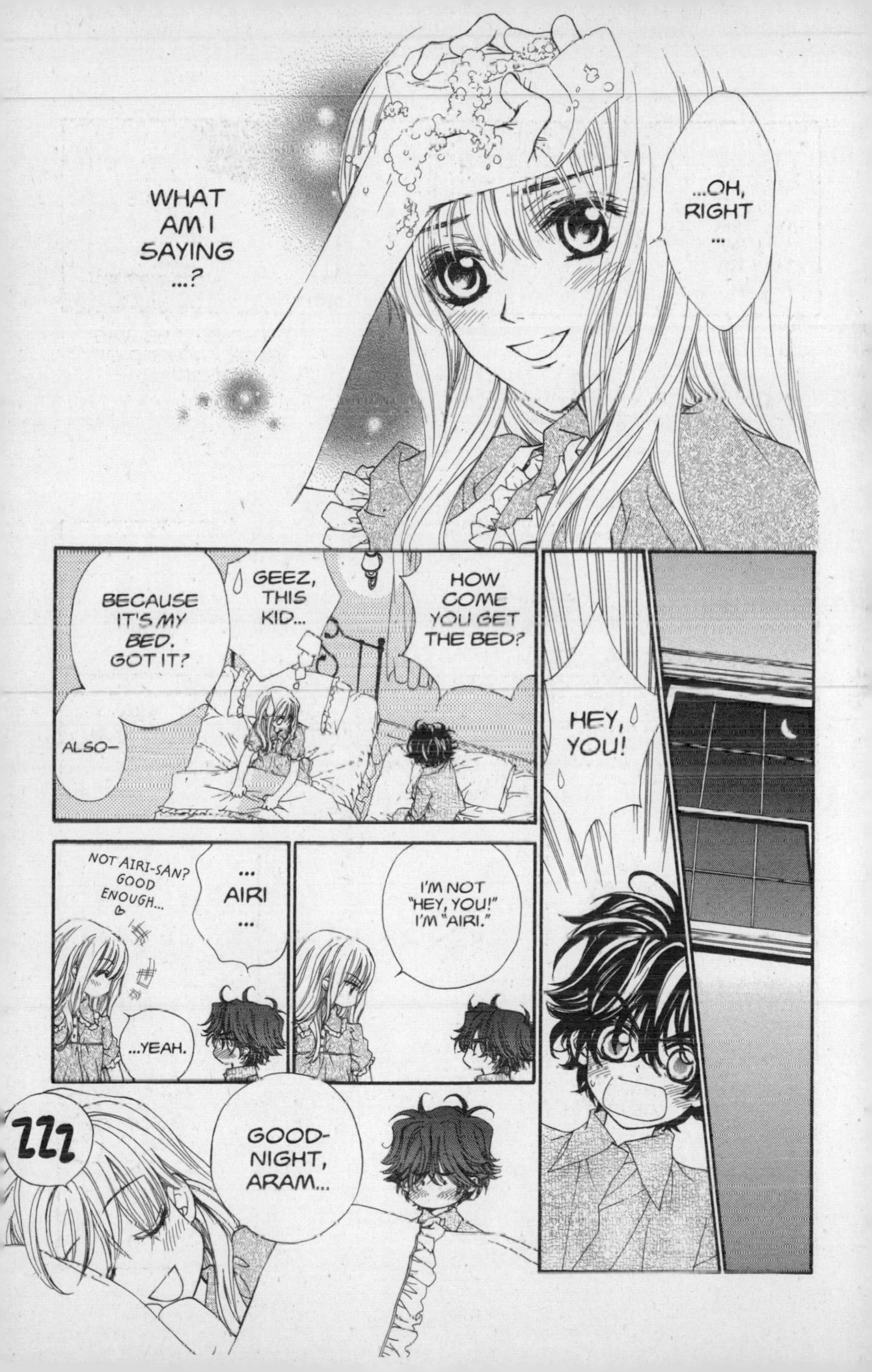
...OH, RIGHT ...
WHAT AM I SAYING ...?
HEY, YOU!
HOW COME YOU GET THE BED?
GEEZ, THIS KID...
BECAUSE IT'S MY BED. GOT IT?
ALSO—
I'M NOT "HEY, YOU!" I'M "AIRI."
... AIRI ...
NOT AIRI-SAN? GOOD ENOUGH...
...YEAH.
GOOD-NIGHT, ARAM...
ZZZ

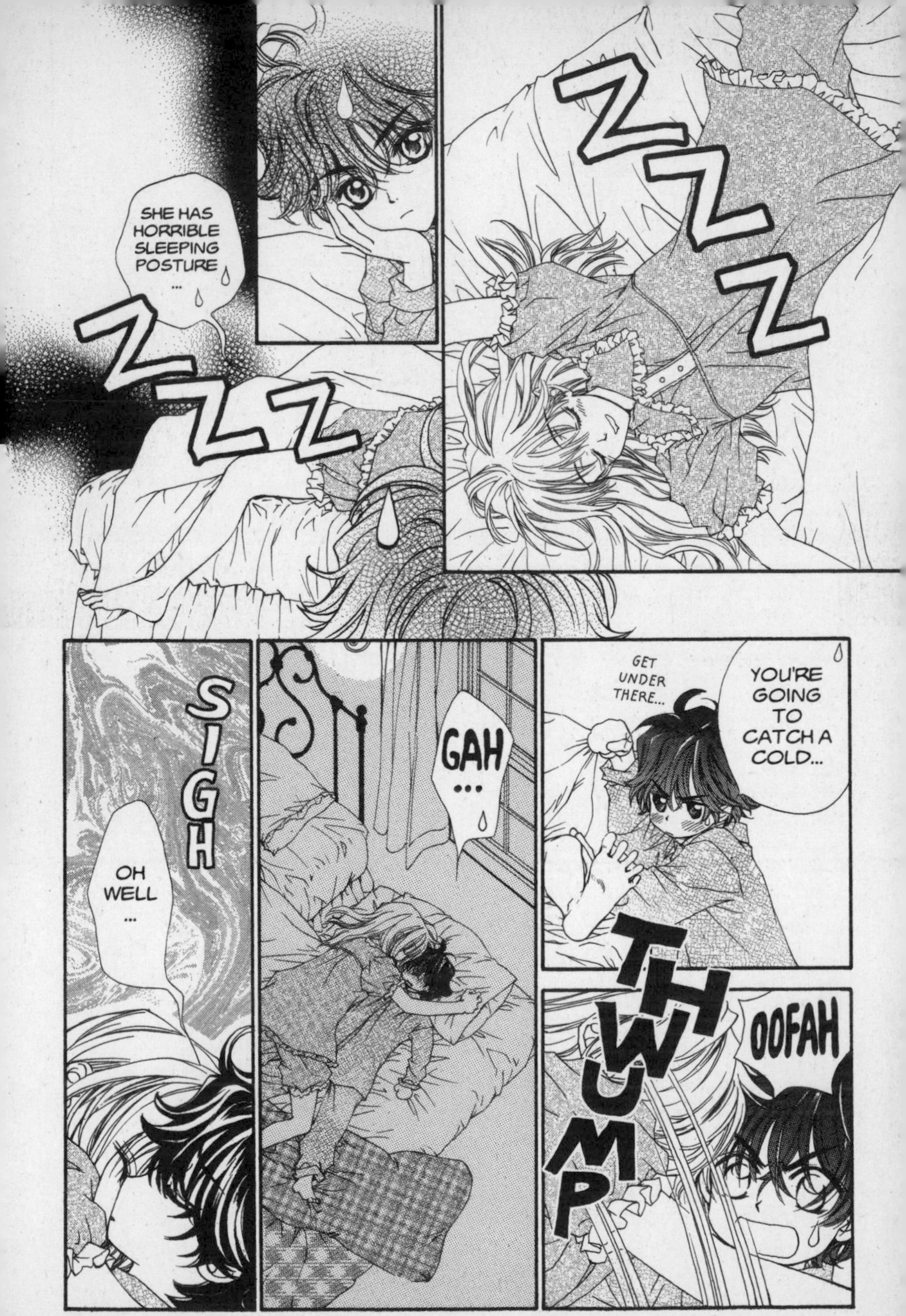
ZZZ
SHE HAS HORRIBLE SLEEPING POSTURE ...
ZZZ
YOU'RE GOING TO CATCH A COLD...
GET UNDER THERE...
GAH ...
SIGH
OH WELL ...
THWUMP
OOFAH

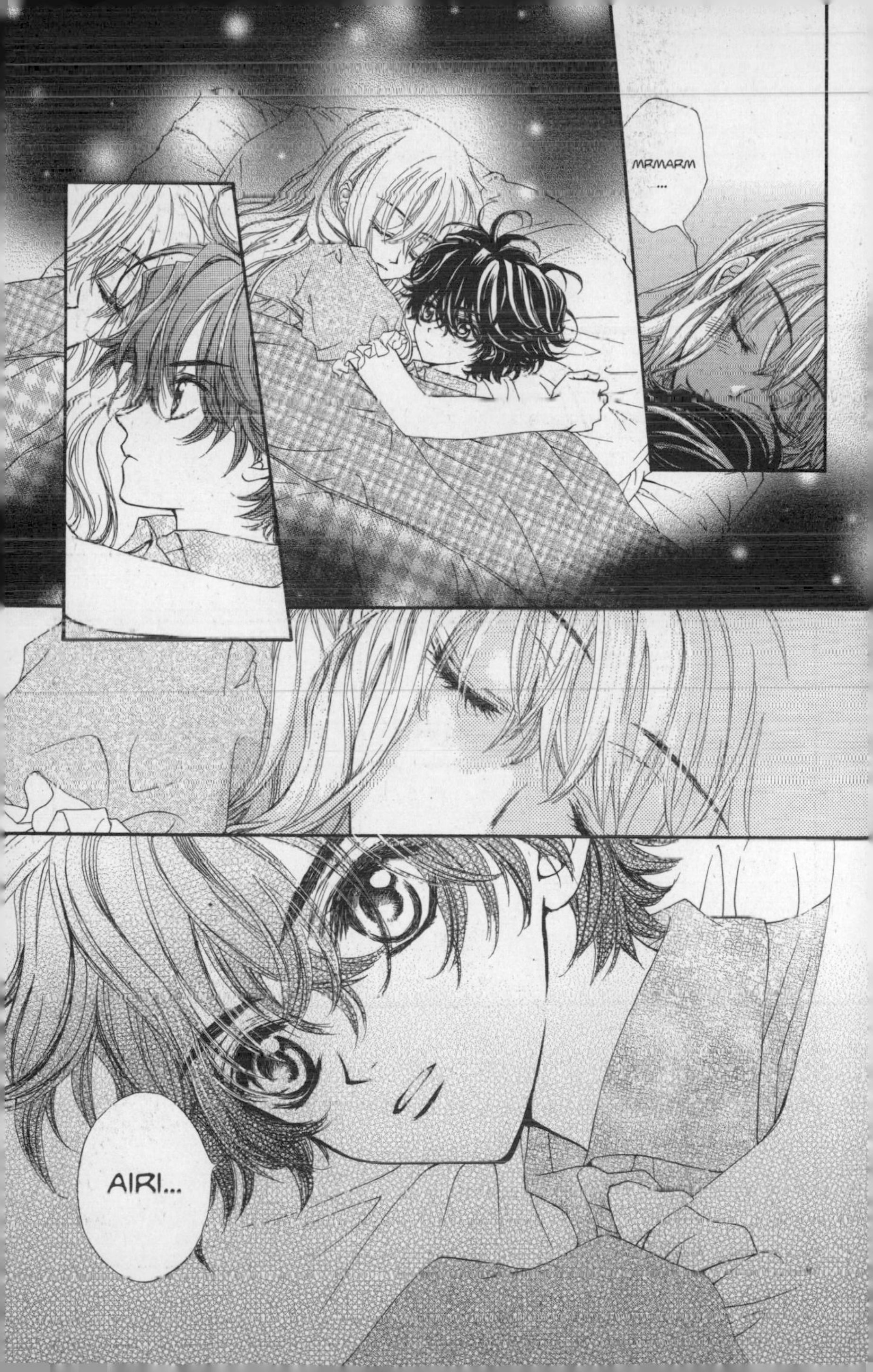
MRMARM ...
AIRI...

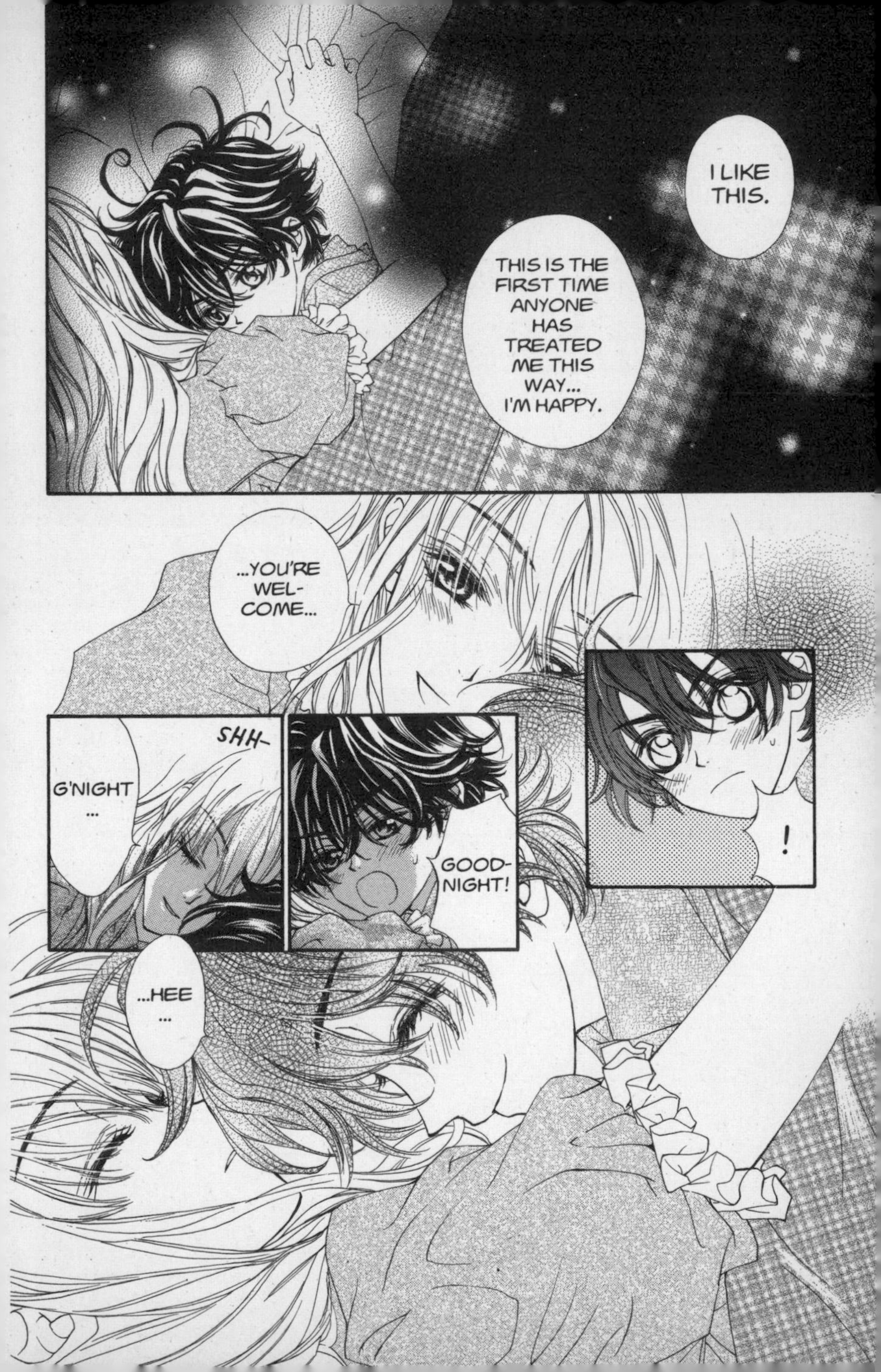
I LIKE THIS.
THIS IS THE FIRST TIME ANYONE HAS TREATED ME THIS WAY... I'M HAPPY.
...YOU'RE WEL-COME...
!
GOOD-NIGHT!
SHH-
G'NIGHT ...
...HEE ...

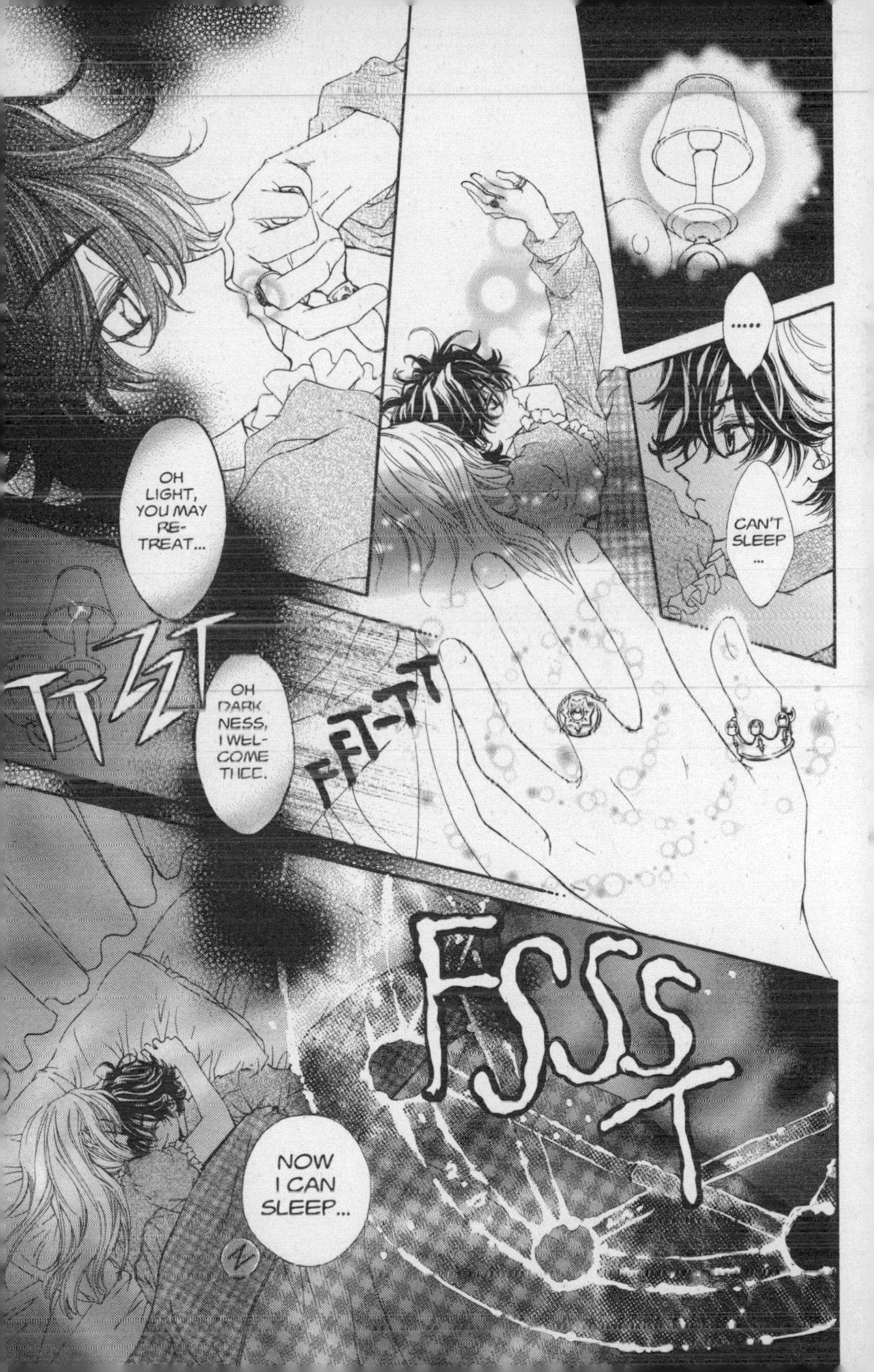
......
CAN'T SLEEP ...
OH LIGHT, YOU MAY RE-TREAT...
FFT-TT
OH DARKNESS, I WEL-COME THEE.
TTZZT
FSSST
NOW I CAN SLEEP...
Z

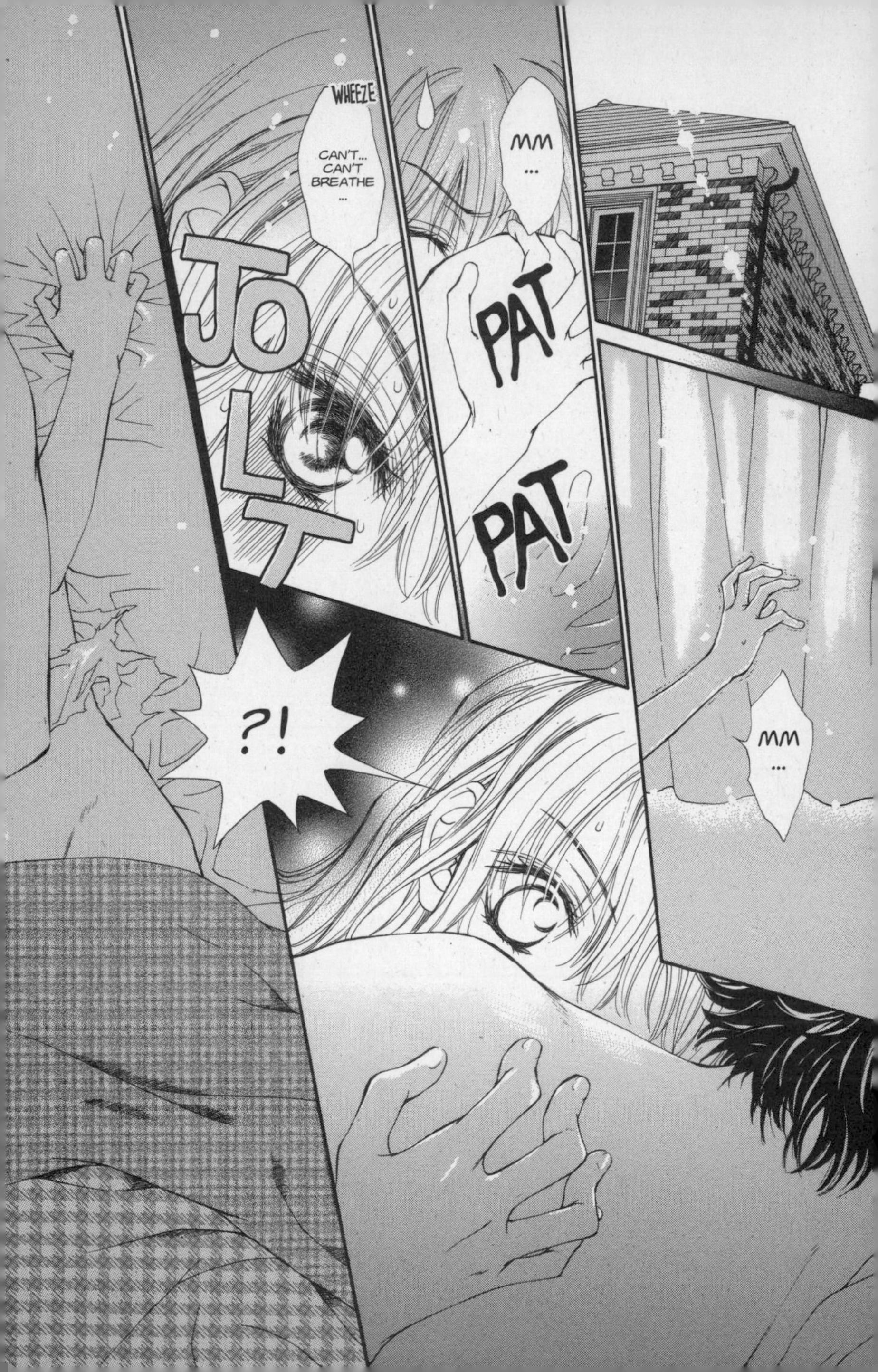
MM ...
MM ...
PAT
PAT
WHEEZE
CAN'T... CAN'T BREATHE ...
JOLT
?!

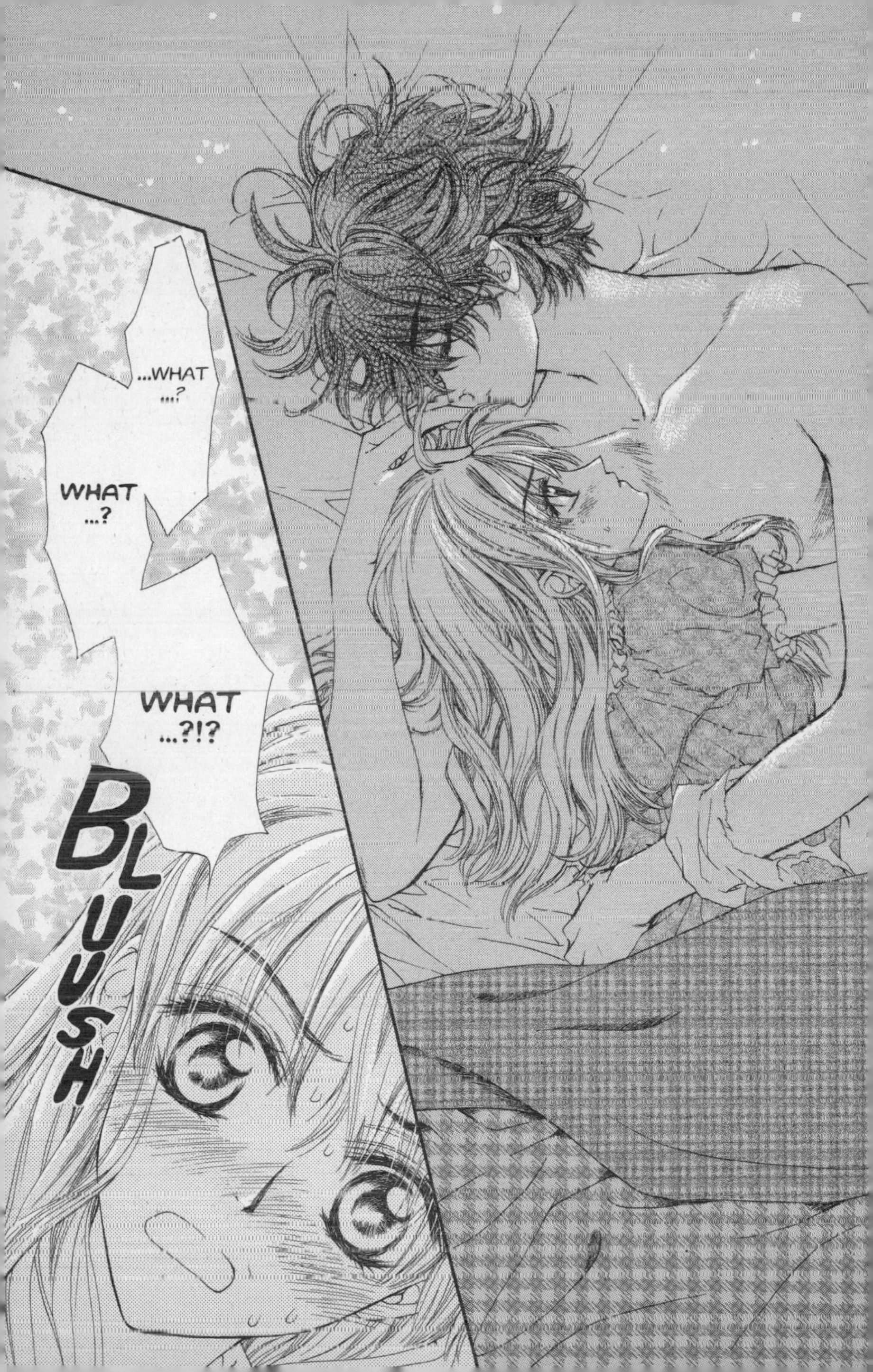
...WHAT ...?
WHAT ...?
WHAT ...?!?
BLUUSH

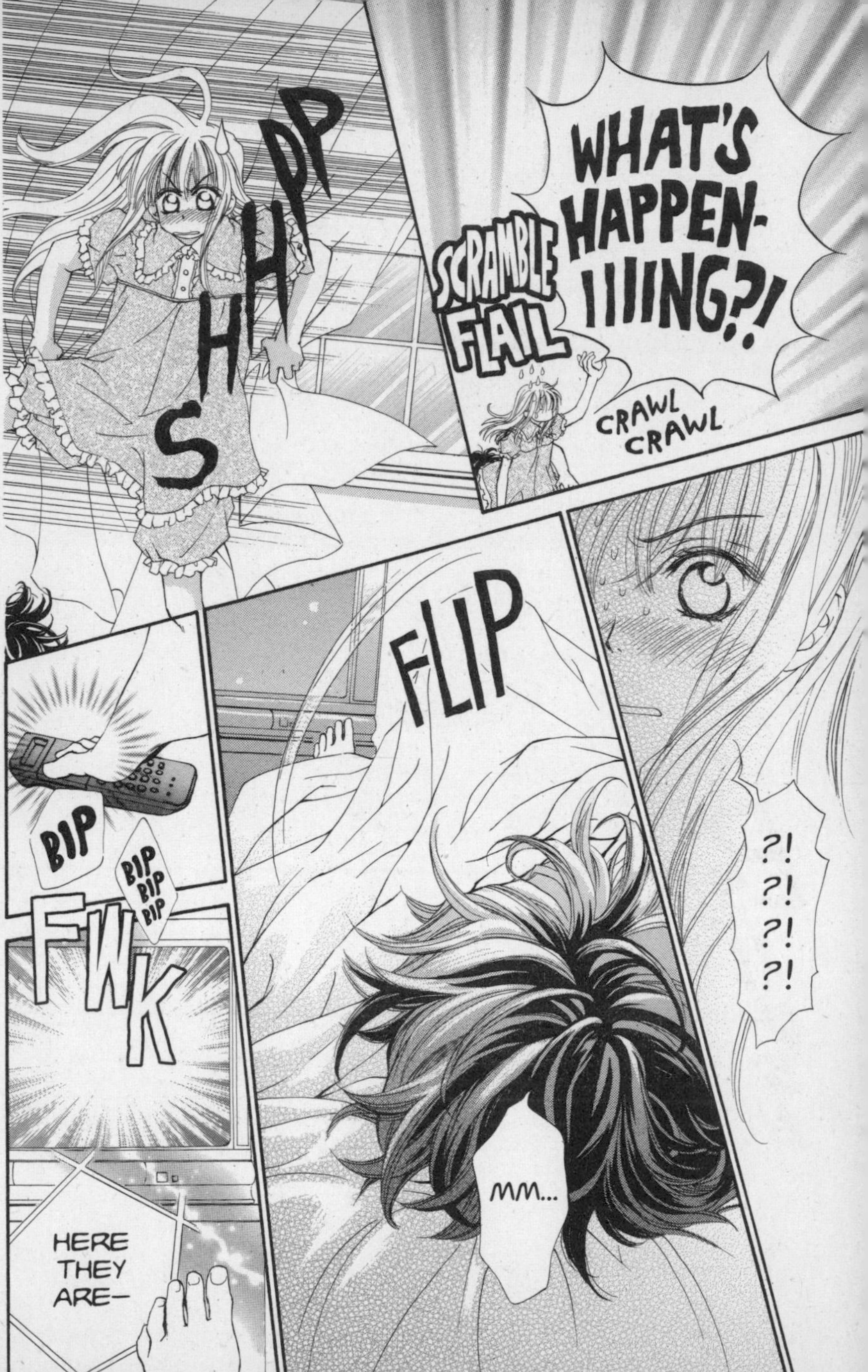
WHAT'S HAPPEN-IIIING?!
SCRAMBLE FLAIL
CRAWL CRAWL
SHHPP
?! ?! ?! ?!
FLIP
MM...
BIP
BIP BIP BIP
FWK
HERE THEY ARE—

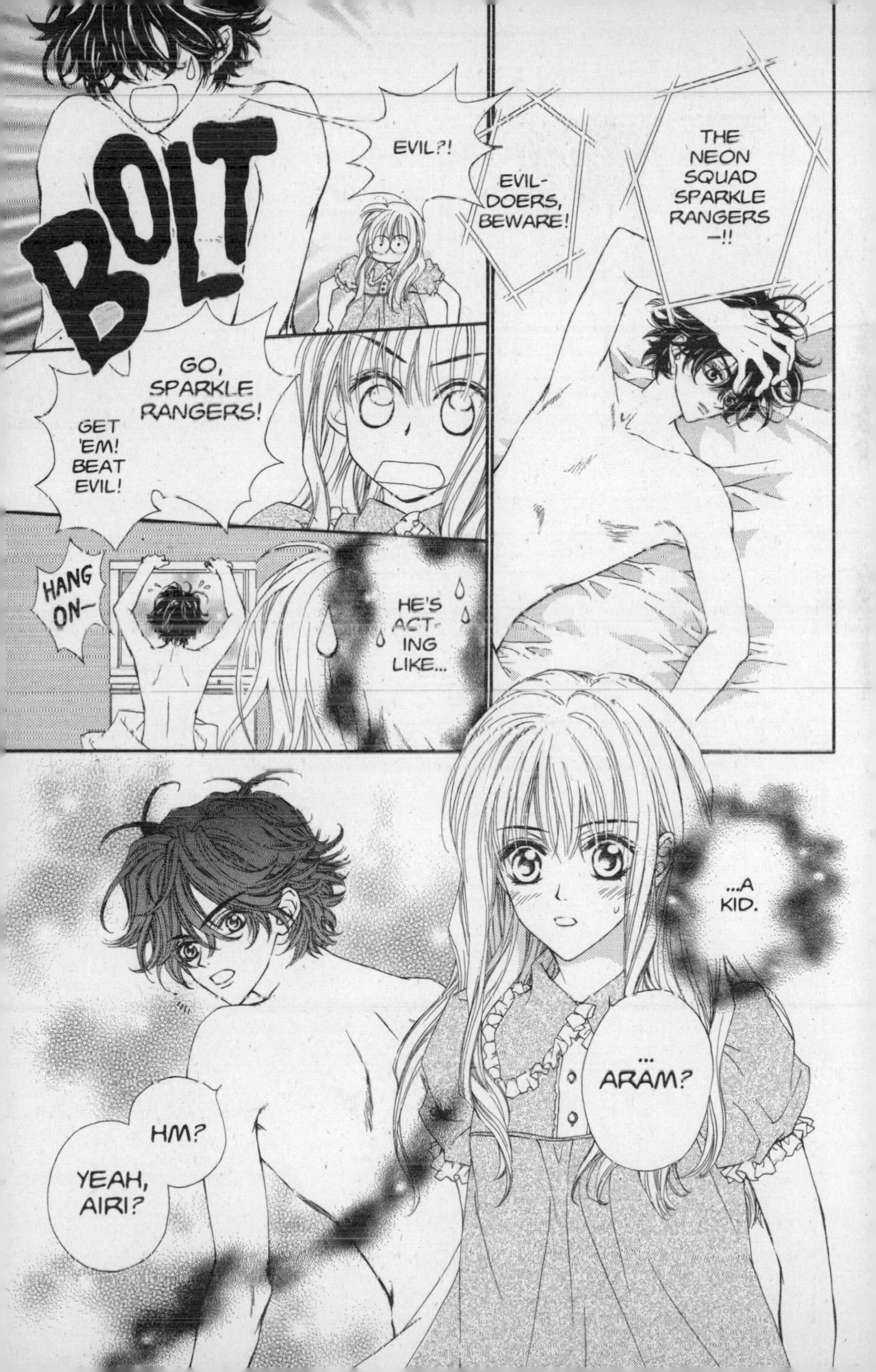
THE NEON SQUAD SPARKLE RANGERS—!!
EVIL-DOERS, BEWARE!
EVIL?!
BOLT
GO, SPARKLE RANGERS!
GET 'EM! BEAT EVIL!
HE'S ACT-ING LIKE...
HANG ON—
...A KID.
...ARAM?
HM? YEAH, AIRI?

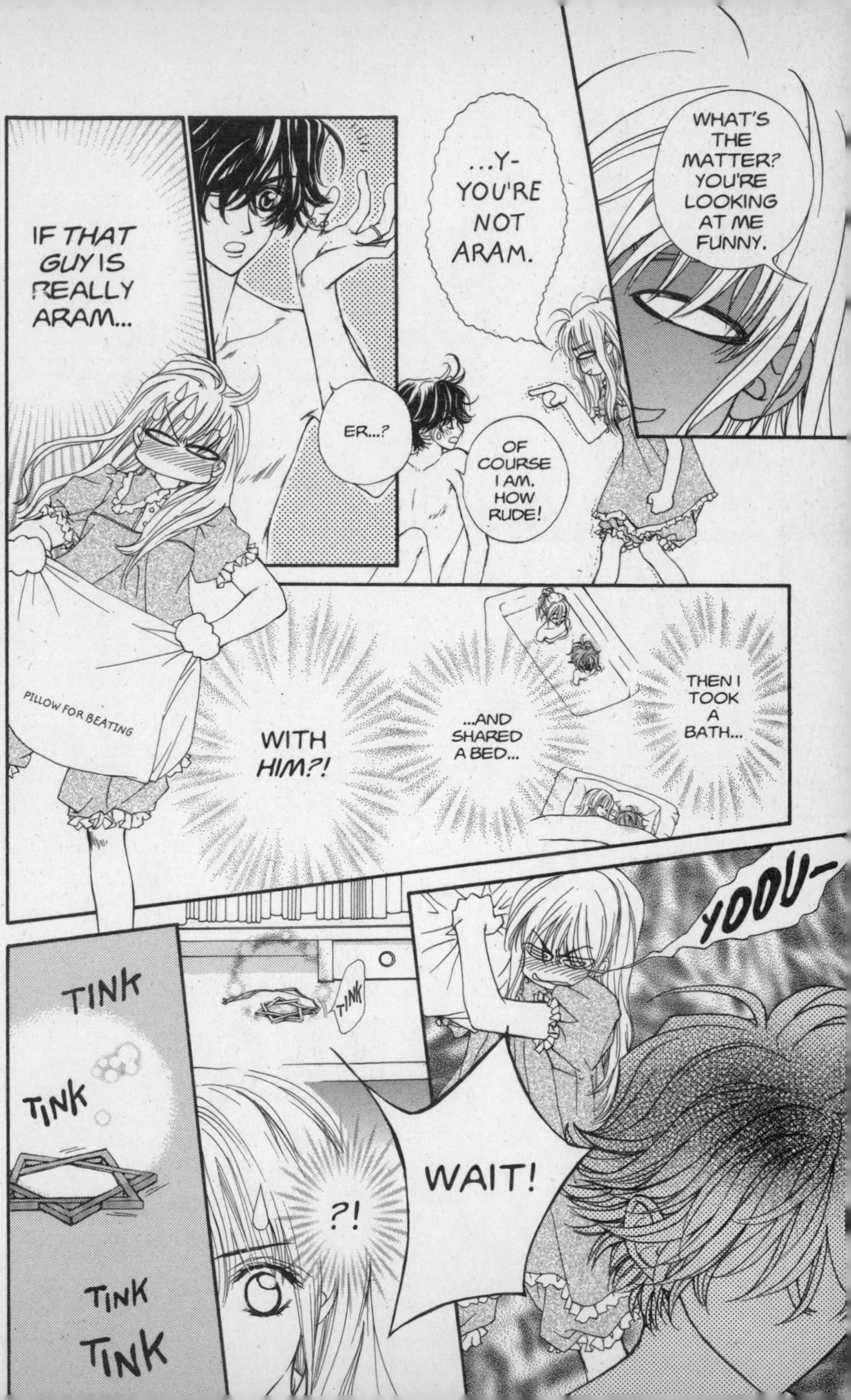
WHAT'S THE MATTER? YOU'RE LOOKING AT ME FUNNY.
...Y- YOU'RE NOT ARAM.
OF COURSE I AM. HOW RUDE!
ER...?
IF THAT GUY IS REALLY ARAM...
THEN I TOOK A BATH...
...AND SHARED A BED...
WITH HIM?!
PILLOW FOR BEATING
YOOU-
WAIT!
?!
TINK
TINK
TINK
TINK
TINK

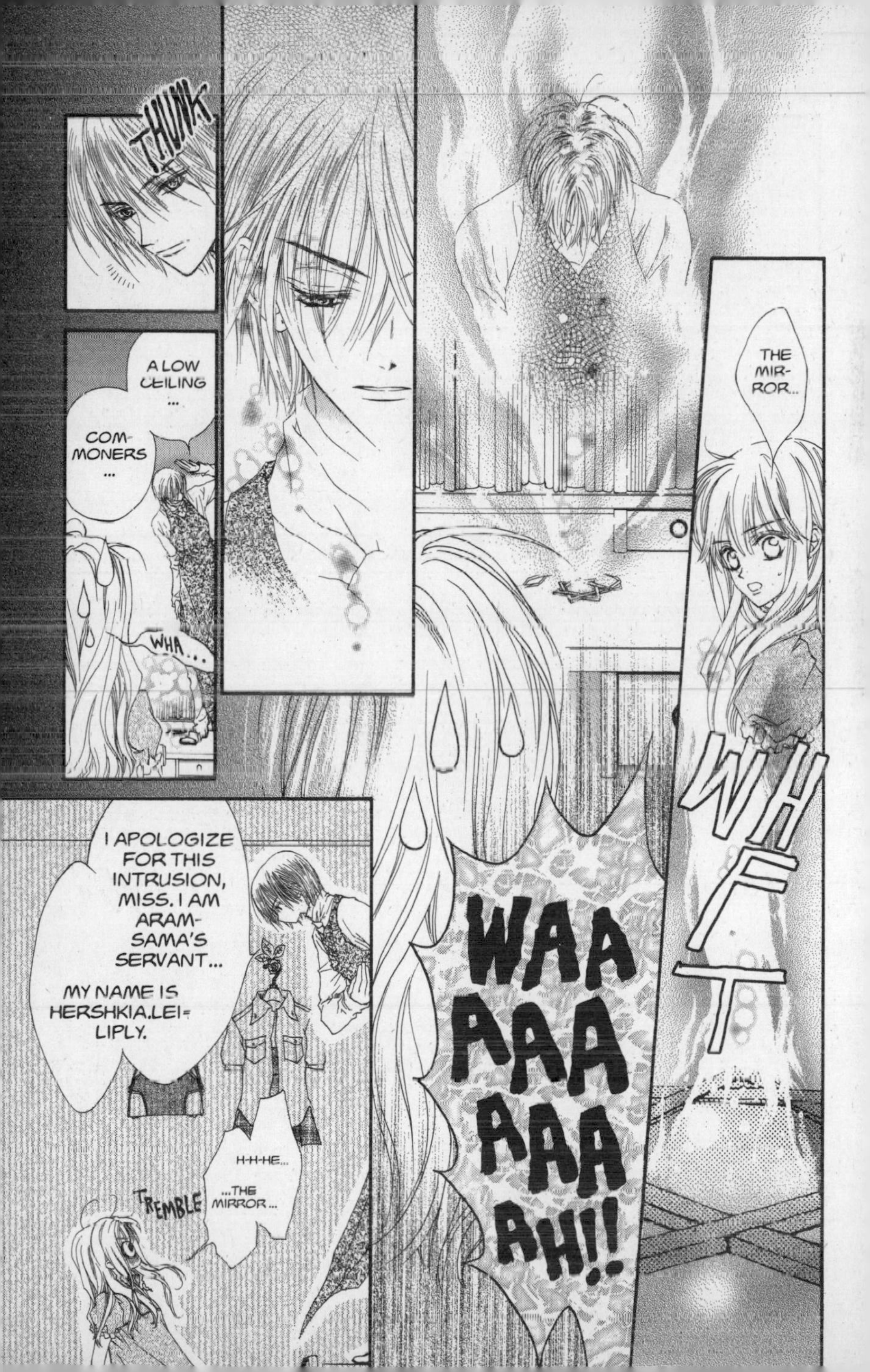
THE MIR-ROR...
WHIFT
WAAAAAAAAAAAH!!
THUNK
A LOW CEILING ...
COM-MONERS ...
WHA...
I APOLOGIZE FOR THIS INTRUSION, MISS. I AM ARAM-SAMA'S SERVANT...
MY NAME IS HERSHKIA.LEI=LIPLY.
H-H-HE...
...THE MIRROR...
TREMBLE

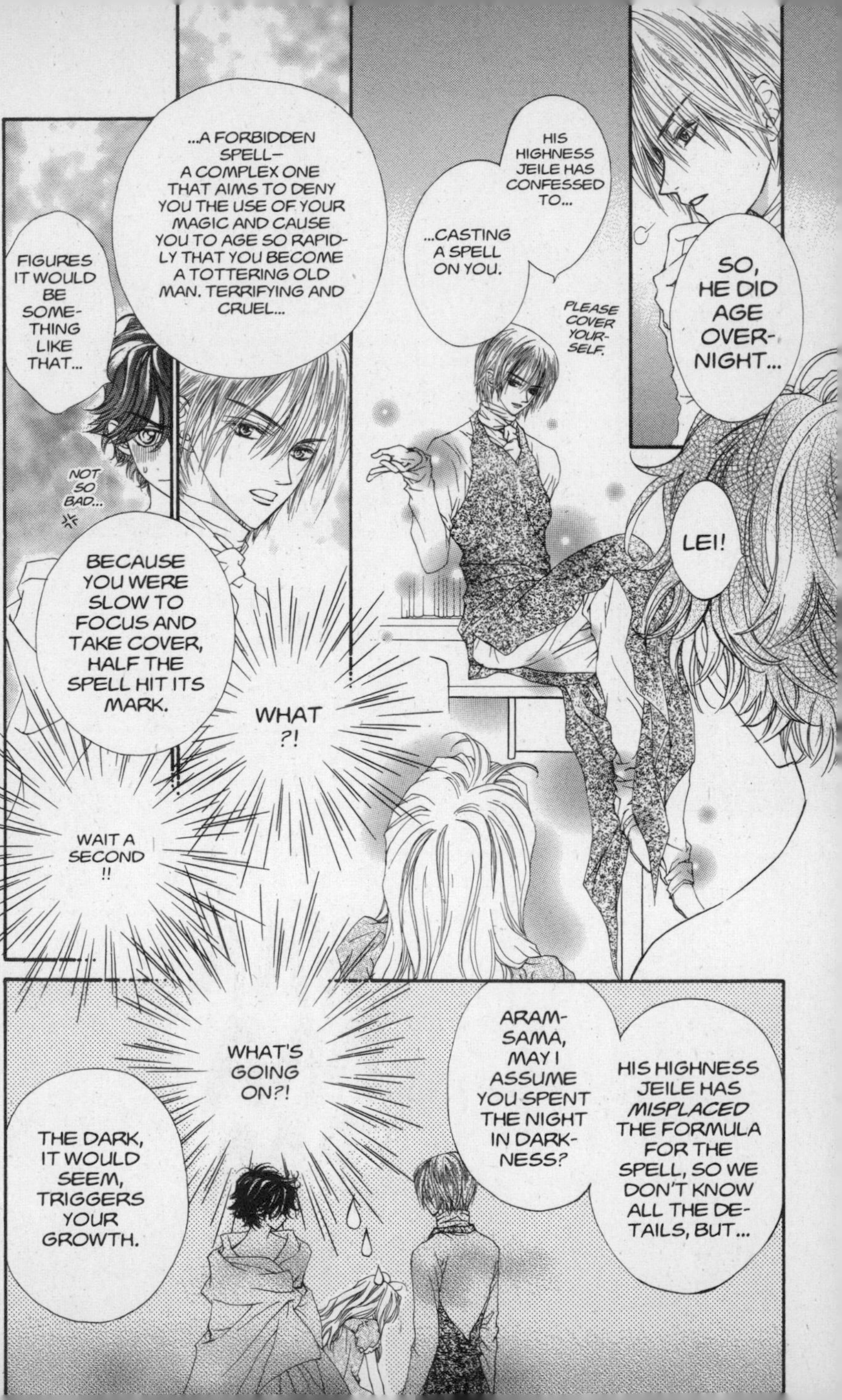
SO, HE DID AGE OVERNIGHT...
LEI!
HIS HIGHNESS JEILE HAS CONFESSED TO...
...CASTING A SPELL ON YOU.
PLEASE COVER YOURSELF.
...A FORBIDDEN SPELL—A COMPLEX ONE THAT AIMS TO DENY YOU THE USE OF YOUR MAGIC AND CAUSE YOU TO AGE SO RAPIDLY THAT YOU BECOME A TOTTERING OLD MAN. TERRIFYING AND CRUEL...
FIGURES IT WOULD BE SOMETHING LIKE THAT...
NOT SO BAD...
BECAUSE YOU WERE SLOW TO FOCUS AND TAKE COVER, HALF THE SPELL HIT ITS MARK.
WHAT?!
WAIT A SECOND!!
HIS HIGHNESS JEILE HAS *MISPLACED* THE FORMULA FOR THE SPELL, SO WE DON'T KNOW ALL THE DETAILS, BUT...
ARAM-SAMA, MAY I ASSUME YOU SPENT THE NIGHT IN DARKNESS?
WHAT'S GOING ON?!
THE DARK, IT WOULD SEEM, TRIGGERS YOUR GROWTH.

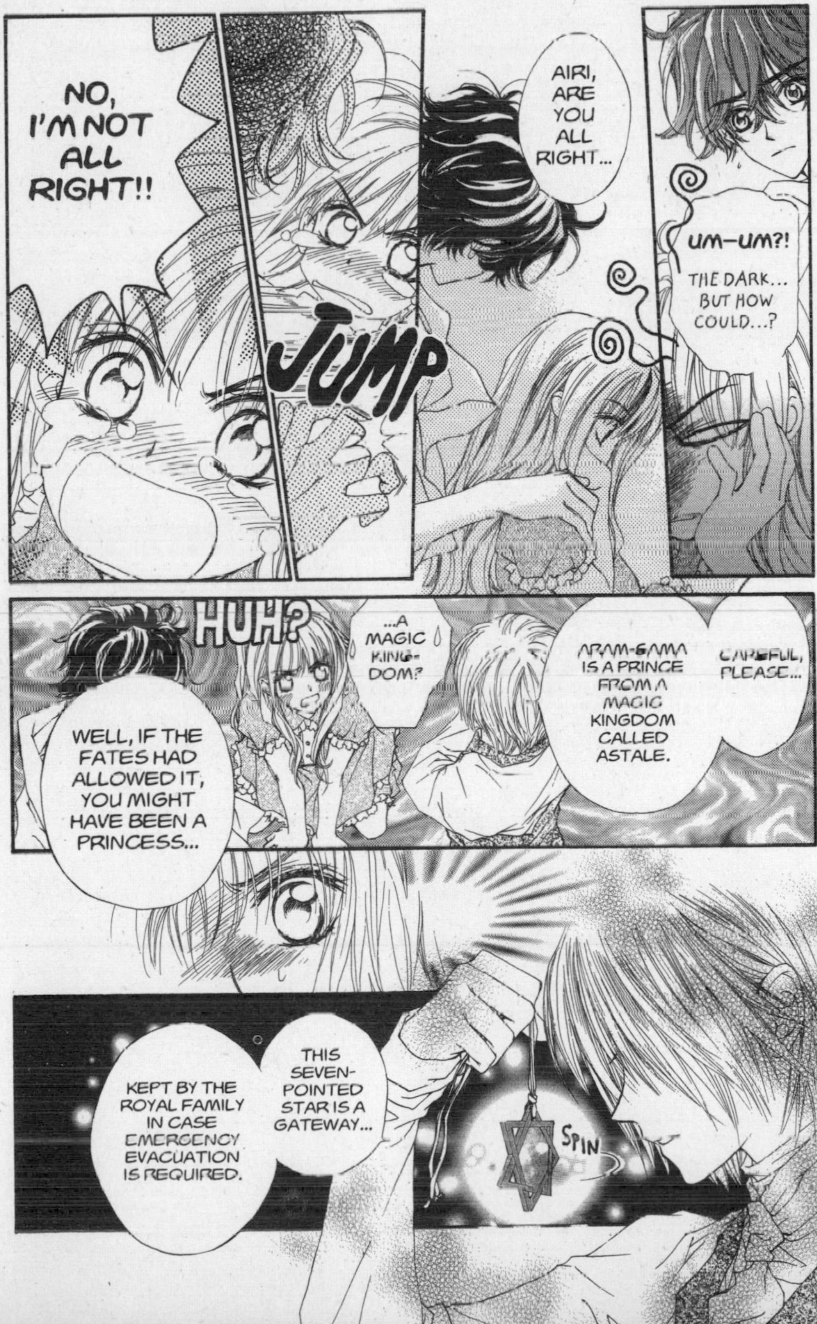
UM-UM?!
THE DARK... BUT HOW COULD...?
AIRI, ARE YOU ALL RIGHT...
JUMP
NO, I'M NOT ALL RIGHT!!
CAREFUL, PLEASE...
ARAM-SAMA IS A PRINCE FROM A MAGIC KINGDOM CALLED ASTALE.
...A MAGIC KING-DOM?
HUH?
WELL, IF THE FATES HAD ALLOWED IT, YOU MIGHT HAVE BEEN A PRINCESS...
SPIN
THIS SEVEN-POINTED STAR IS A GATEWAY...
KEPT BY THE ROYAL FAMILY IN CASE EMERGENCY EVACUATION IS REQUIRED.

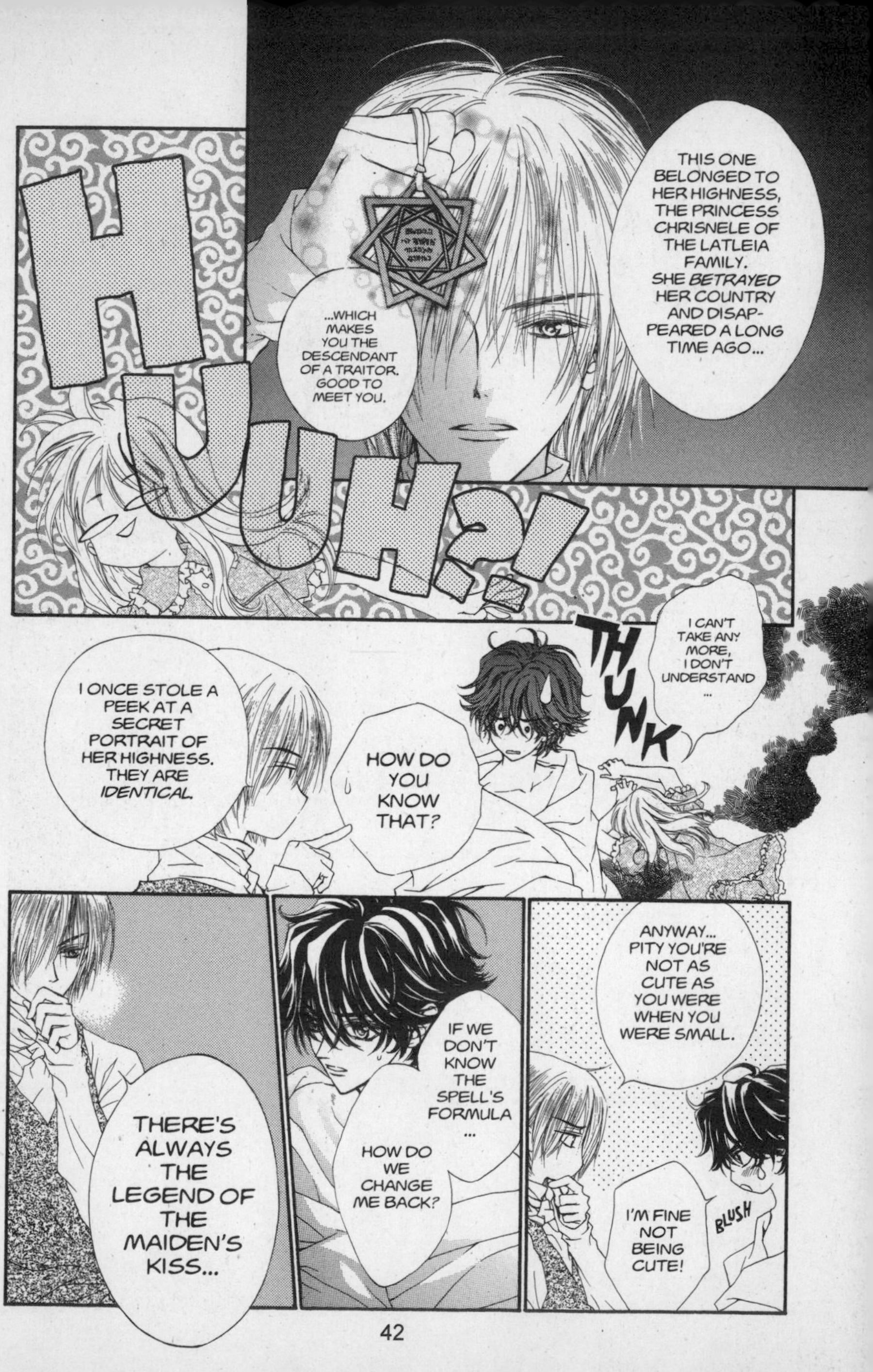
THIS ONE BELONGED TO HER HIGHNESS, THE PRINCESS CHRISNELE OF THE LATLEIA FAMILY. SHE *BETRAYED* HER COUNTRY AND DISAPPEARED A LONG TIME AGO...
...WHICH MAKES YOU THE DESCENDANT OF A TRAITOR. GOOD TO MEET YOU.
HUUH?!
I CAN'T TAKE ANY MORE, I DON'T UNDERSTAND ...
THUNK
HOW DO YOU KNOW THAT?
I ONCE STOLE A PEEK AT A SECRET PORTRAIT OF HER HIGHNESS. THEY ARE *IDENTICAL*.
ANYWAY... PITY YOU'RE NOT AS CUTE AS YOU WERE WHEN YOU WERE SMALL.
I'M FINE NOT BEING CUTE!
BLUSH
IF WE DON'T KNOW THE SPELL'S FORMULA ...
HOW DO WE CHANGE ME BACK?
THERE'S ALWAYS THE LEGEND OF THE MAIDEN'S KISS...

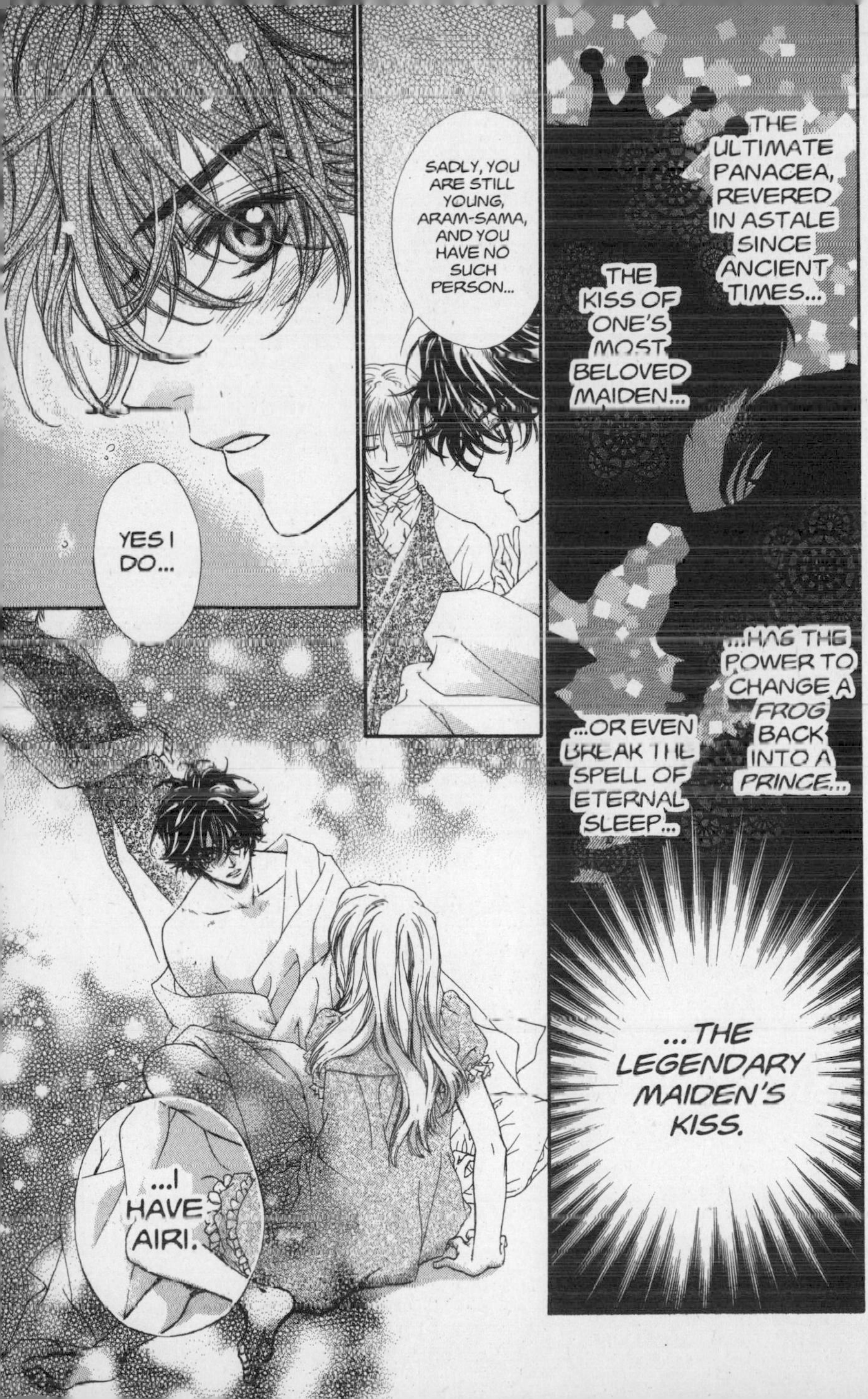
THE ULTIMATE PANACEA, REVERED IN ASTALE SINCE ANCIENT TIMES...
THE KISS OF ONE'S MOST BELOVED MAIDEN...
...HAS THE POWER TO CHANGE A FROG BACK INTO A PRINCE...
...OR EVEN BREAK THE SPELL OF ETERNAL SLEEP...
...THE LEGENDARY MAIDEN'S KISS.
SADLY, YOU ARE STILL YOUNG, ARAM-SAMA, AND YOU HAVE NO SUCH PERSON...
YES I DO...
...I HAVE AIRI.

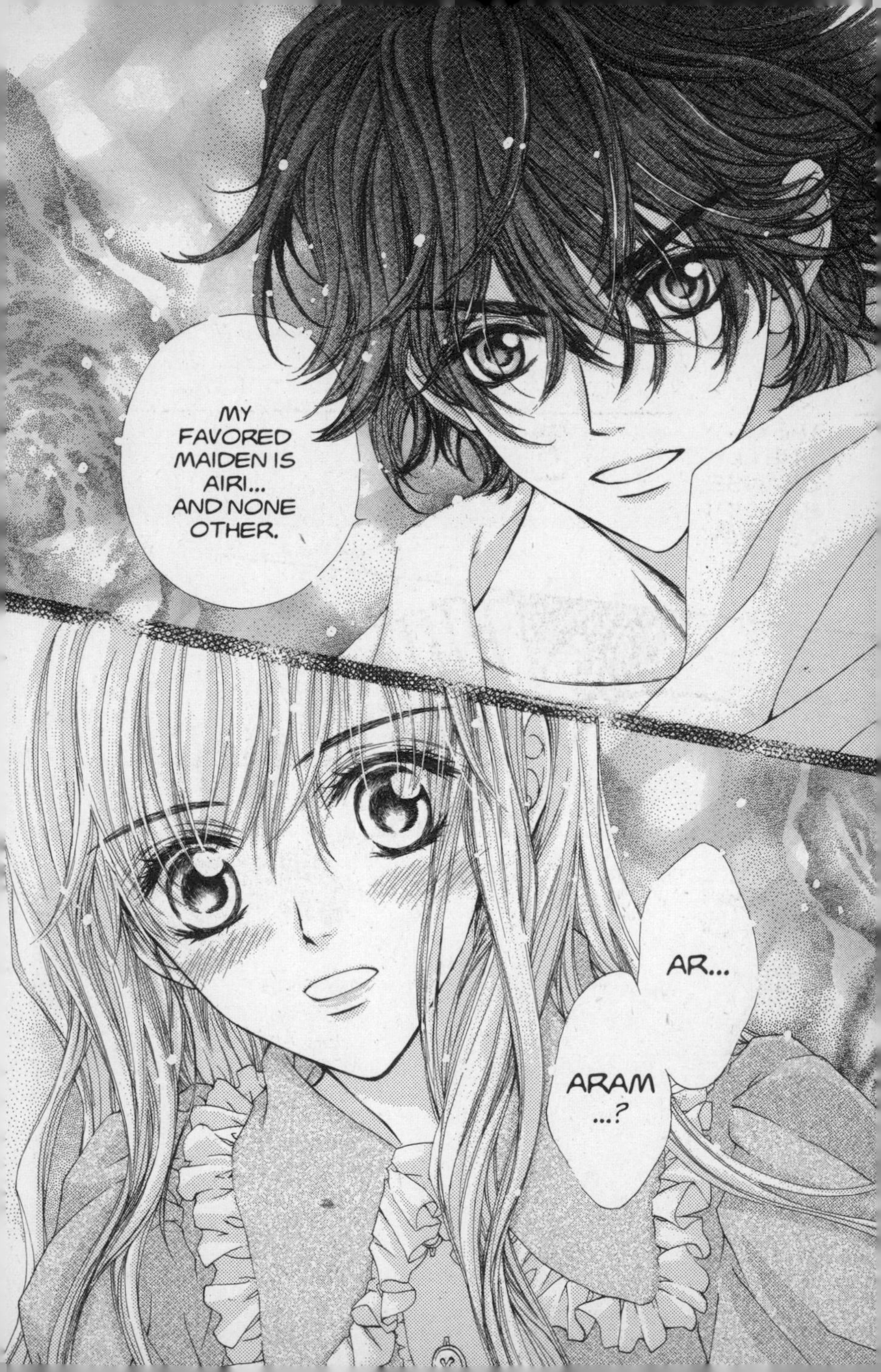
MY FAVORED MAIDEN IS AIRI... AND NONE OTHER.
AR...
ARAM ...?

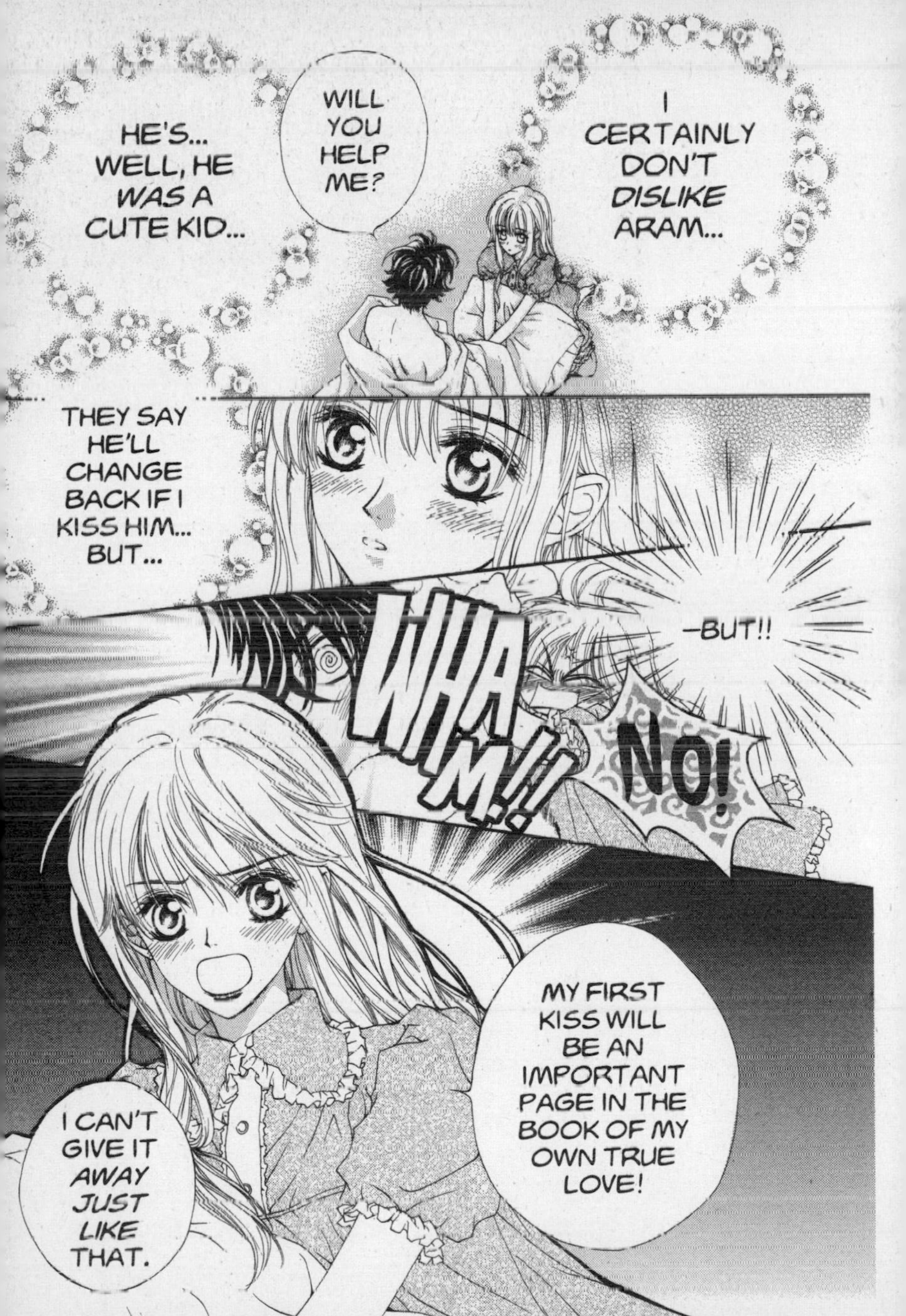
I CERTAINLY DON'T DISLIKE ARAM...
WILL YOU HELP ME?
HE'S... WELL, HE WAS A CUTE KID...
THEY SAY HE'LL CHANGE BACK IF I KISS HIM... BUT...
—BUT!!
WHAM!!
NO!
MY FIRST KISS WILL BE AN IMPORTANT PAGE IN THE BOOK OF MY OWN TRUE LOVE!
I CAN'T GIVE IT AWAY JUST LIKE THAT.

MERUPURI CHAPTER 1/END

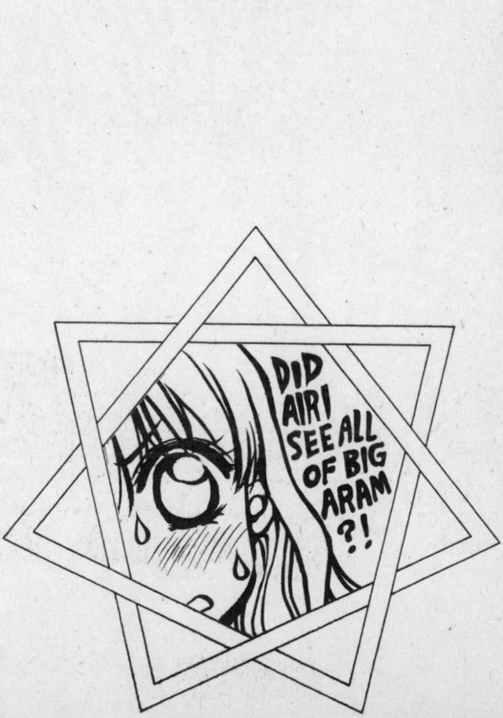
DID AIRI SEE ALL OF BIG ARAM ?!

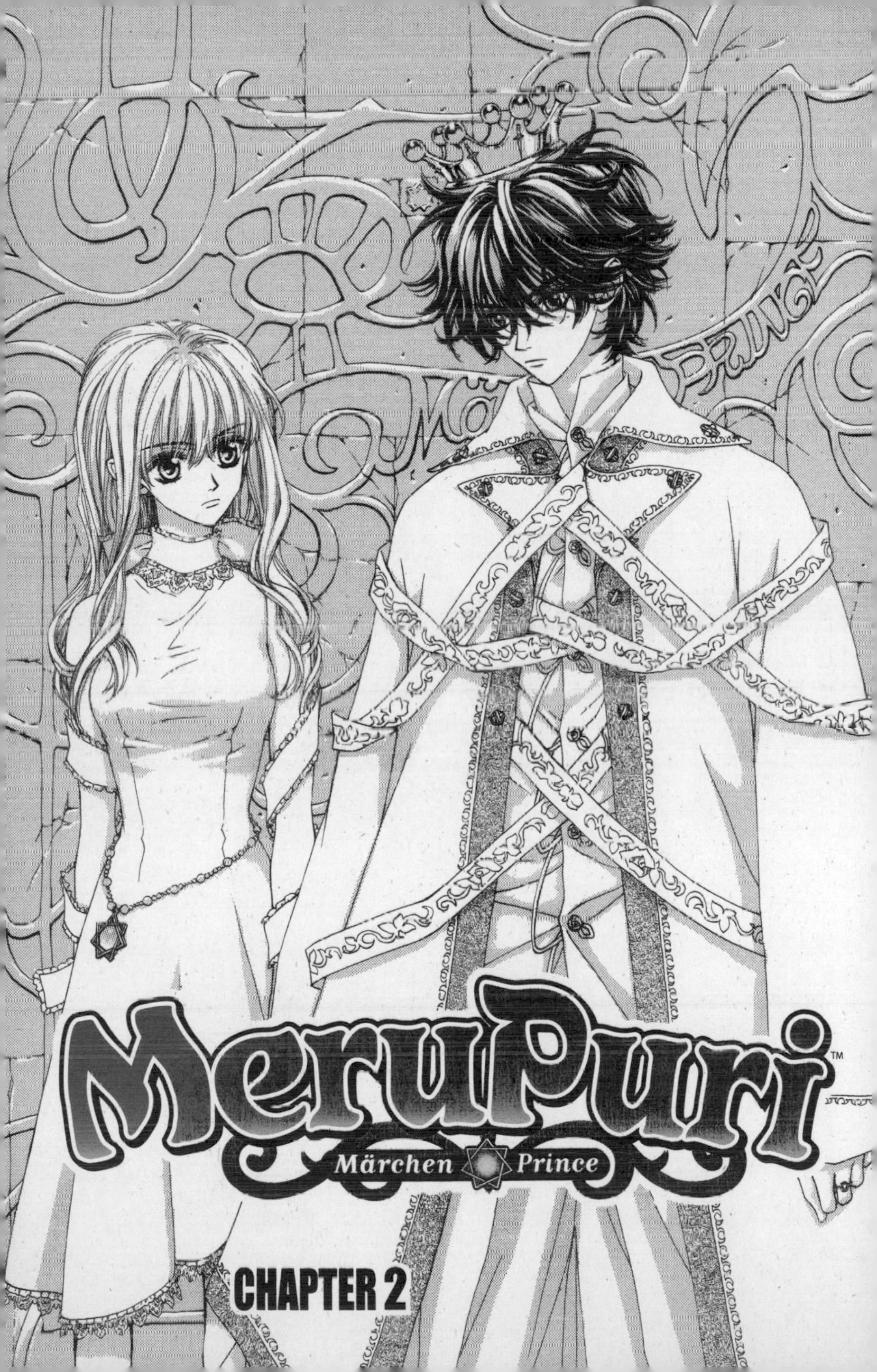
MeruPuri™
Märchen Prince
CHAPTER 2

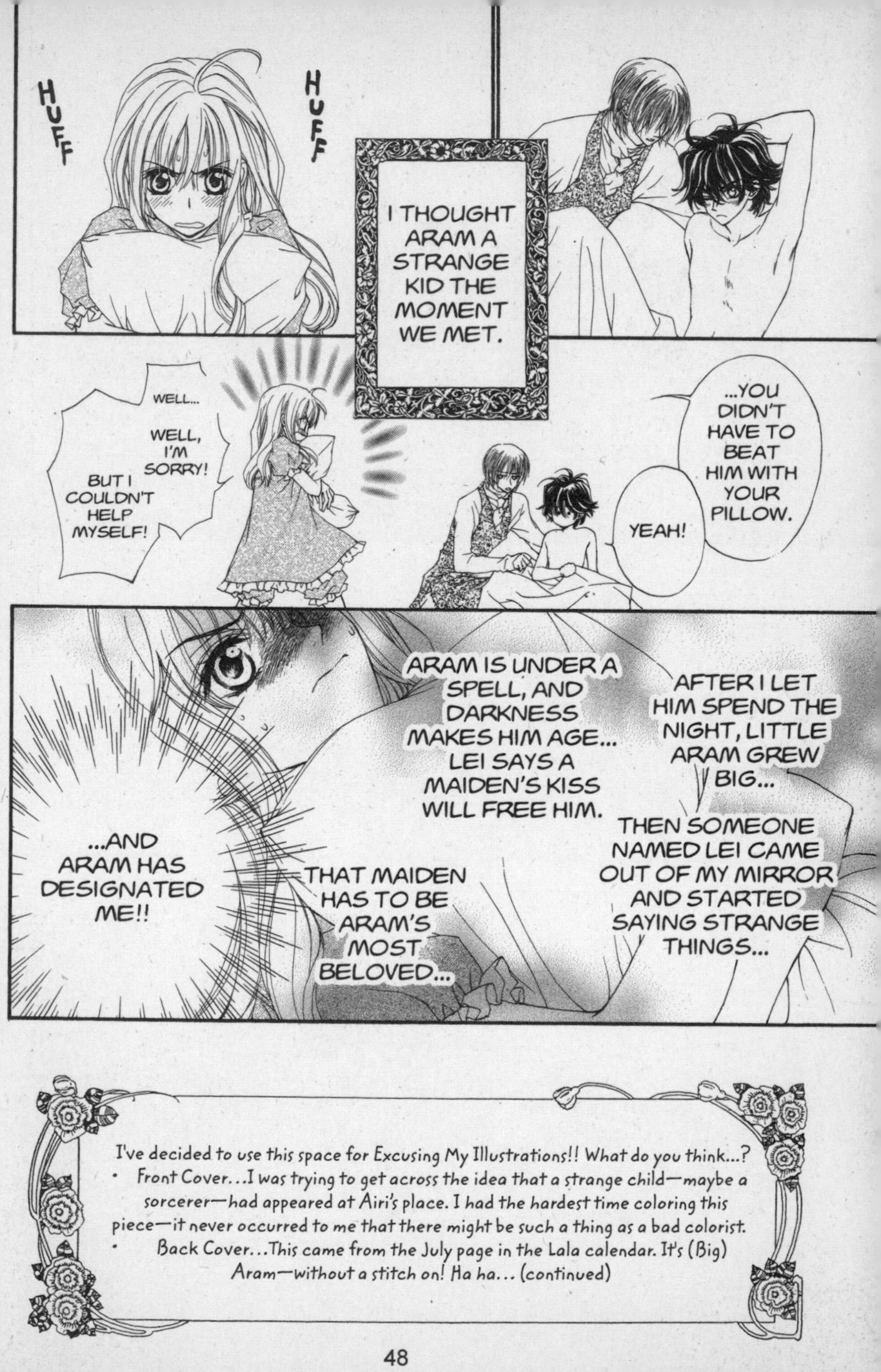
I THOUGHT ARAM A STRANGE KID THE MOMENT WE MET.
HUFF
HUFF
...YOU DIDN'T HAVE TO BEAT HIM WITH YOUR PILLOW.
YEAH!
WELL...
WELL, I'M SORRY!
BUT I COULDN'T HELP MYSELF!
AFTER I LET HIM SPEND THE NIGHT, LITTLE ARAM GREW BIG...
THEN SOMEONE NAMED LEI CAME OUT OF MY MIRROR AND STARTED SAYING STRANGE THINGS...
ARAM IS UNDER A SPELL, AND DARKNESS MAKES HIM AGE... LEI SAYS A MAIDEN'S KISS WILL FREE HIM.
THAT MAIDEN HAS TO BE ARAM'S MOST BELOVED...
...AND ARAM HAS DESIGNATED ME!!

I've decided to use this space for Excusing My Illustrations!! What do you think...?

- Front Cover...I was trying to get across the idea that a strange child—maybe a sorcerer—had appeared at Airi's place. I had the hardest time coloring this piece—it never occurred to me that there might be such a thing as a bad colorist.
- Back Cover...This came from the July page in the Lala calendar. It's (Big) Aram—without a stitch on! Ha ha... (continued)

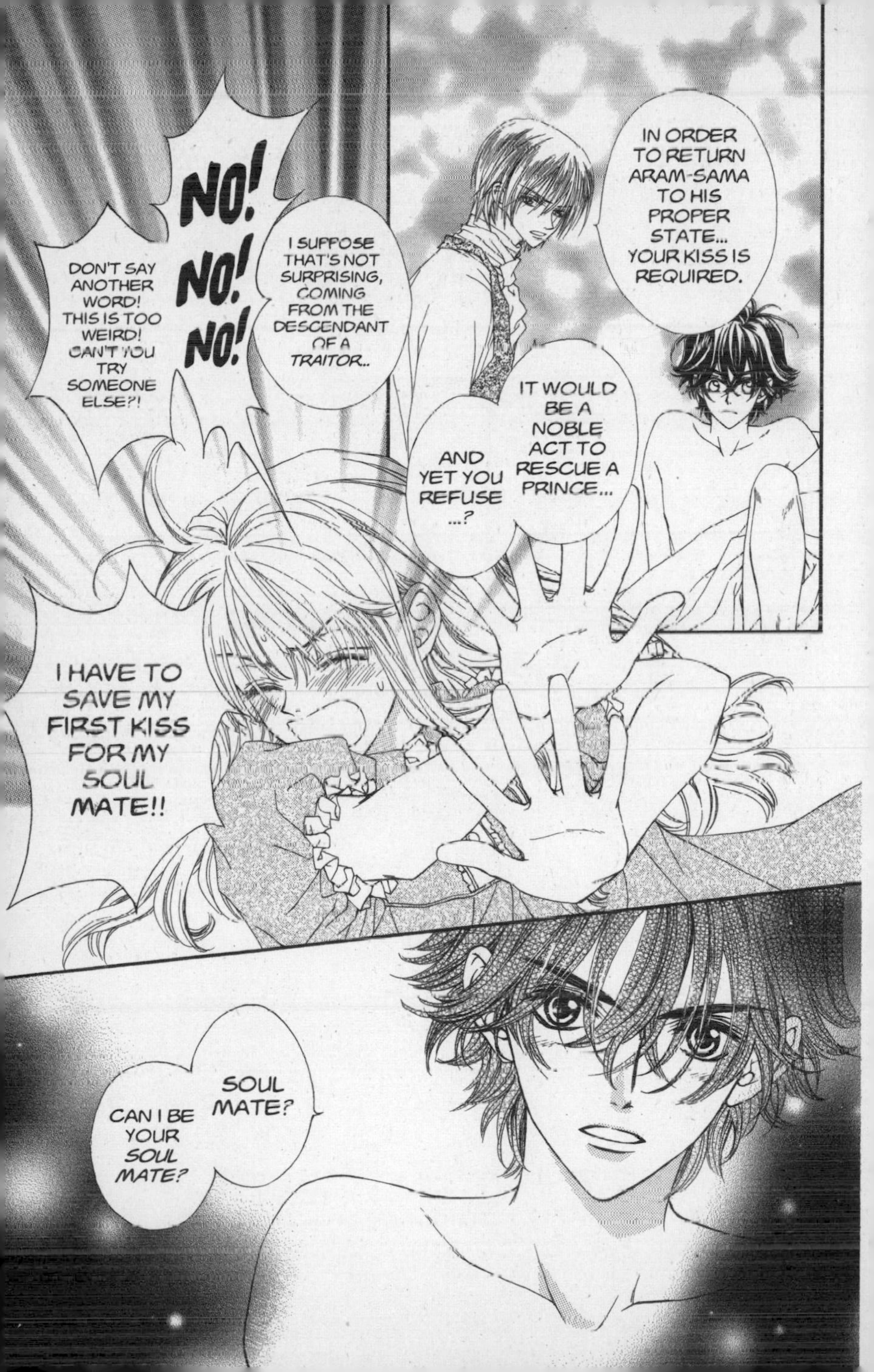
IN ORDER TO RETURN ARAM-SAMA TO HIS PROPER STATE... YOUR KISS IS REQUIRED.
IT WOULD BE A NOBLE ACT TO RESCUE A PRINCE...
AND YET YOU REFUSE ...?
I SUPPOSE THAT'S NOT SURPRISING, COMING FROM THE DESCENDANT OF A TRAITOR...
NO! NO! NO!
DON'T SAY ANOTHER WORD! THIS IS TOO WEIRD! CAN'T YOU TRY SOMEONE ELSE?!
I HAVE TO SAVE MY FIRST KISS FOR MY SOUL MATE!!
SOUL MATE?
CAN I BE YOUR SOUL MATE?

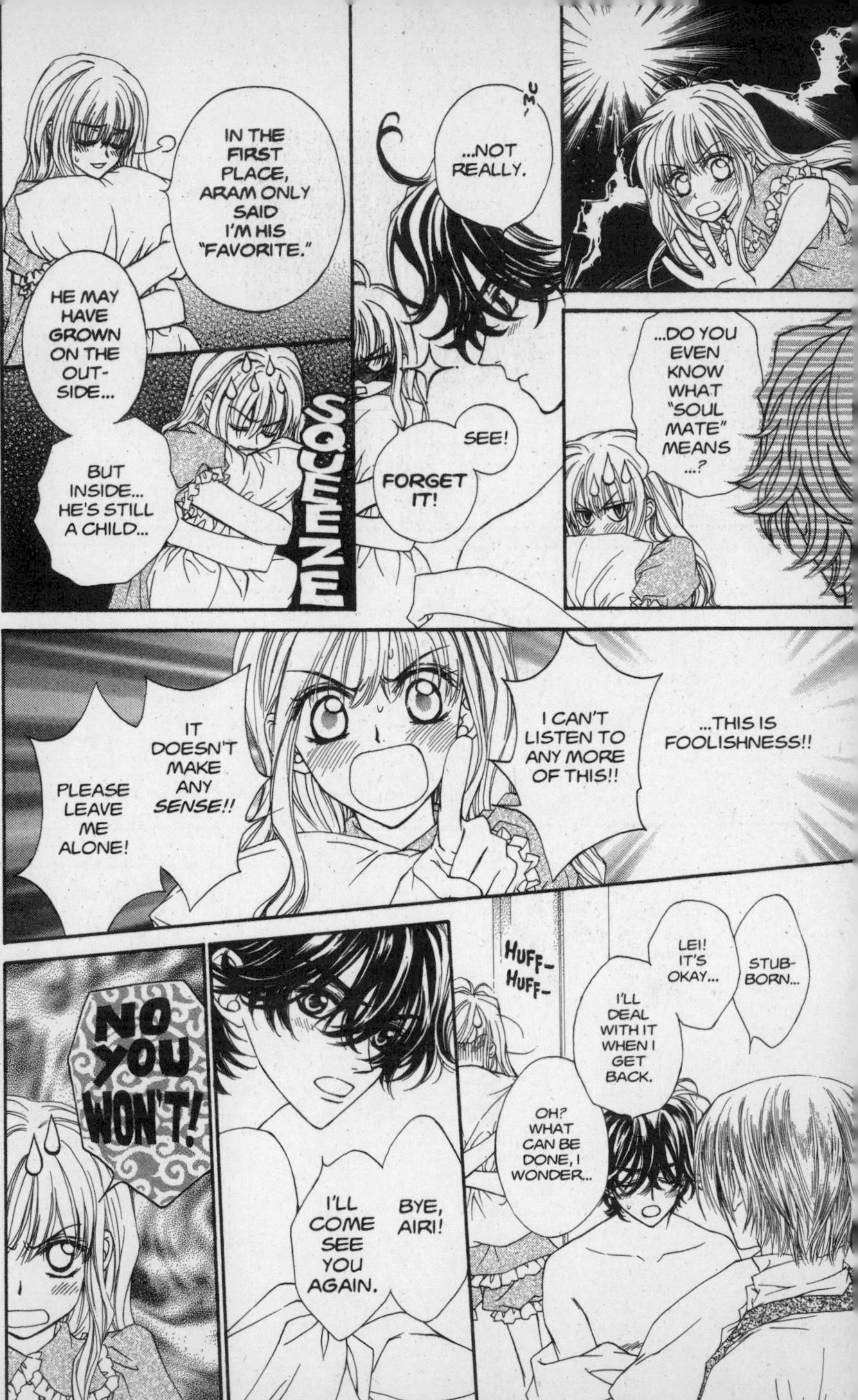
...DO YOU EVEN KNOW WHAT "SOUL MATE" MEANS ...?
UM, ...NOT REALLY.
SEE! FORGET IT!
IN THE FIRST PLACE, ARAM ONLY SAID I'M HIS "FAVORITE."
HE MAY HAVE GROWN ON THE OUT-SIDE...
BUT INSIDE... HE'S STILL A CHILD...
SQUEEZE
...THIS IS FOOLISHNESS!!
I CAN'T LISTEN TO ANY MORE OF THIS!!
IT DOESN'T MAKE ANY SENSE!!
PLEASE LEAVE ME ALONE!
STUB-BORN...
LEI! IT'S OKAY...
I'LL DEAL WITH IT WHEN I GET BACK.
OH? WHAT CAN BE DONE, I WONDER...
HUFF- HUFF-
BYE, AIRI!
I'LL COME SEE YOU AGAIN.
NO YOU WON'T!

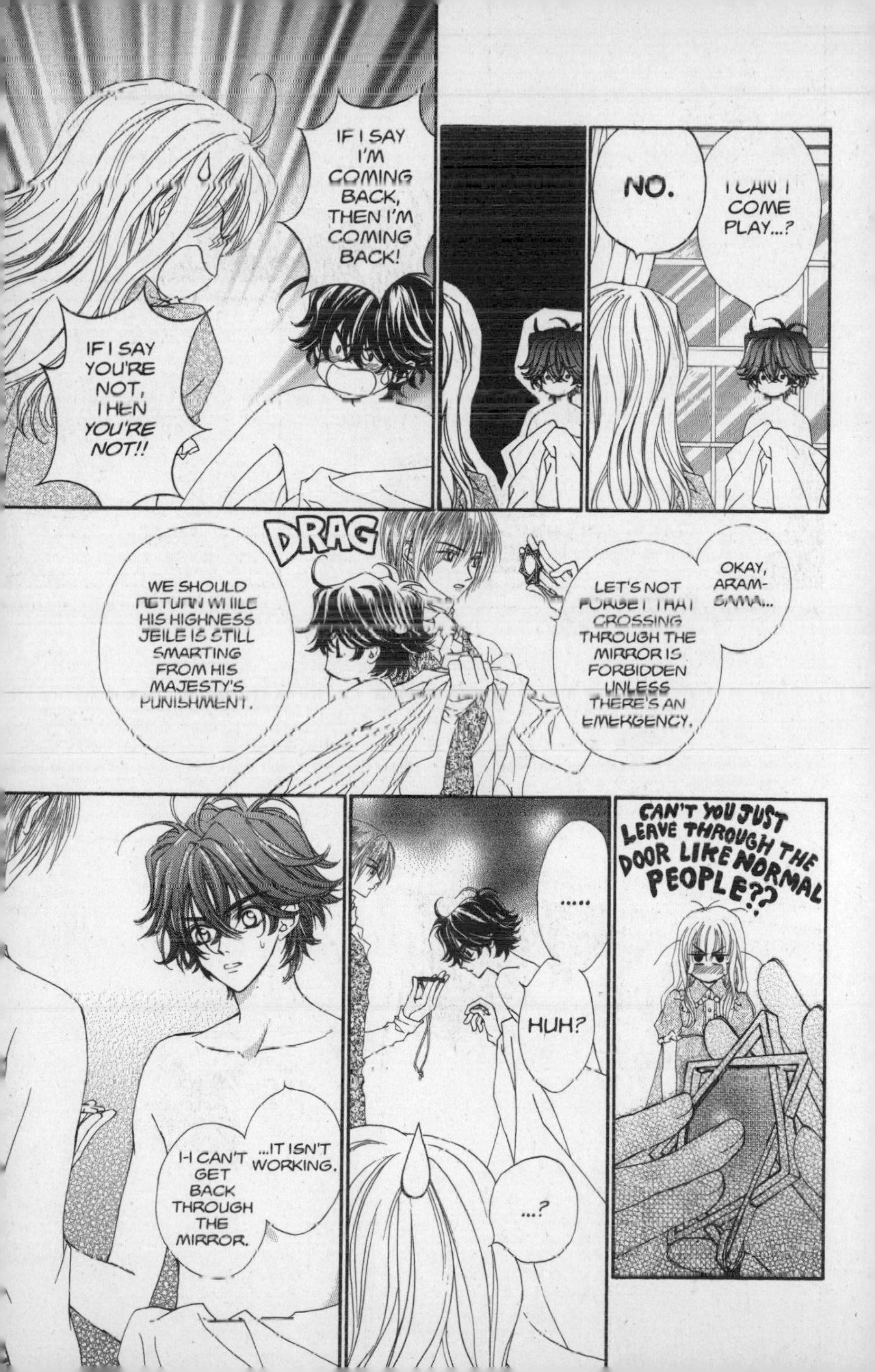
I CAN'T COME PLAY...?
NO.
IF I SAY I'M COMING BACK, THEN I'M COMING BACK!
IF I SAY YOU'RE NOT, THEN YOU'RE NOT!!
OKAY, ARAM-SAMA...
LET'S NOT FORGET THAT CROSSING THROUGH THE MIRROR IS FORBIDDEN UNLESS THERE'S AN EMERGENCY.
DRAG
WE SHOULD RETURN WHILE HIS HIGHNESS JEILE IS STILL SMARTING FROM HIS MAJESTY'S PUNISHMENT.
CAN'T YOU JUST LEAVE THROUGH THE DOOR LIKE NORMAL PEOPLE??
.....
HUH?
...?
...IT ISN'T WORKING.
I-I CAN'T GET BACK THROUGH THE MIRROR.

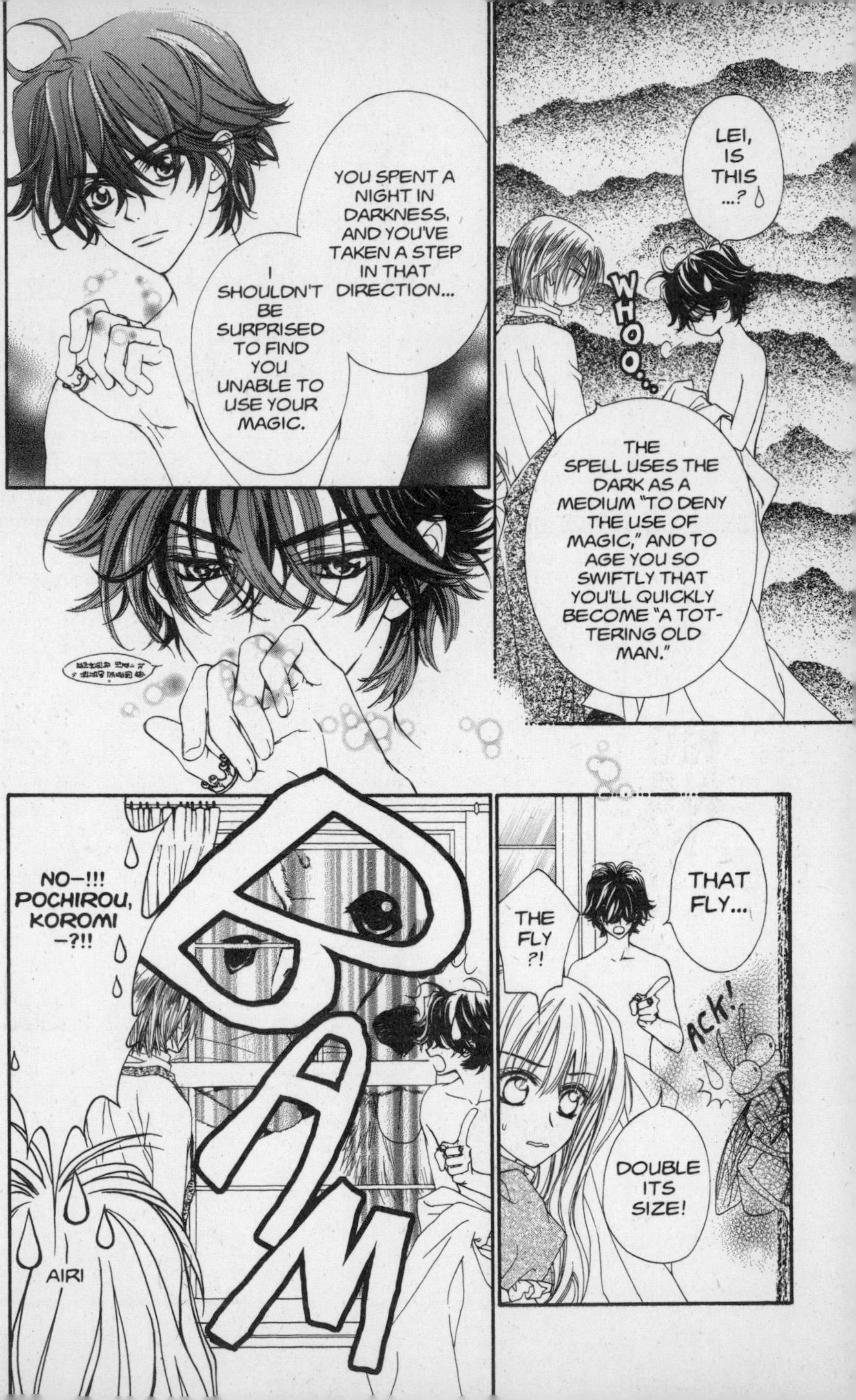
LEI, IS THIS ...?
WHOO...
THE SPELL USES THE DARK AS A MEDIUM "TO DENY THE USE OF MAGIC," AND TO AGE YOU SO SWIFTLY THAT YOU'LL QUICKLY BECOME "A TOTTERING OLD MAN."
YOU SPENT A NIGHT IN DARKNESS, AND YOU'VE TAKEN A STEP IN THAT DIRECTION...
I SHOULDN'T BE SURPRISED TO FIND YOU UNABLE TO USE YOUR MAGIC.
THAT FLY...
THE FLY ?!
ACK!
DOUBLE ITS SIZE!
NO-!!! POCHIROU, KOROMI-?!!
PAM
AIRI

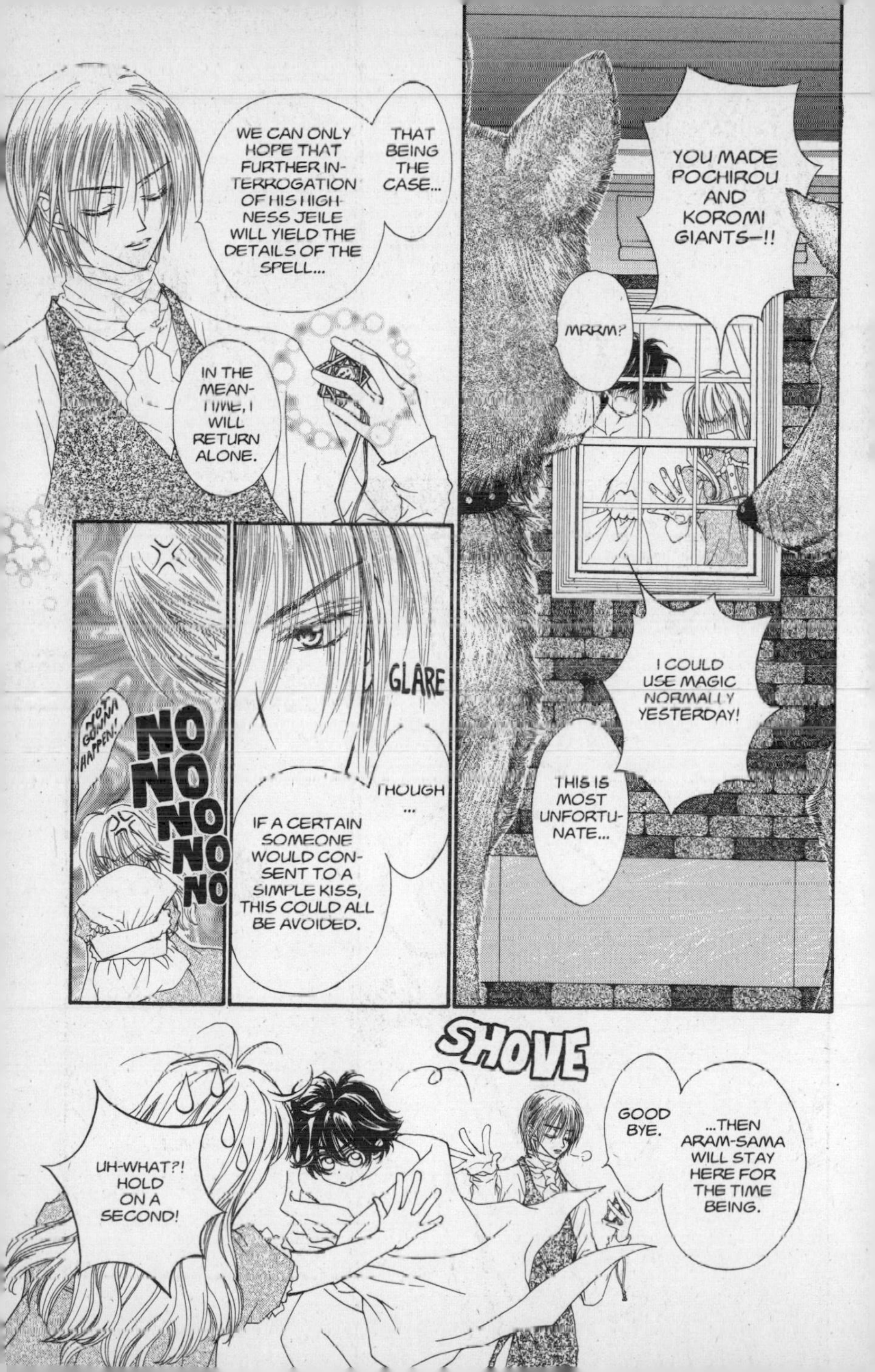
YOU MADE POCHIROU AND KOROMI GIANTS—!!
MRRM?
I COULD USE MAGIC NORMALLY YESTERDAY!
THIS IS MOST UNFORTUNATE...
THAT BEING THE CASE...
WE CAN ONLY HOPE THAT FURTHER INTERROGATION OF HIS HIGHNESS JEILE WILL YIELD THE DETAILS OF THE SPELL...
IN THE MEANTIME, I WILL RETURN ALONE.
GLARE
THOUGH ...
IF A CERTAIN SOMEONE WOULD CONSENT TO A SIMPLE KISS, THIS COULD ALL BE AVOIDED.
NOT GONNA HAPPEN!
NO NO NO NO NO NO
SHOVE
...THEN ARAM-SAMA WILL STAY HERE FOR THE TIME BEING.
GOOD BYE.
UH-WHAT?! HOLD ON A SECOND!

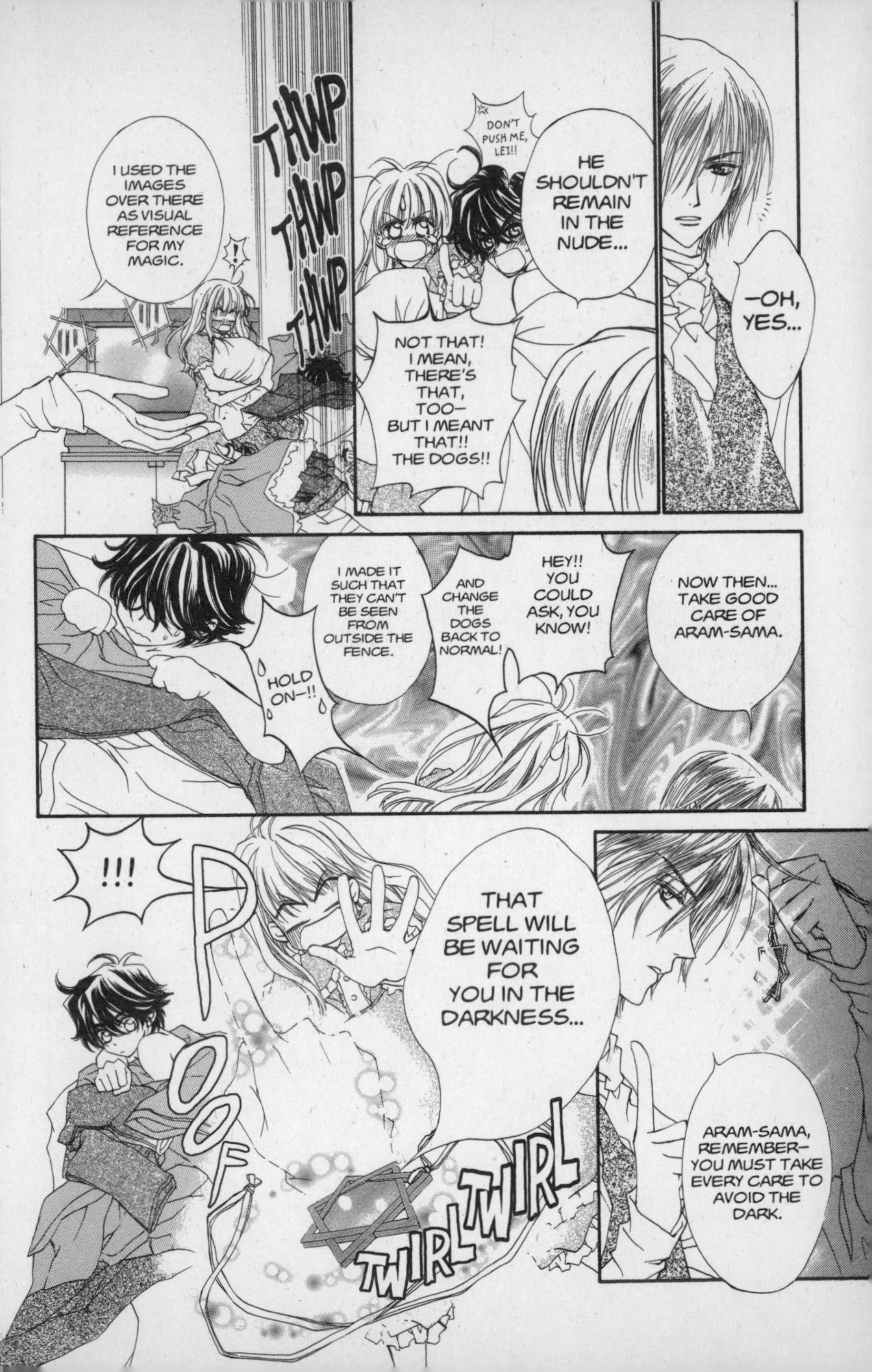
—OH, YES...
HE SHOULDN'T REMAIN IN THE NUDE...
DON'T PUSH ME, LEI!!
NOT THAT! I MEAN, THERE'S THAT, TOO— BUT I MEANT THAT!! THE DOGS!!
THWP THWP THWP
I USED THE IMAGES OVER THERE AS VISUAL REFERENCE FOR MY MAGIC.
!
NOW THEN... TAKE GOOD CARE OF ARAM-SAMA.
HEY!! YOU COULD ASK, YOU KNOW!
AND CHANGE THE DOGS BACK TO NORMAL!
I MADE IT SUCH THAT THEY CAN'T BE SEEN FROM OUTSIDE THE FENCE.
HOLD ON—!!
ARAM-SAMA, REMEMBER— YOU MUST TAKE EVERY CARE TO AVOID THE DARK.
THAT SPELL WILL BE WAITING FOR YOU IN THE DARKNESS...
!!!
POOF
TWIRL TWIRL

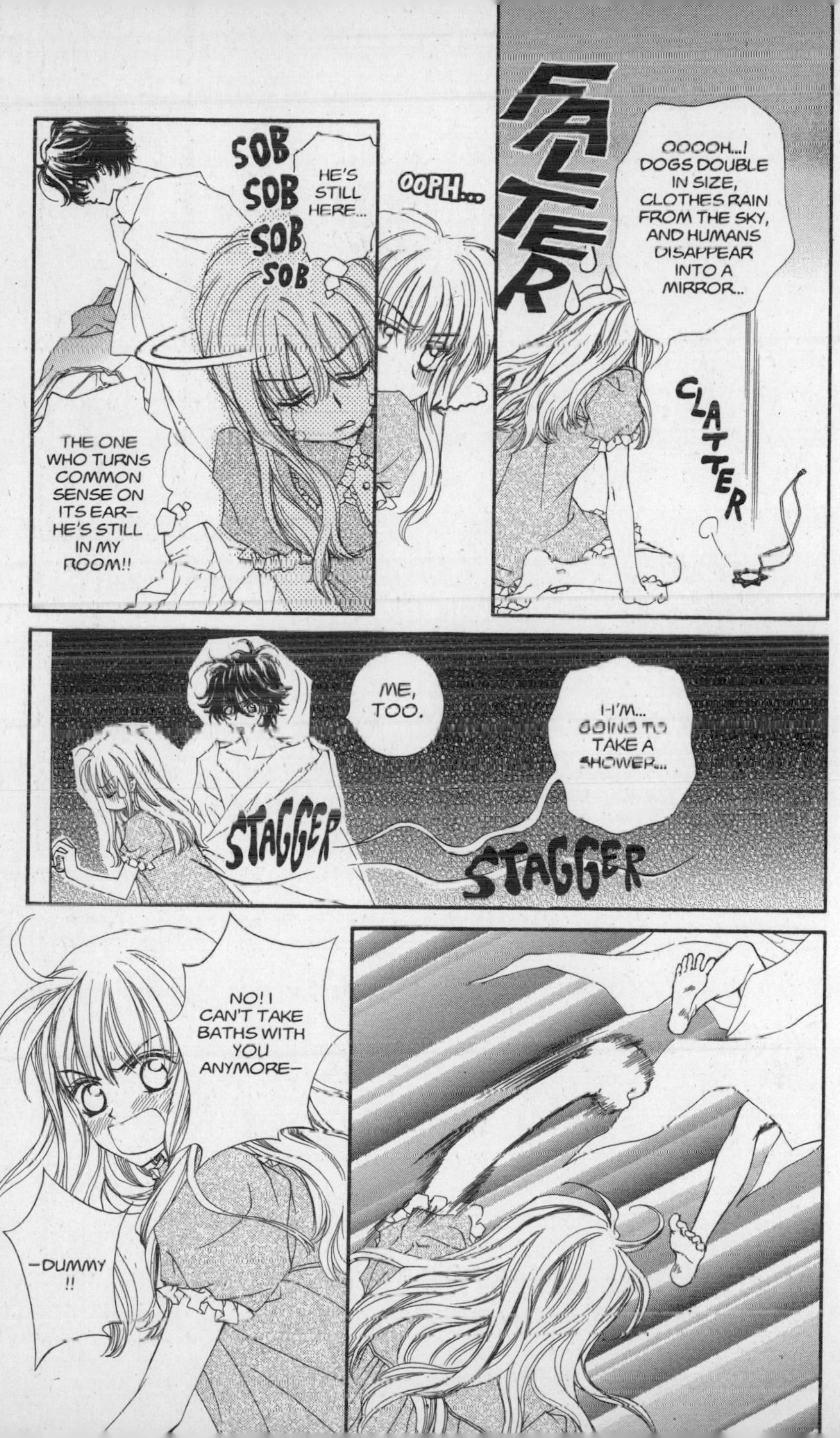
FALTER
OOOOH...I DOGS DOUBLE IN SIZE, CLOTHES RAIN FROM THE SKY, AND HUMANS DISAPPEAR INTO A MIRROR...
CLATTER
OOPH...
SOB SOB SOB SOB
HE'S STILL HERE...
THE ONE WHO TURNS COMMON SENSE ON ITS EAR— HE'S STILL IN MY ROOM!!
I'M... GOING TO TAKE A SHOWER...
ME, TOO.
STAGGER
STAGGER
NO! I CAN'T TAKE BATHS WITH YOU ANYMORE—
—DUMMY!!

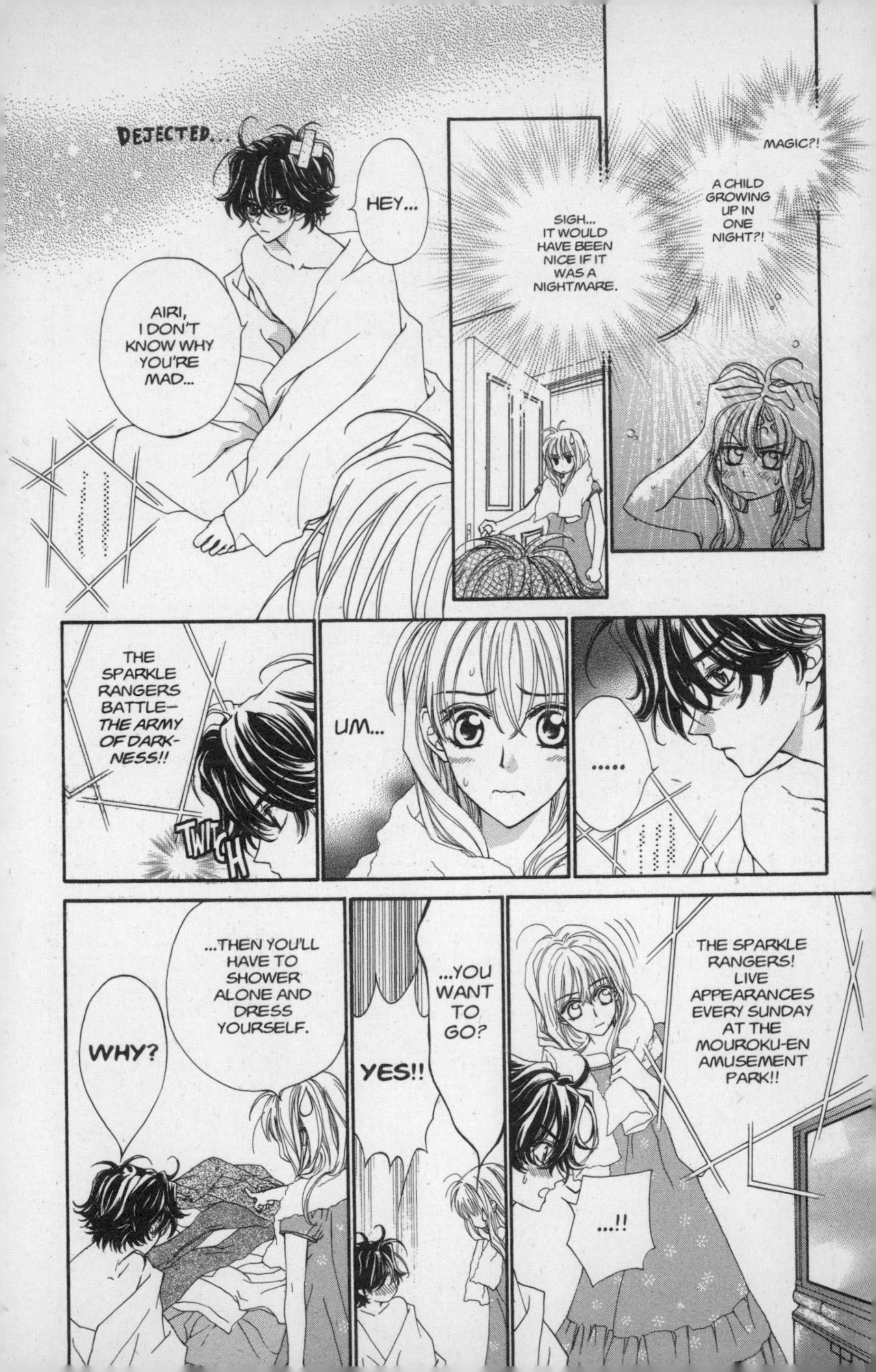
MAGIC?!
A CHILD GROWING UP IN ONE NIGHT?!
SIGH... IT WOULD HAVE BEEN NICE IF IT WAS A NIGHTMARE.
DEJECTED...
HEY...
AIRI, I DON'T KNOW WHY YOU'RE MAD...
.....
UM...
THE SPARKLE RANGERS BATTLE—THE ARMY OF DARKNESS!!
TWITCH
THE SPARKLE RANGERS! LIVE APPEARANCES EVERY SUNDAY AT THE MOUROKU-EN AMUSEMENT PARK!!
...!!
...YOU WANT TO GO?
YES!!
...THEN YOU'LL HAVE TO SHOWER ALONE AND DRESS YOURSELF.
WHY?

Aram

Astale=Ei=Daemonia Eucharistia Aram. Explaining the name in earth terms:

- Astale=Ei=Daemonia → Because he's a member of the royal family, the name of the kingdom comes first. ("Ei=Daemonia" means something like "hoping for the happiness of the Kingdom of Astale")
- Eucharistia → family name
- Aram → given name

Aram is here to fill the role of "child prince" and still manages, when he's big, to be "sexy" and—often enough—"nude." (He's a babe, sure, but he's also a baby, so the skin on his bottom is as smooth and soft as, well, a baby's bottom!) He's a prince, so sometimes he's a little hard to take. He lives in a fairytale world and he's kind of an idiot.

(Yes, that is the way it has to be. Blame the prejudice of the author!)

His hair is designed to reflect his character: it's lively, curly, and it flips out. (And it's troublesome to draw!) In contrast to his older brother, Aram is serious (actually, Jeile is serious, too—in his own way) and he's calm for his age.

Because he's still a child, there are a lot of changes in store for him. Who knows what kind of person he'll grow up to be? ...This scares me, of course, but I'm also looking forward to it.

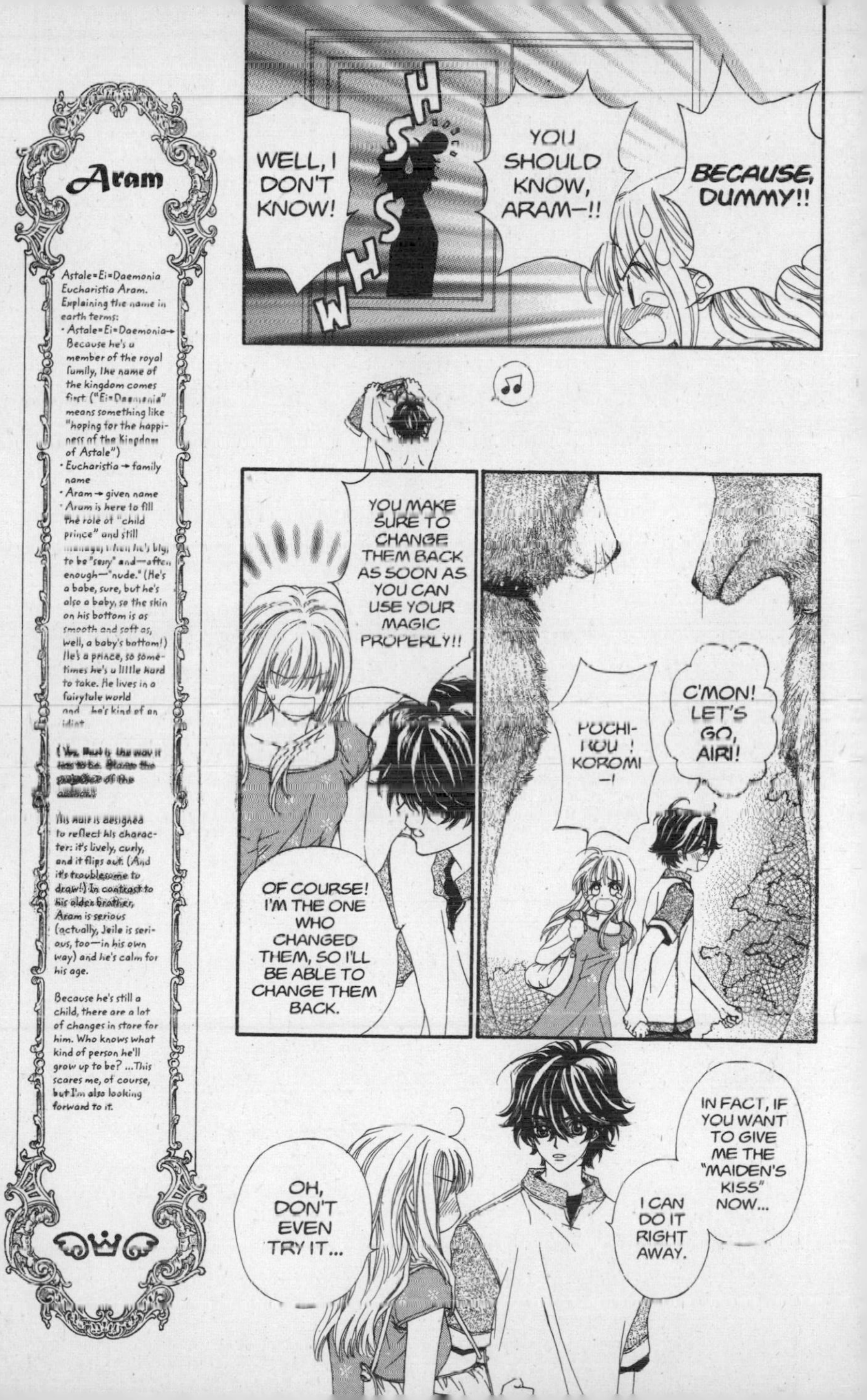
BECAUSE, DUMMY!!
YOU SHOULD KNOW, ARAM—!!
WELL, I DON'T KNOW!
WHSSH
C'MON! LET'S GO, AIRI!
POCHI-KOU! KOROMI—!
YOU MAKE SURE TO CHANGE THEM BACK AS SOON AS YOU CAN USE YOUR MAGIC PROPERLY!!
OF COURSE! I'M THE ONE WHO CHANGED THEM, SO I'LL BE ABLE TO CHANGE THEM BACK.
IN FACT, IF YOU WANT TO GIVE ME THE "MAIDEN'S KISS" NOW...
I CAN DO IT RIGHT AWAY.
OH, DON'T EVEN TRY IT...

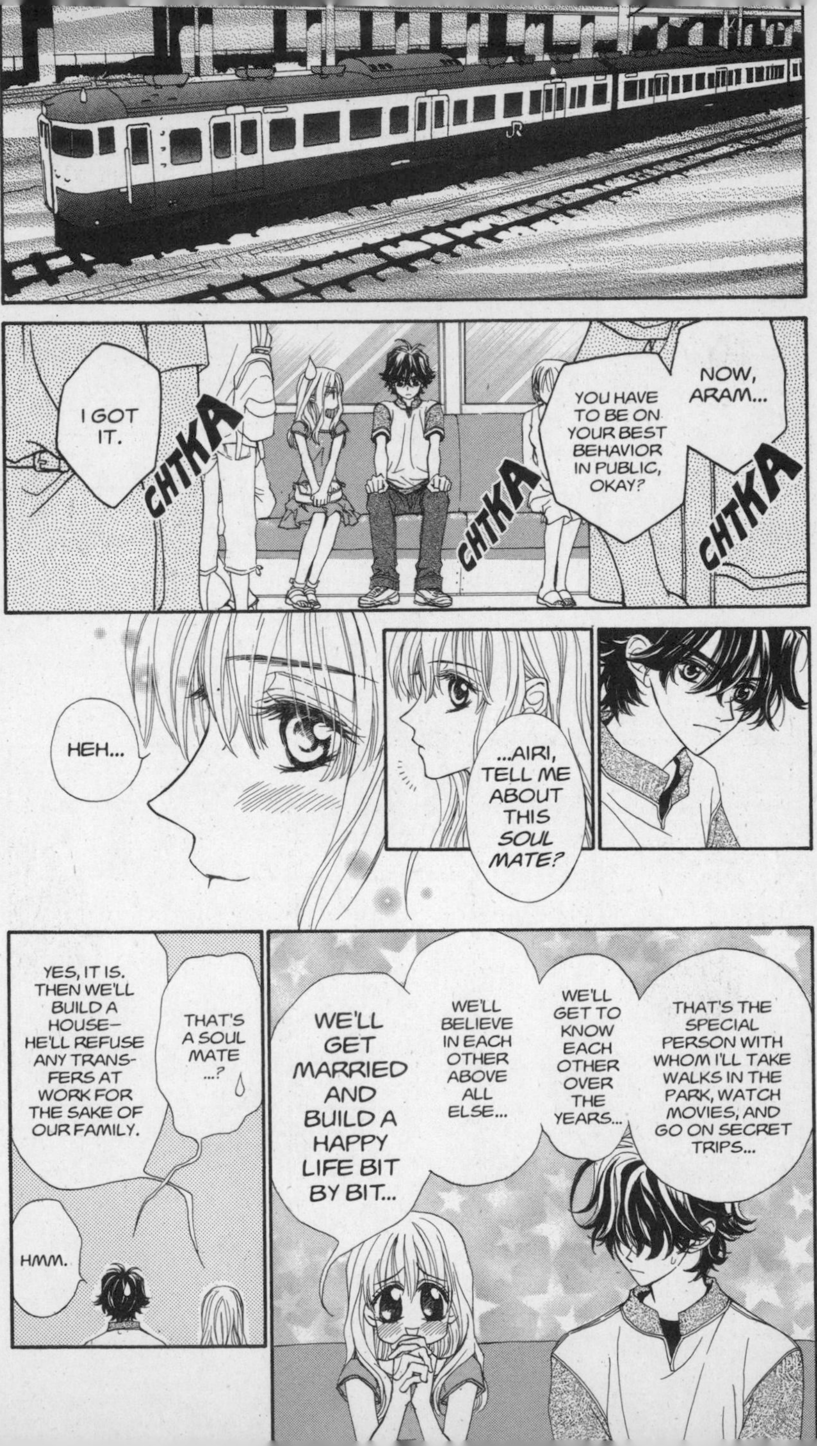
NOW, ARAM...
YOU HAVE TO BE ON YOUR BEST BEHAVIOR IN PUBLIC, OKAY?
CHTKA
CHTKA
I GOT IT.
CHTKA
...AIRI, TELL ME ABOUT THIS SOUL MATE?
HEH...
THAT'S THE SPECIAL PERSON WITH WHOM I'LL TAKE WALKS IN THE PARK, WATCH MOVIES, AND GO ON SECRET TRIPS...
WE'LL GET TO KNOW EACH OTHER OVER THE YEARS...
WE'LL BELIEVE IN EACH OTHER ABOVE ALL ELSE...
WE'LL GET MARRIED AND BUILD A HAPPY LIFE BIT BY BIT...
THAT'S A SOUL MATE ...?
YES, IT IS. THEN WE'LL BUILD A HOUSE— HE'LL REFUSE ANY TRANS-FERS AT WORK FOR THE SAKE OF OUR FAMILY.
HMM.

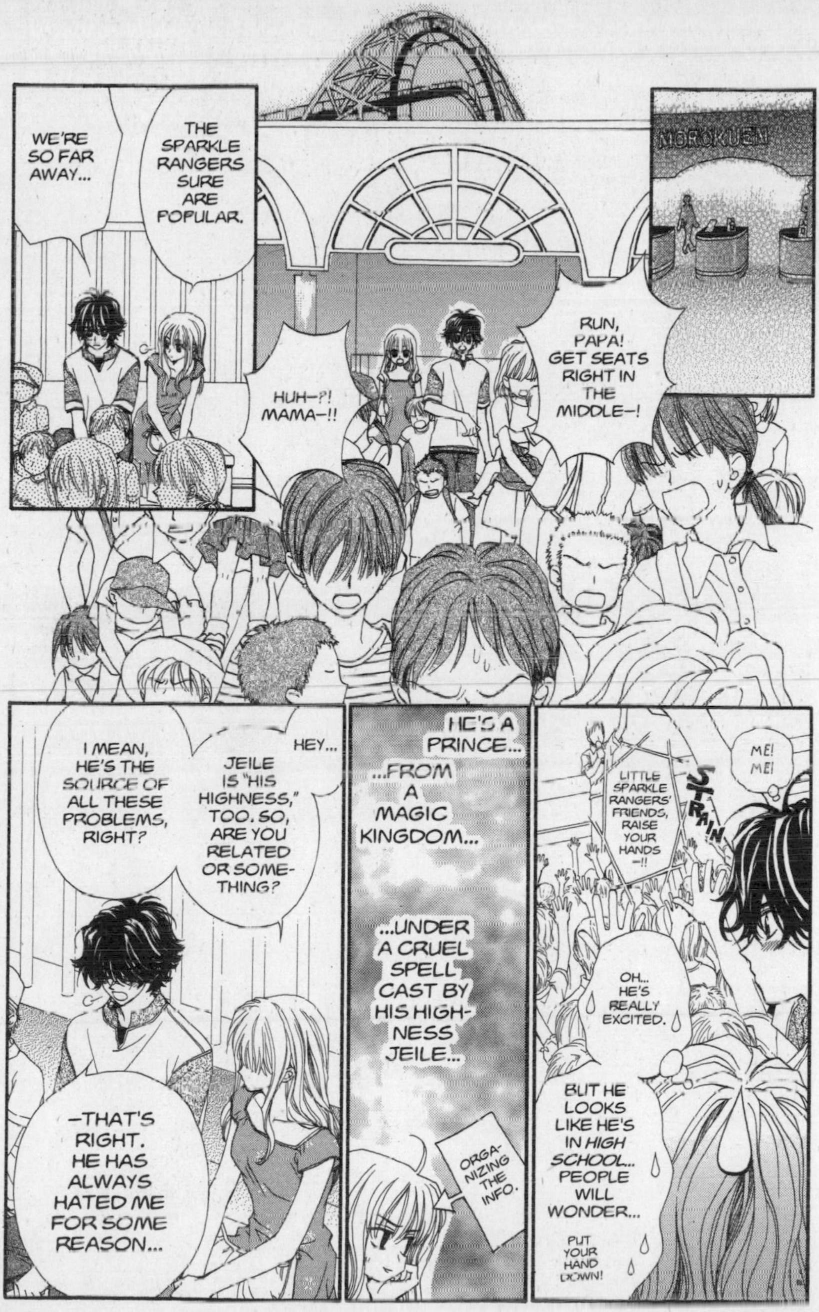
MOROKUEN
RUN, PAPA! GET SEATS RIGHT IN THE MIDDLE-!
HUH-?! MAMA-!!
THE SPARKLE RANGERS SURE ARE POPULAR.
WE'RE SO FAR AWAY...
LITTLE SPARKLE RANGERS' FRIENDS, RAISE YOUR HANDS-!!
STRAIN
ME! ME!
OH... HE'S REALLY EXCITED.
BUT HE LOOKS LIKE HE'S IN *HIGH SCHOOL*... PEOPLE WILL WONDER...
PUT YOUR HAND DOWN!
HE'S A PRINCE...
...FROM A MAGIC KINGDOM...
...UNDER A CRUEL SPELL CAST BY HIS HIGHNESS JEILE...
ORGANIZING THE INFO.
HEY...
JEILE IS "HIS HIGHNESS," TOO. SO, ARE YOU RELATED OR SOMETHING?
I MEAN, HE'S THE SOURCE OF ALL THESE PROBLEMS, RIGHT?
-THAT'S RIGHT. HE HAS ALWAYS HATED ME FOR SOME REASON...

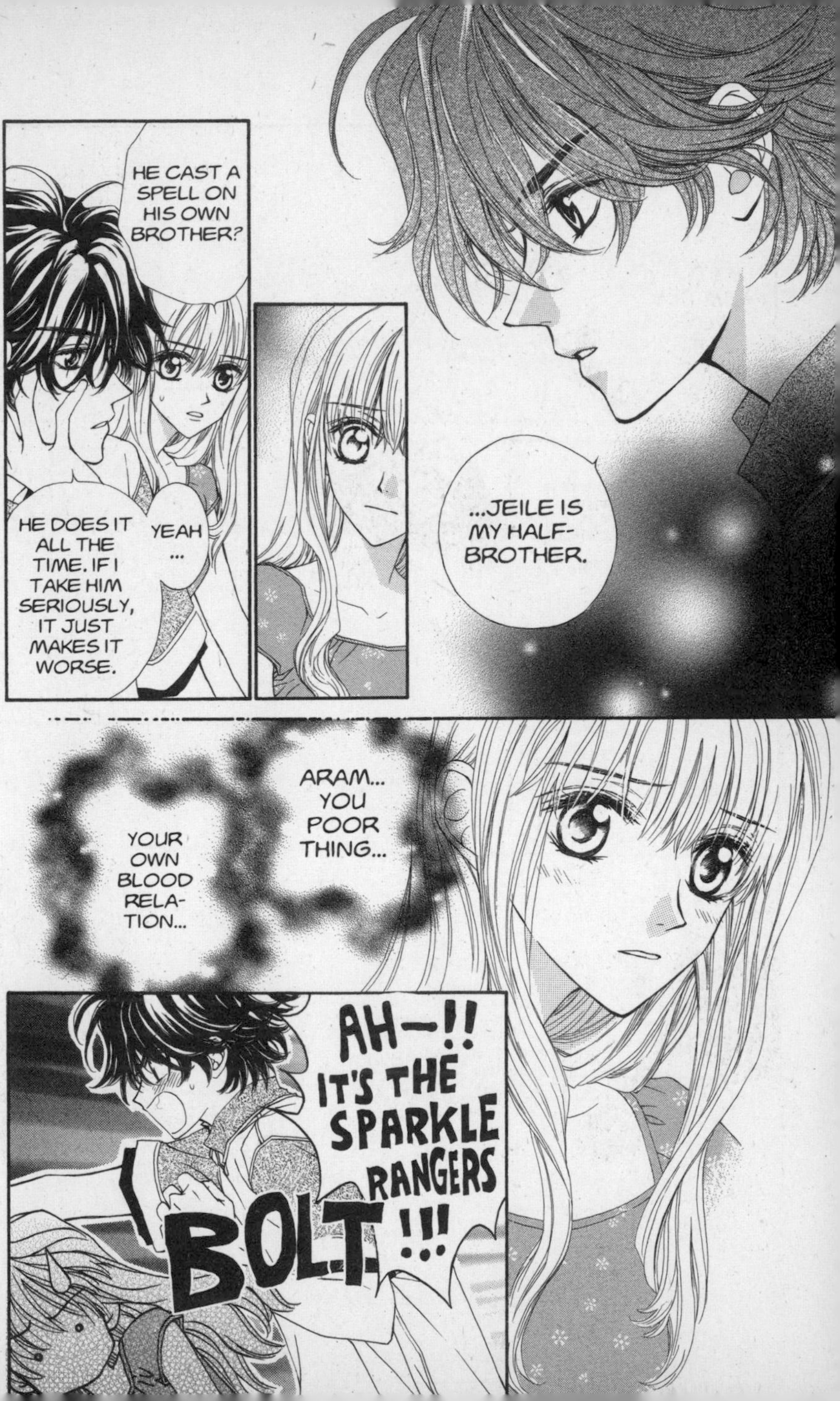
...JEILE IS MY HALF-BROTHER.
HE CAST A SPELL ON HIS OWN BROTHER?
YEAH ...
HE DOES IT ALL THE TIME. IF I TAKE HIM SERIOUSLY, IT JUST MAKES IT WORSE.
ARAM... YOU POOR THING...
YOUR OWN BLOOD RELA-TION...
AH—!! IT'S THE SPARKLE RANGERS BOLT. !!!

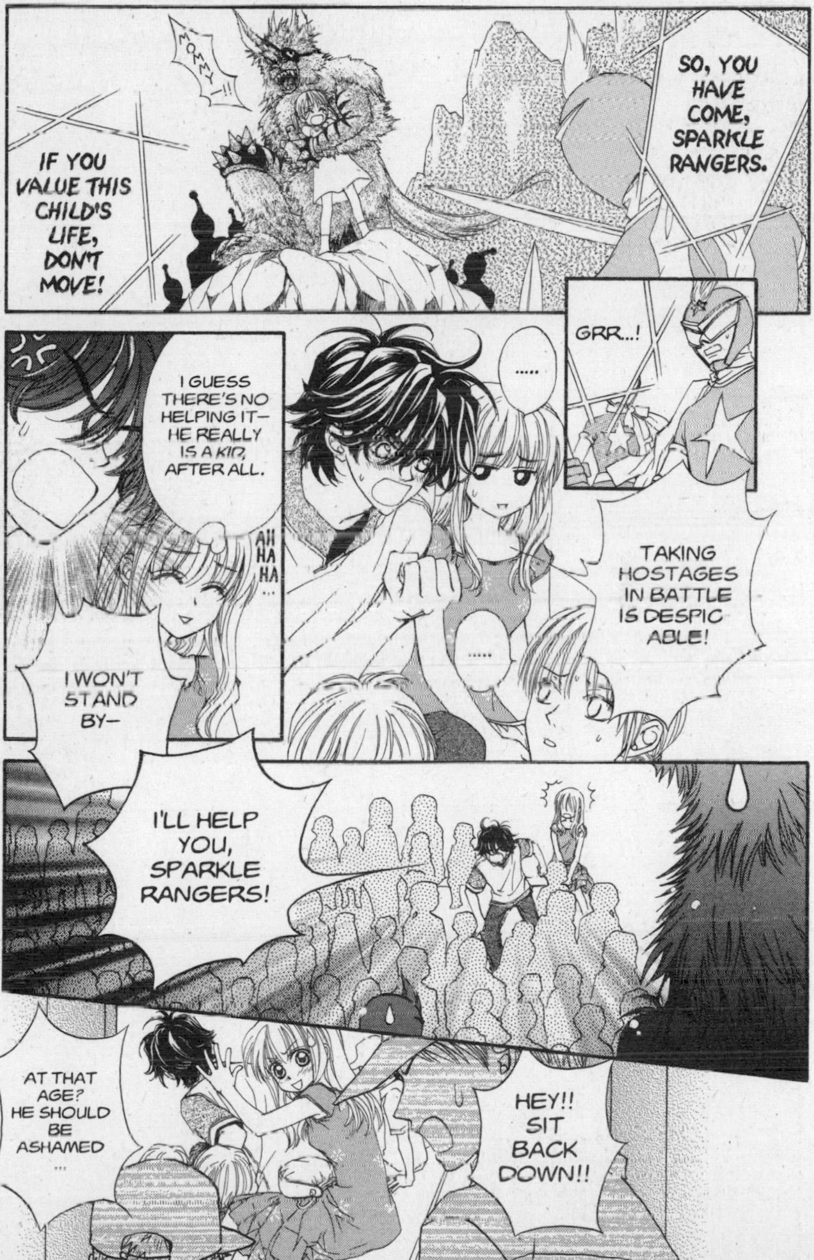

SO, YOU HAVE COME, SPARKLE RANGERS.
MOMMY—!!
IF YOU VALUE THIS CHILD'S LIFE, DON'T MOVE!
GRR...!
.....
TAKING HOSTAGES IN BATTLE IS DESPIC ABLE!
.....
I GUESS THERE'S NO HELPING IT— HE REALLY IS A KID, AFTER ALL.
AH HA HA ...
I WON'T STAND BY—
I'LL HELP YOU, SPARKLE RANGERS!
HEY!! SIT BACK DOWN!!
AT THAT AGE? HE SHOULD BE ASHAMED ...

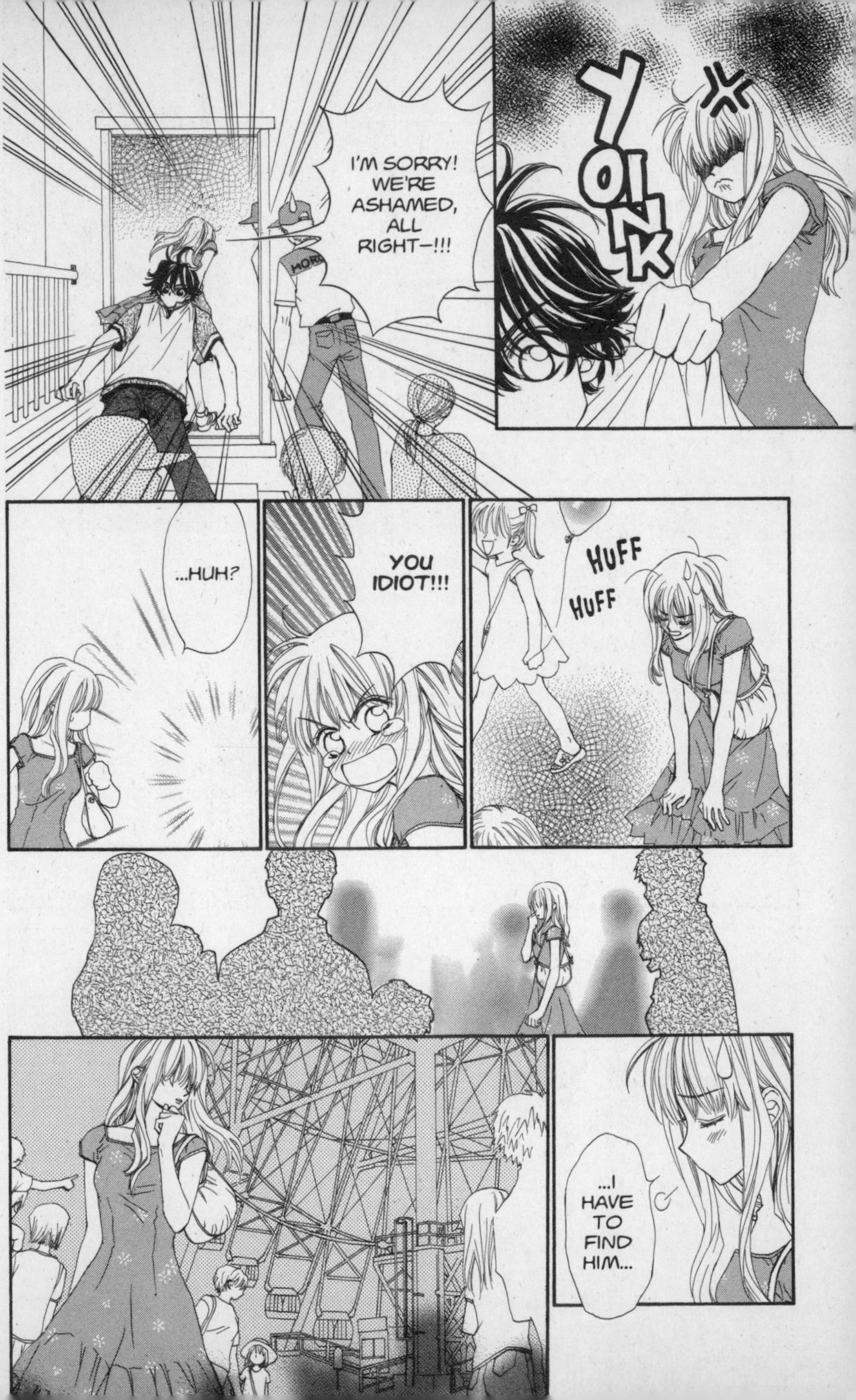
YOINK
I'M SORRY! WE'RE ASHAMED, ALL RIGHT–!!!
HUFF HUFF
YOU IDIOT!!!
...HUH?
...I HAVE TO FIND HIM...

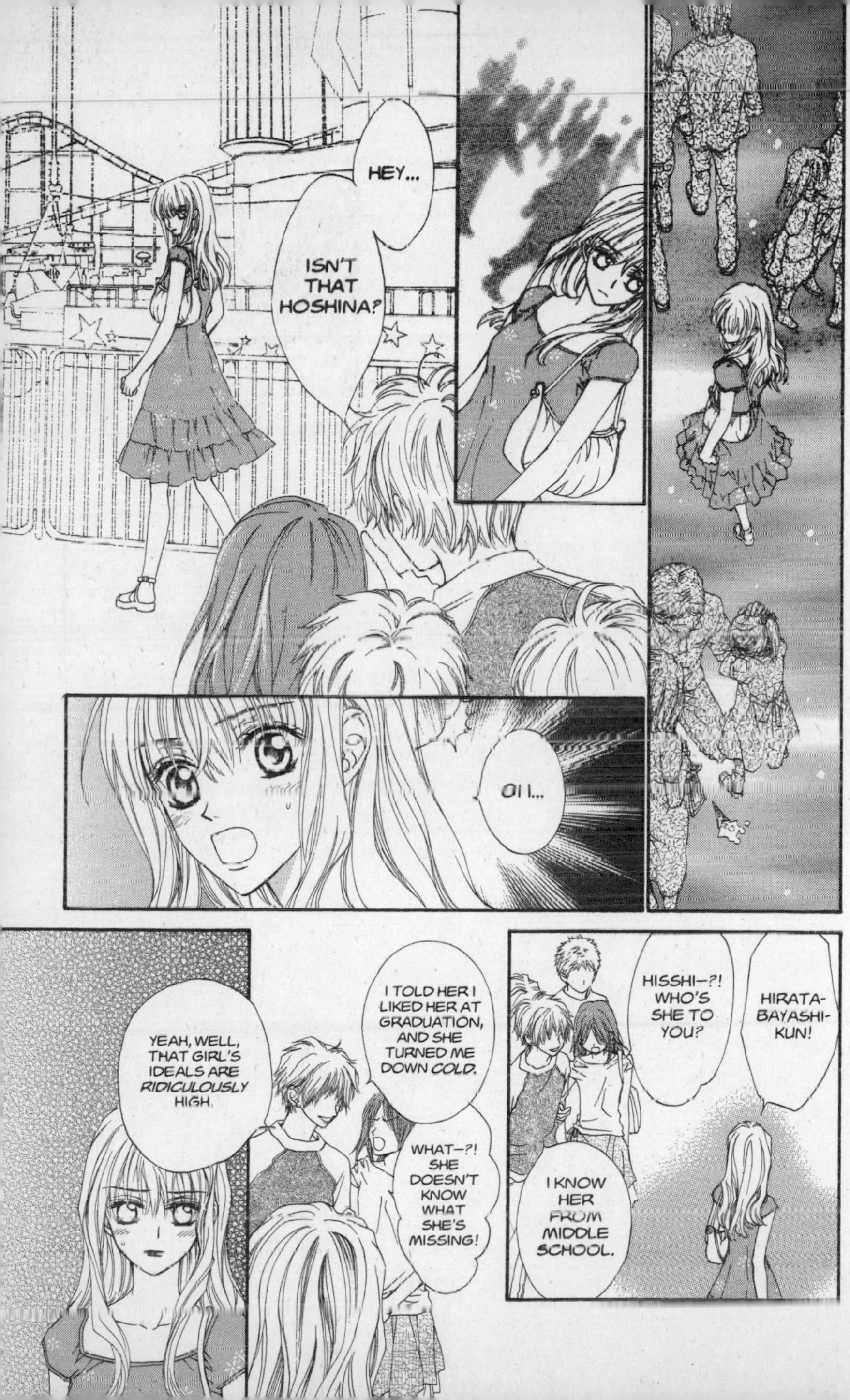
HEY... ISN'T THAT HOSHINA?
OI I...
HIRATA-BAYASHI-KUN!
HISSHI-?! WHO'S SHE TO YOU?
I KNOW HER FROM MIDDLE SCHOOL.
I TOLD HER I LIKED HER AT GRADUATION, AND SHE TURNED ME DOWN *COLD*.
WHAT-?! SHE DOESN'T KNOW WHAT SHE'S MISSING!
YEAH, WELL, THAT GIRL'S IDEALS ARE *RIDICULOUSLY* HIGH.

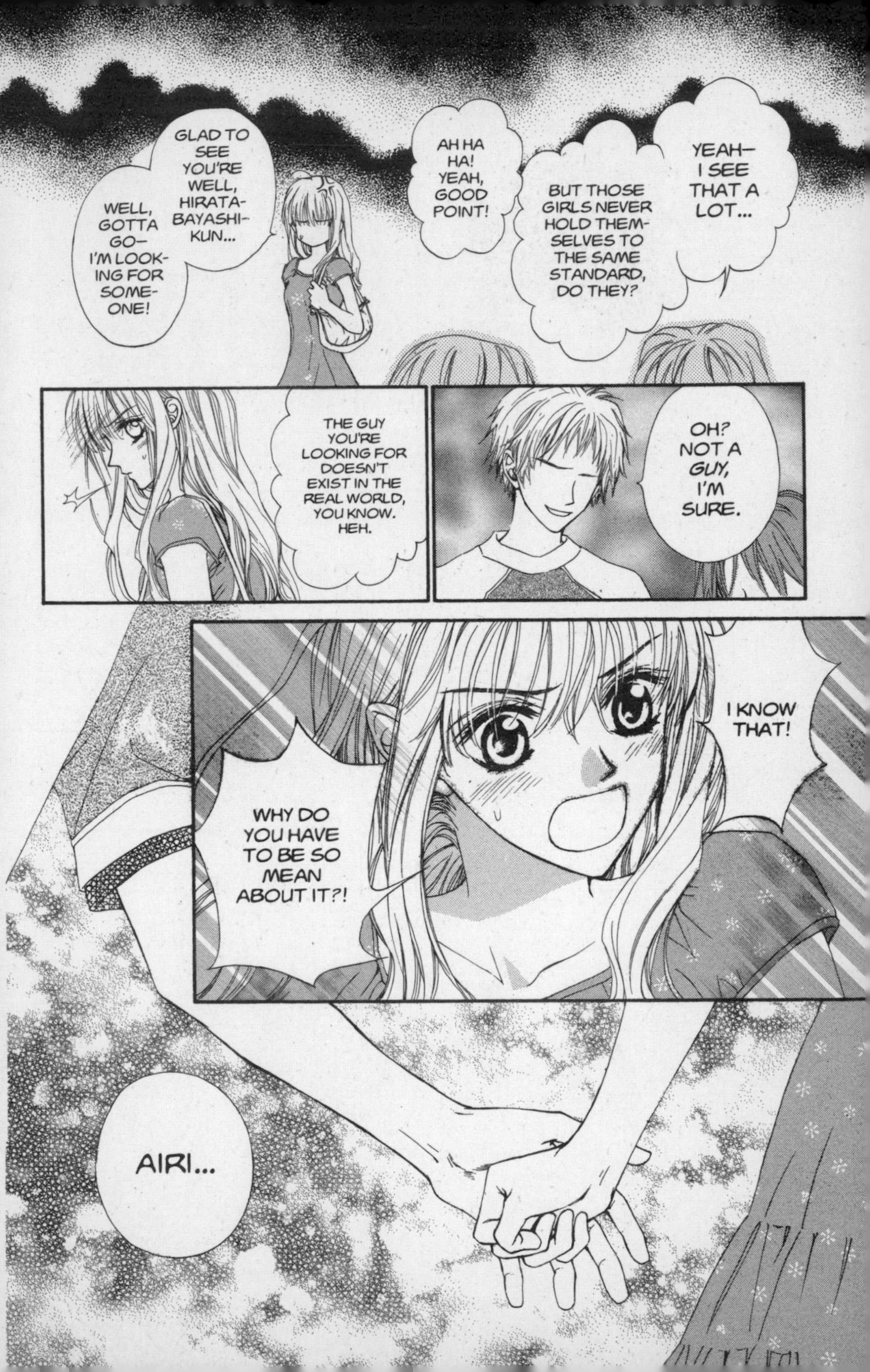
YEAH— I SEE THAT A LOT...
BUT THOSE GIRLS NEVER HOLD THEMSELVES TO THE SAME STANDARD, DO THEY?
AH HA HA! YEAH, GOOD POINT!
GLAD TO SEE YOU'RE WELL, HIRATA-BAYASHI-KUN...
WELL, GOTTA GO— I'M LOOKING FOR SOMEONE!
OH? NOT A GUY, I'M SURE.
THE GUY YOU'RE LOOKING FOR DOESN'T EXIST IN THE REAL WORLD, YOU KNOW. HEH.
I KNOW THAT!
WHY DO YOU HAVE TO BE SO MEAN ABOUT IT?!
AIRI...

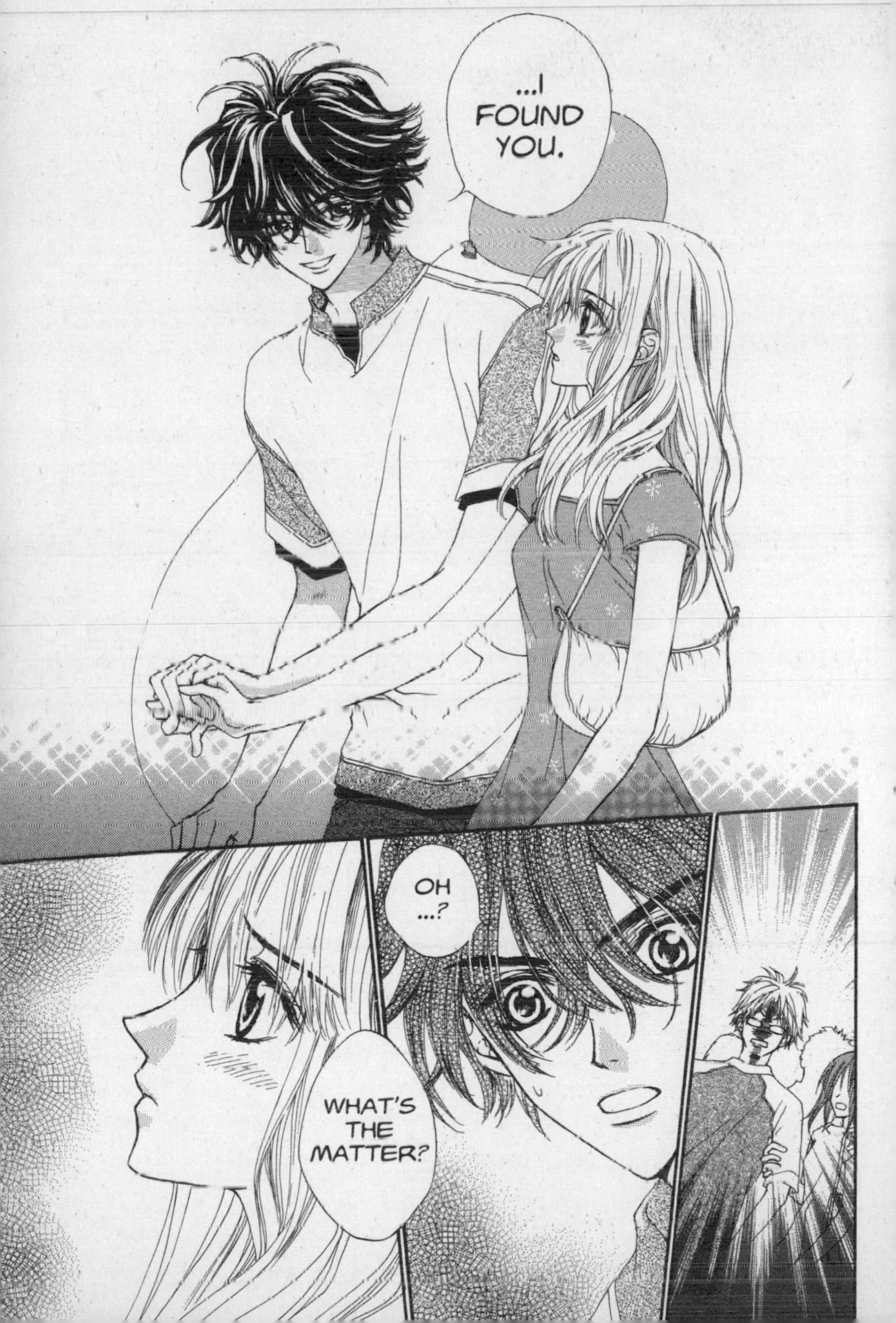
...I FOUND YOU.
OH ...?
WHAT'S THE MATTER?

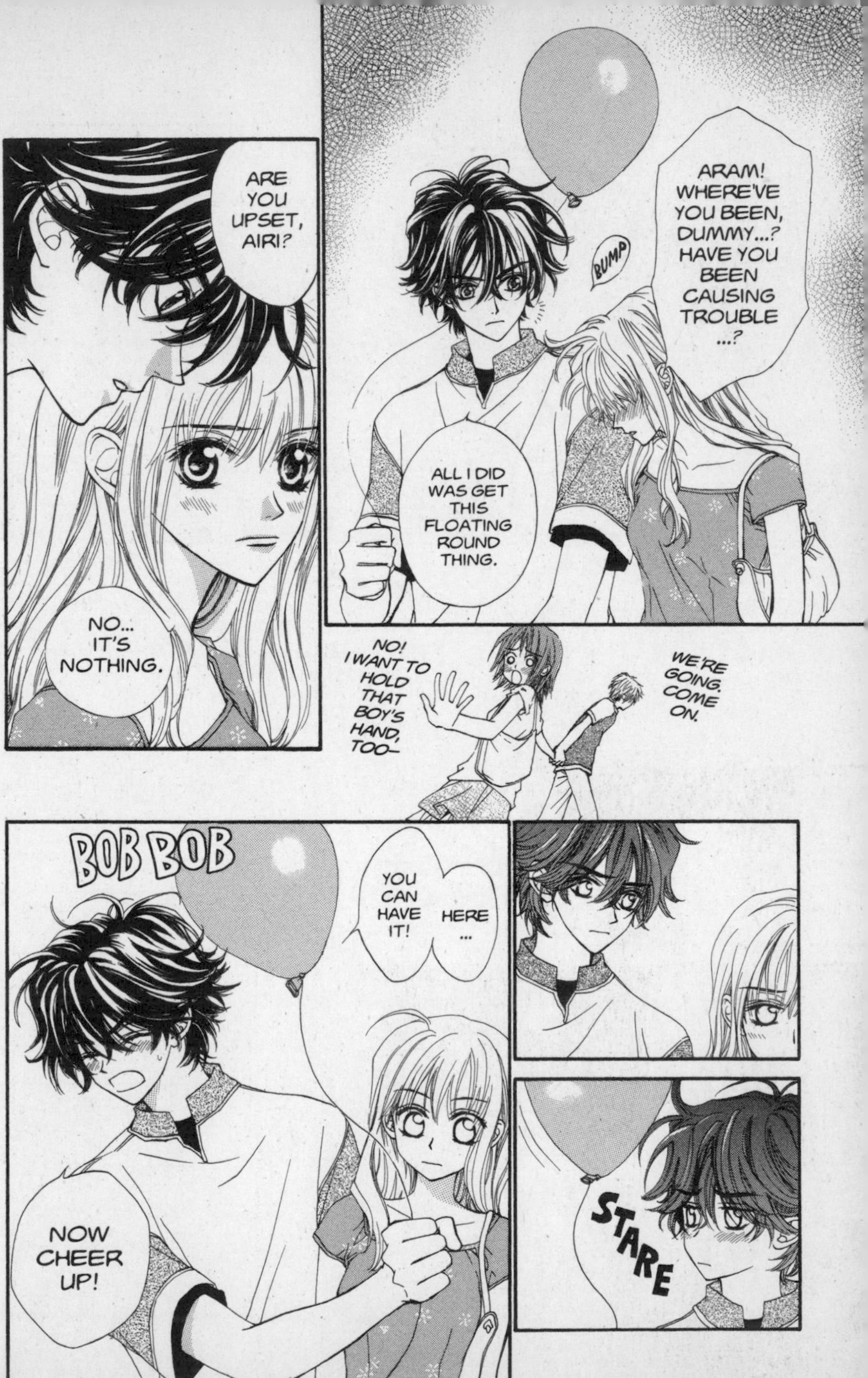
ARAM! WHERE'VE YOU BEEN, DUMMY...? HAVE YOU BEEN CAUSING TROUBLE ...?
BUMP
ALL I DID WAS GET THIS FLOATING ROUND THING.
WE'RE GOING. COME ON.
NO! I WANT TO HOLD THAT BOY'S HAND, TOO–
ARE YOU UPSET, AIRI?
NO... IT'S NOTHING.
STARE
HERE ...
YOU CAN HAVE IT!
BOB BOB
NOW CHEER UP!

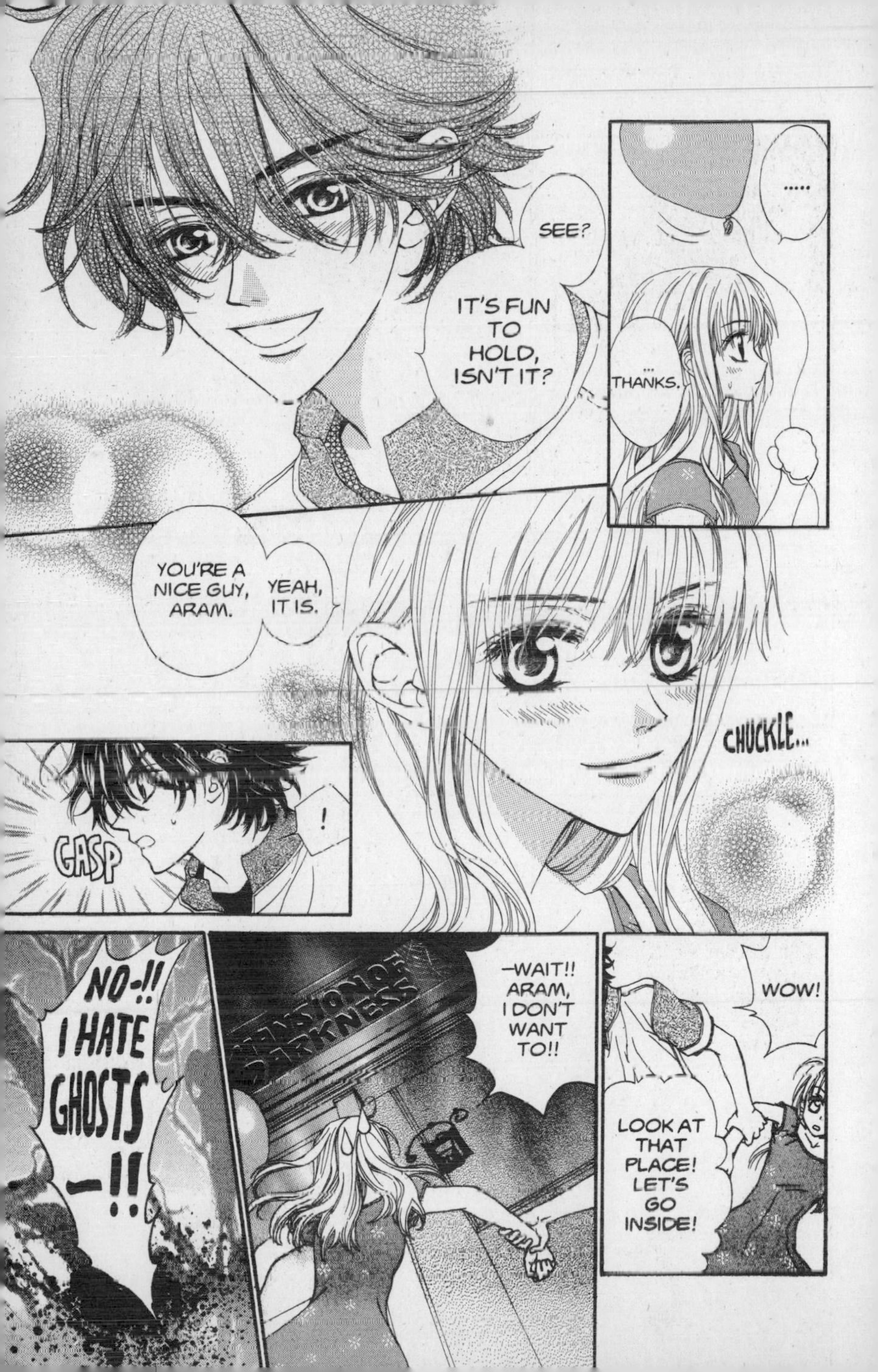
.....
...THANKS.
SEE?
IT'S FUN TO HOLD, ISN'T IT?
YEAH, IT IS.
YOU'RE A NICE GUY, ARAM.
CHUCKLE...
!
GASP
WOW!
LOOK AT THAT PLACE! LET'S GO INSIDE!
—WAIT!! ARAM, I DON'T WANT TO!!
MANSION OF DARKNESS
NO-!! I HATE GHOSTS—!!

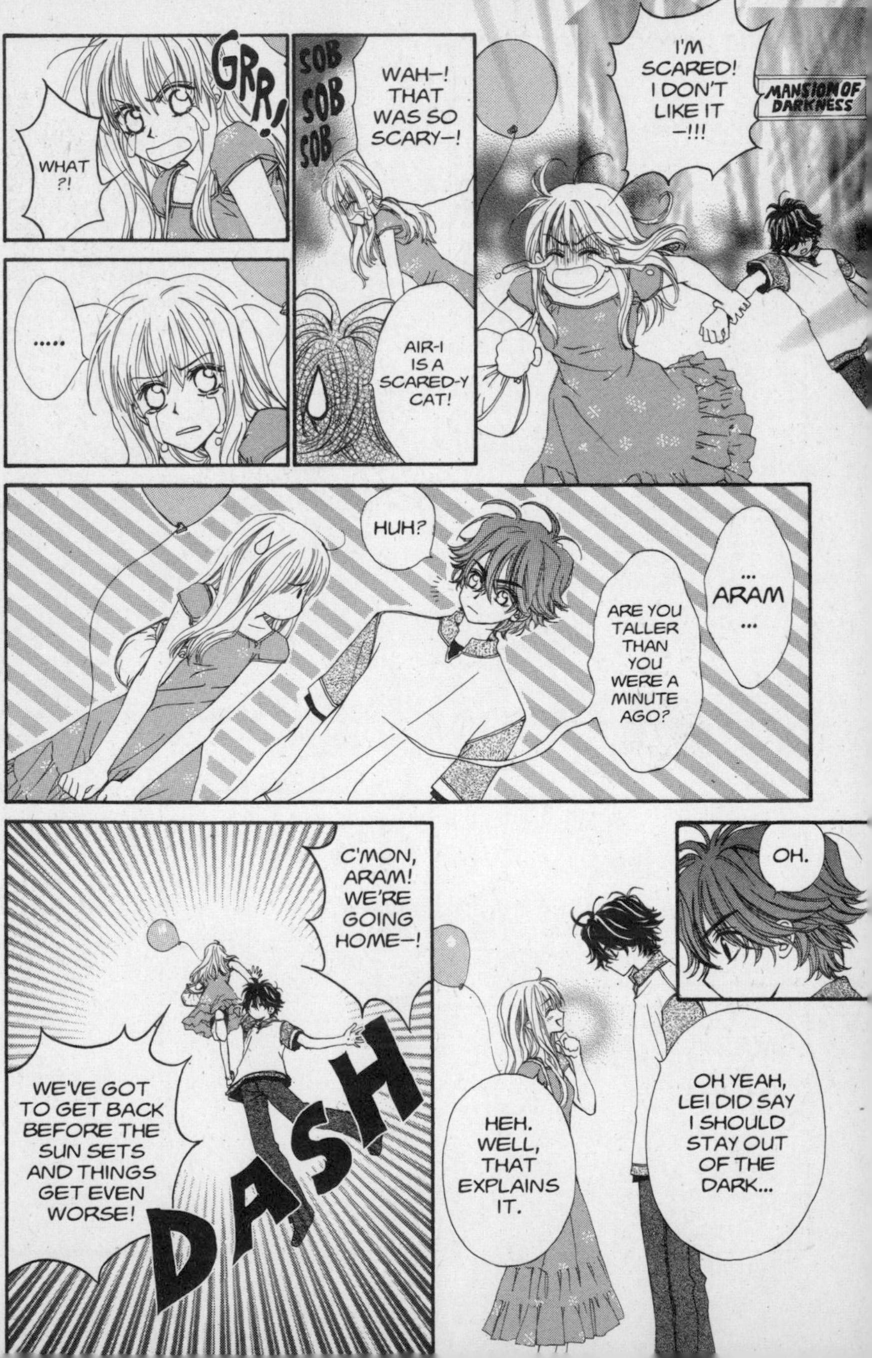
I'M SCARED! I DON'T LIKE IT —!!!
MANSION OF DARKNESS
SOB SOB SOB
WAH—! THAT WAS SO SCARY—!
AIR-I IS A SCARED-Y CAT!
GRR!
WHAT ?!
......
... ARAM ...
ARE YOU TALLER THAN YOU WERE A MINUTE AGO?
HUH?
OH.
OH YEAH, LEI DID SAY I SHOULD STAY OUT OF THE DARK...
HEH. WELL, THAT EXPLAINS IT.
C'MON, ARAM! WE'RE GOING HOME—!
WE'VE GOT TO GET BACK BEFORE THE SUN SETS AND THINGS GET EVEN WORSE!
DASH

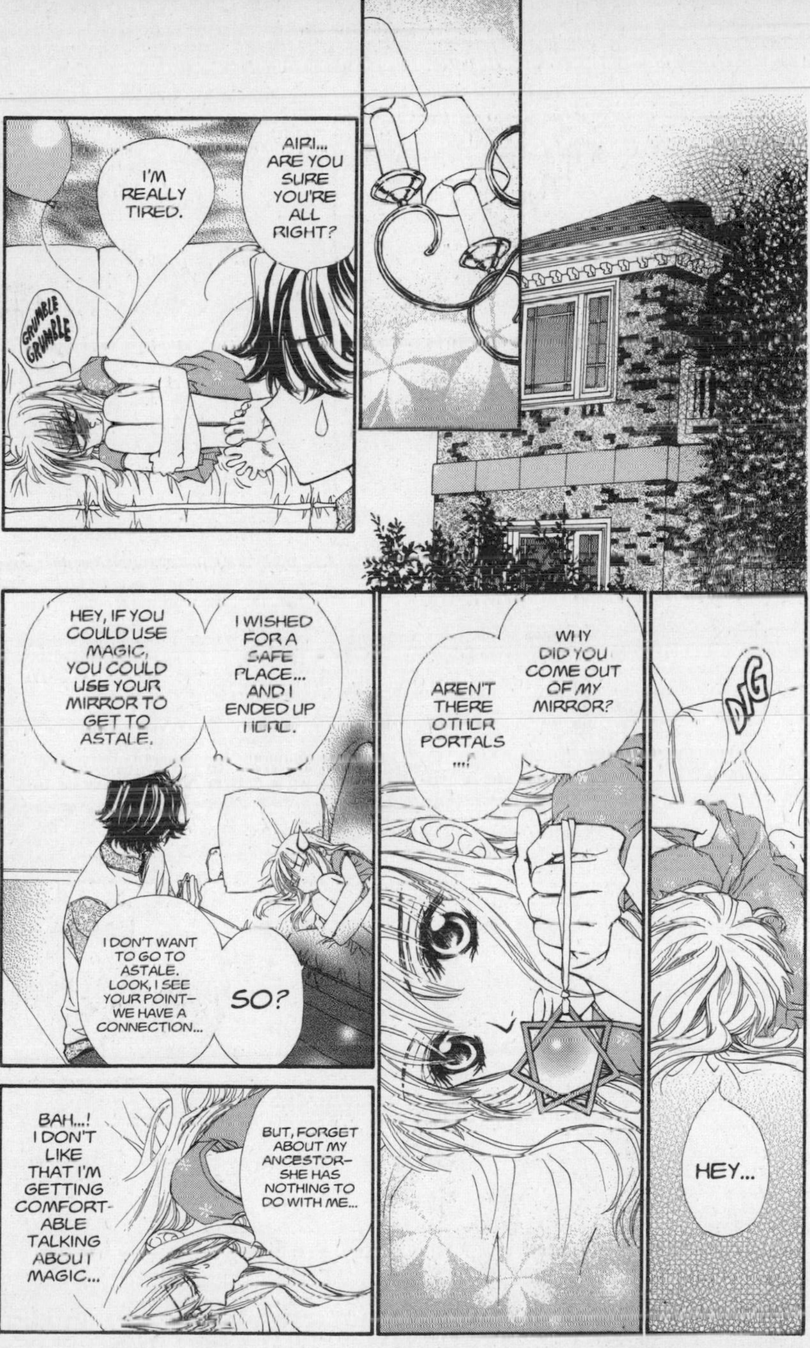
AIRI... ARE YOU SURE YOU'RE ALL RIGHT?
I'M REALLY TIRED.
GRUMBLE GRUMBLE
DIG
HEY...
WHY DID YOU COME OUT OF MY MIRROR?
AREN'T THERE OTHER PORTALS ...?
I WISHED FOR A SAFE PLACE... AND I ENDED UP HERE.
HEY, IF YOU COULD USE MAGIC, YOU COULD USE YOUR MIRROR TO GET TO ASTALE.
SO?
I DON'T WANT TO GO TO ASTALE. LOOK, I SEE YOUR POINT– WE HAVE A CONNECTION...
BUT, FORGET ABOUT MY ANCESTOR– SHE HAS NOTHING TO DO WITH ME...
BAH...! I DON'T LIKE THAT I'M GETTING COMFORT-ABLE TALKING ABOUT MAGIC...

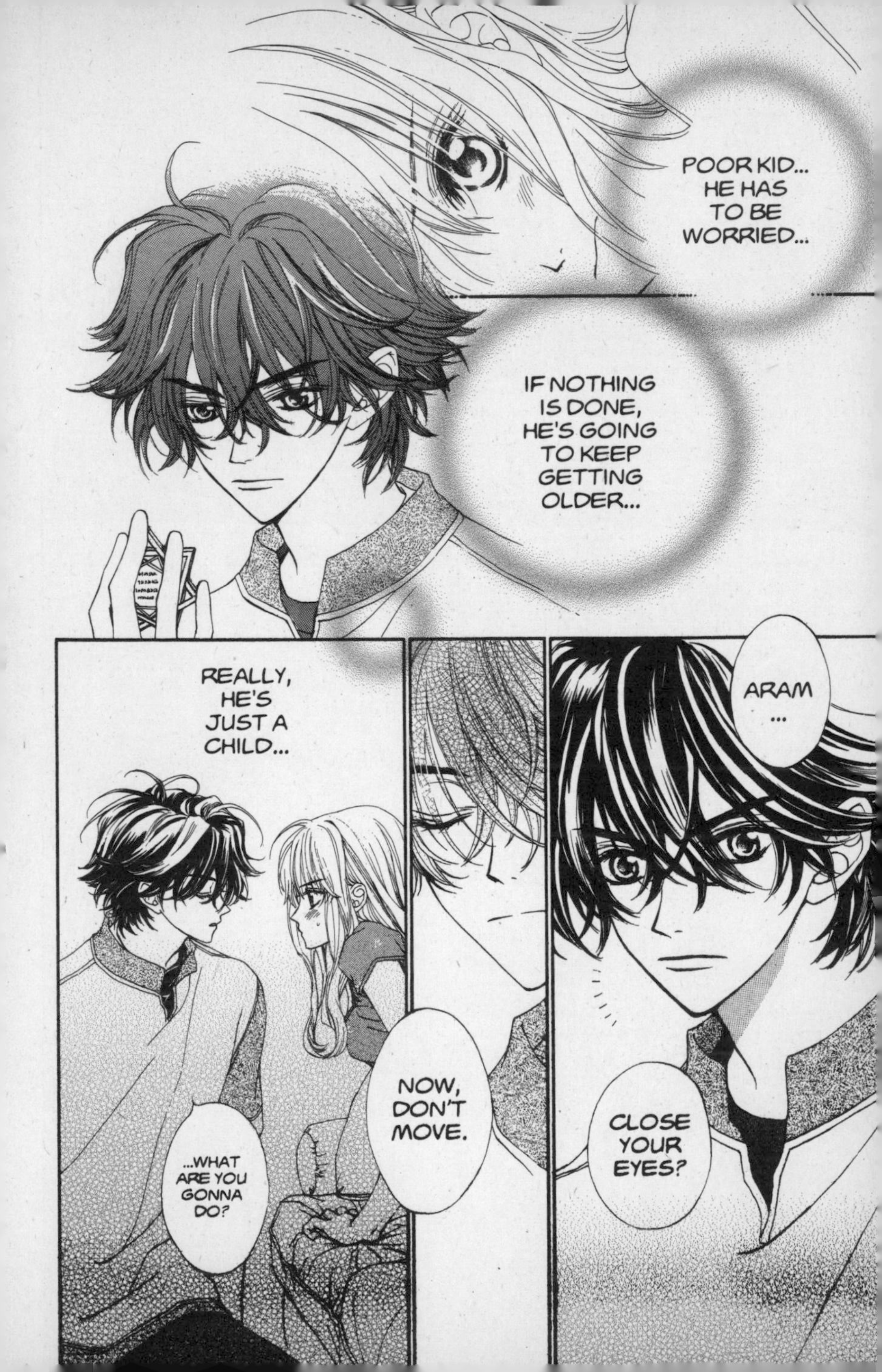
POOR KID... HE HAS TO BE WORRIED...
IF NOTHING IS DONE, HE'S GOING TO KEEP GETTING OLDER...
ARAM ...
CLOSE YOUR EYES?
NOW, DON'T MOVE.
REALLY, HE'S JUST A CHILD...
...WHAT ARE YOU GONNA DO?

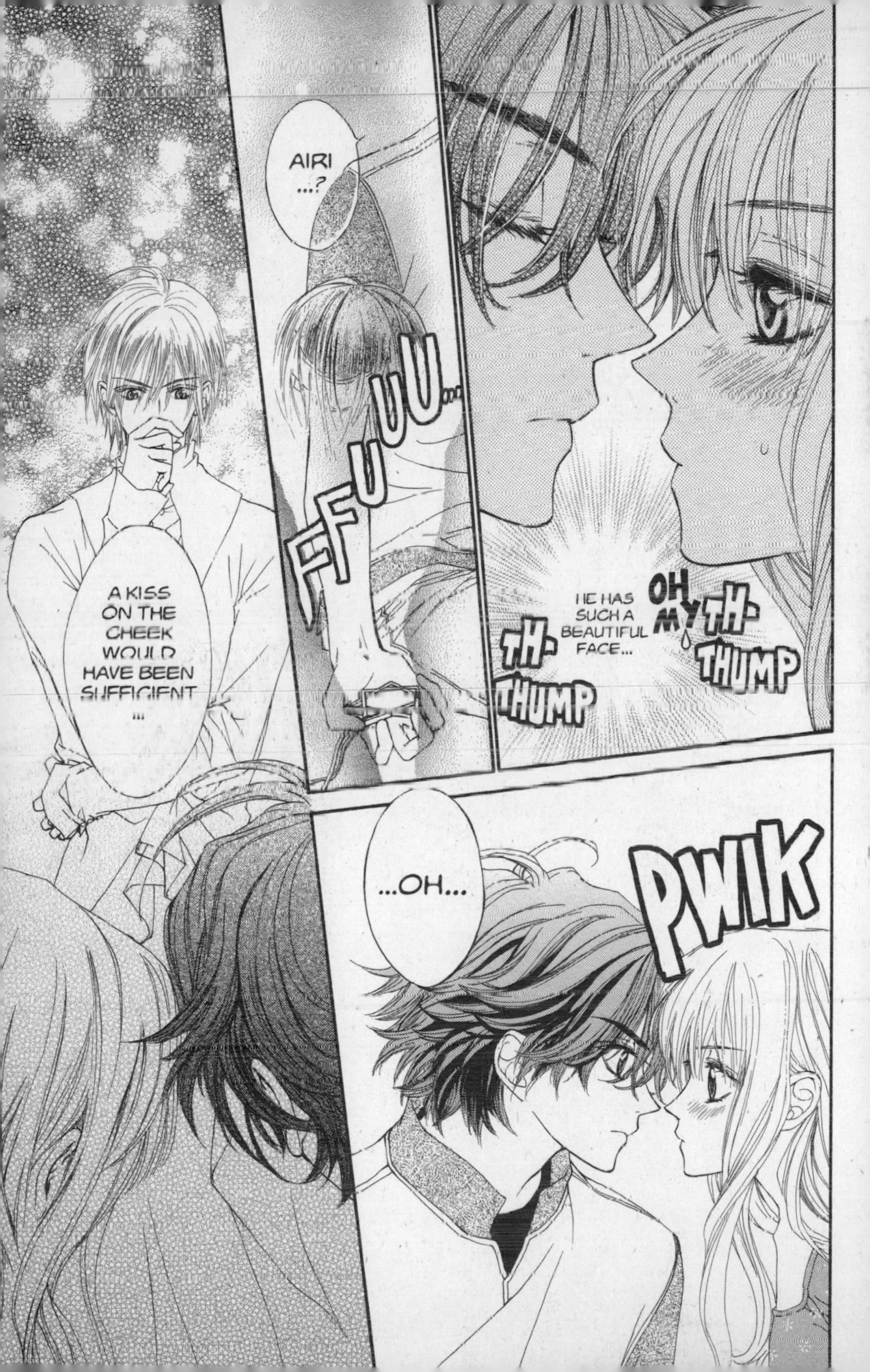
TH-THUMP
HE HAS SUCH A BEAUTIFUL FACE...
OH MY
TH-THUMP
AIRI ...?
FFUUU...
PWIK
...OH...
A KISS ON THE CHEEK WOULD HAVE BEEN SUFFICIENT ...

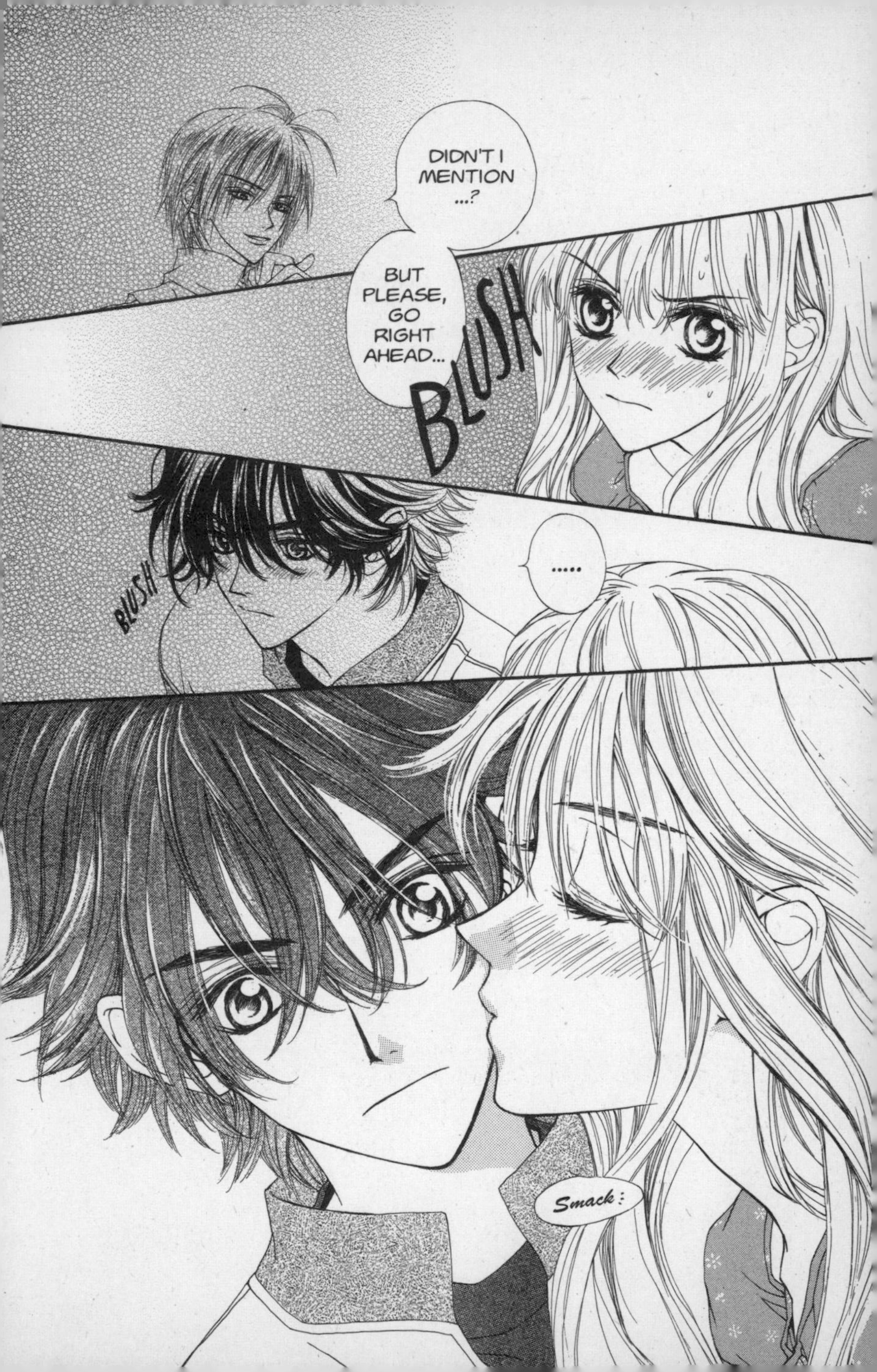
DIDN'T I MENTION ...?
BUT PLEASE, GO RIGHT AHEAD...
BLUSH
BLUSH
......
Smack

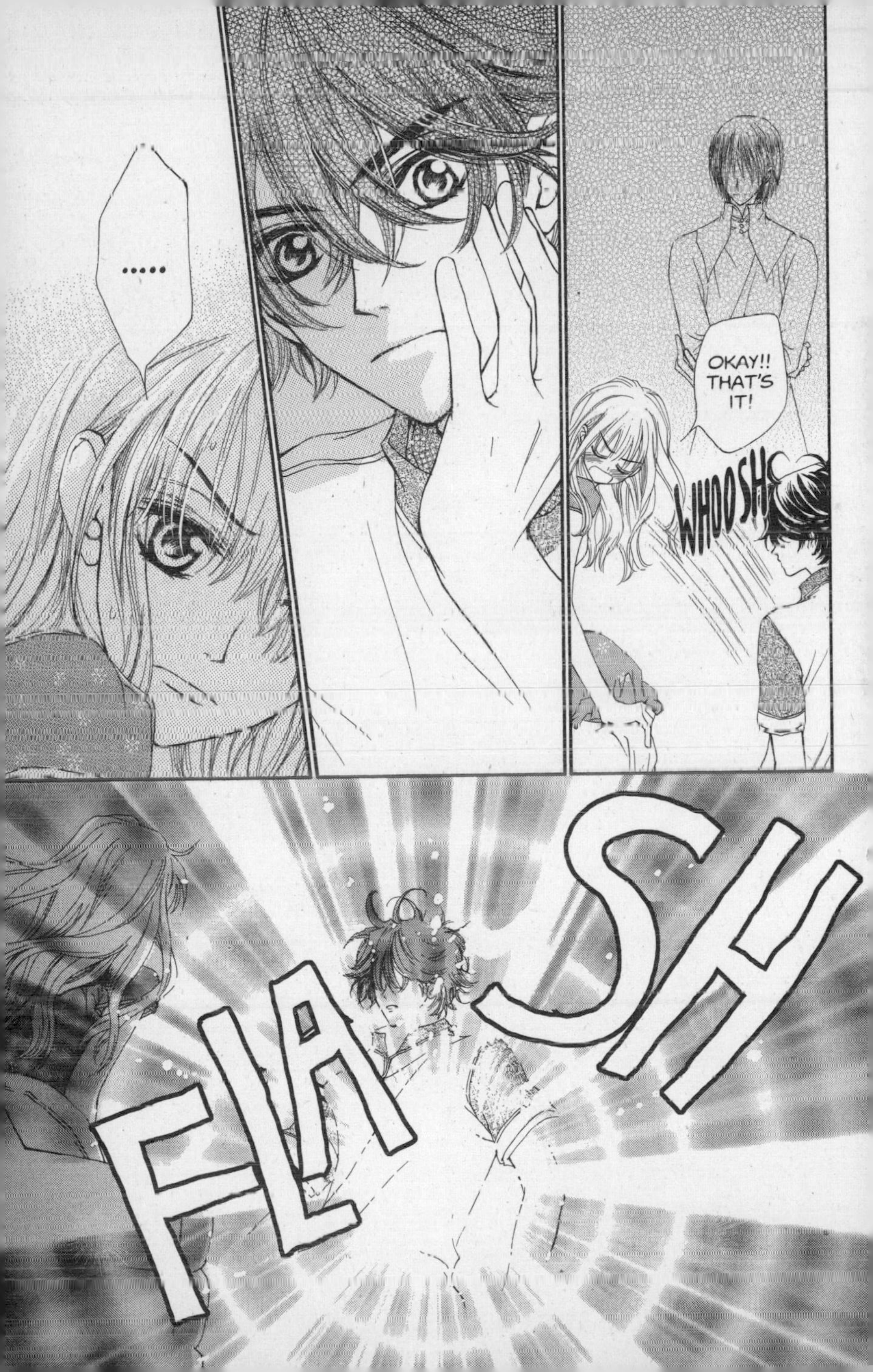
OKAY!! THAT'S IT!
WHOOSH
.....
FLASH

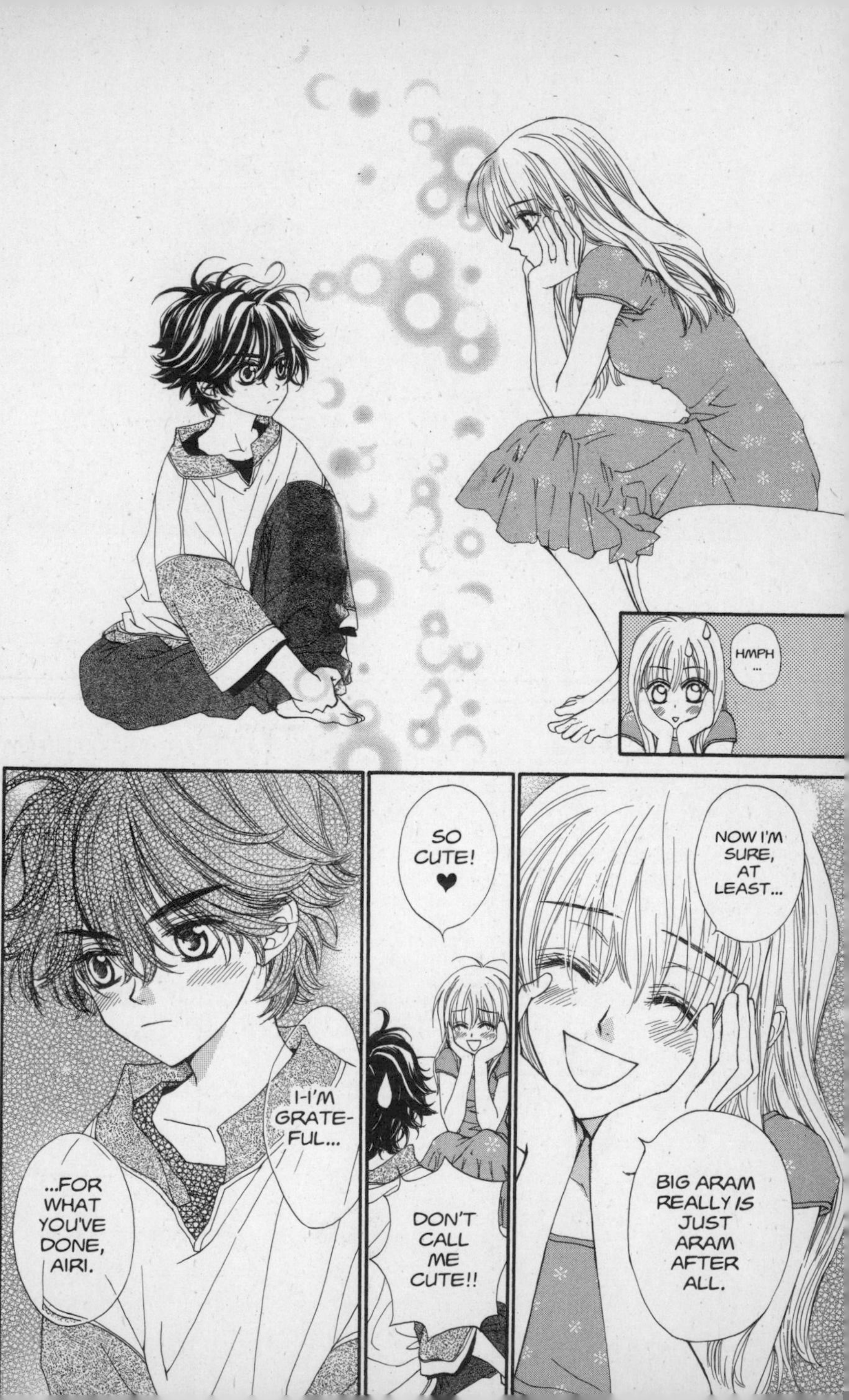
HMPH ...
NOW I'M SURE, AT LEAST...
BIG ARAM REALLY IS JUST ARAM AFTER ALL.
SO CUTE! ♥
DON'T CALL ME CUTE!!
I-I'M GRATE-FUL...
...FOR WHAT YOU'VE DONE, AIRI.

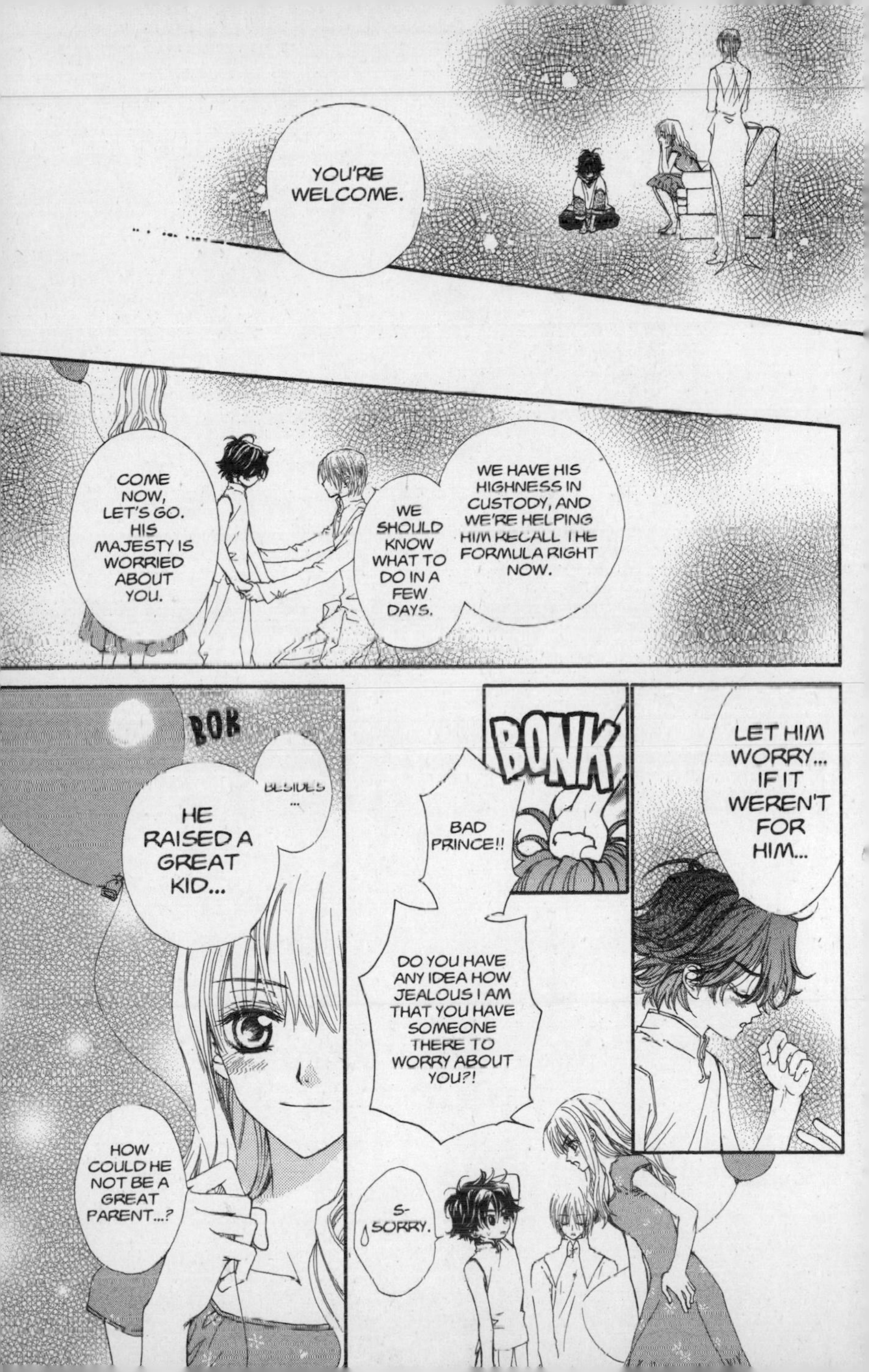
YOU'RE WELCOME.
WE HAVE HIS HIGHNESS IN CUSTODY, AND WE'RE HELPING HIM RECALL THE FORMULA RIGHT NOW.
WE SHOULD KNOW WHAT TO DO IN A FEW DAYS.
COME NOW, LET'S GO. HIS MAJESTY IS WORRIED ABOUT YOU.
LET HIM WORRY... IF IT WEREN'T FOR HIM...
BONK
BAD PRINCE!!
DO YOU HAVE ANY IDEA HOW JEALOUS I AM THAT YOU HAVE SOMEONE THERE TO WORRY ABOUT YOU?!
S-SORRY.
BOK
BESIDES...
HE RAISED A GREAT KID...
HOW COULD HE NOT BE A GREAT PARENT...?

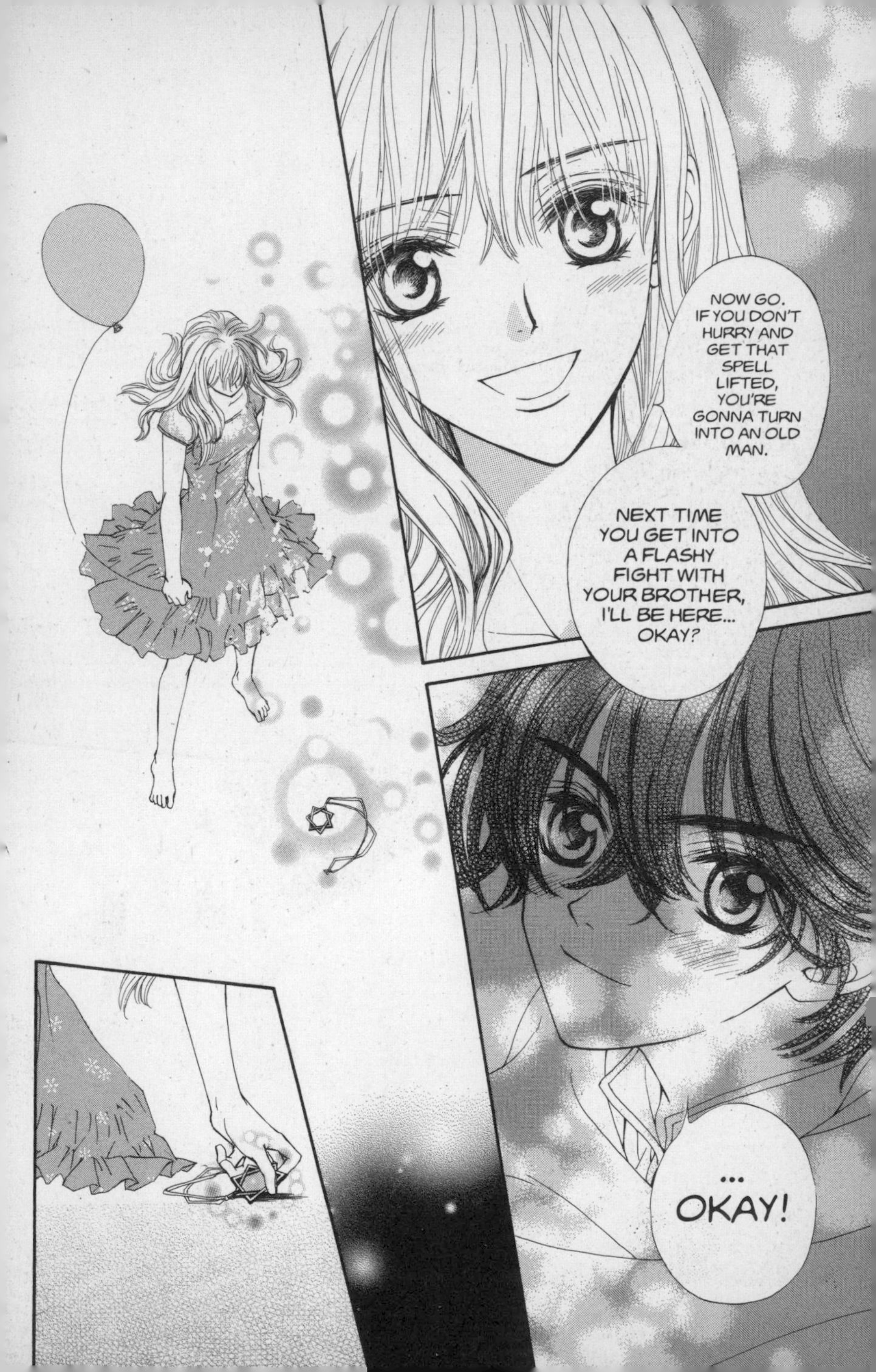
NOW GO. IF YOU DON'T HURRY AND GET THAT SPELL LIFTED, YOU'RE GONNA TURN INTO AN OLD MAN.
NEXT TIME YOU GET INTO A FLASHY FIGHT WITH YOUR BROTHER, I'LL BE HERE... OKAY?
...OKAY!

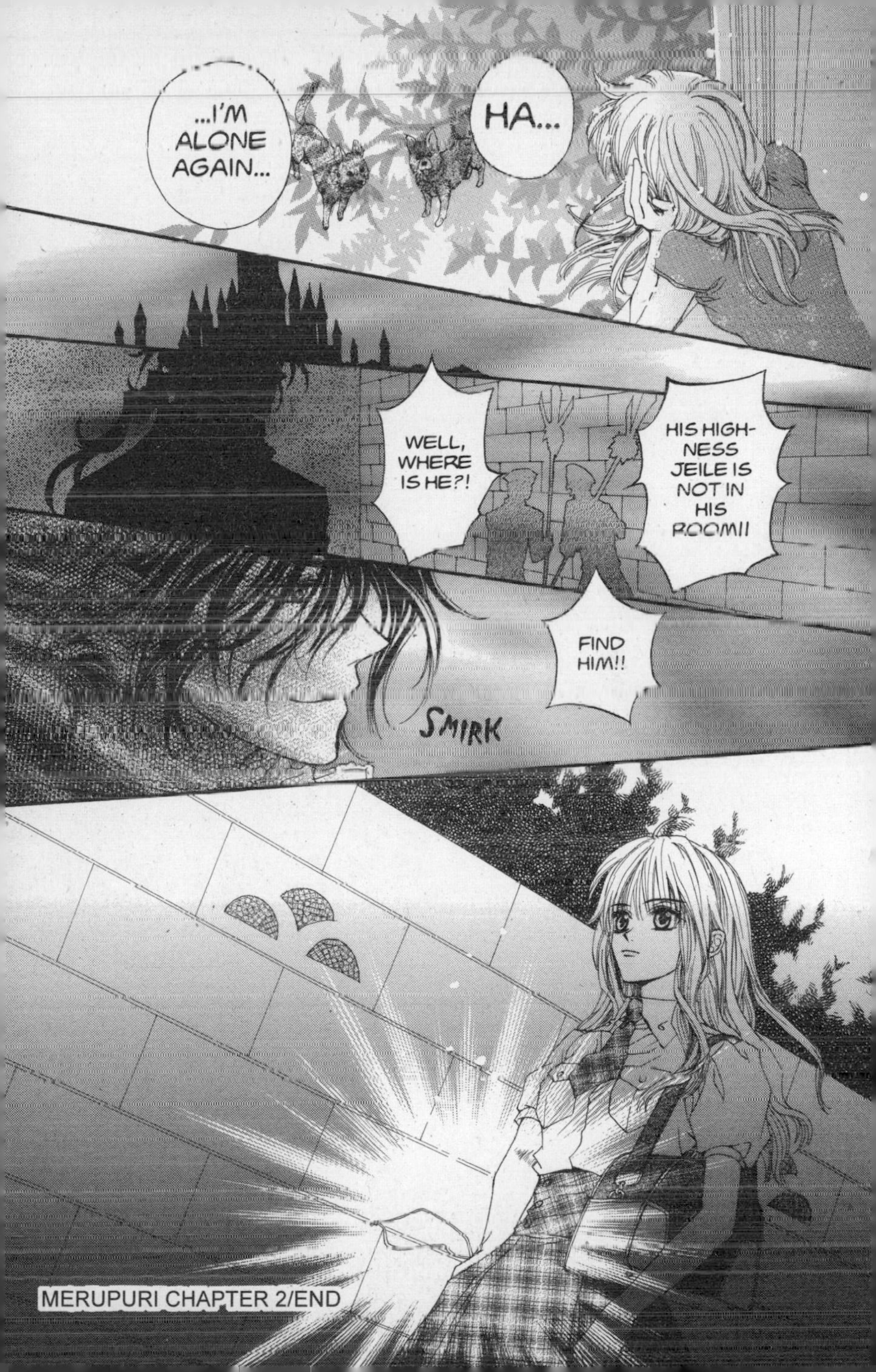
HA...
...I'M ALONE AGAIN...
HIS HIGH-NESS JEILE IS NOT IN HIS ROOM!!
WELL, WHERE IS HE?!
FIND HIM!!
SMIRK
MERUPURI CHAPTER 2/END

MYSTERIOUS
BEINGS WHO
HAVE YET TO SHOW
THEMSELVES...
AIRI'S GRAND-
PARENTS.

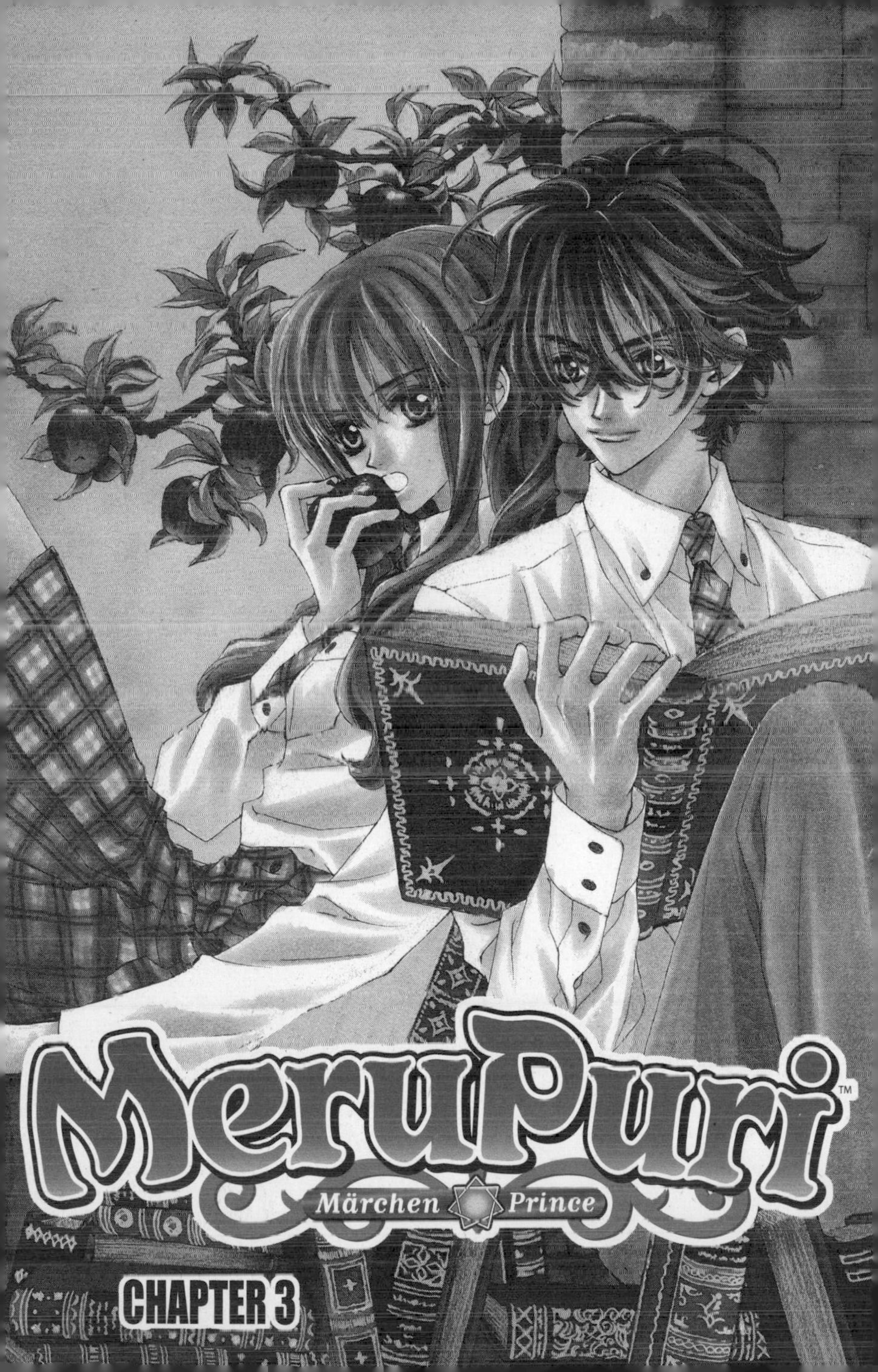
MeruPuri™
Märchen Prince
CHAPTER 3

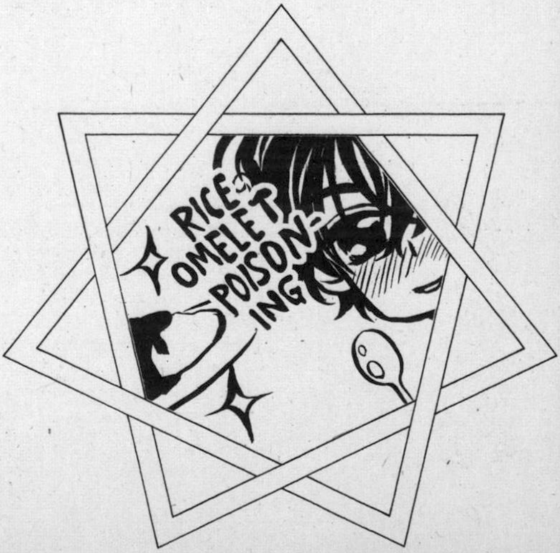
RICE-
OMELET
POISON-
ING

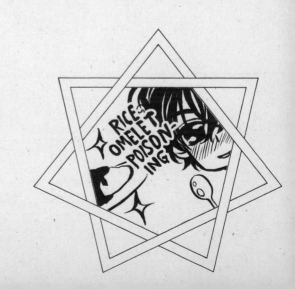

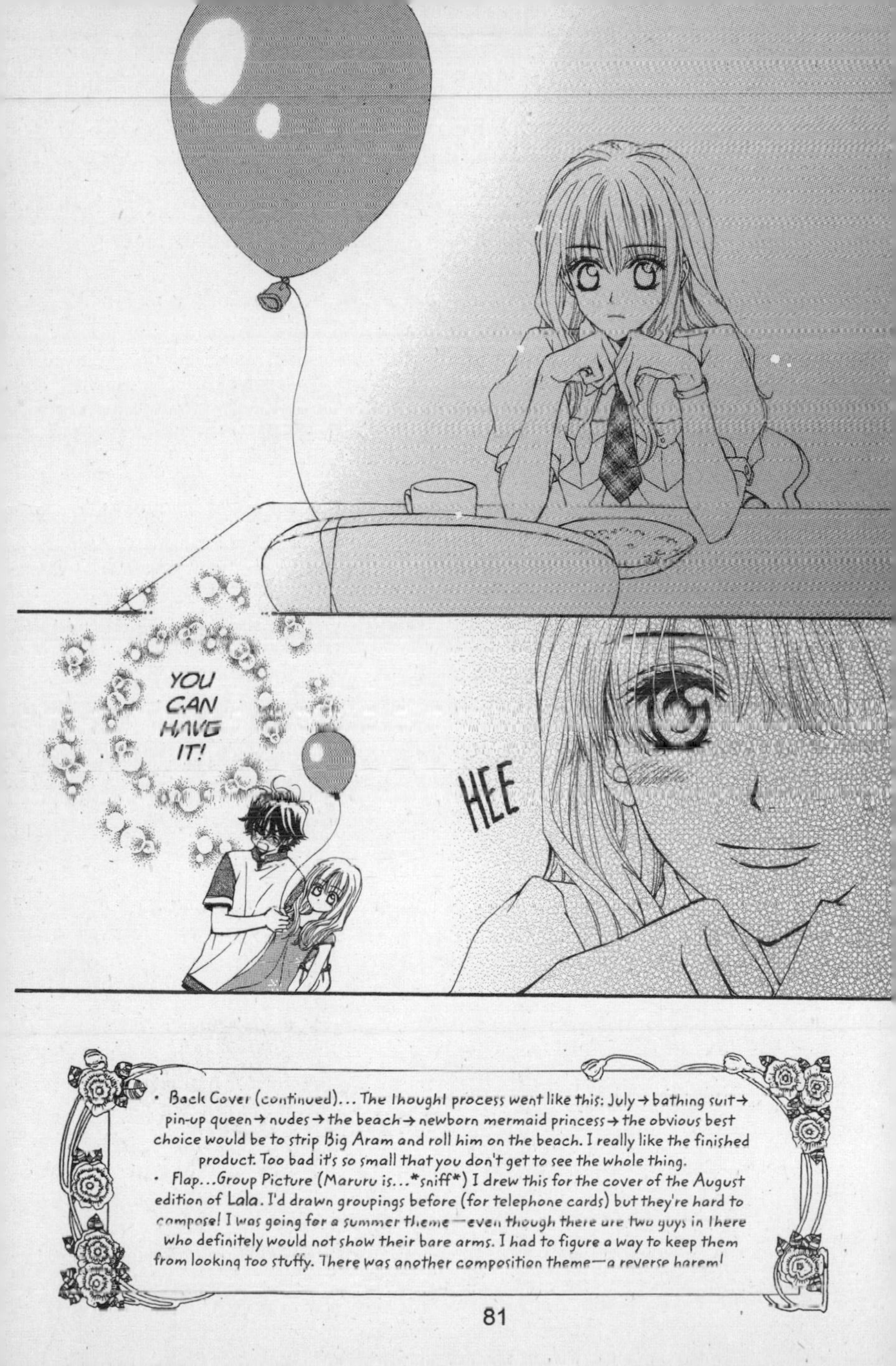
HEE
YOU CAN HAVE IT!

• Back Cover (continued)... The thought process went like this: July → bathing suit → pin-up queen → nudes → the beach → newborn mermaid princess → the obvious best choice would be to strip Big Aram and roll him on the beach. I really like the finished product. Too bad it's so small that you don't get to see the whole thing.

• Flap...Group Picture (Maruru is...*sniff*) I drew this for the cover of the August edition of *Lala*. I'd drawn groupings before (for telephone cards) but they're hard to compose! I was going for a summer theme—even though there are two guys in there who definitely would not show their bare arms. I had to figure a way to keep them from looking too stuffy. There was another composition theme—a reverse harem!

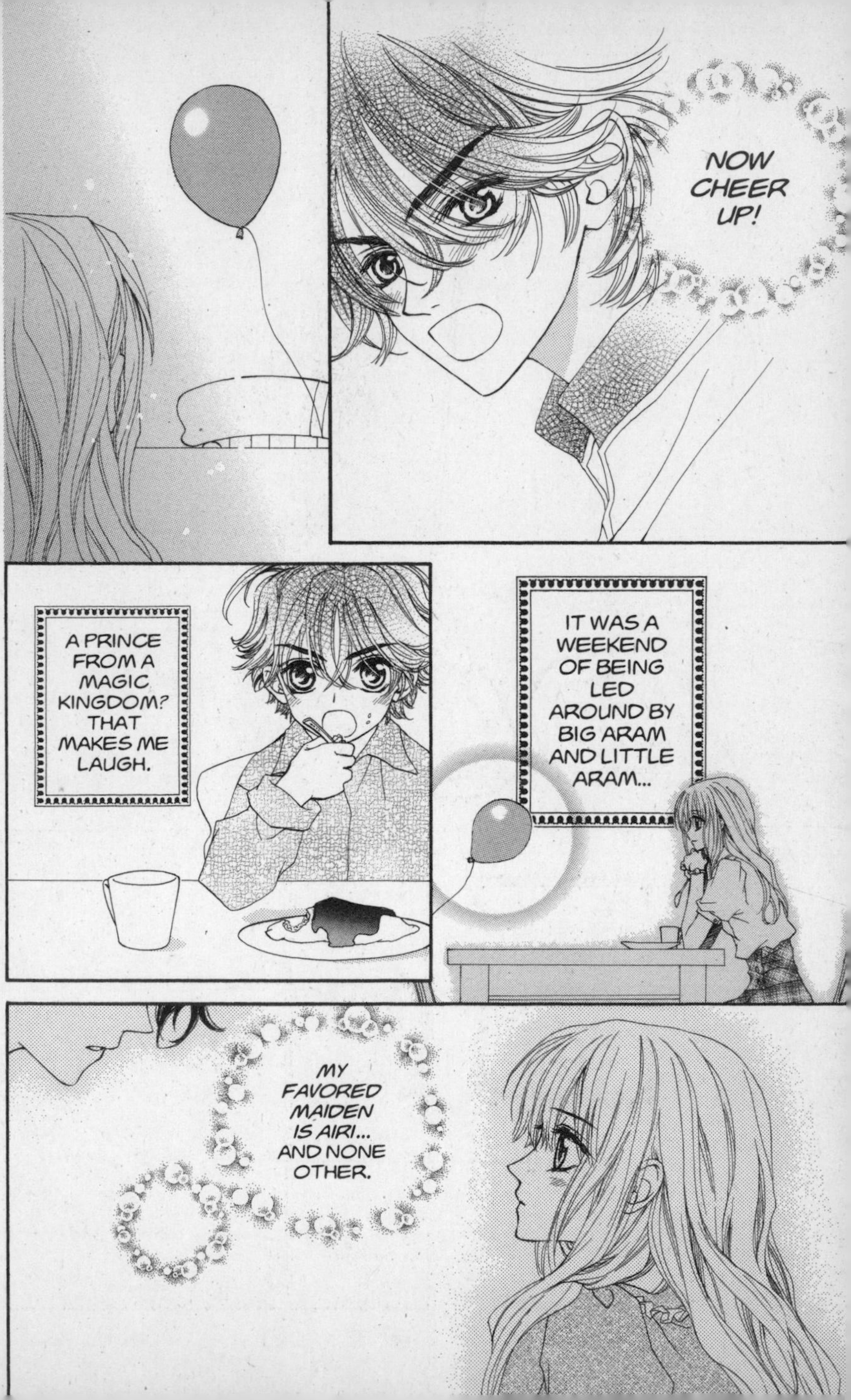
NOW CHEER UP!
IT WAS A WEEKEND OF BEING LED AROUND BY BIG ARAM AND LITTLE ARAM...
A PRINCE FROM A MAGIC KINGDOM? THAT MAKES ME LAUGH.
MY FAVORED MAIDEN IS AIRI... AND NONE OTHER.

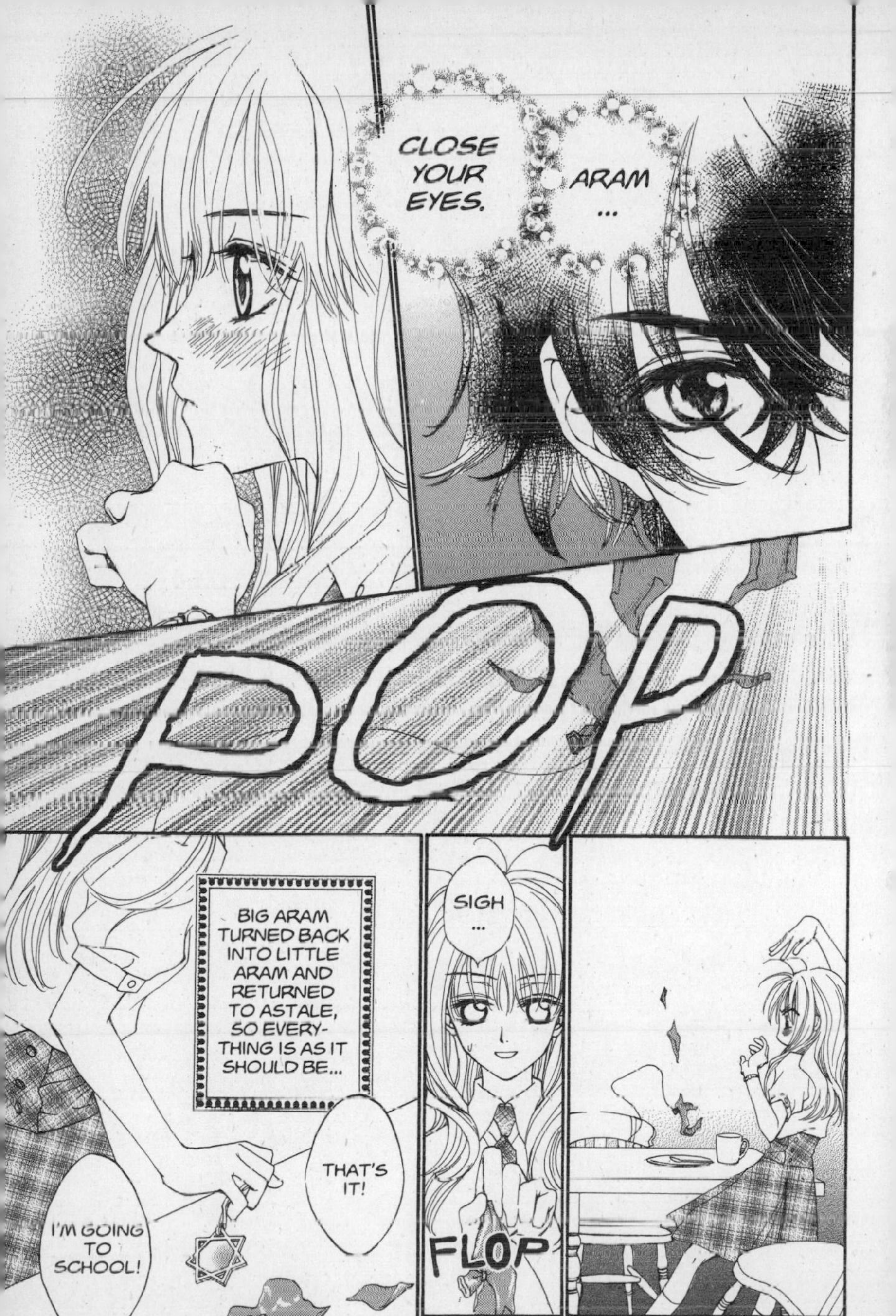
ARAM ...
CLOSE YOUR EYES.
POP
SIGH ...
FLOP
BIG ARAM TURNED BACK INTO LITTLE ARAM AND RETURNED TO ASTALE, SO EVERY-THING IS AS IT SHOULD BE...
THAT'S IT!
I'M GOING TO SCHOOL!

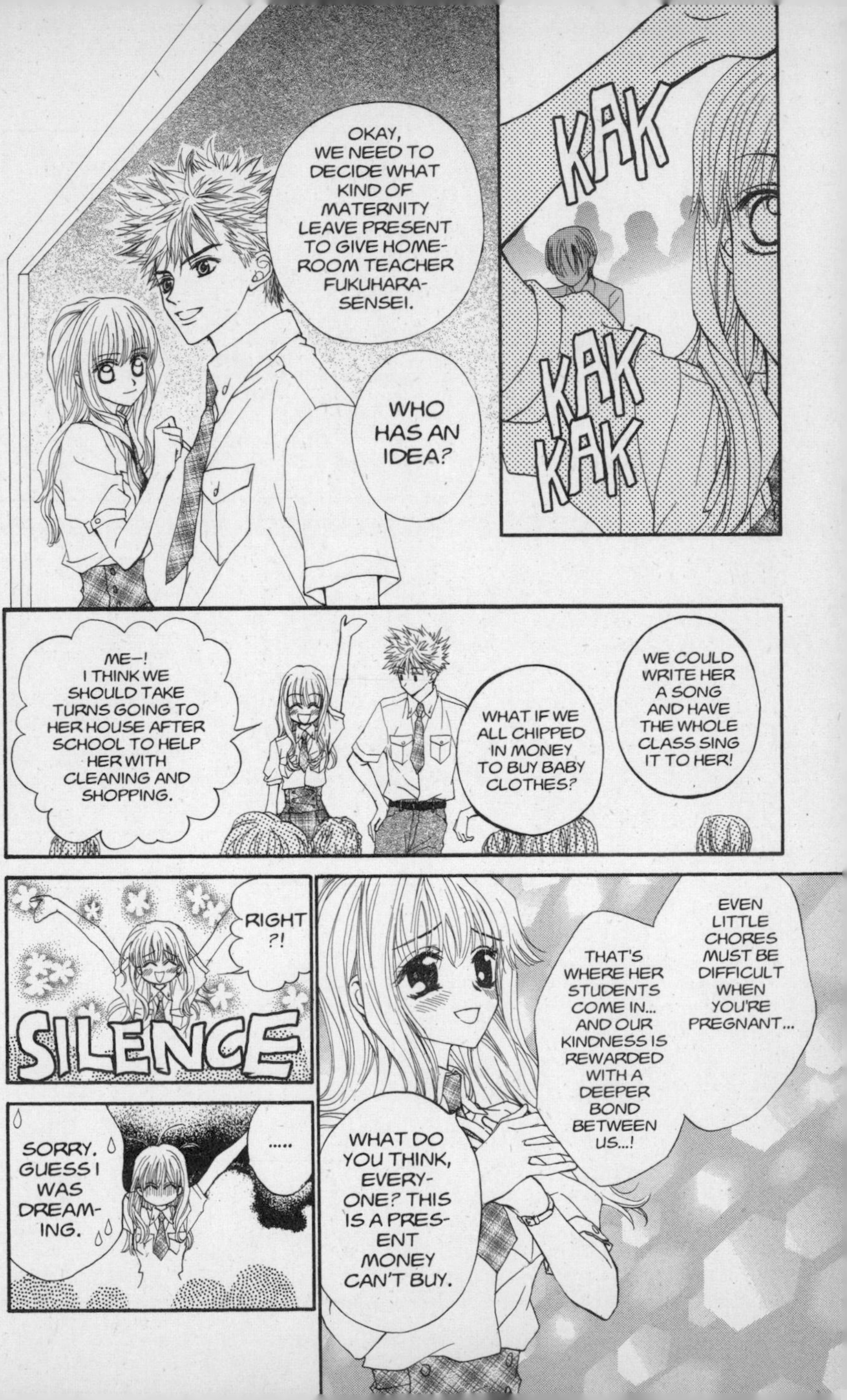
KAK
KAK KAK KAK
OKAY, WE NEED TO DECIDE WHAT KIND OF MATERNITY LEAVE PRESENT TO GIVE HOME-ROOM TEACHER FUKUHARA-SENSEI.
WHO HAS AN IDEA?
WE COULD WRITE HER A SONG AND HAVE THE WHOLE CLASS SING IT TO HER!
WHAT IF WE ALL CHIPPED IN MONEY TO BUY BABY CLOTHES?
ME--! I THINK WE SHOULD TAKE TURNS GOING TO HER HOUSE AFTER SCHOOL TO HELP HER WITH CLEANING AND SHOPPING.
EVEN LITTLE CHORES MUST BE DIFFICULT WHEN YOU'RE PREGNANT...
THAT'S WHERE HER STUDENTS COME IN... AND OUR KINDNESS IS REWARDED WITH A DEEPER BOND BETWEEN US...!
WHAT DO YOU THINK, EVERY-ONE? THIS IS A PRES-ENT MONEY CAN'T BUY.
RIGHT ?!
SILENCE
.....
SORRY. GUESS I WAS DREAM-ING.

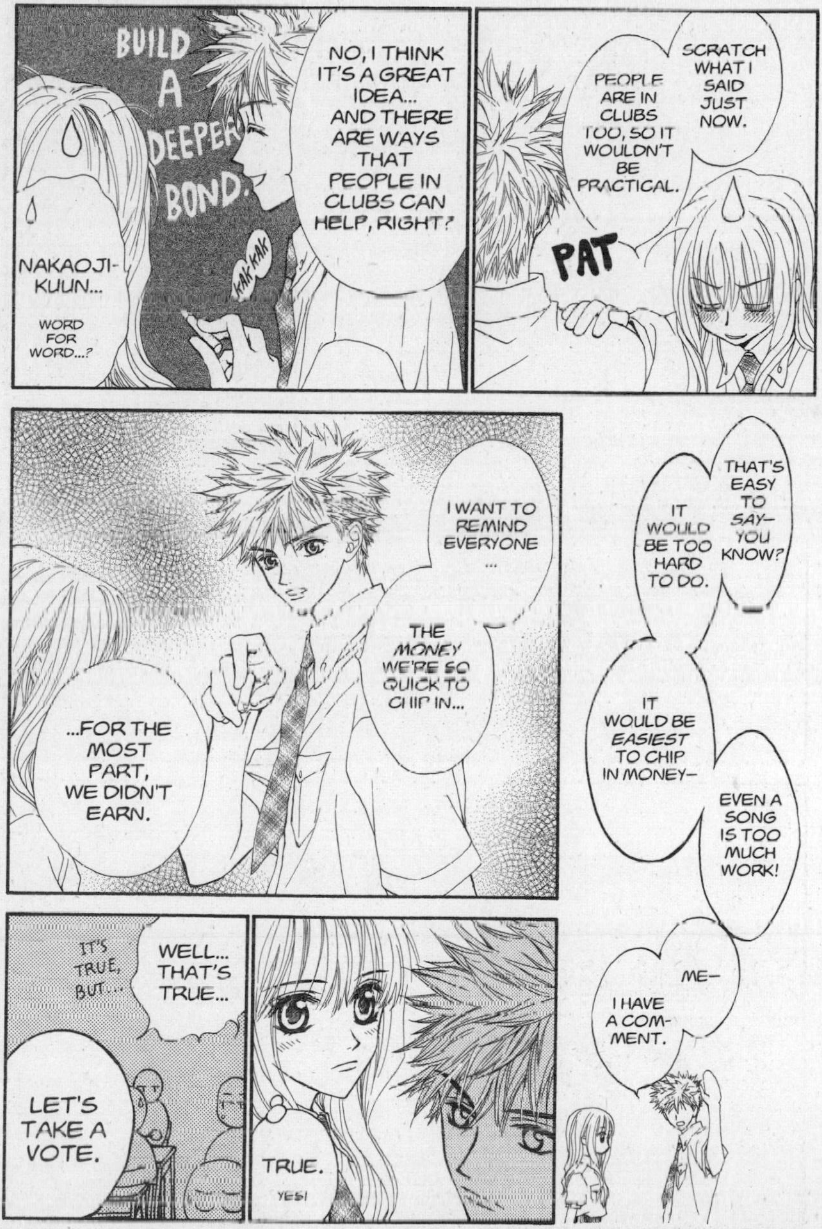
SCRATCH WHAT I SAID JUST NOW.
PEOPLE ARE IN CLUBS TOO, SO IT WOULDN'T BE PRACTICAL.
PAT
NO, I THINK IT'S A GREAT IDEA... AND THERE ARE WAYS THAT PEOPLE IN CLUBS CAN HELP, RIGHT?
BUILD A DEEPER BOND.
KAK KAK
NAKAOJI-KUUN...
WORD FOR WORD...?
THAT'S EASY TO SAY—YOU KNOW?
IT WOULD BE TOO HARD TO DO.
IT WOULD BE EASIEST TO CHIP IN MONEY—
EVEN A SONG IS TOO MUCH WORK!
ME—
I HAVE A COMMENT.
I WANT TO REMIND EVERYONE ...
THE MONEY WE'RE SO QUICK TO CHIP IN...
...FOR THE MOST PART, WE DIDN'T EARN.
TRUE.
YES!
WELL... THAT'S TRUE...
IT'S TRUE, BUT...
LET'S TAKE A VOTE.

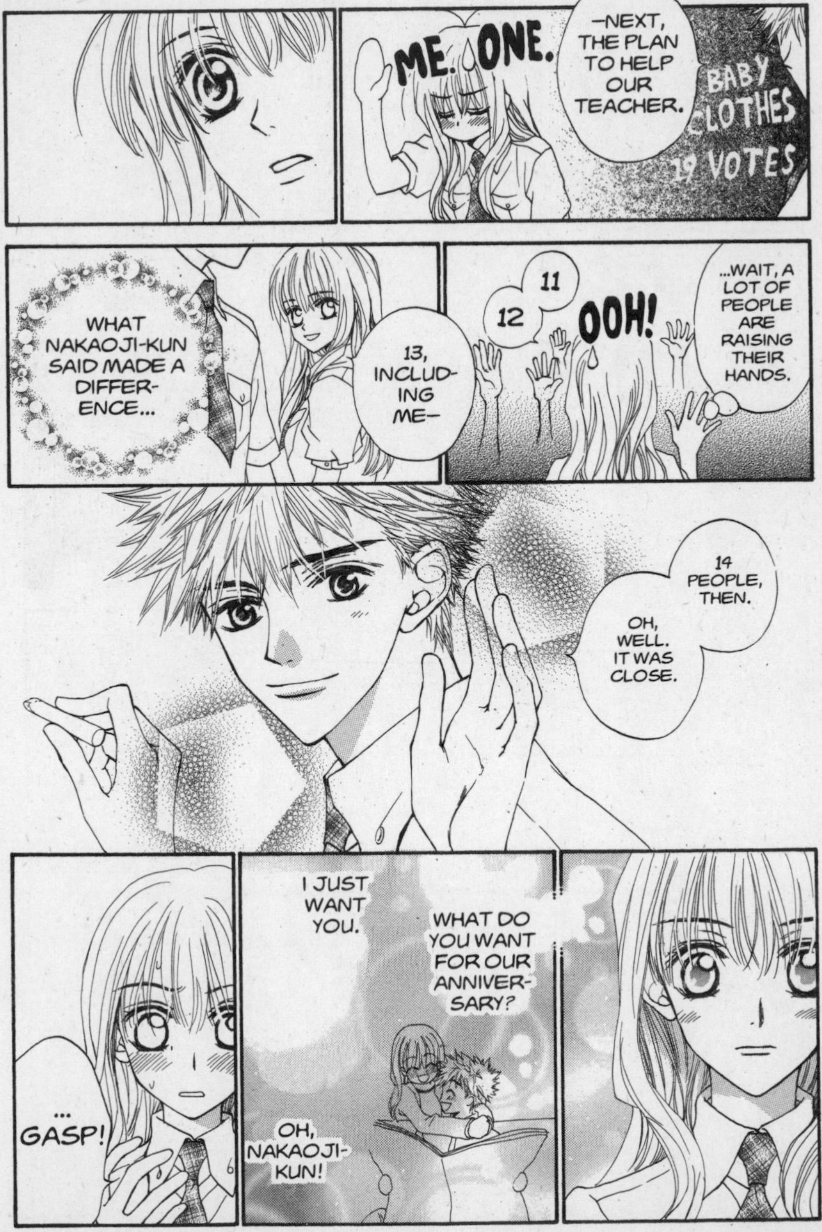
BABY CLOTHES 19 VOTES
—NEXT, THE PLAN TO HELP OUR TEACHER.
ME. ONE.
...WAIT, A LOT OF PEOPLE ARE RAISING THEIR HANDS.
OOH!
11
12
13, INCLUDING ME—
WHAT NAKAOJI-KUN SAID MADE A DIFFERENCE...
14 PEOPLE, THEN.
OH, WELL. IT WAS CLOSE.
WHAT DO YOU WANT FOR OUR ANNIVERSARY?
I JUST WANT YOU.
OH, NAKAOJI-KUN!
...GASP!

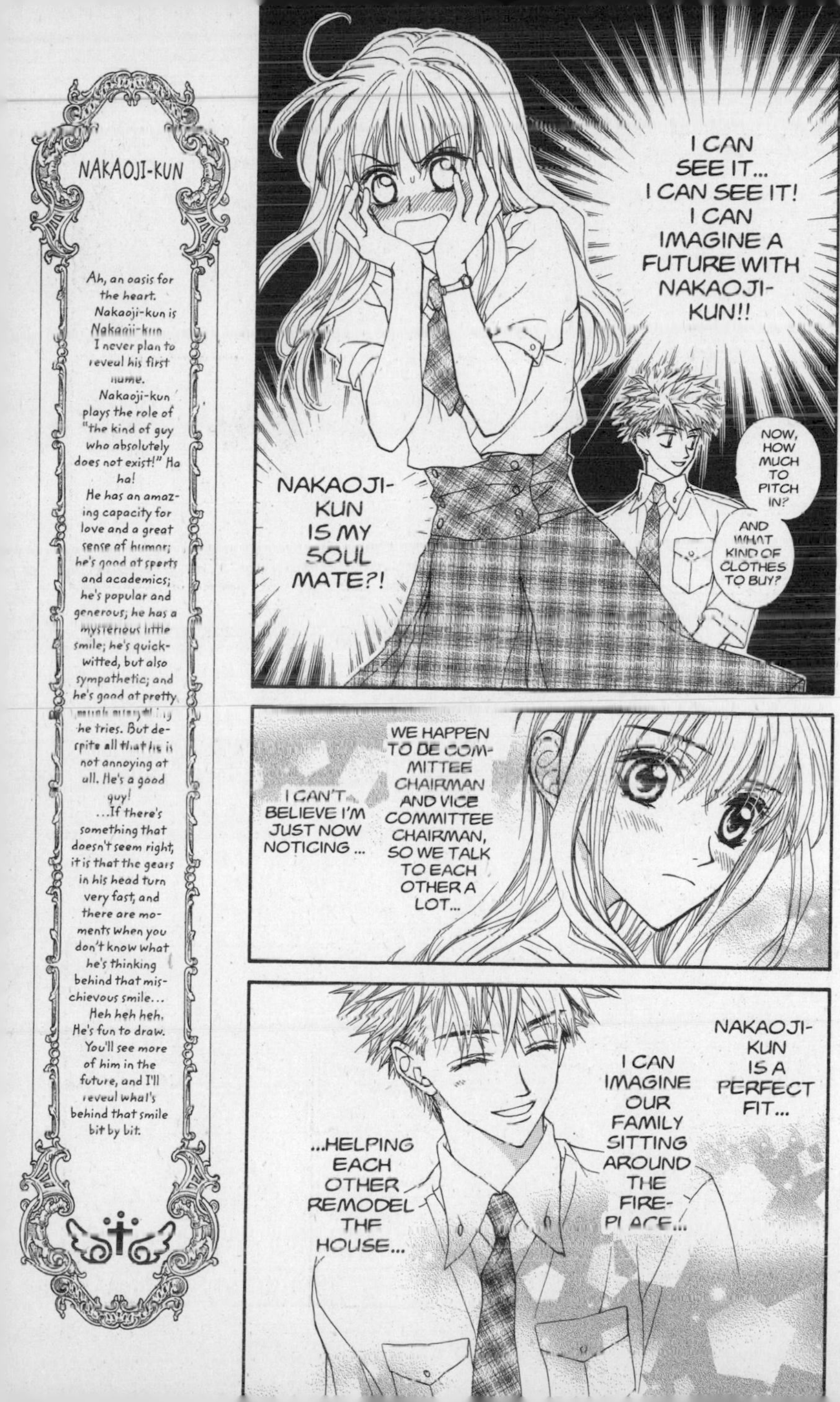
I CAN SEE IT... I CAN SEE IT! I CAN IMAGINE A FUTURE WITH NAKAOJI-KUN!!
NOW, HOW MUCH TO PITCH IN?
AND WHAT KIND OF CLOTHES TO BUY?
NAKAOJI-KUN IS MY SOUL MATE?!
WE HAPPEN TO BE COMMITTEE CHAIRMAN AND VICE COMMITTEE CHAIRMAN, SO WE TALK TO EACH OTHER A LOT...
I CAN'T BELIEVE I'M JUST NOW NOTICING ...
NAKAOJI-KUN IS A PERFECT FIT...
I CAN IMAGINE OUR FAMILY SITTING AROUND THE FIRE-PLACE...
...HELPING EACH OTHER REMODEL THE HOUSE...

NAKAOJI-KUN

Ah, an oasis for the heart. Nakaoji-kun is Nakaoji-kun. I never plan to reveal his first name. Nakaoji-kun plays the role of "the kind of guy who absolutely does not exist!" Ha ha! He has an amazing capacity for love and a great sense of humor; he's good at sports and academics; he's popular and generous; he has a mysterious little smile; he's quick-witted, but also sympathetic; and he's good at pretty much anything he tries. But despite all that he is not annoying at all. He's a good guy! ...If there's something that doesn't seem right, it is that the gears in his head turn very fast, and there are moments when you don't know what he's thinking behind that mischievous smile... Heh heh heh. He's fun to draw. You'll see more of him in the future, and I'll reveal what's behind that smile bit by bit.

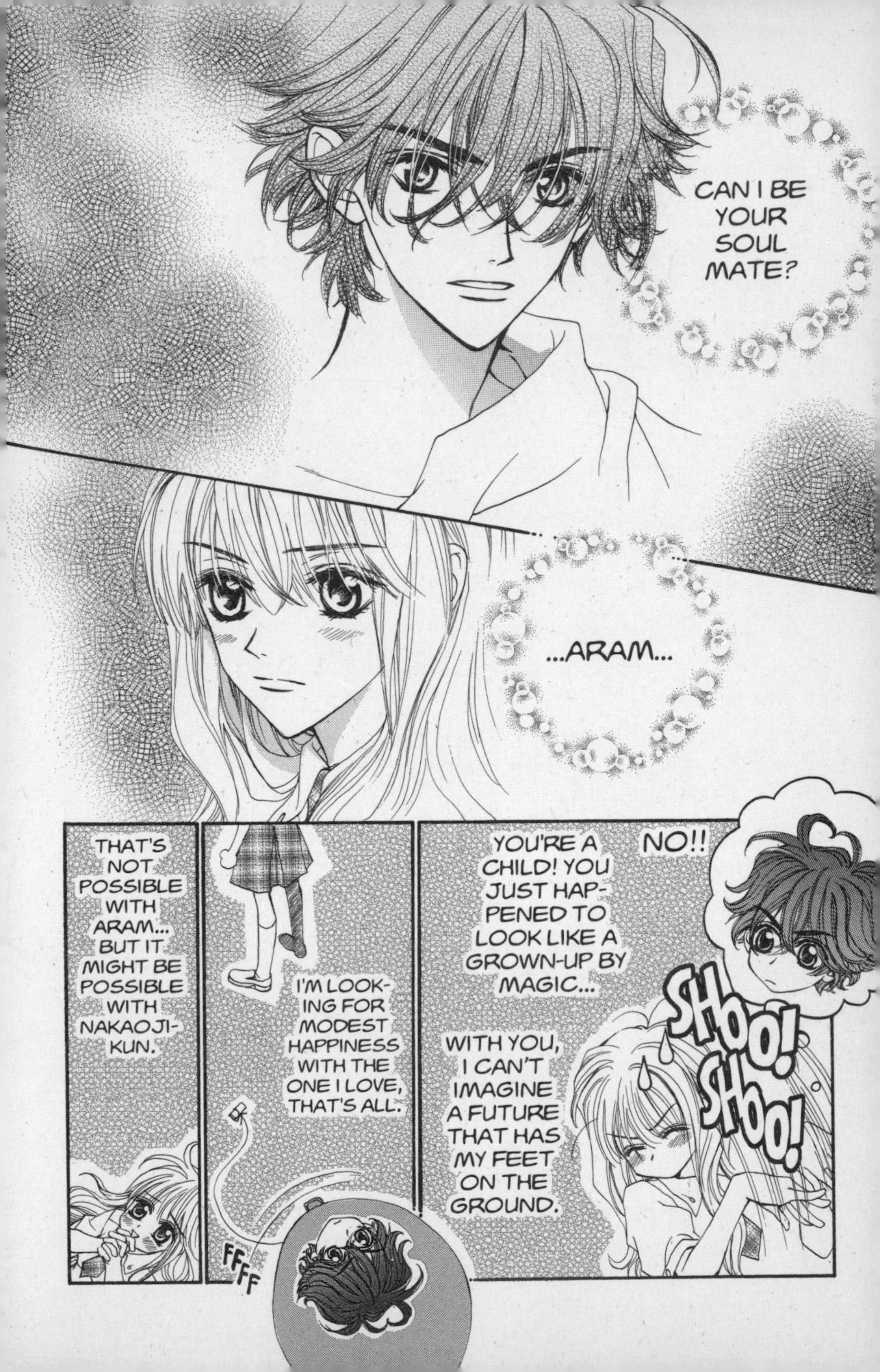
CAN I BE YOUR SOUL MATE?
...ARAM...
NO!!
YOU'RE A CHILD! YOU JUST HAP-PENED TO LOOK LIKE A GROWN-UP BY MAGIC...
SHOO! SHOO!
WITH YOU, I CAN'T IMAGINE A FUTURE THAT HAS MY FEET ON THE GROUND.
I'M LOOK-ING FOR MODEST HAPPINESS WITH THE ONE I LOVE, THAT'S ALL.
FFFF
THAT'S NOT POSSIBLE WITH ARAM... BUT IT MIGHT BE POSSIBLE WITH NAKAOJI-KUN.

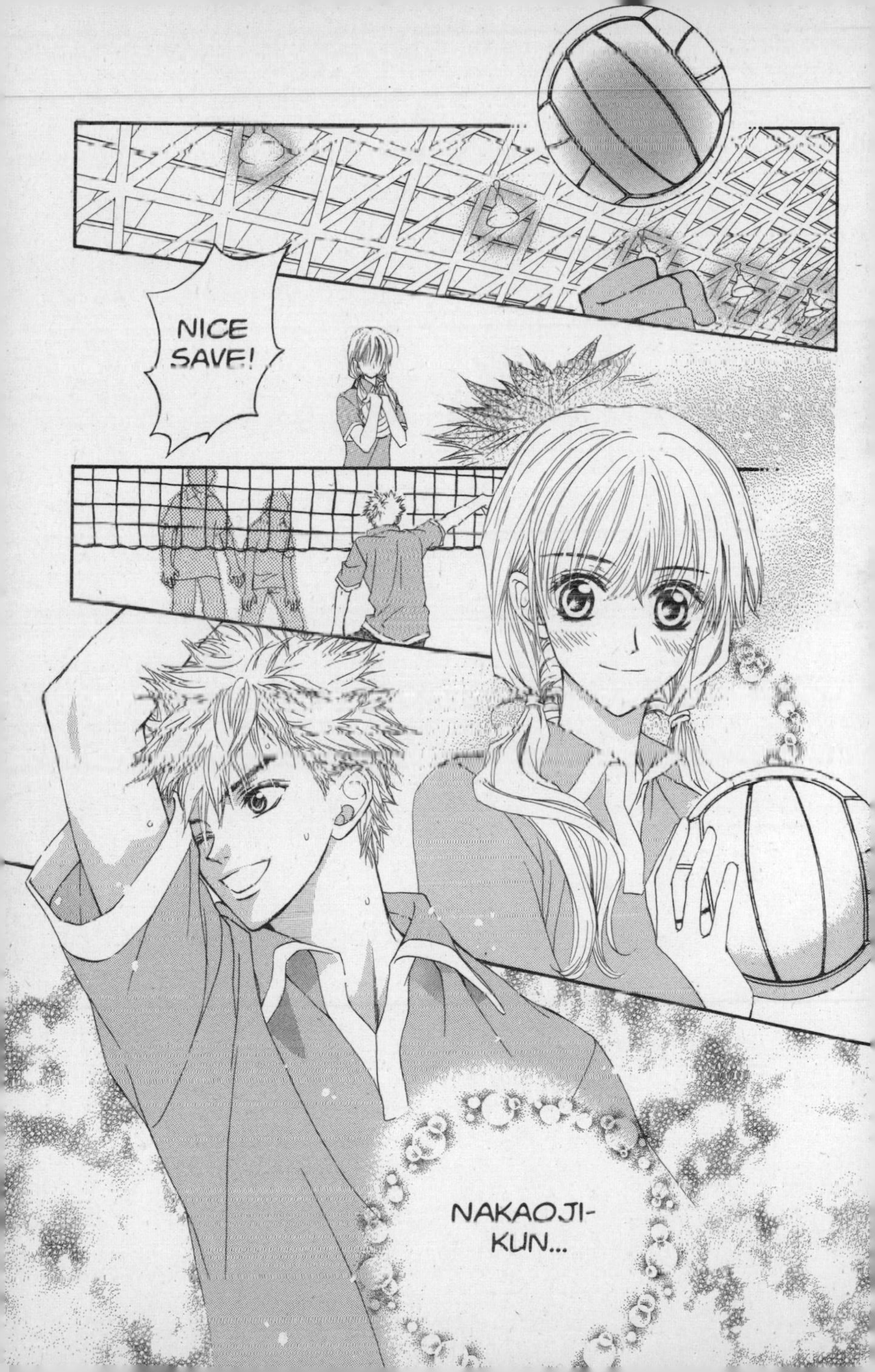
NICE SAVE!
NAKAOJI-KUN...

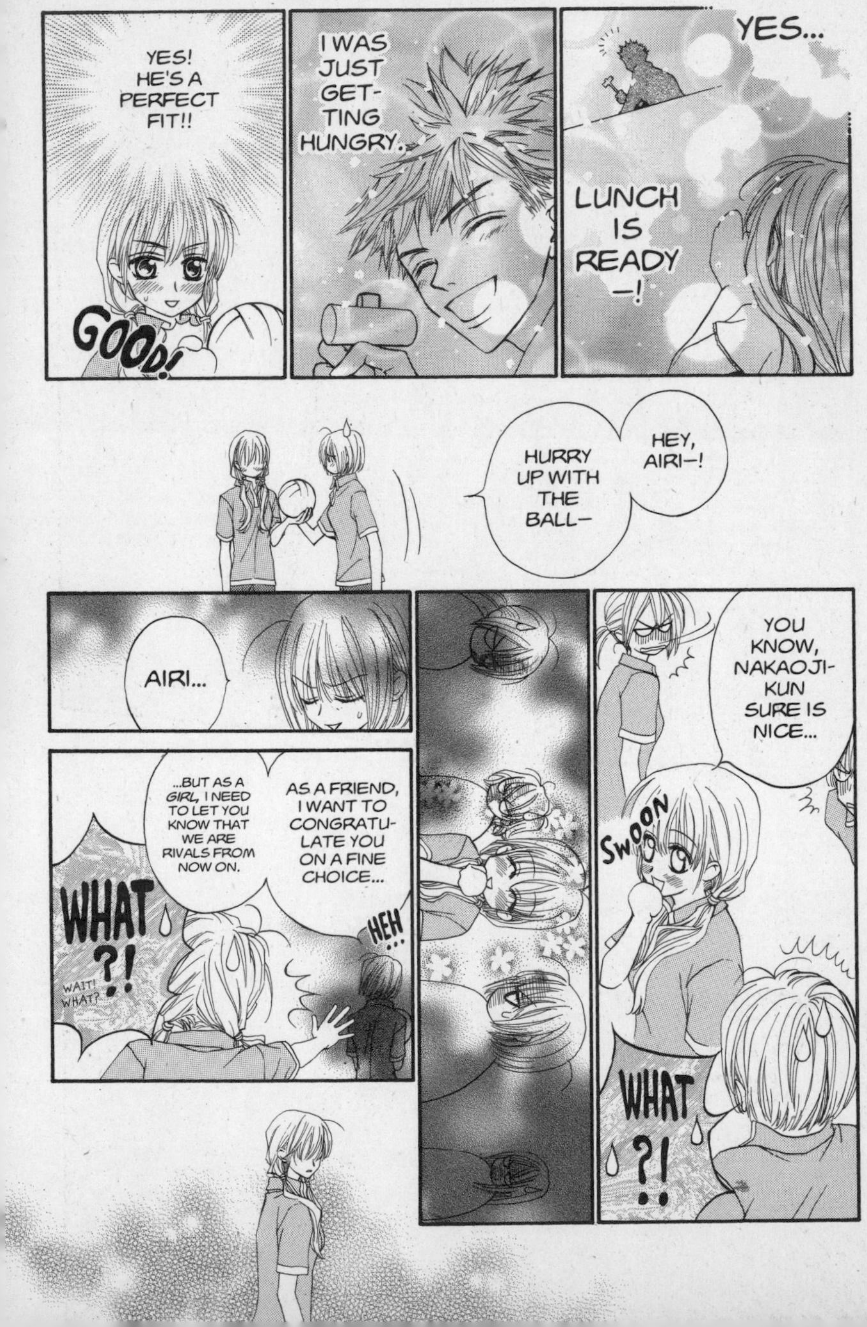
YES...
LUNCH IS READY—!
I WAS JUST GET-TING HUNGRY..
YES! HE'S A PERFECT FIT!!
GOOD!
HEY, AIRI—!
HURRY UP WITH THE BALL—
YOU KNOW, NAKAOJI-KUN SURE IS NICE...
SWOON
WHAT ?!
AIRI...
AS A FRIEND, I WANT TO CONGRATU-LATE YOU ON A FINE CHOICE...
...BUT AS A GIRL, I NEED TO LET YOU KNOW THAT WE ARE RIVALS FROM NOW ON.
HEH...
WHAT ?!
WAIT! WHAT?

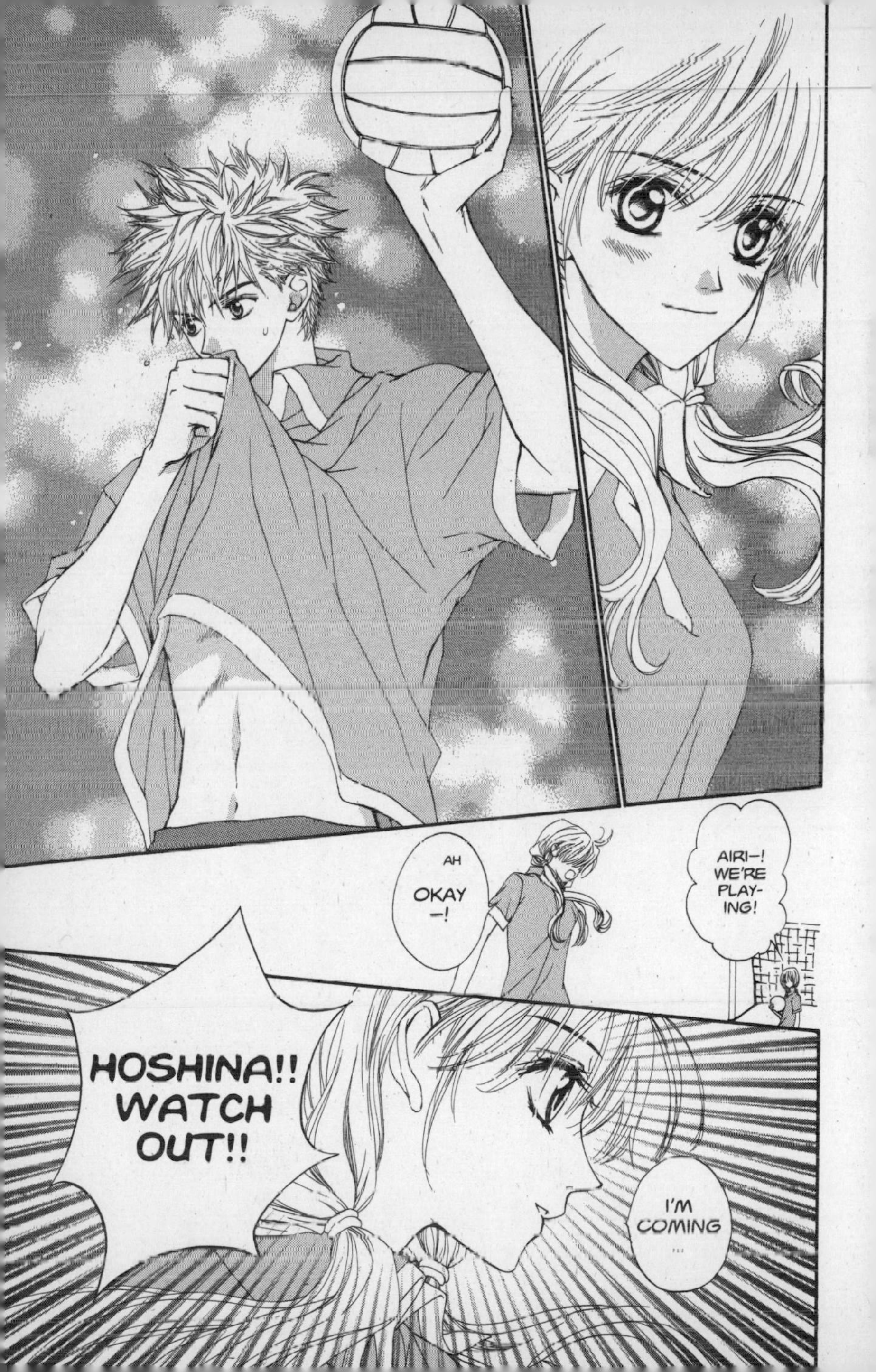
AIRI—! WE'RE PLAY-ING!
AH OKAY —!
I'M COMING
HOSHINA!! WATCH OUT!!

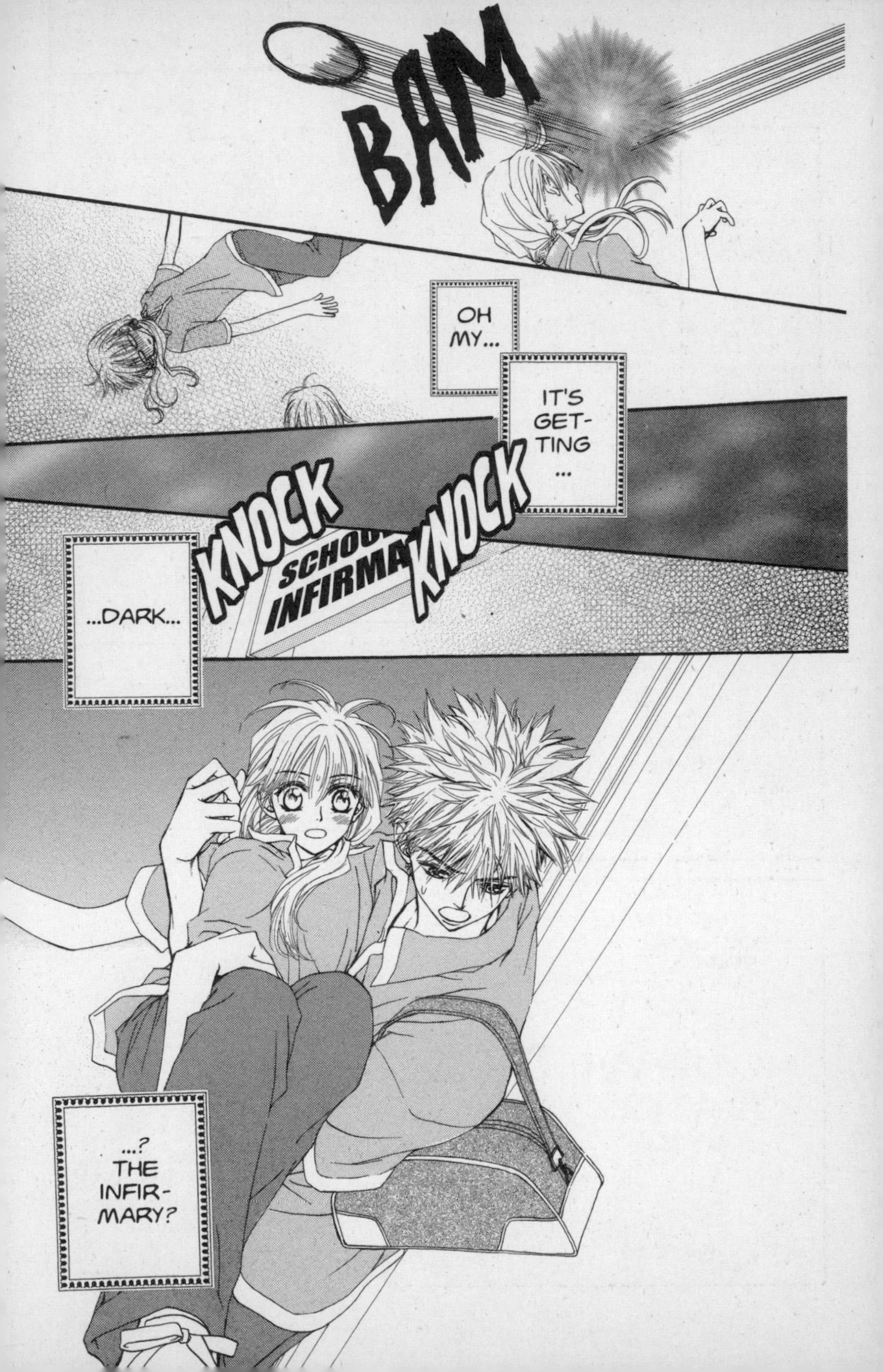
BAM
OH MY...
IT'S GET-TING ...
KNOCK KNOCK
SCHOO
INFIRMA
...DARK...
...? THE INFIR-MARY?

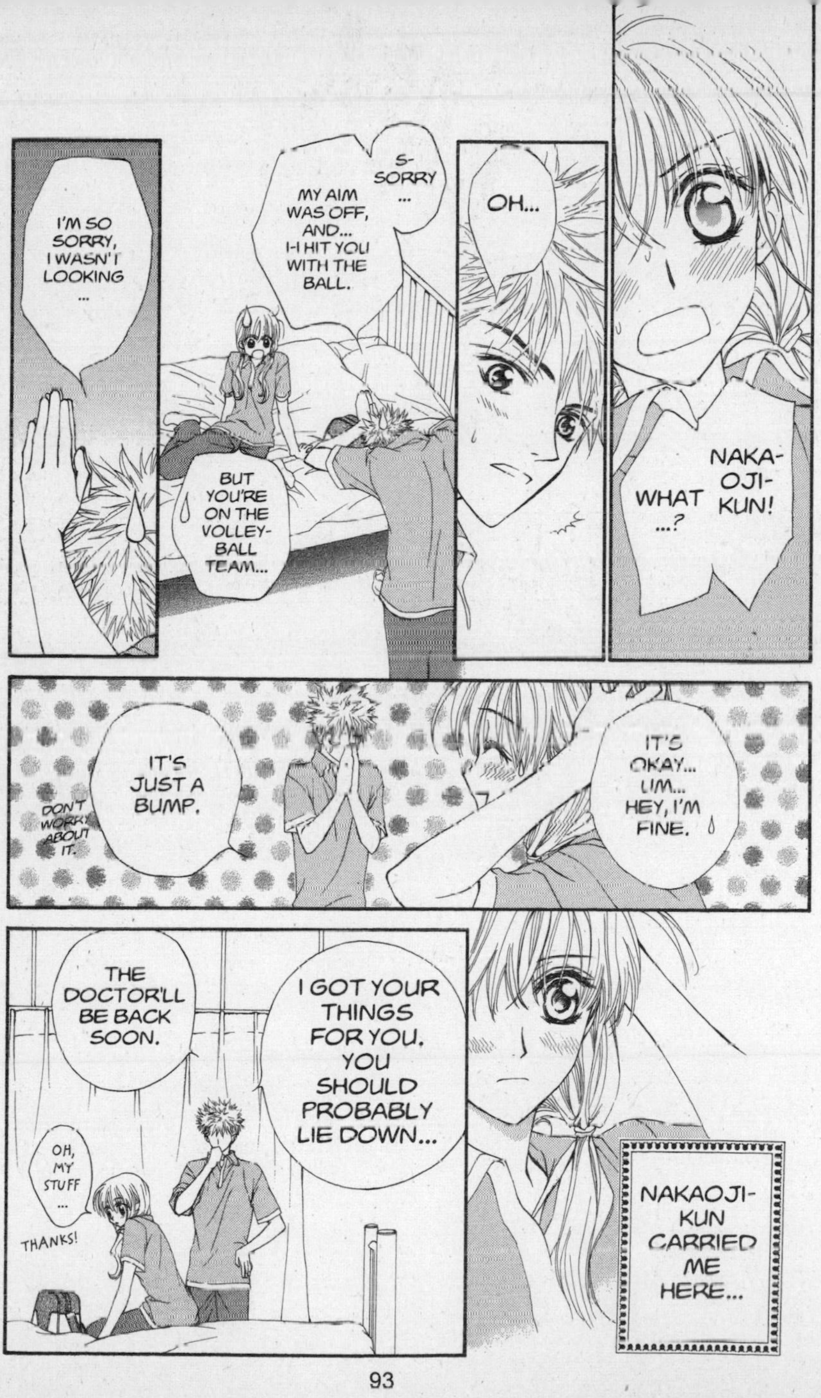
NAKA-OJI-KUN!
WHAT ...?
OH...
S-SORRY ...
MY AIM WAS OFF, AND... I-I HIT YOU WITH THE BALL.
BUT YOU'RE ON THE VOLLEY-BALL TEAM...
I'M SO SORRY, I WASN'T LOOKING ...
IT'S OKAY... UM... HEY, I'M FINE.
IT'S JUST A BUMP.
DON'T WORRY ABOUT IT.
NAKAOJI-KUN CARRIED ME HERE...
I GOT YOUR THINGS FOR YOU. YOU SHOULD PROBABLY LIE DOWN...
THE DOCTOR'LL BE BACK SOON.
OH, MY STUFF ...
THANKS!

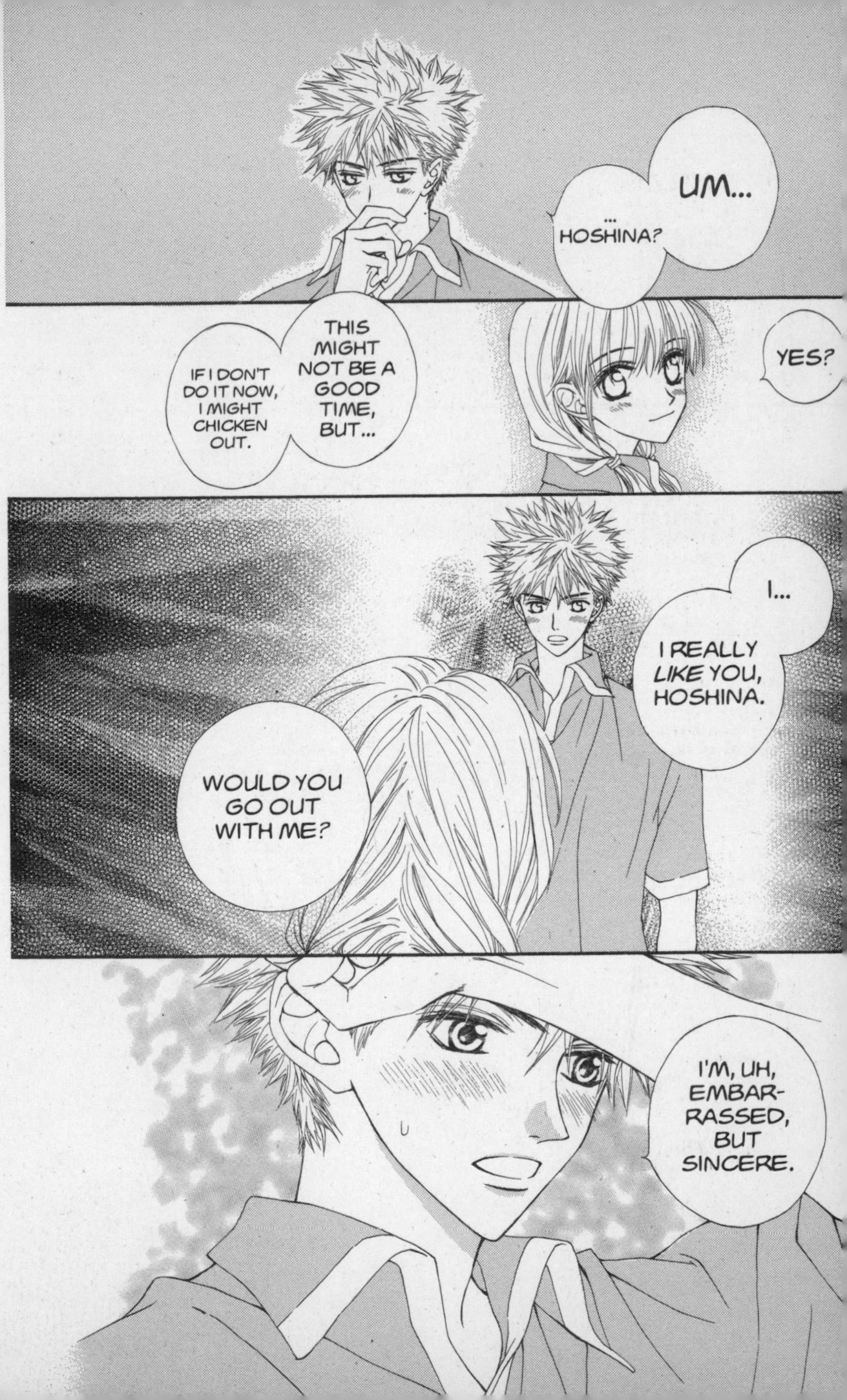
UM...
...HOSHINA?
YES?
THIS MIGHT NOT BE A GOOD TIME, BUT...
IF I DON'T DO IT NOW, I MIGHT CHICKEN OUT.
I...
I REALLY *LIKE* YOU, HOSHINA.
WOULD YOU GO OUT WITH ME?
I'M, UH, EMBAR-RASSED, BUT SINCERE.

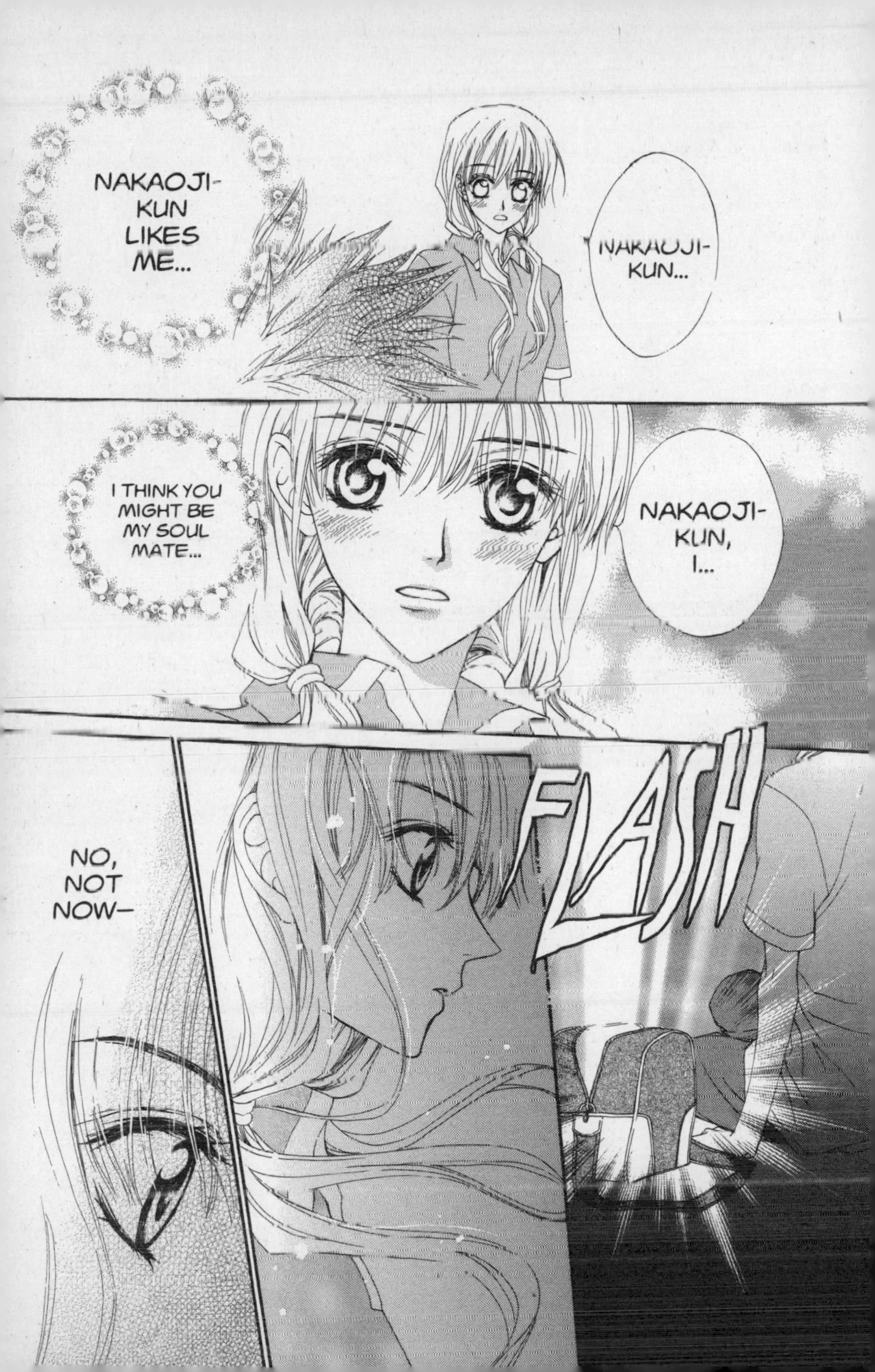
NAKAOJI-KUN...
NAKAOJI-KUN LIKES ME...
NAKAOJI-KUN, I...
I THINK YOU MIGHT BE MY SOUL MATE...
FLASH
NO, NOT NOW–

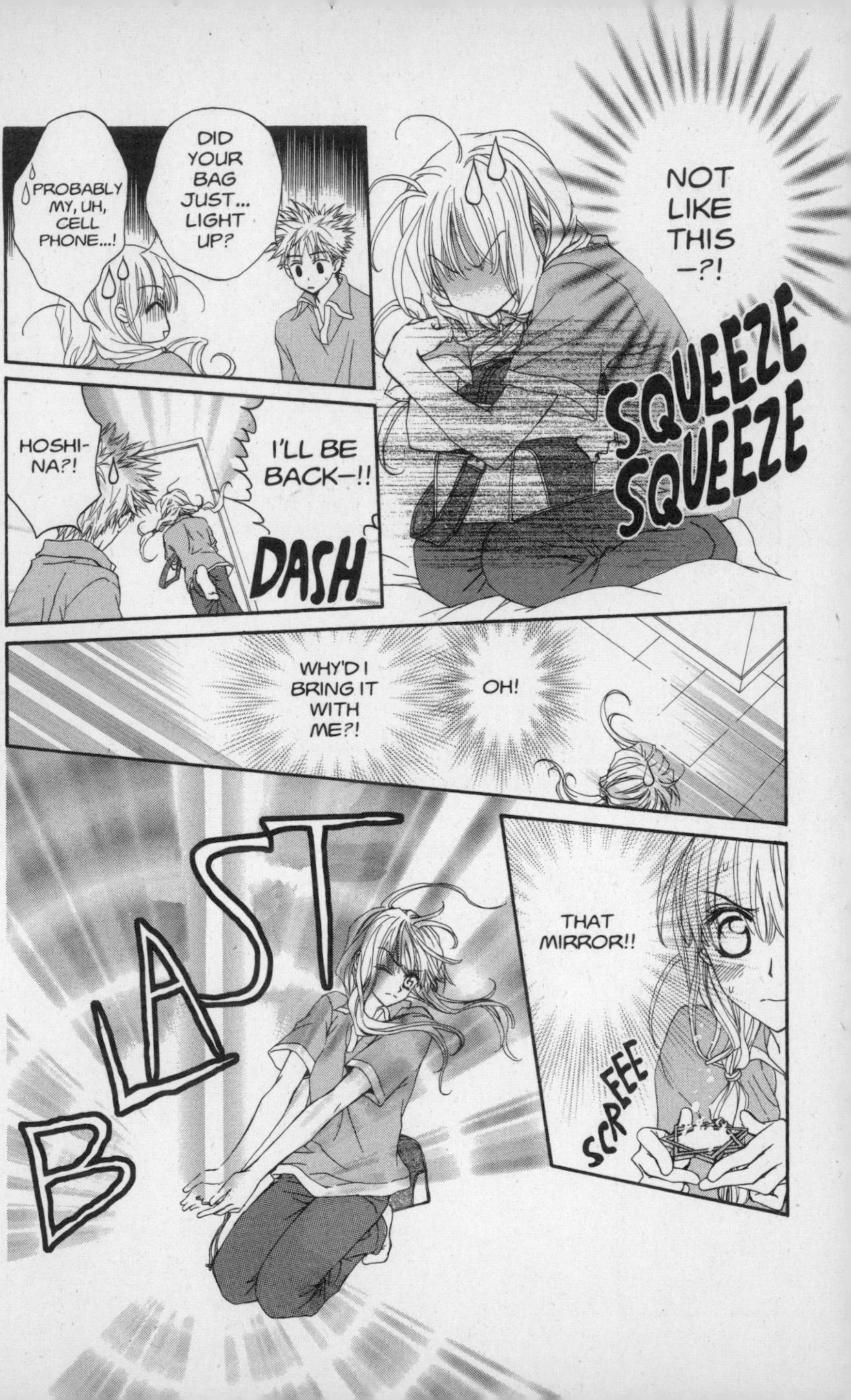
NOT LIKE THIS—?!
SQUEEZE SQUEEZE
DID YOUR BAG JUST... LIGHT UP?
PROBABLY MY, UH, CELL PHONE...!
I'LL BE BACK—!!
DASH
HOSHI-NA?!
OH!
WHY'D I BRING IT WITH ME?!
THAT MIRROR!!
SCREEE
BLAST

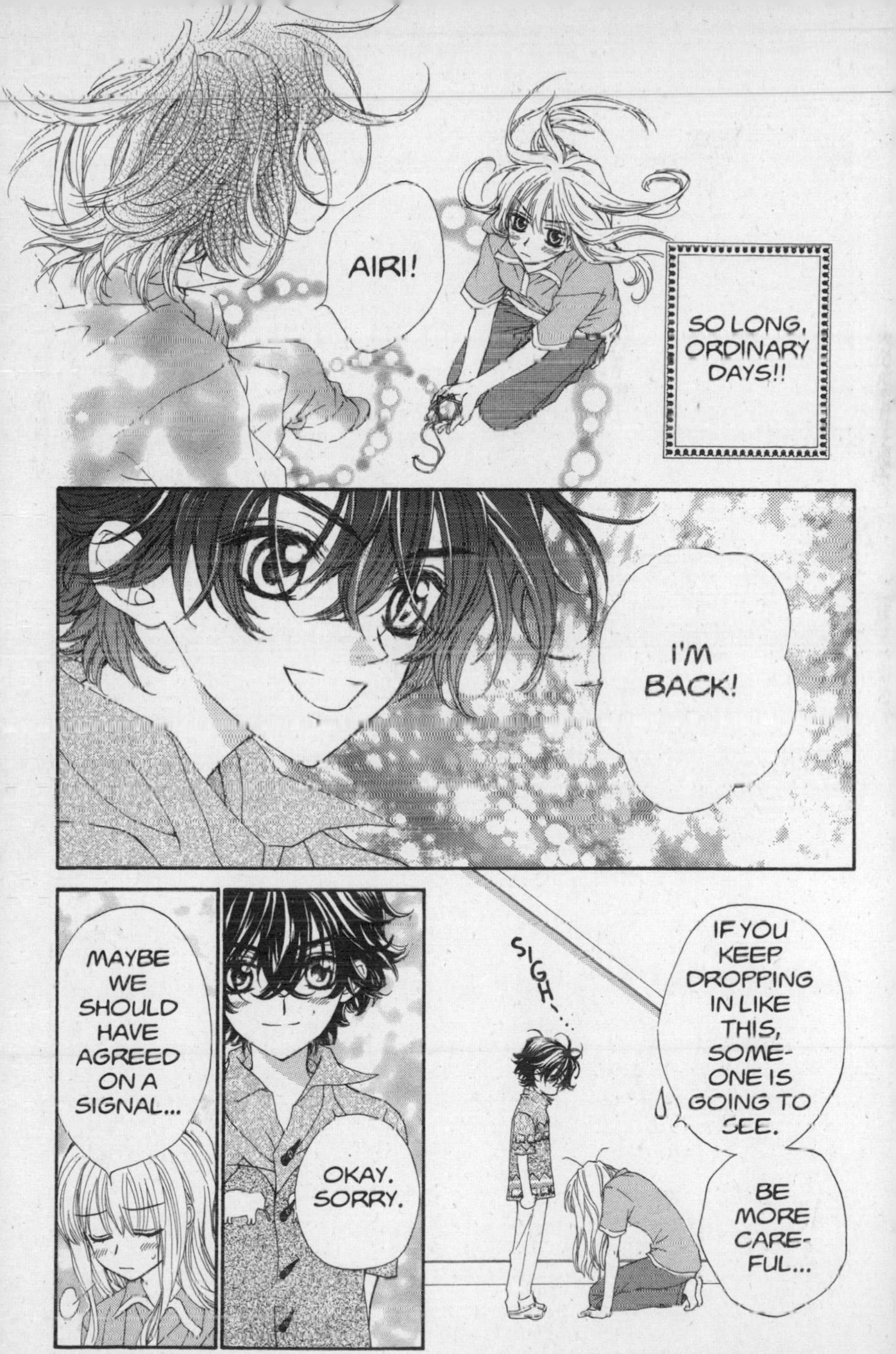
SO LONG, ORDINARY DAYS!!
AIRI!
I'M BACK!
IF YOU KEEP DROPPING IN LIKE THIS, SOME-ONE IS GOING TO SEE.
SIGH...
BE MORE CARE-FUL...
OKAY. SORRY.
MAYBE WE SHOULD HAVE AGREED ON A SIGNAL...

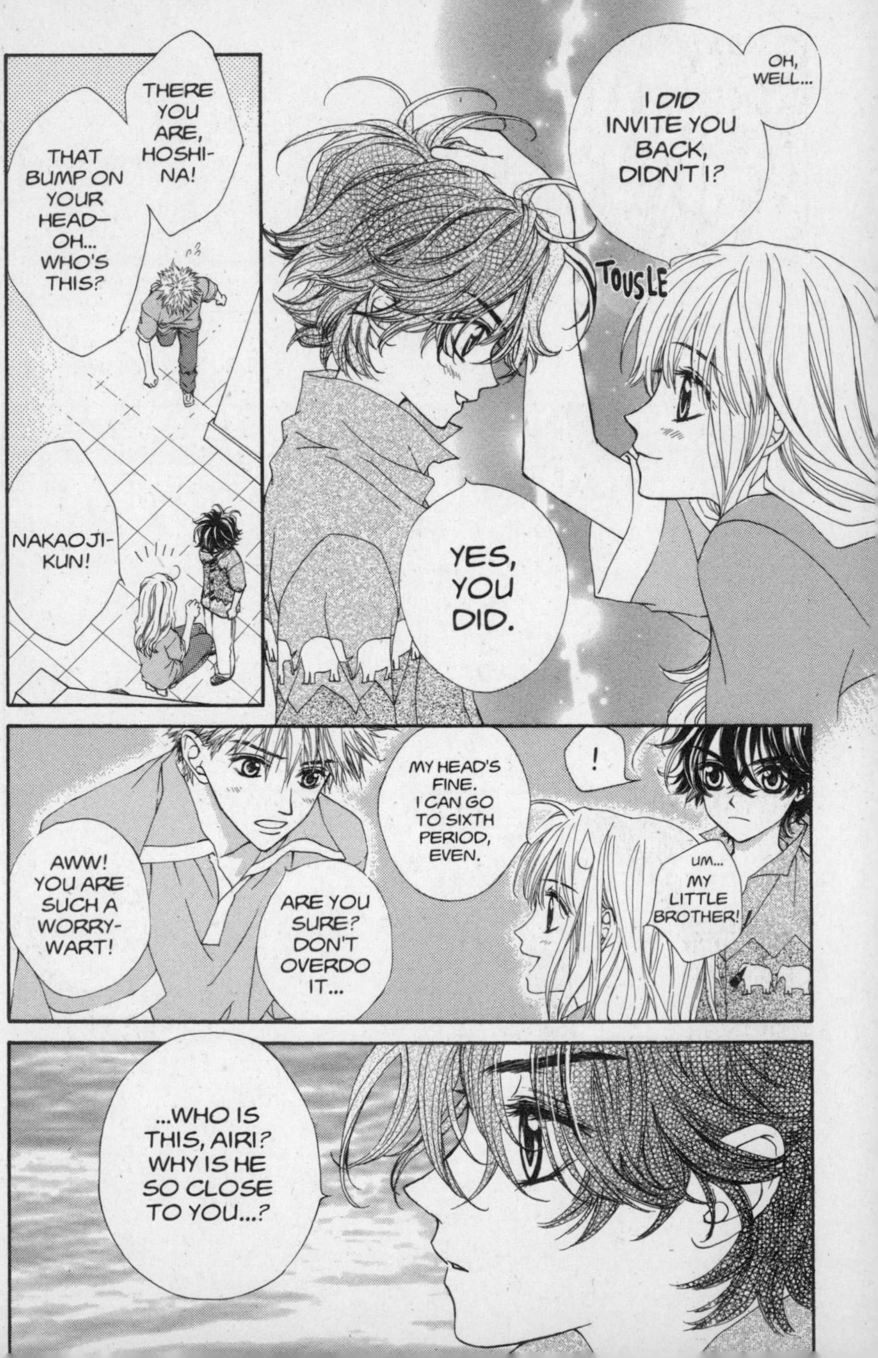
OH, WELL...
I DID INVITE YOU BACK, DIDN'T I?
TOUSLE
YES, YOU DID.
THERE YOU ARE, HOSHINA!
THAT BUMP ON YOUR HEAD— OH... WHO'S THIS?
NAKAOJI-KUN!
!
UM... MY LITTLE BROTHER!
MY HEAD'S FINE. I CAN GO TO SIXTH PERIOD, EVEN.
ARE YOU SURE? DON'T OVERDO IT...
AWW! YOU ARE SUCH A WORRY-WART!
...WHO IS THIS, AIRI? WHY IS HE SO CLOSE TO YOU...?

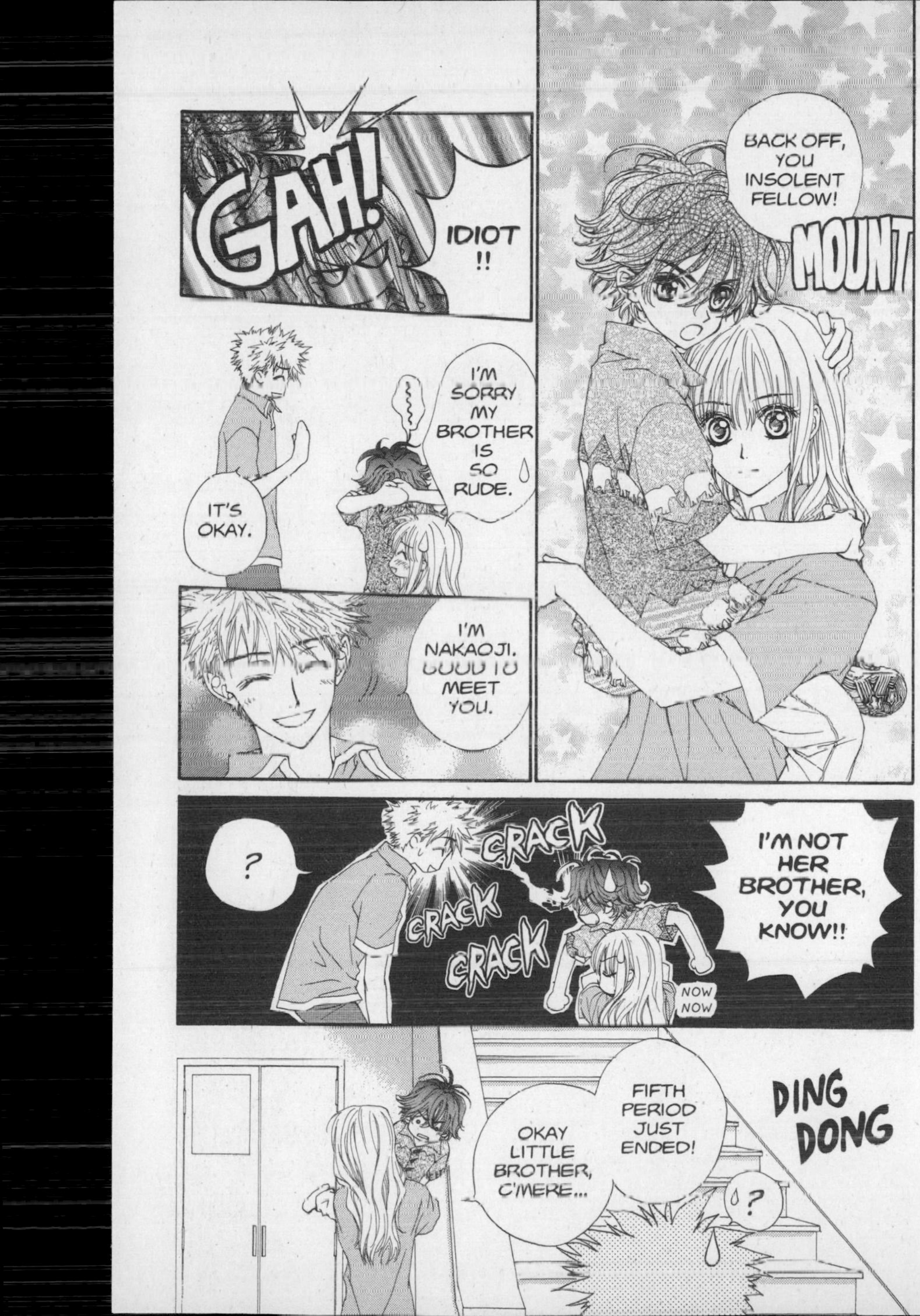
BACK OFF, YOU INSOLENT FELLOW!
MOUNT
GAH!
IDIOT !!
I'M SORRY MY BROTHER IS SO RUDE.
IT'S OKAY.
I'M NAKAOJI. GOOD TO MEET YOU.
I'M NOT HER BROTHER, YOU KNOW!!
CRACK
CRACK
CRACK
NOW NOW
?
DING DONG
FIFTH PERIOD JUST ENDED!
OKAY LITTLE BROTHER, C'MERE...
?

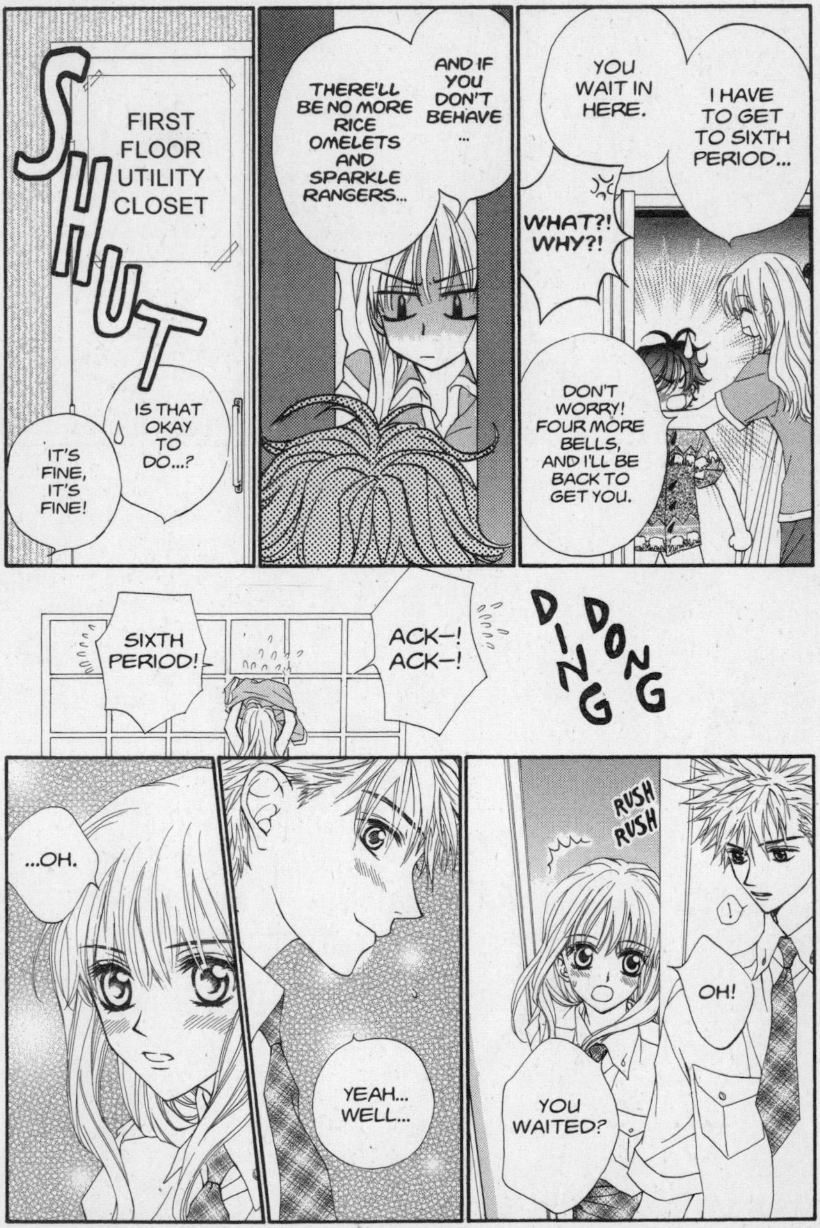
I HAVE TO GET TO SIXTH PERIOD...
YOU WAIT IN HERE.
WHAT?! WHY?!
DON'T WORRY! FOUR MORE BELLS, AND I'LL BE BACK TO GET YOU.
AND IF YOU DON'T BEHAVE...
THERE'LL BE NO MORE RICE OMELETS AND SPARKLE RANGERS...
SHUT
FIRST FLOOR UTILITY CLOSET
IS THAT OKAY TO DO...?
IT'S FINE, IT'S FINE!
DING DONG
ACK—! ACK—!
SIXTH PERIOD!
RUSH RUSH
!
OH!
YOU WAITED?
YEAH... WELL...
...OH.

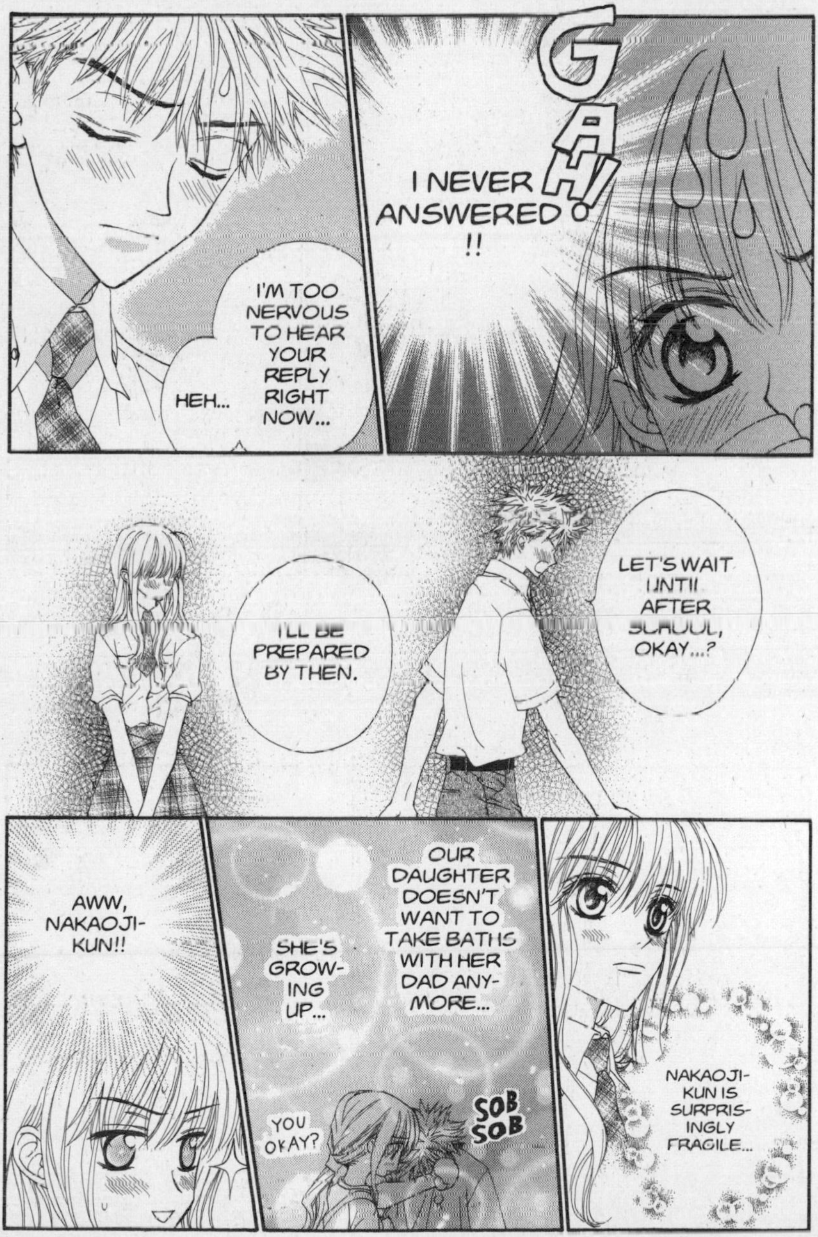
GAH!
I NEVER ANSWERED!!
I'M TOO NERVOUS TO HEAR YOUR REPLY RIGHT NOW...
HEH...
LET'S WAIT UNTIL AFTER SCHOOL, OKAY...?
I'LL BE PREPARED BY THEN.
NAKAOJI-KUN IS SURPRIS-INGLY FRAGILE...
OUR DAUGHTER DOESN'T WANT TO TAKE BATHS WITH HER DAD ANY-MORE...
SHE'S GROW-ING UP...
SOB SOB
YOU OKAY?
AWW, NAKAOJI-KUN!!

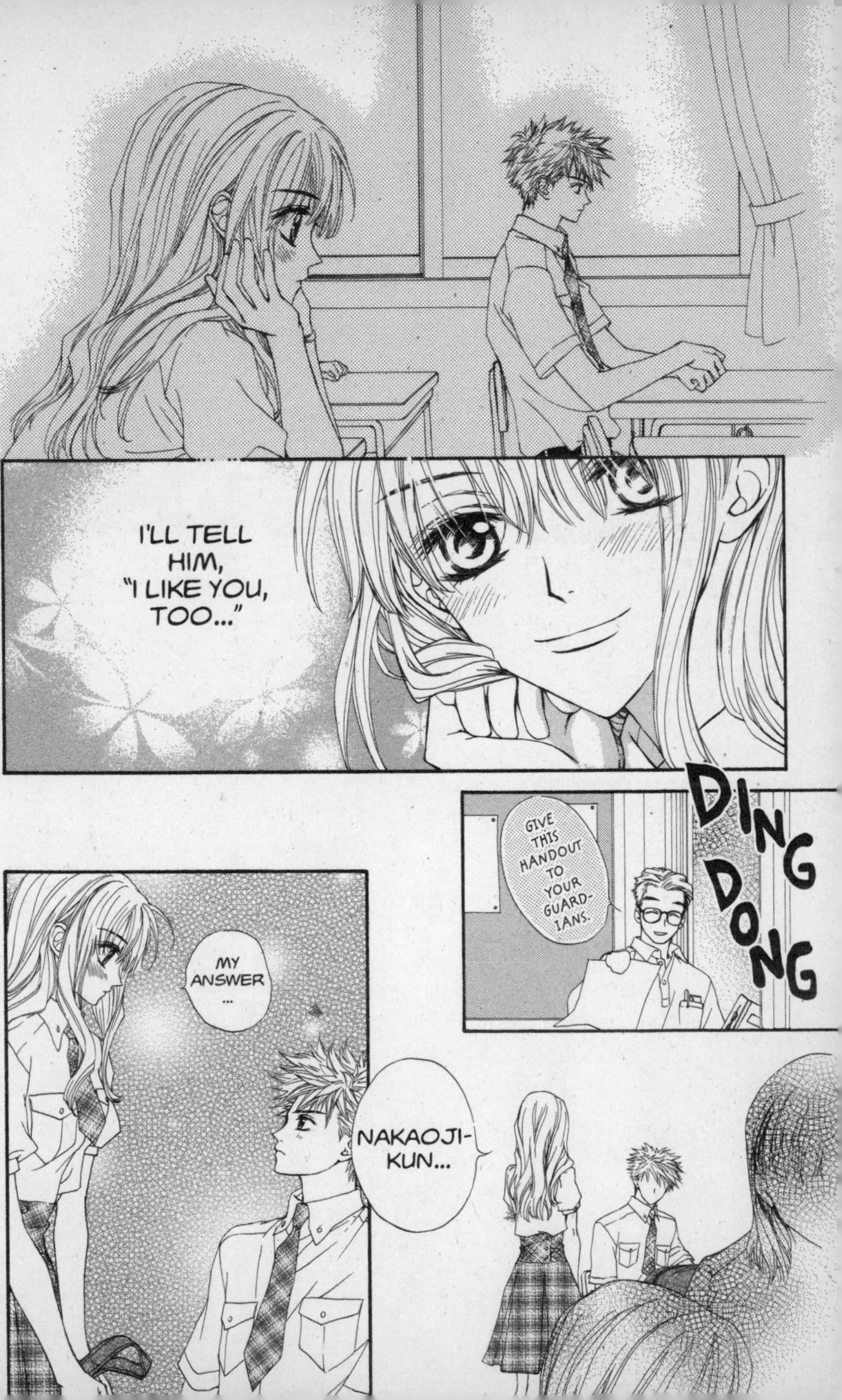
I'LL TELL HIM, "I LIKE YOU, TOO..."
DING DONG
GIVE THIS HANDOUT TO YOUR GUARD-IANS.
NAKAOJI-KUN...
MY ANSWER ...

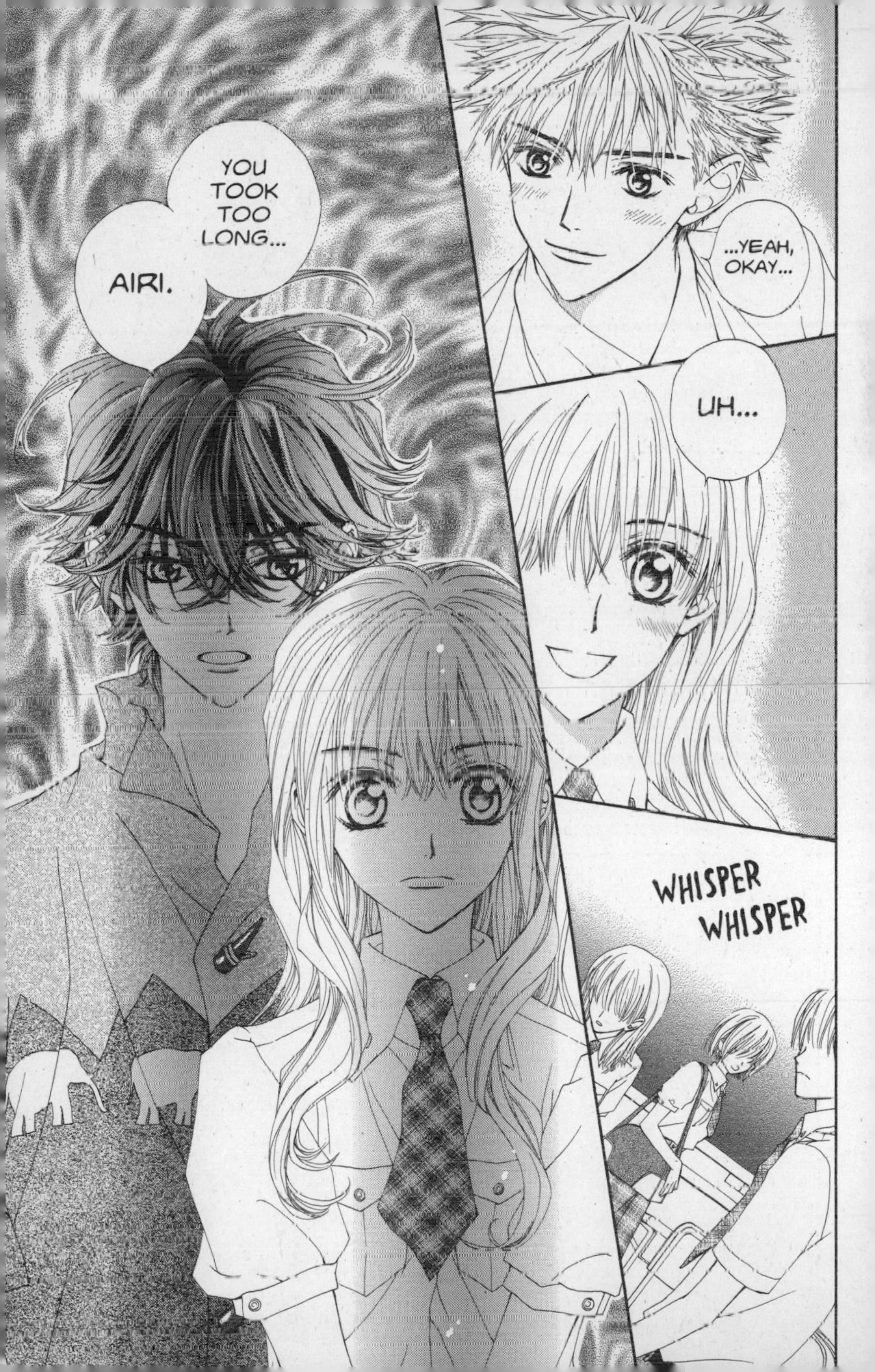
...YEAH, OKAY...
UH...
WHISPER WHISPER
YOU TOOK TOO LONG...
AIRI.

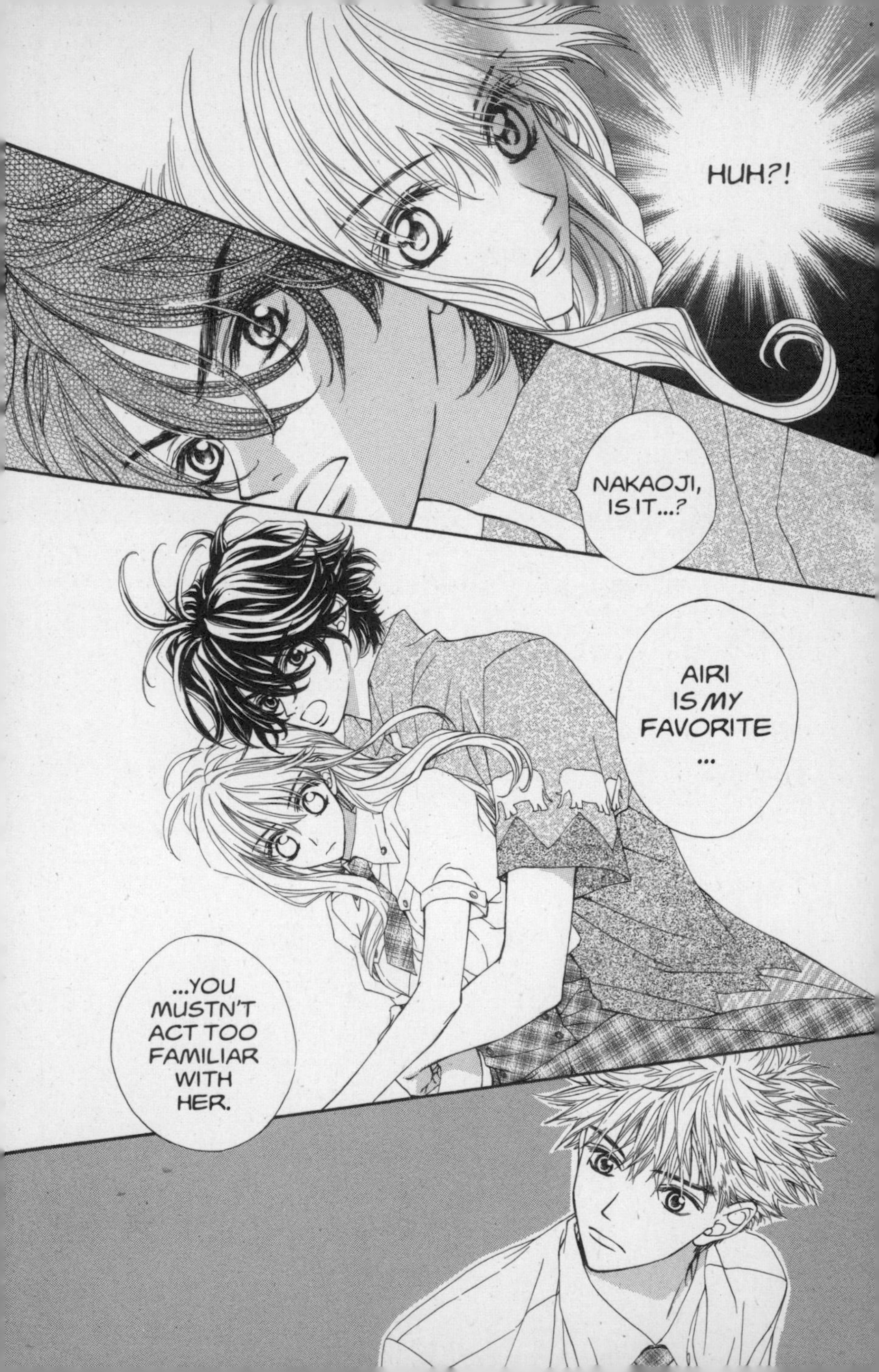
HUH?!
NAKAOJI, IS IT...?
AIRI IS MY FAVORITE ...
...YOU MUSTN'T ACT TOO FAMILIAR WITH HER.

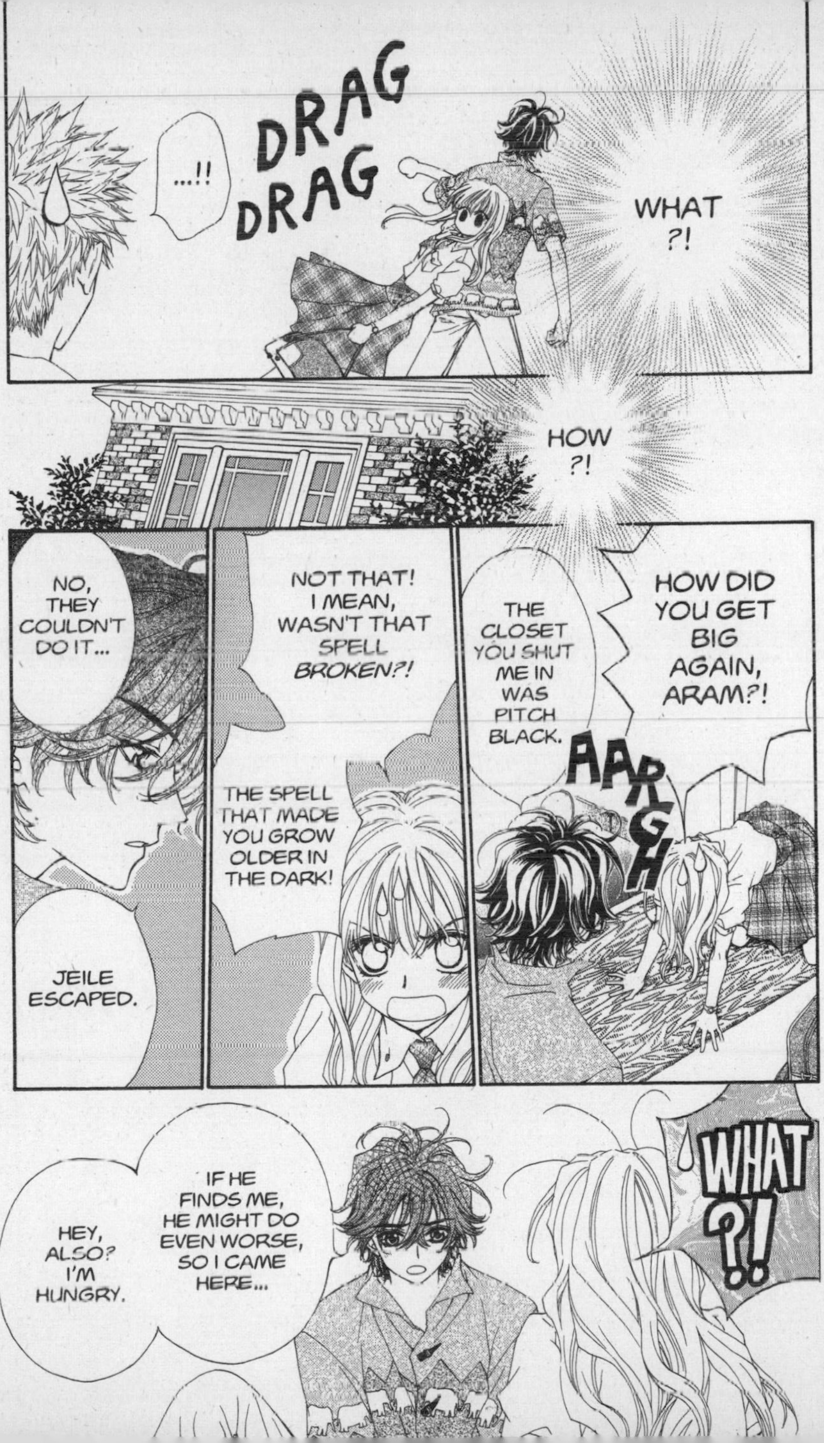
WHAT ?!
DRAG DRAG
...!!
HOW ?!
HOW DID YOU GET BIG AGAIN, ARAM?!
THE CLOSET YOU SHUT ME IN WAS PITCH BLACK.
AARGH
NOT THAT! I MEAN, WASN'T THAT SPELL BROKEN?!
THE SPELL THAT MADE YOU GROW OLDER IN THE DARK!
NO, THEY COULDN'T DO IT...
JEILE ESCAPED.
WHAT ?!
IF HE FINDS ME, HE MIGHT DO EVEN WORSE, SO I CAME HERE...
HEY, ALSO? I'M HUNGRY.

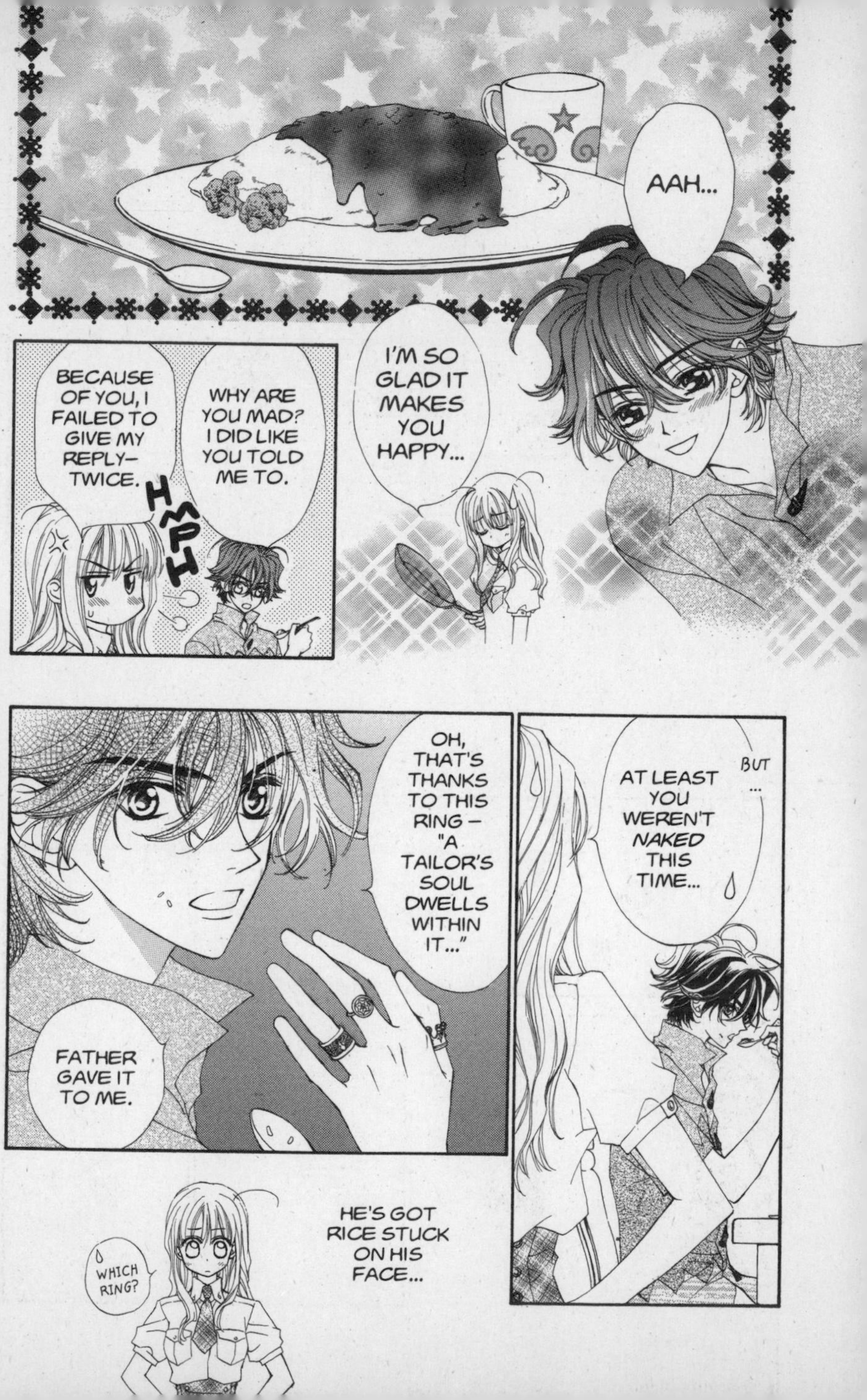
AAH...
I'M SO GLAD IT MAKES YOU HAPPY...
WHY ARE YOU MAD? I DID LIKE YOU TOLD ME TO.
BECAUSE OF YOU, I FAILED TO GIVE MY REPLY— TWICE.
HMPH
BUT ...
AT LEAST YOU WEREN'T *NAKED* THIS TIME...
OH, THAT'S THANKS TO THIS RING— "A TAILOR'S SOUL DWELLS WITHIN IT..."
FATHER GAVE IT TO ME.
HE'S GOT RICE STUCK ON HIS FACE...
WHICH RING?

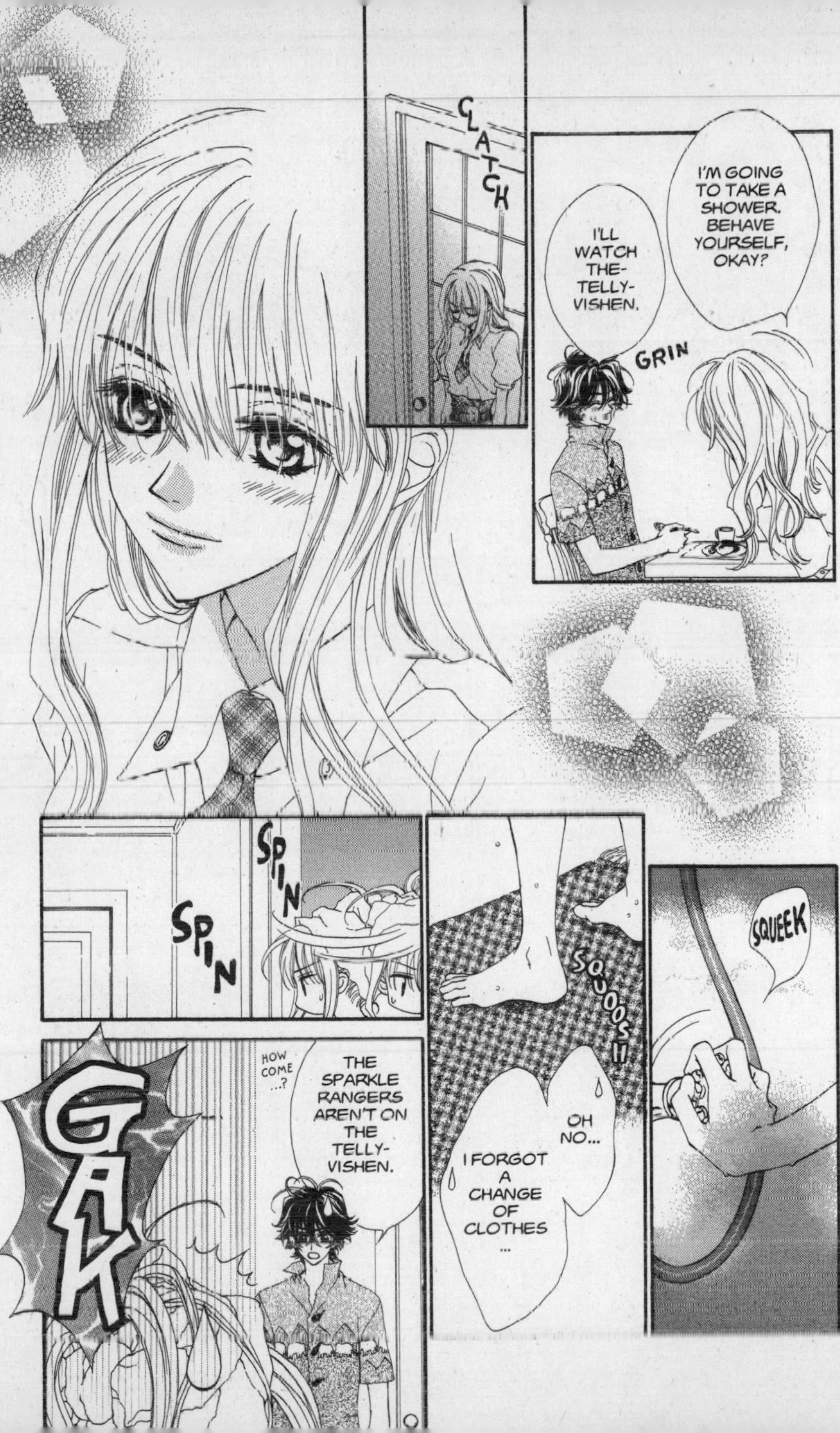
I'M GOING TO TAKE A SHOWER. BEHAVE YOURSELF, OKAY?
I'LL WATCH THE-TELLY-VISHEN.
GRIN
CLATCH
SQUEEK
SQUOOSH
OH NO...
I FORGOT A CHANGE OF CLOTHES ...
SPIN
SPIN
THE SPARKLE RANGERS AREN'T ON THE TELLY-VISHEN.
HOW COME ...?
GAK

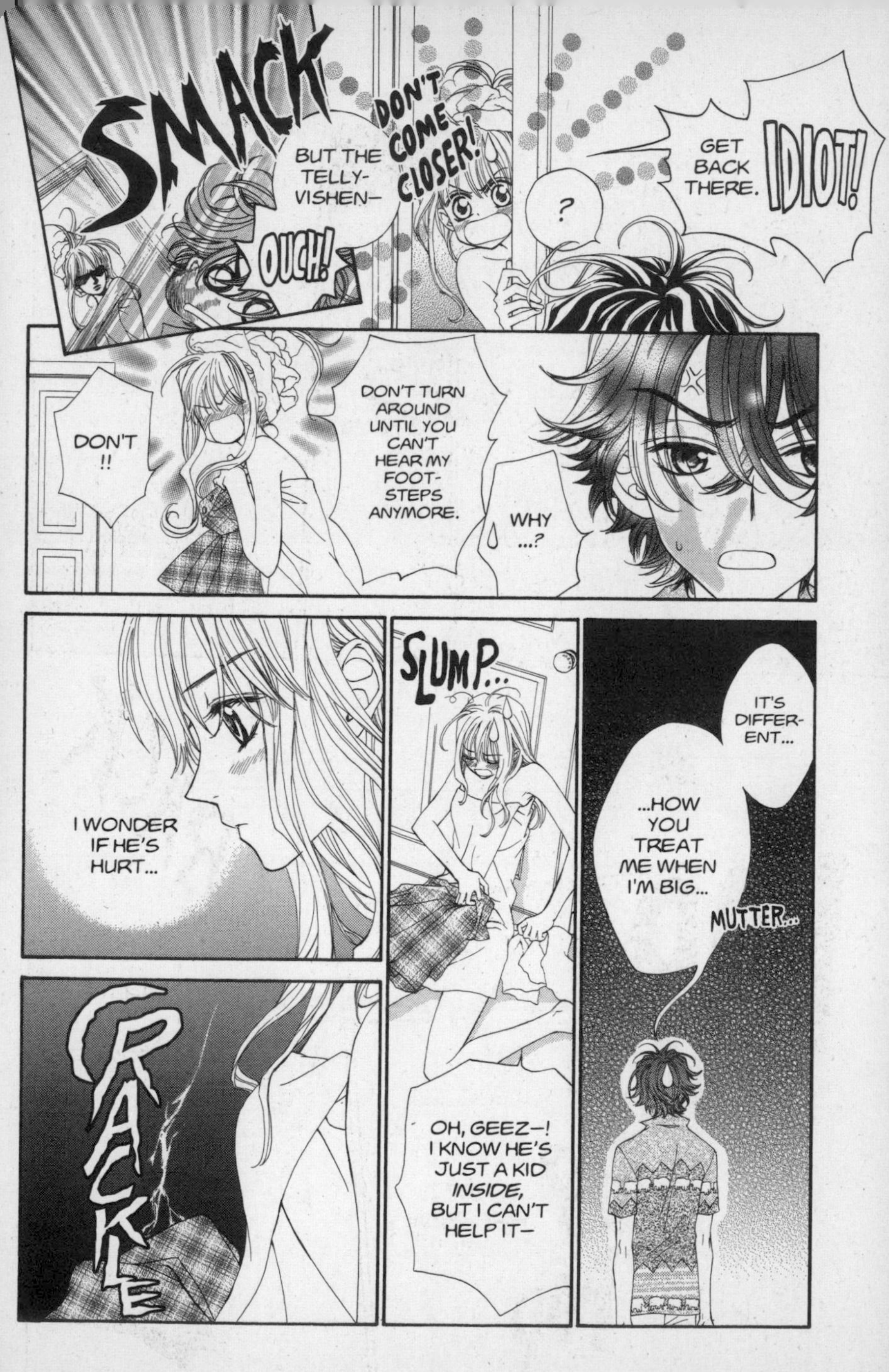
IDIOT!
GET BACK THERE.
?
DON'T COME CLOSER!
BUT THE TELLY-VISHEN—
SMACK
OUCH!
WHY ...?
DON'T !!
DON'T TURN AROUND UNTIL YOU CAN'T HEAR MY FOOT-STEPS ANYMORE.
IT'S DIFFER-ENT...
...HOW YOU TREAT ME WHEN I'M BIG...
MUTTER...
SLUMP...
OH, GEEZ—! I KNOW HE'S JUST A KID *INSIDE*, BUT I CAN'T HELP IT—
I WONDER IF HE'S HURT...
CRACKLE

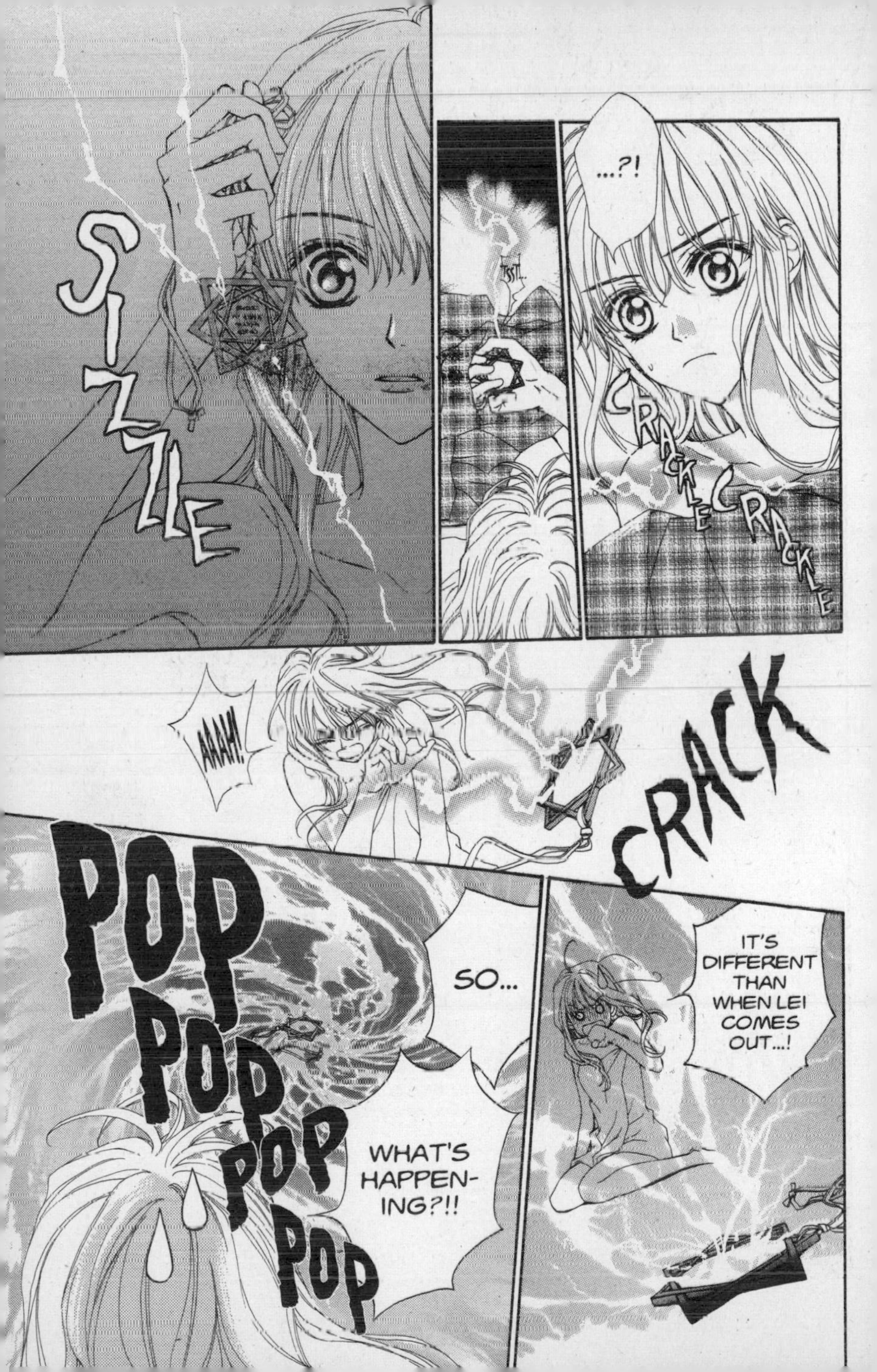
...?!
CRACKLE CRACKLE
TSST...
SIZZLE
CRACK
AAAH!
IT'S DIFFERENT THAN WHEN LEI COMES OUT...!
SO...
WHAT'S HAPPEN-ING?!!
POP POP POP POP POP

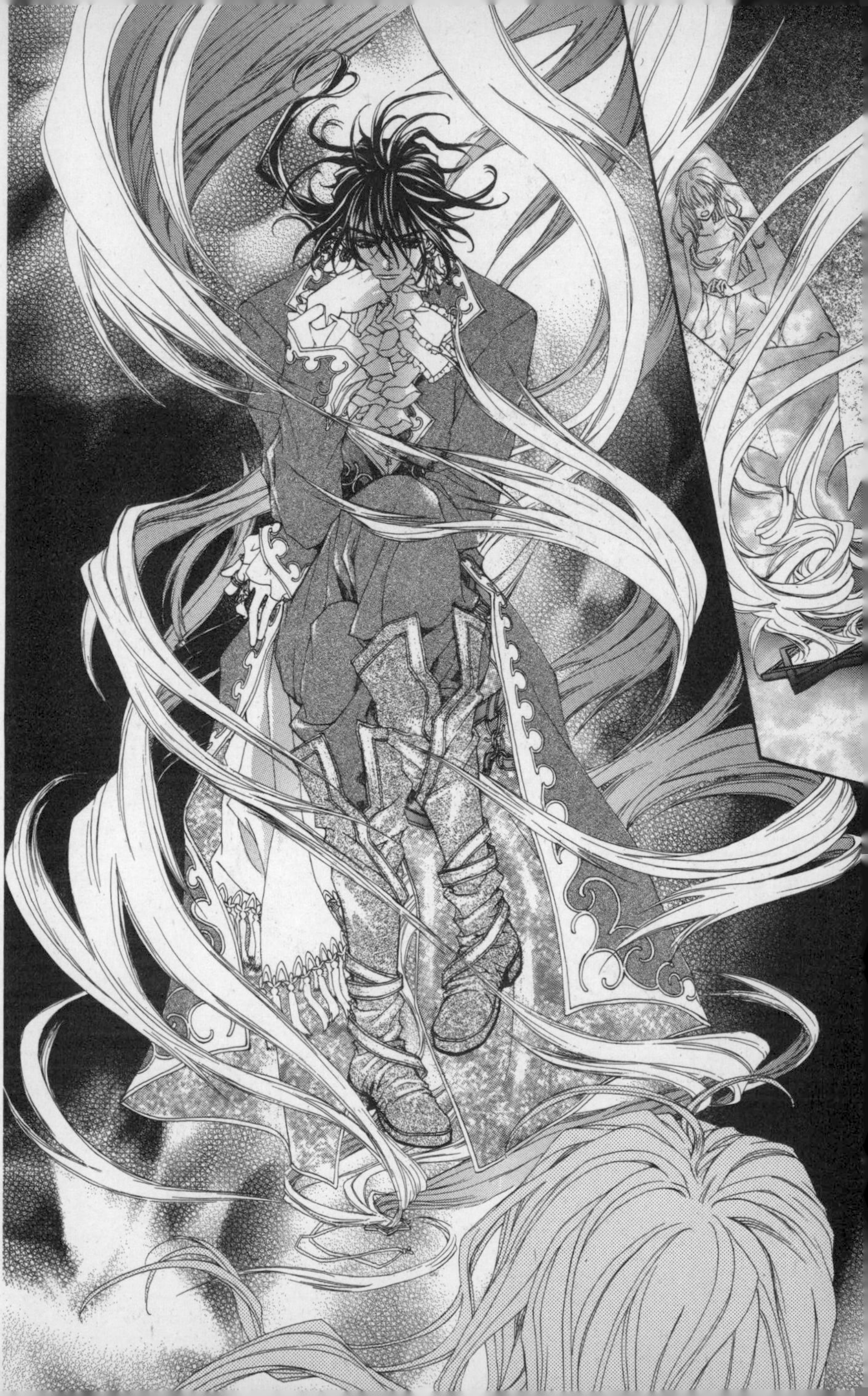

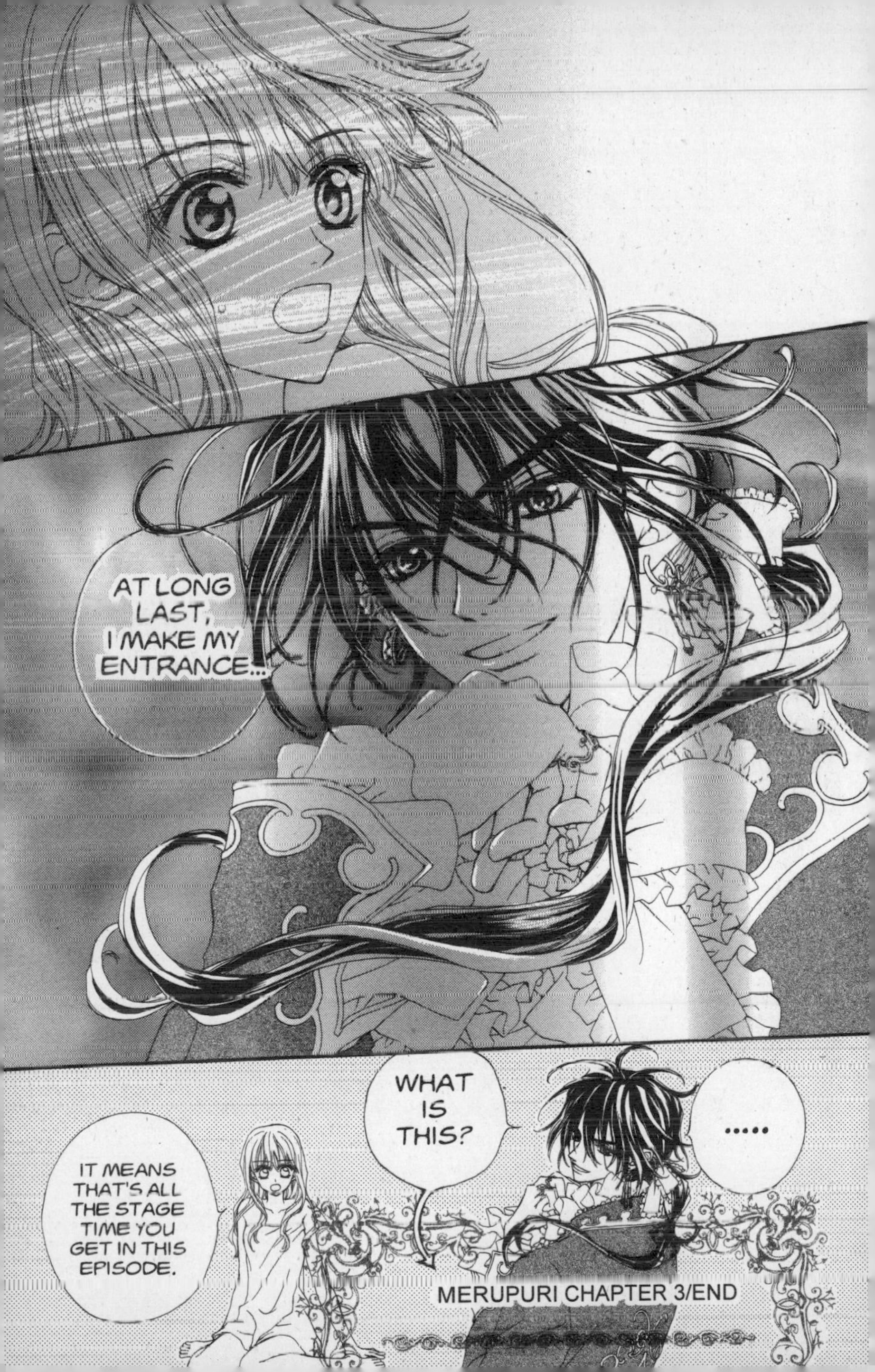
AT LONG LAST, I MAKE MY ENTRANCE...
.....
WHAT IS THIS?
IT MEANS THAT'S ALL THE STAGE TIME YOU GET IN THIS EPISODE.
MERUPURI CHAPTER 3/END

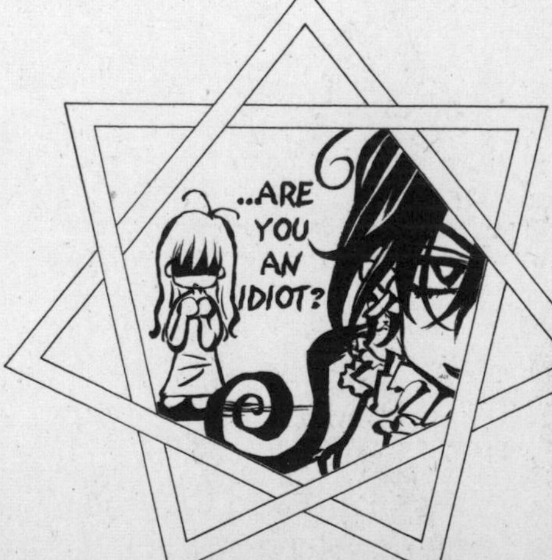
..ARE YOU AN IDIOT?

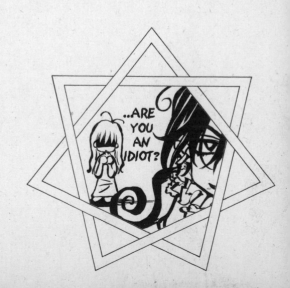

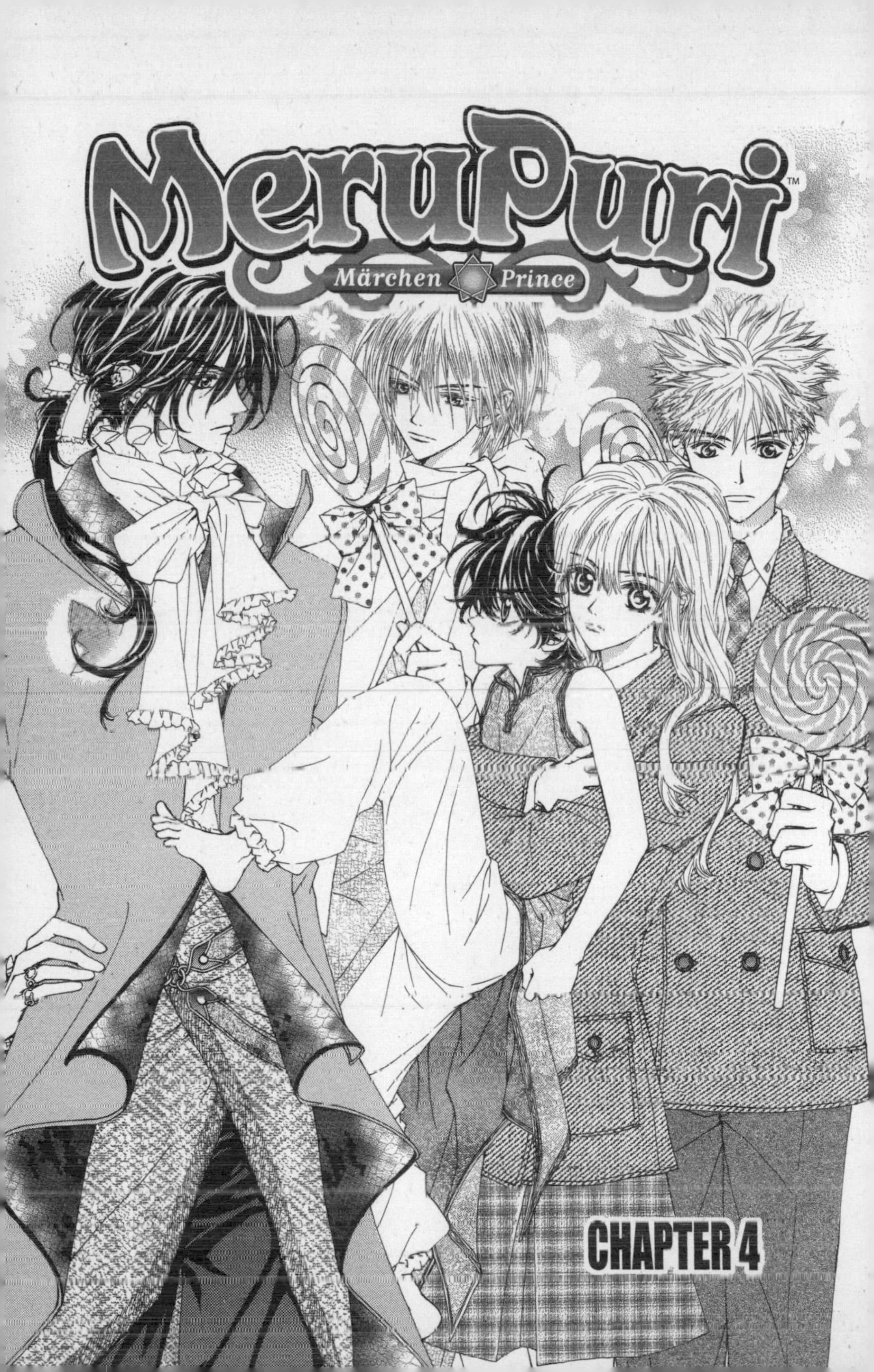
MeruPuri™
Märchen Prince
CHAPTER 4

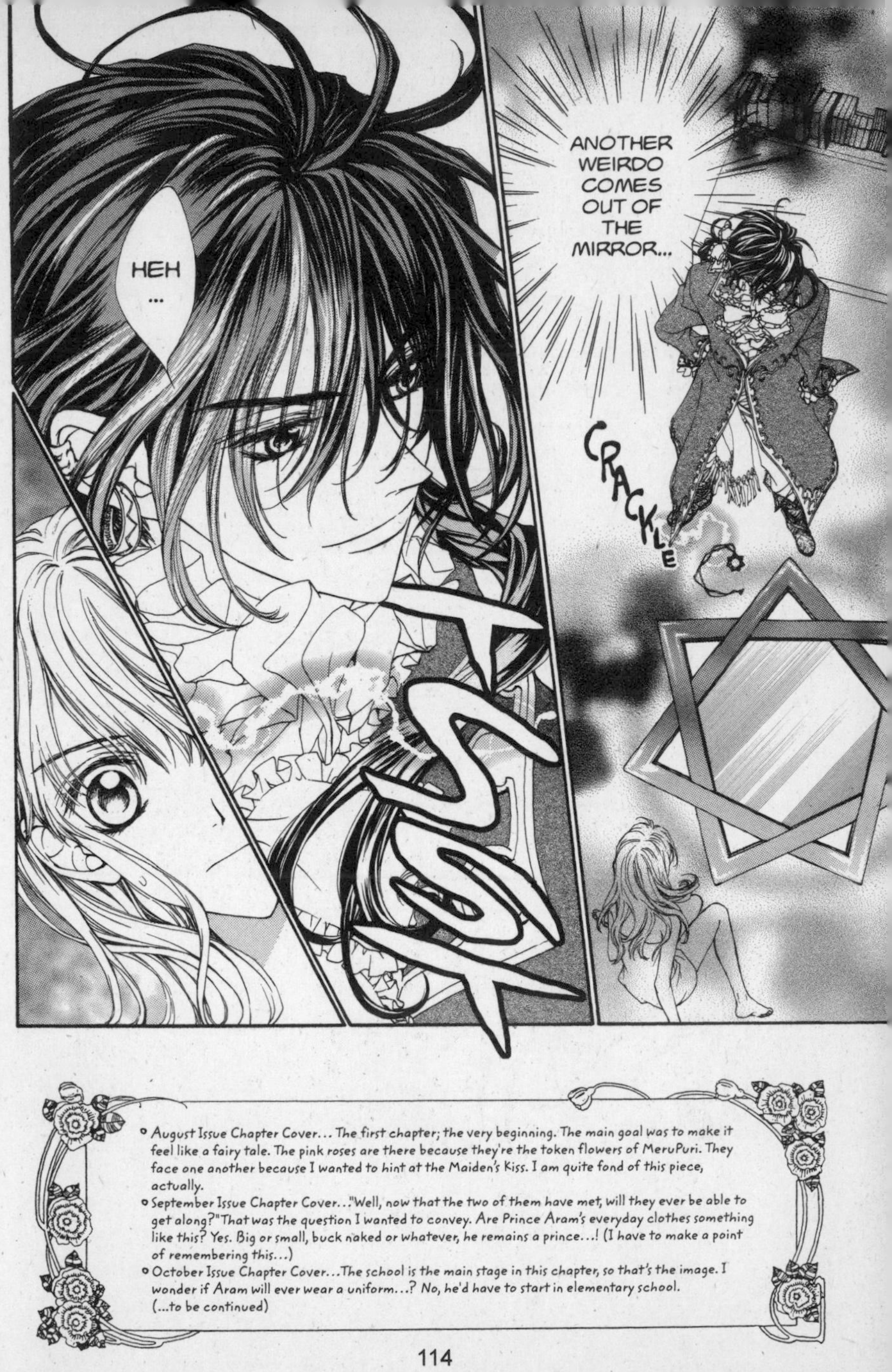
ANOTHER WEIRDO COMES OUT OF THE MIRROR...
CRACKLE
HEH ...

- August Issue Chapter Cover... The first chapter; the very beginning. The main goal was to make it feel like a fairy tale. The pink roses are there because they're the token flowers of MeruPuri. They face one another because I wanted to hint at the Maiden's Kiss. I am quite fond of this piece, actually.
- September Issue Chapter Cover..."Well, now that the two of them have met, will they ever be able to get along?" That was the question I wanted to convey. Are Prince Aram's everyday clothes something like this? Yes. Big or small, buck naked or whatever, he remains a prince...! (I have to make a point of remembering this...)
- October Issue Chapter Cover...The school is the main stage in this chapter, so that's the image. I wonder if Aram will ever wear a uniform...? No, he'd have to start in elementary school.

(...to be continued)

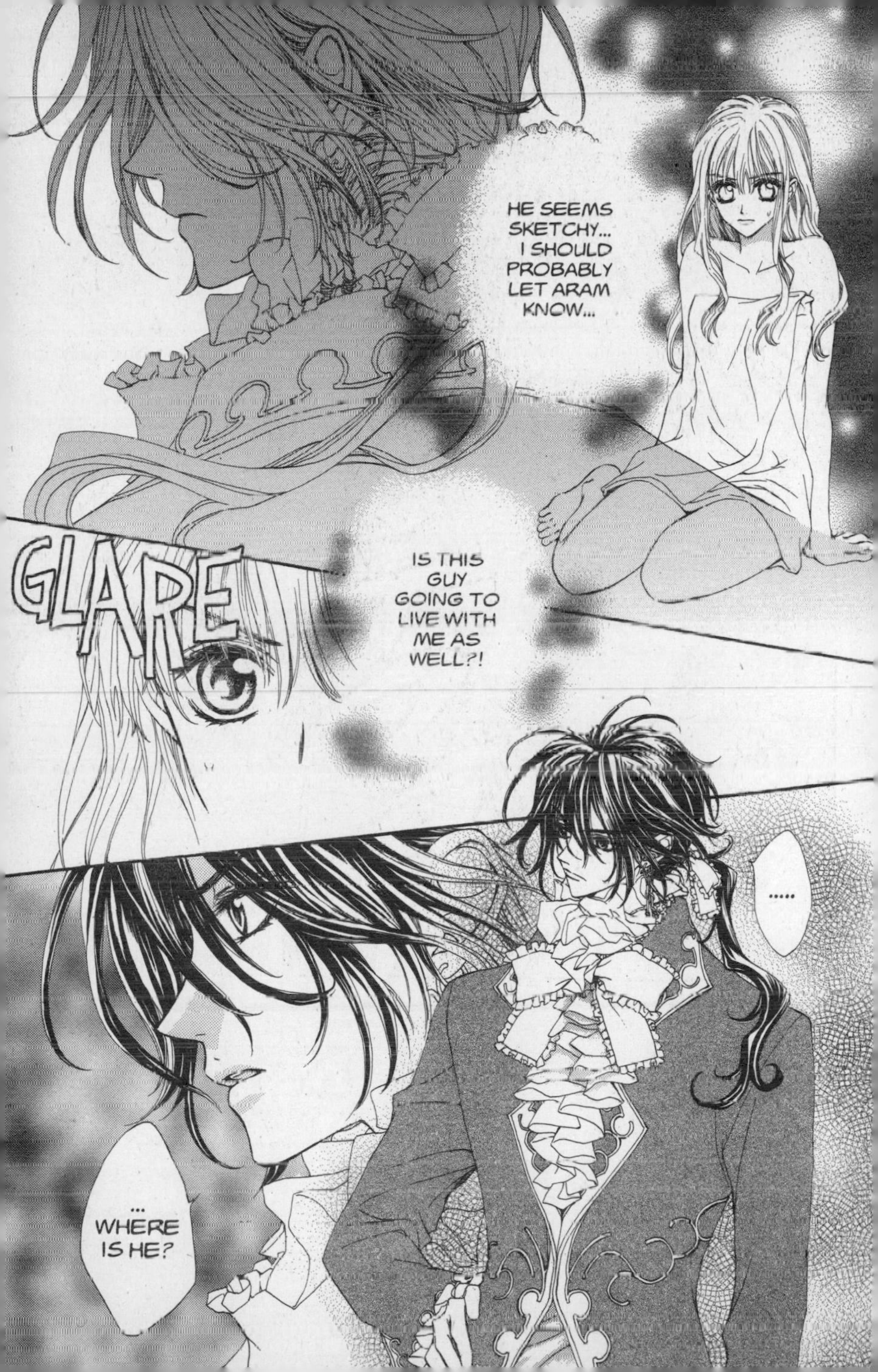
HE SEEMS SKETCHY... I SHOULD PROBABLY LET ARAM KNOW...
IS THIS GUY GOING TO LIVE WITH ME AS WELL?!
GLARE
......
... WHERE IS HE?

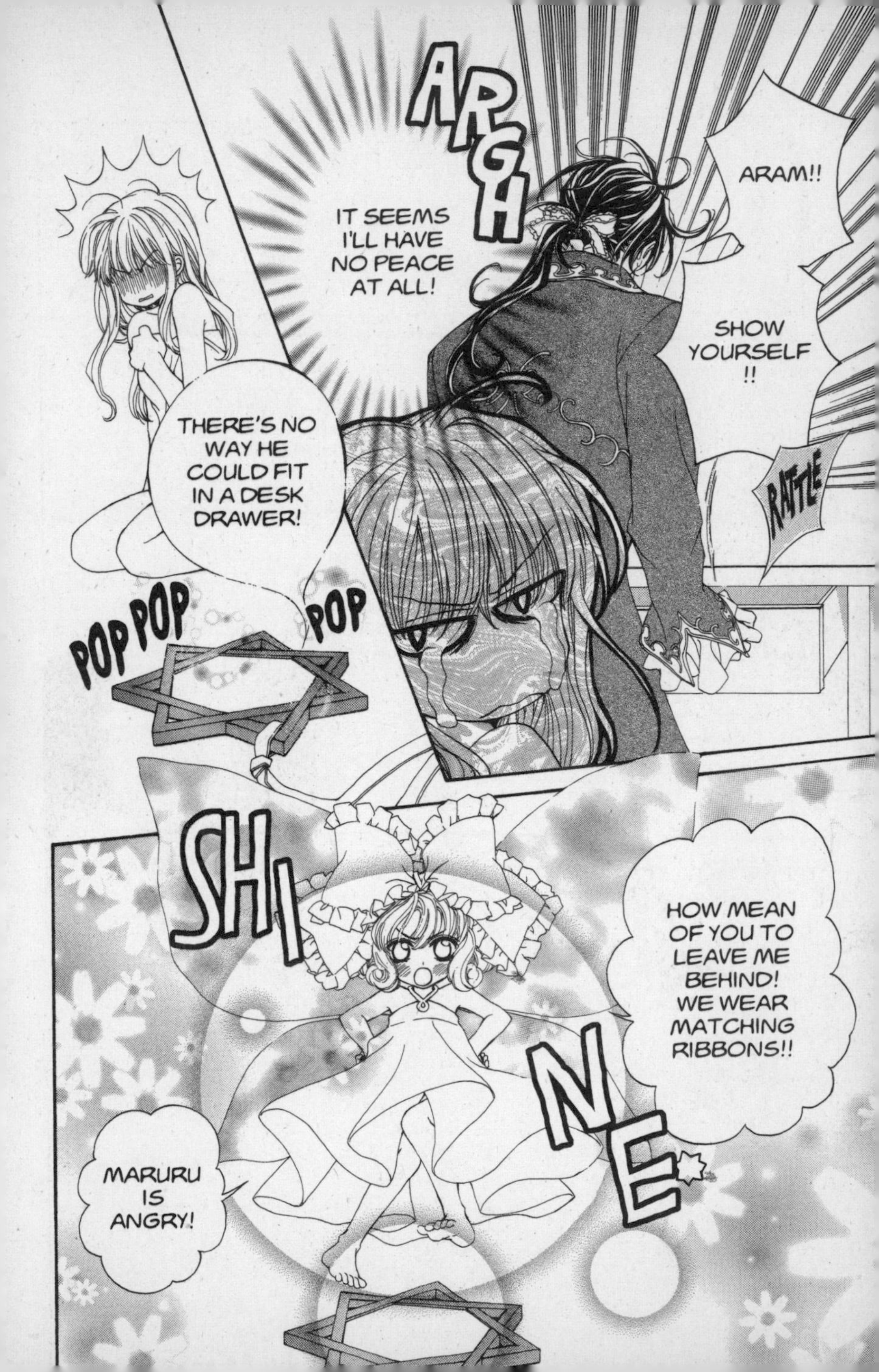
ARAM!!
SHOW YOURSELF !!
RATTLE
ARGH
IT SEEMS I'LL HAVE NO PEACE AT ALL!
THERE'S NO WAY HE COULD FIT IN A DESK DRAWER!
POP POP POP
SHINE
HOW MEAN OF YOU TO LEAVE ME BEHIND! WE WEAR MATCHING RIBBONS!!
MARURU IS ANGRY!

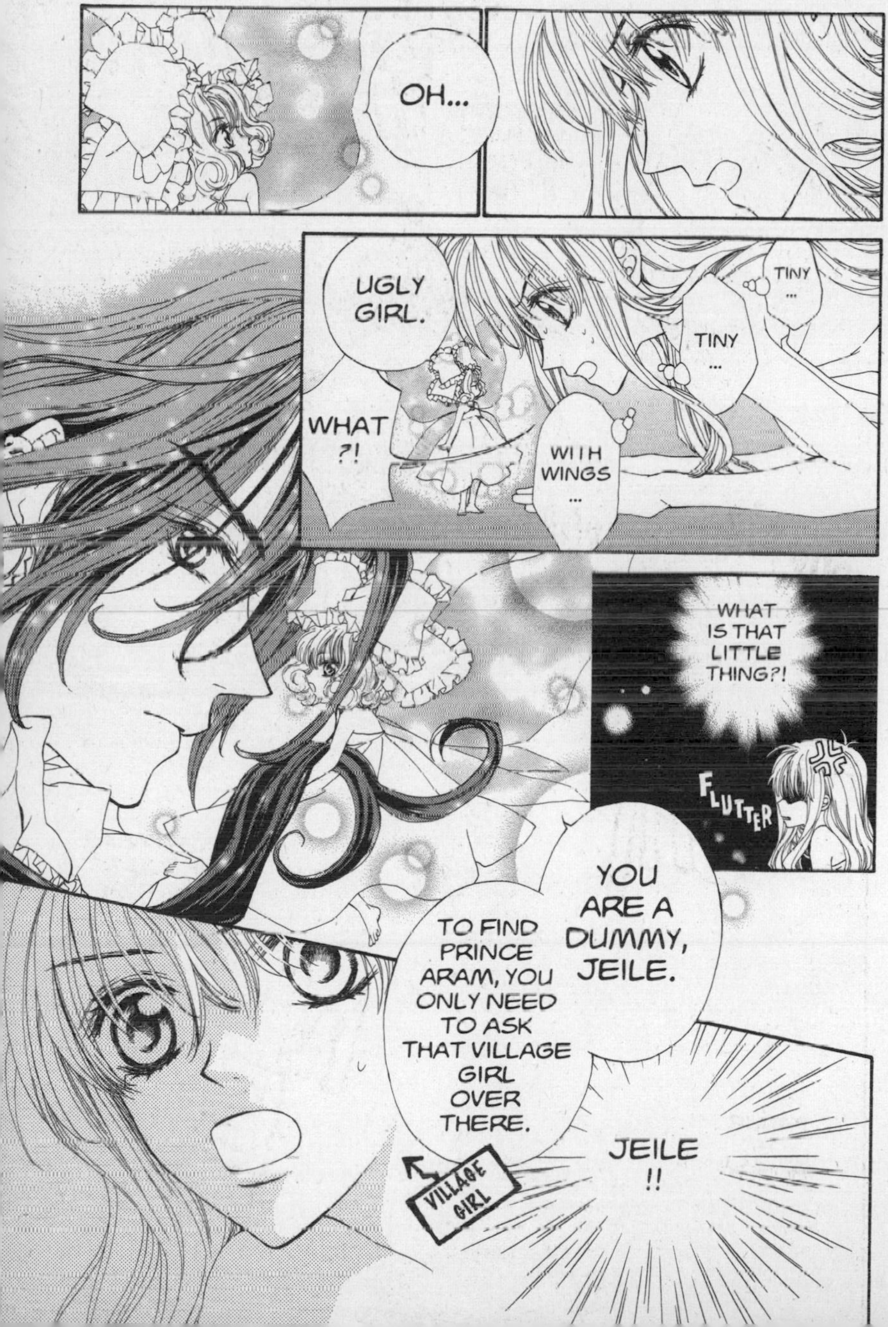
OH...
TINY ...
TINY ...
WITH WINGS ...
UGLY GIRL.
WHAT ?!
WHAT IS THAT LITTLE THING?!
FLUTTER
YOU ARE A DUMMY, JEILE.
TO FIND PRINCE ARAM, YOU ONLY NEED TO ASK THAT VILLAGE GIRL OVER THERE.
JEILE !!
VILLAGE GIRL

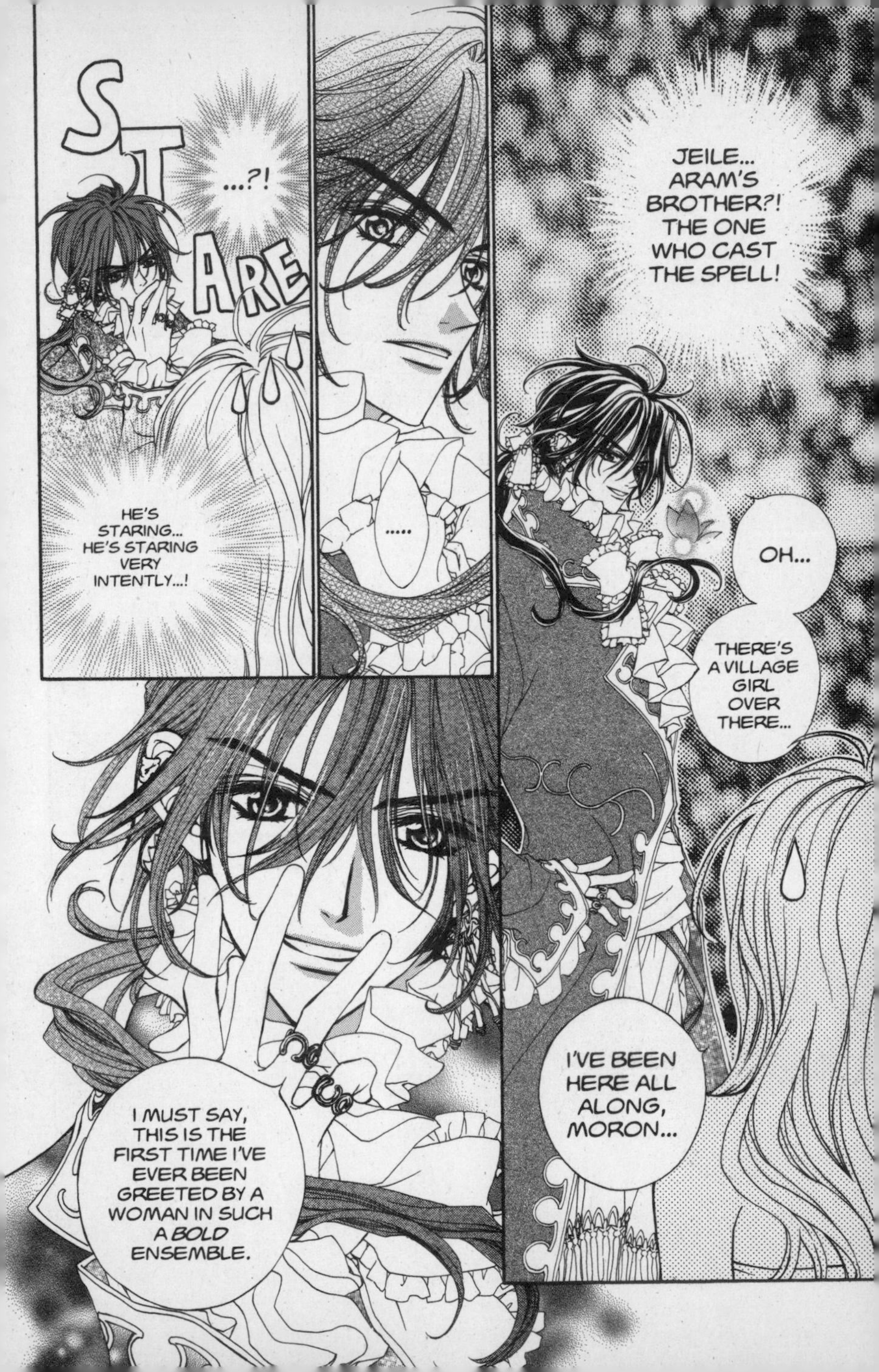
JEILE... ARAM'S BROTHER?! THE ONE WHO CAST THE SPELL!
OH...
THERE'S A VILLAGE GIRL OVER THERE...
I'VE BEEN HERE ALL ALONG, MORON...
.....
STARE
...?!
HE'S STARING... HE'S STARING VERY INTENTLY...!
I MUST SAY, THIS IS THE FIRST TIME I'VE EVER BEEN GREETED BY A WOMAN IN SUCH A *BOLD* ENSEMBLE.

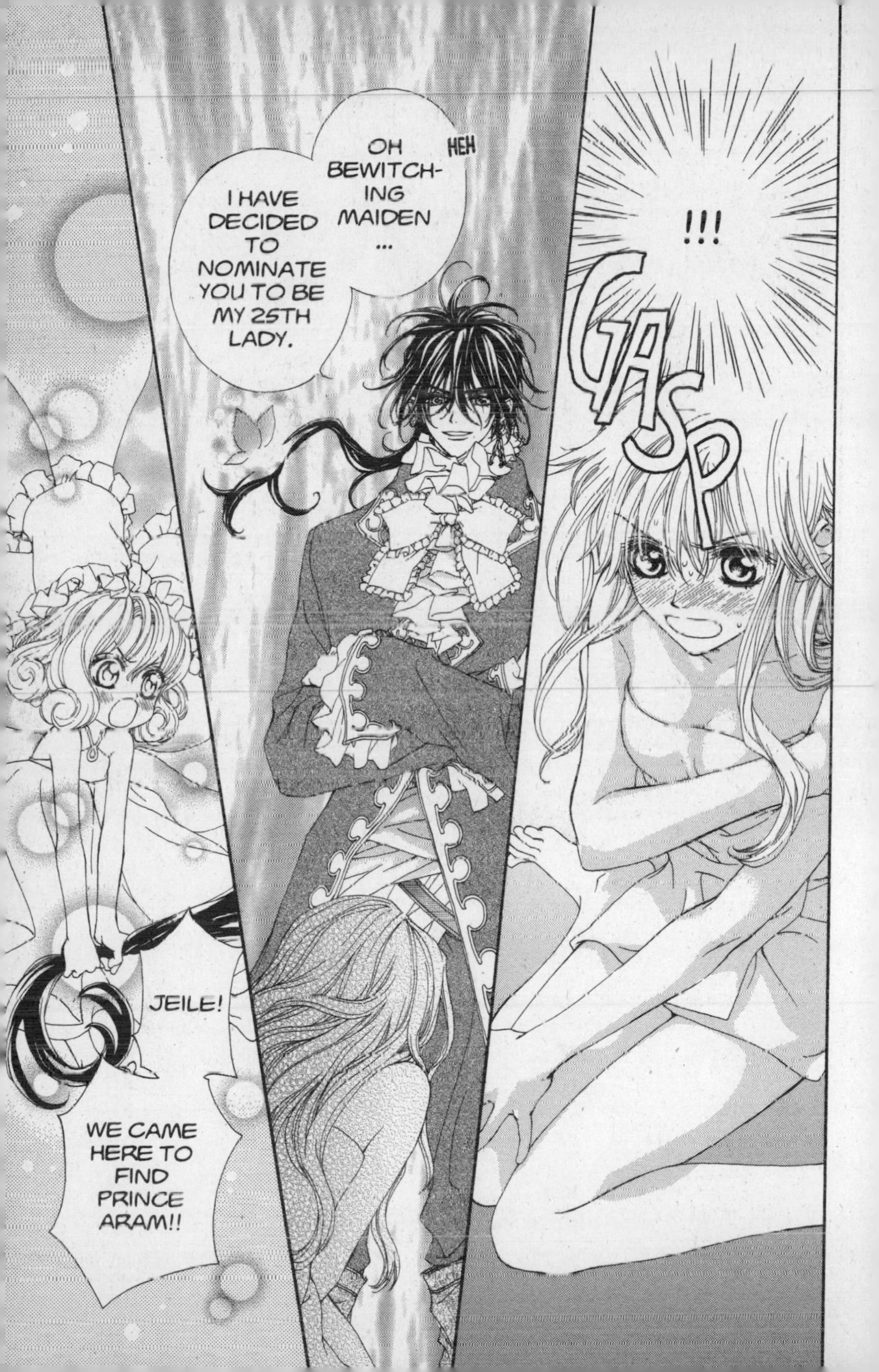
!!!
GASP
HEH
OH BEWITCHING MAIDEN...
I HAVE DECIDED TO NOMINATE YOU TO BE MY 25TH LADY.
JEILE!
WE CAME HERE TO FIND PRINCE ARAM!!

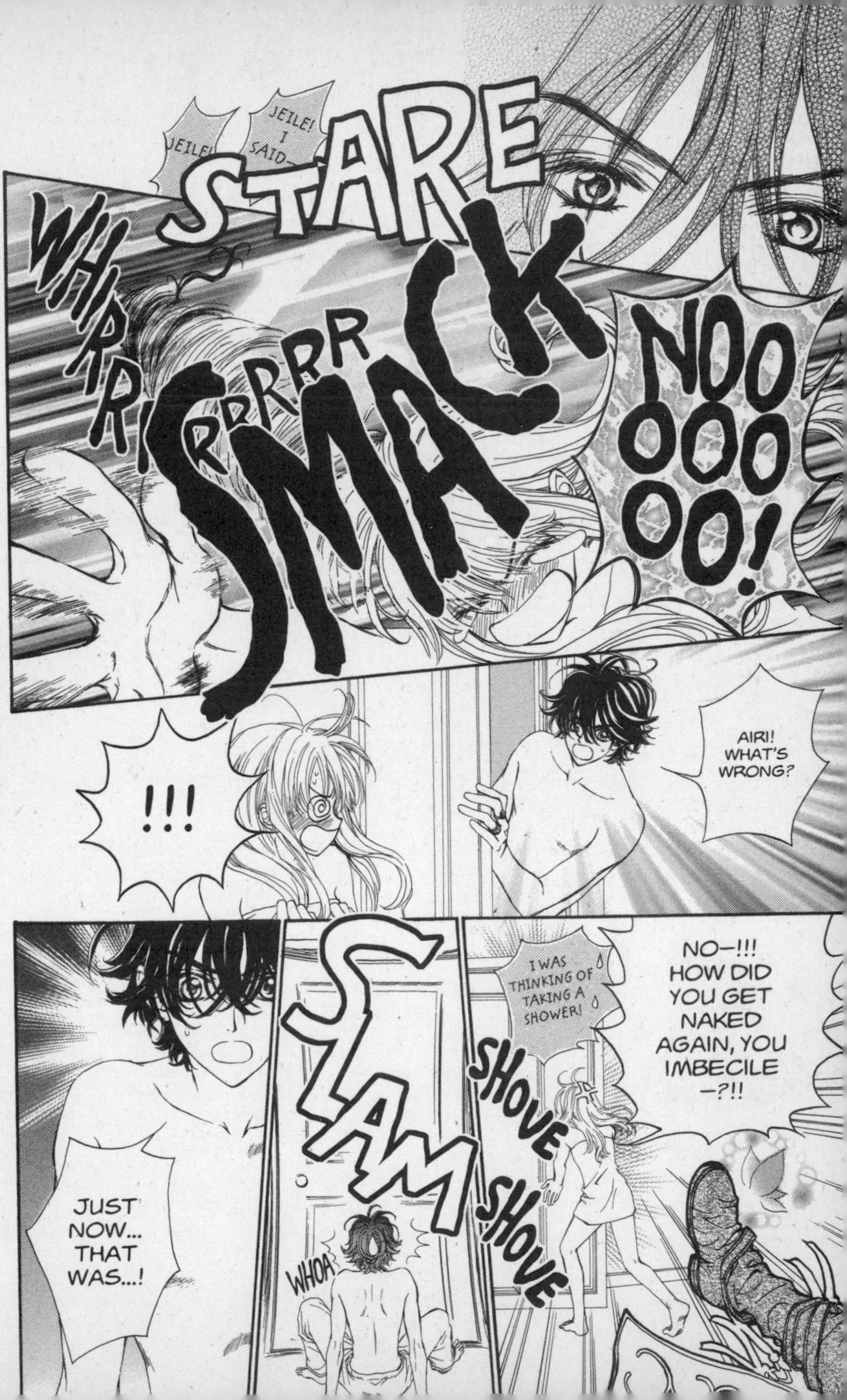
STARE
JEILE! I SAID—
JEILE!
NOOOOOOOO!
SMACK
WHIRRRRRRR
AIRI! WHAT'S WRONG?
!!!
NO—!!! HOW DID YOU GET NAKED AGAIN, YOU IMBECILE—?!!
I WAS THINKING OF TAKING A SHOWER!
SHOVE
SHOVE
SLAM
WHOA
JUST NOW... THAT WAS...!

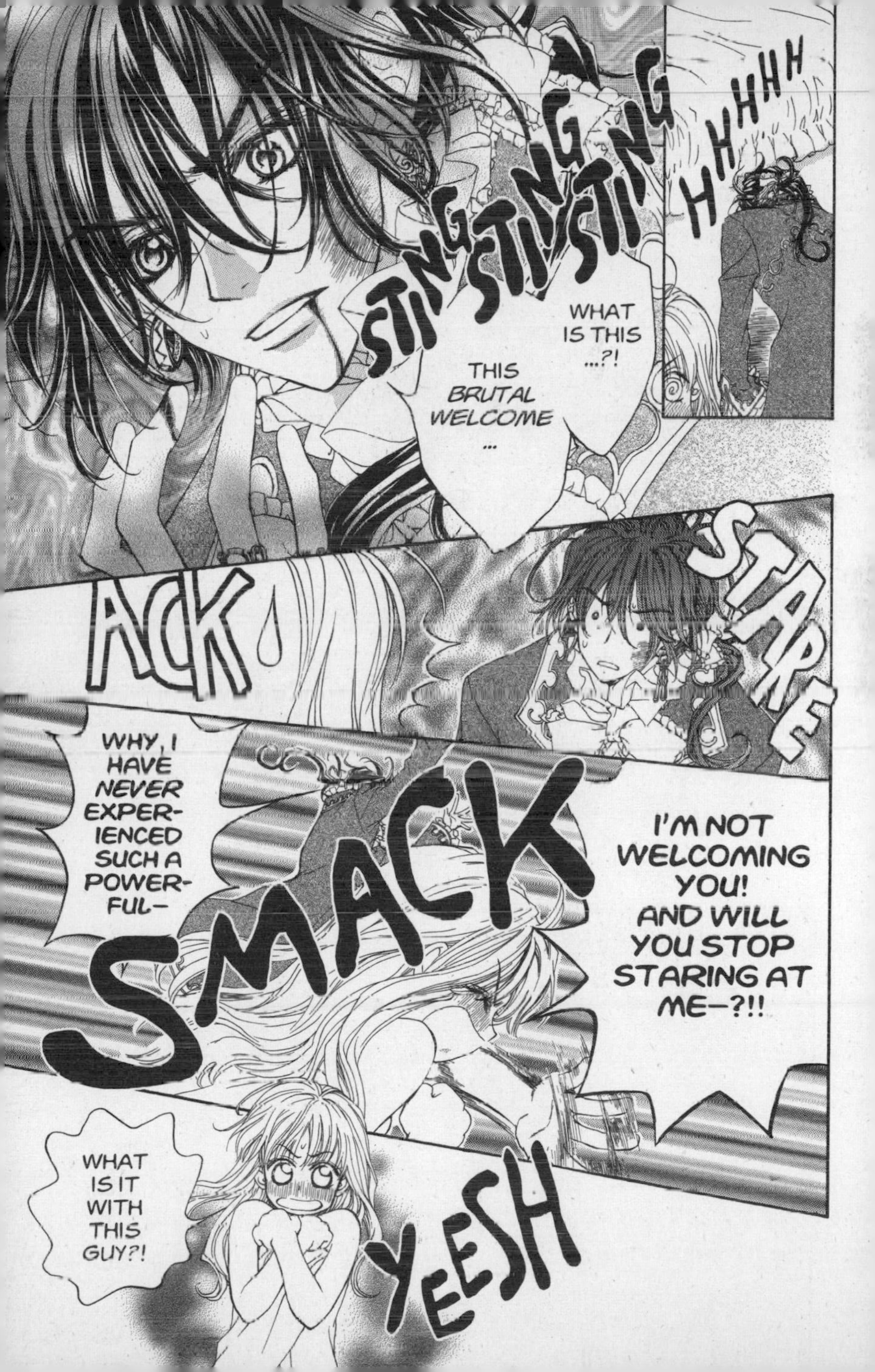
HHHHHHH
STING STING STING
WHAT IS THIS ...?!
THIS BRUTAL WELCOME ...
STARE
ACK
I'M NOT WELCOMING YOU! AND WILL YOU STOP STARING AT ME-?!!
SMACK
WHY, I HAVE NEVER EXPERIENCED SUCH A POWERFUL-
YEESH
WHAT IS IT WITH THIS GUY?!

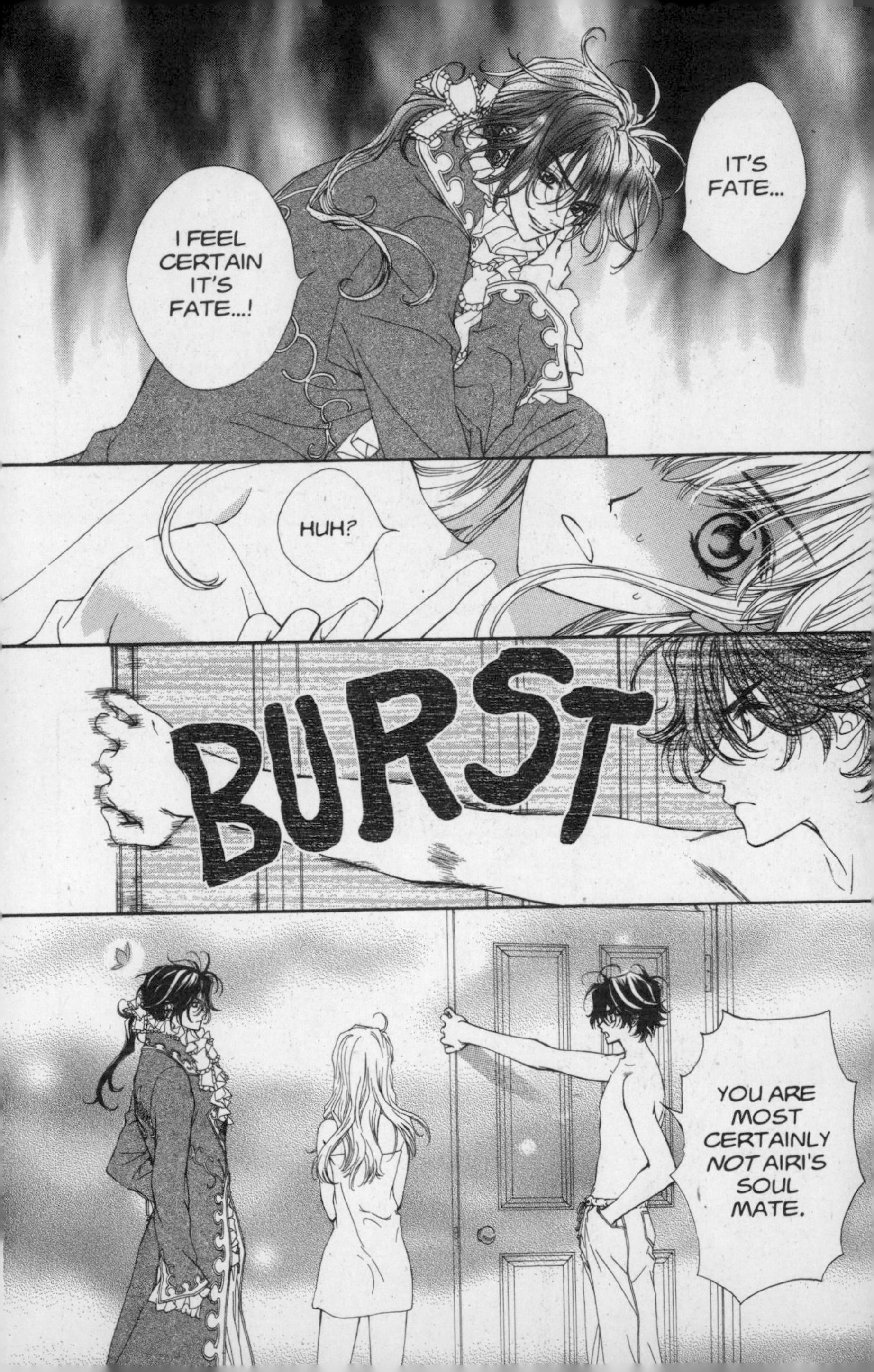
IT'S FATE...
I FEEL CERTAIN IT'S FATE...!
HUH?
BURST
YOU ARE MOST CERTAINLY NOT AIRI'S SOUL MATE.

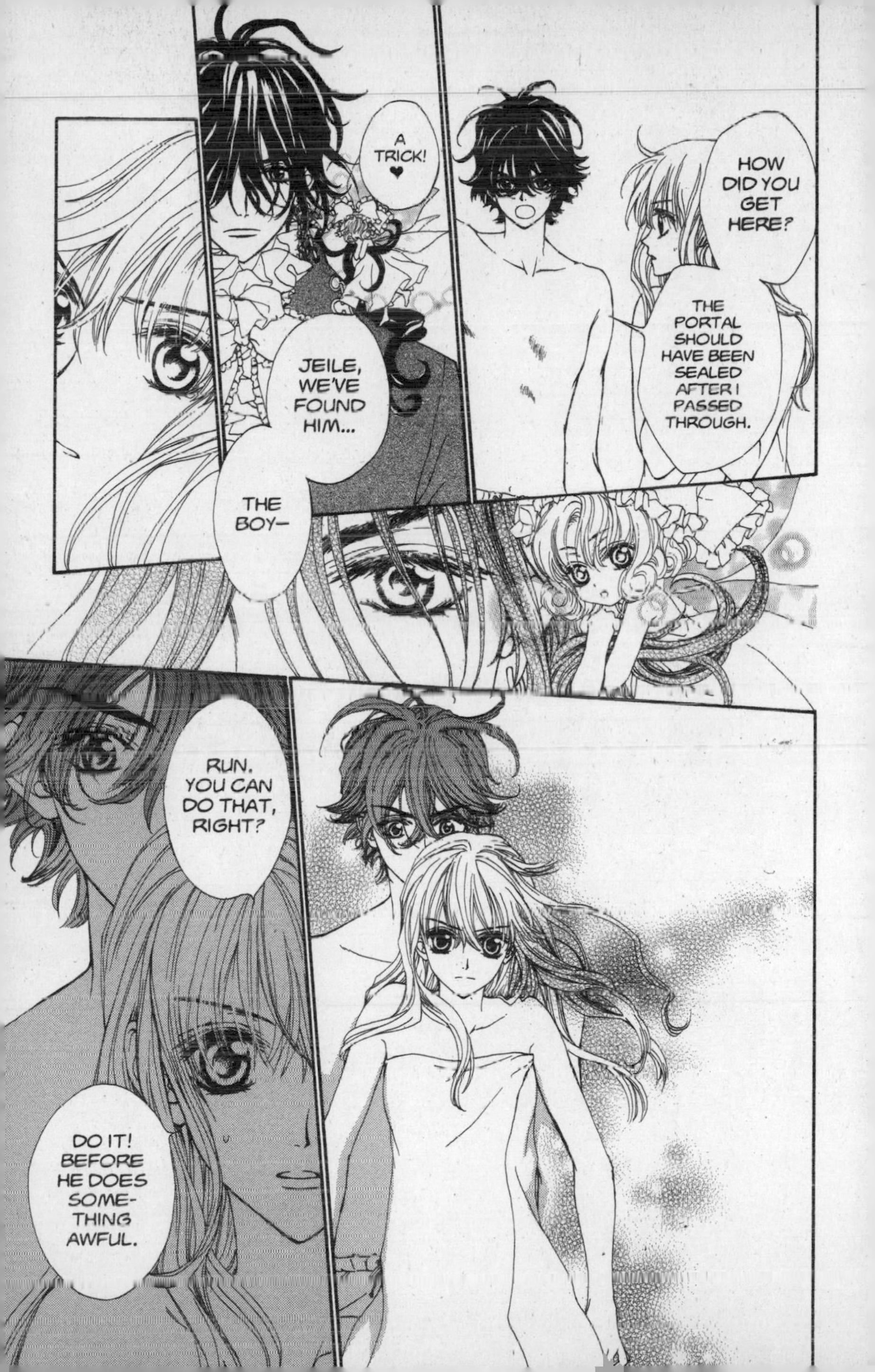
HOW DID YOU GET HERE?
THE PORTAL SHOULD HAVE BEEN SEALED AFTER I PASSED THROUGH.
A TRICK! ♥
JEILE, WE'VE FOUND HIM...
THE BOY—
RUN. YOU CAN DO THAT, RIGHT?
DO IT! BEFORE HE DOES SOME-THING AWFUL.

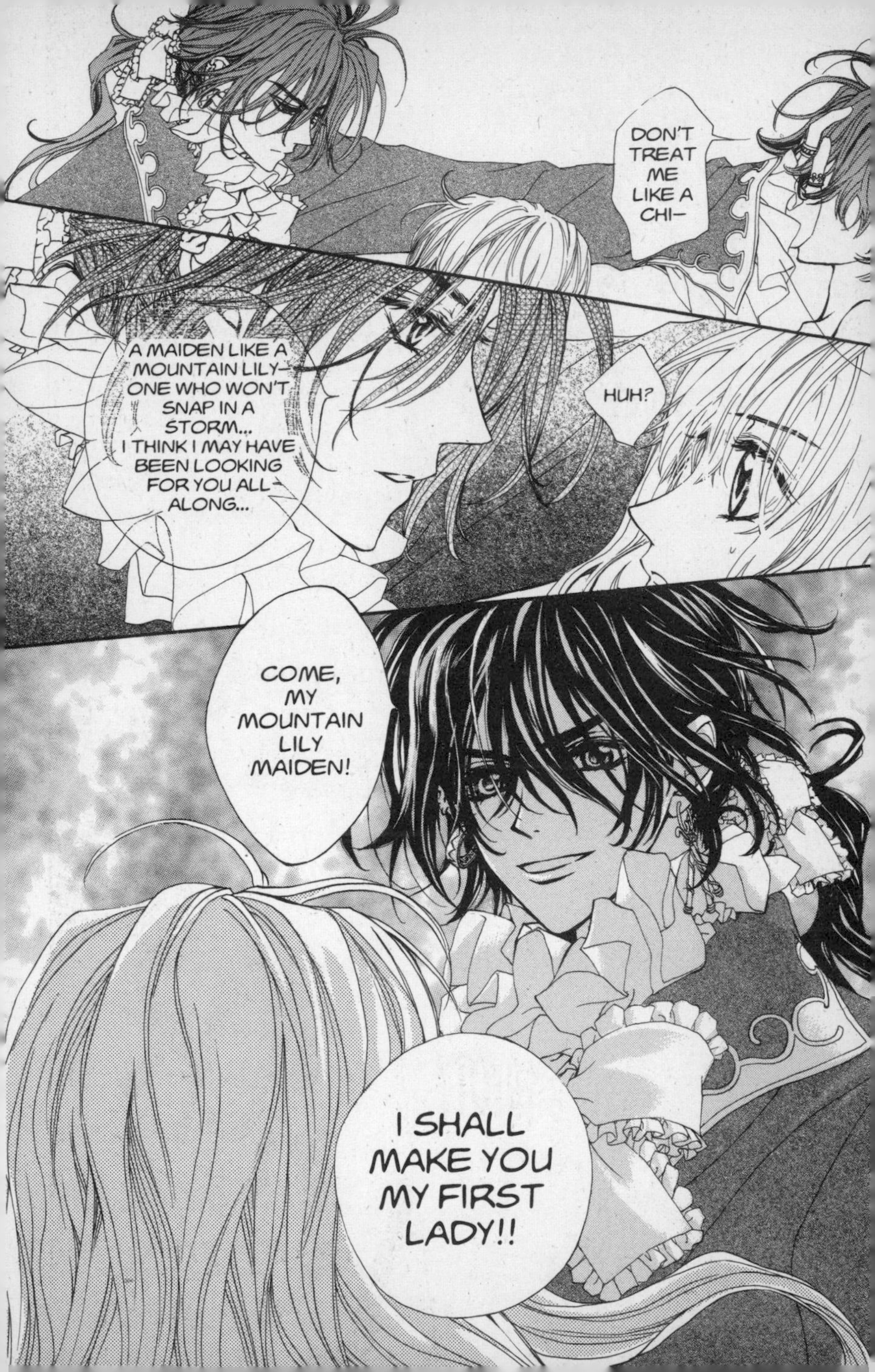
DON'T TREAT ME LIKE A CHI—
A MAIDEN LIKE A MOUNTAIN LILY—ONE WHO WON'T SNAP IN A STORM... I THINK I MAY HAVE BEEN LOOKING FOR YOU ALL ALONG...
HUH?
COME, MY MOUNTAIN LILY MAIDEN!
I SHALL MAKE YOU MY FIRST LADY!!

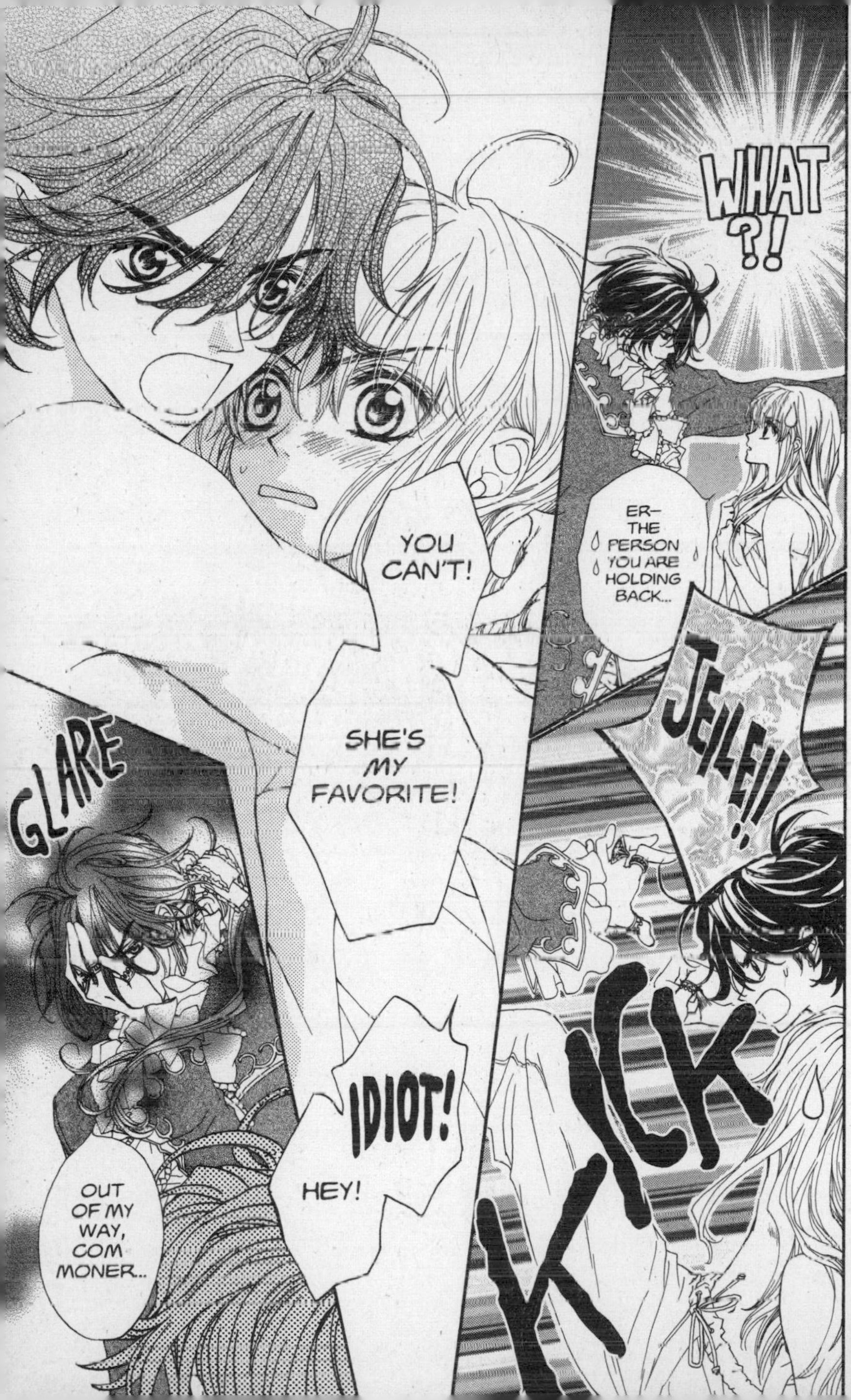
WHAT?!
ER– THE PERSON YOU ARE HOLDING BACK...
JEILE!!
KICK
YOU CAN'T!
SHE'S MY FAVORITE!
IDIOT!
HEY!
GLARE
OUT OF MY WAY, COM MONER...

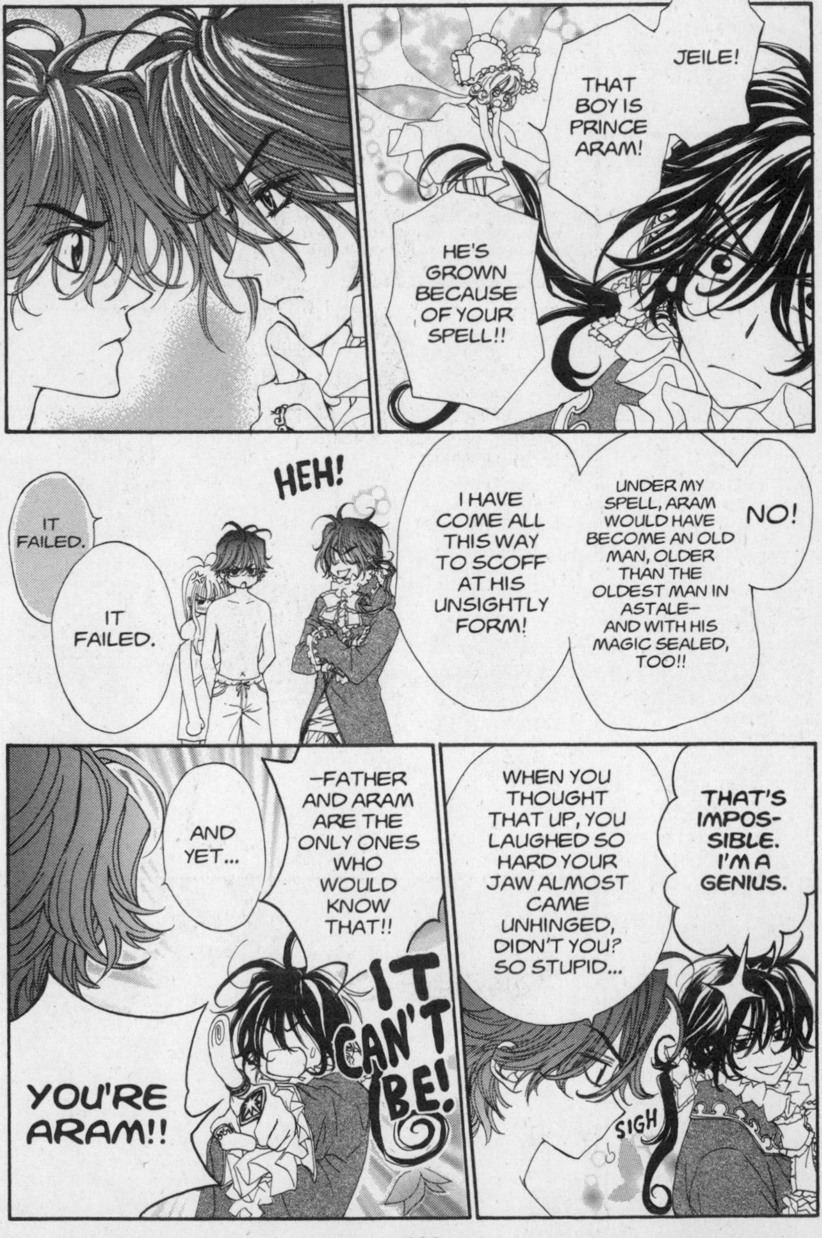
JEILE!
THAT BOY IS PRINCE ARAM!
HE'S GROWN BECAUSE OF YOUR SPELL!!
NO!
UNDER MY SPELL, ARAM WOULD HAVE BECOME AN OLD MAN, OLDER THAN THE OLDEST MAN IN ASTALE— AND WITH HIS MAGIC SEALED, TOO!!
I HAVE COME ALL THIS WAY TO SCOFF AT HIS UNSIGHTLY FORM!
HEH!
IT FAILED.
IT FAILED.
THAT'S IMPOSSIBLE. I'M A GENIUS.
WHEN YOU THOUGHT THAT UP, YOU LAUGHED SO HARD YOUR JAW ALMOST CAME UNHINGED, DIDN'T YOU? SO STUPID...
SIGH
AND YET...
—FATHER AND ARAM ARE THE ONLY ONES WHO WOULD KNOW THAT!!
IT CAN'T BE!
YOU'RE ARAM!!

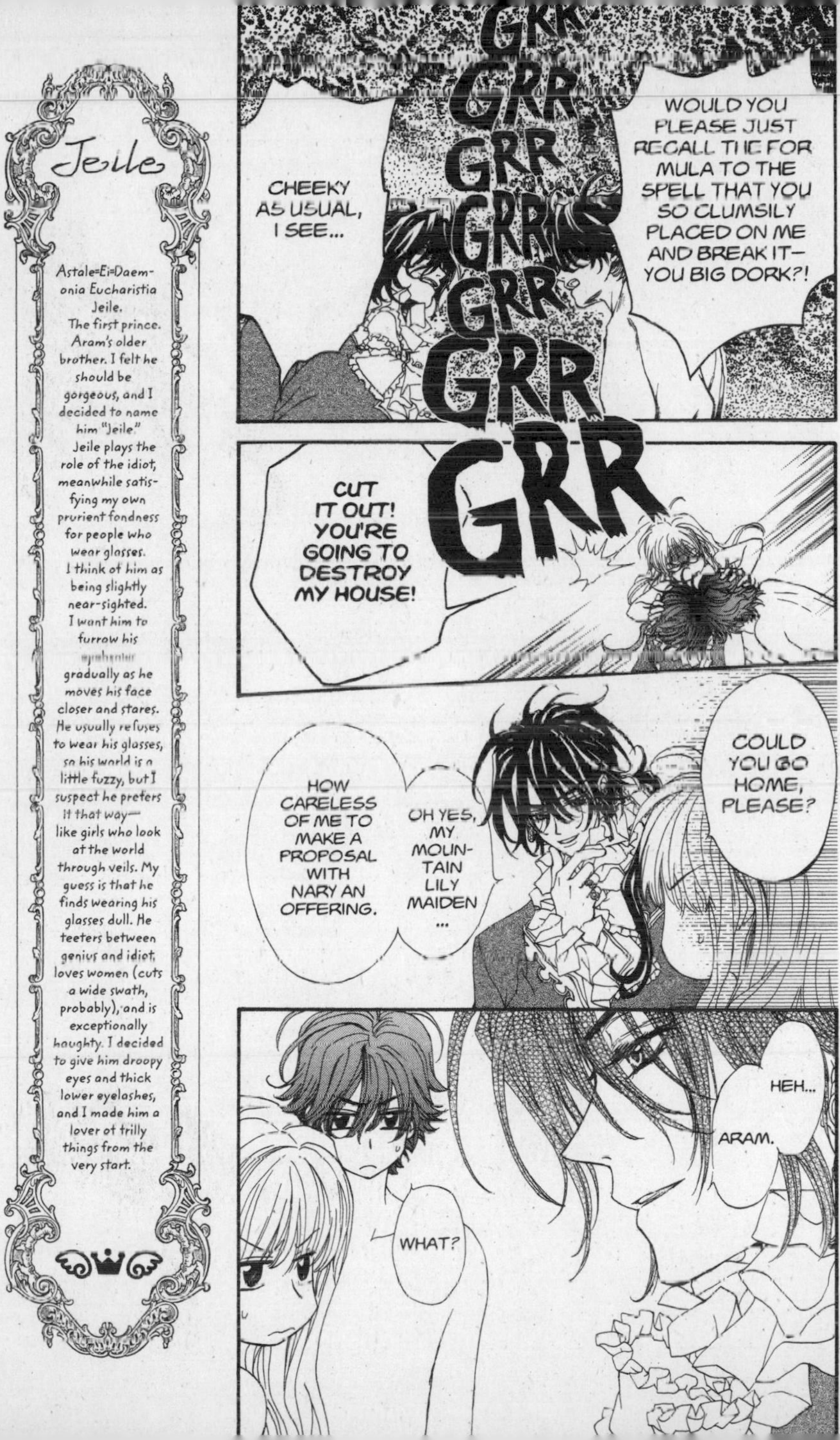
GKK
GRR
GRR
GRR
GRR
GRR
WOULD YOU PLEASE JUST RECALL THE FOR MULA TO THE SPELL THAT YOU SO CLUMSILY PLACED ON ME AND BREAK IT—YOU BIG DORK?!
CHEEKY AS USUAL, I SEE...
GRR
CUT IT OUT! YOU'RE GOING TO DESTROY MY HOUSE!
COULD YOU GO HOME, PLEASE?
OH YES, MY MOUNTAIN LILY MAIDEN ...
HOW CARELESS OF ME TO MAKE A PROPOSAL WITH NARY AN OFFERING.
HEH...
ARAM.
WHAT?

Jeile

Astale=Ei=Daemonia Eucharistia Jeile.
The first prince. Aram's older brother. I felt he should be gorgeous, and I decided to name him "Jeile."
Jeile plays the role of the idiot, meanwhile satisfying my own prurient fondness for people who wear glasses.
I think of him as being slightly near-sighted.
I want him to furrow his eyebrows gradually as he moves his face closer and stares. He usually refuses to wear his glasses, so his world is a little fuzzy, but I suspect he prefers it that way—like girls who look at the world through veils. My guess is that he finds wearing his glasses dull. He teeters between genius and idiot, loves women (cuts a wide swath, probably), and is exceptionally haughty. I decided to give him droopy eyes and thick lower eyelashes, and I made him a lover of frilly things from the very start.

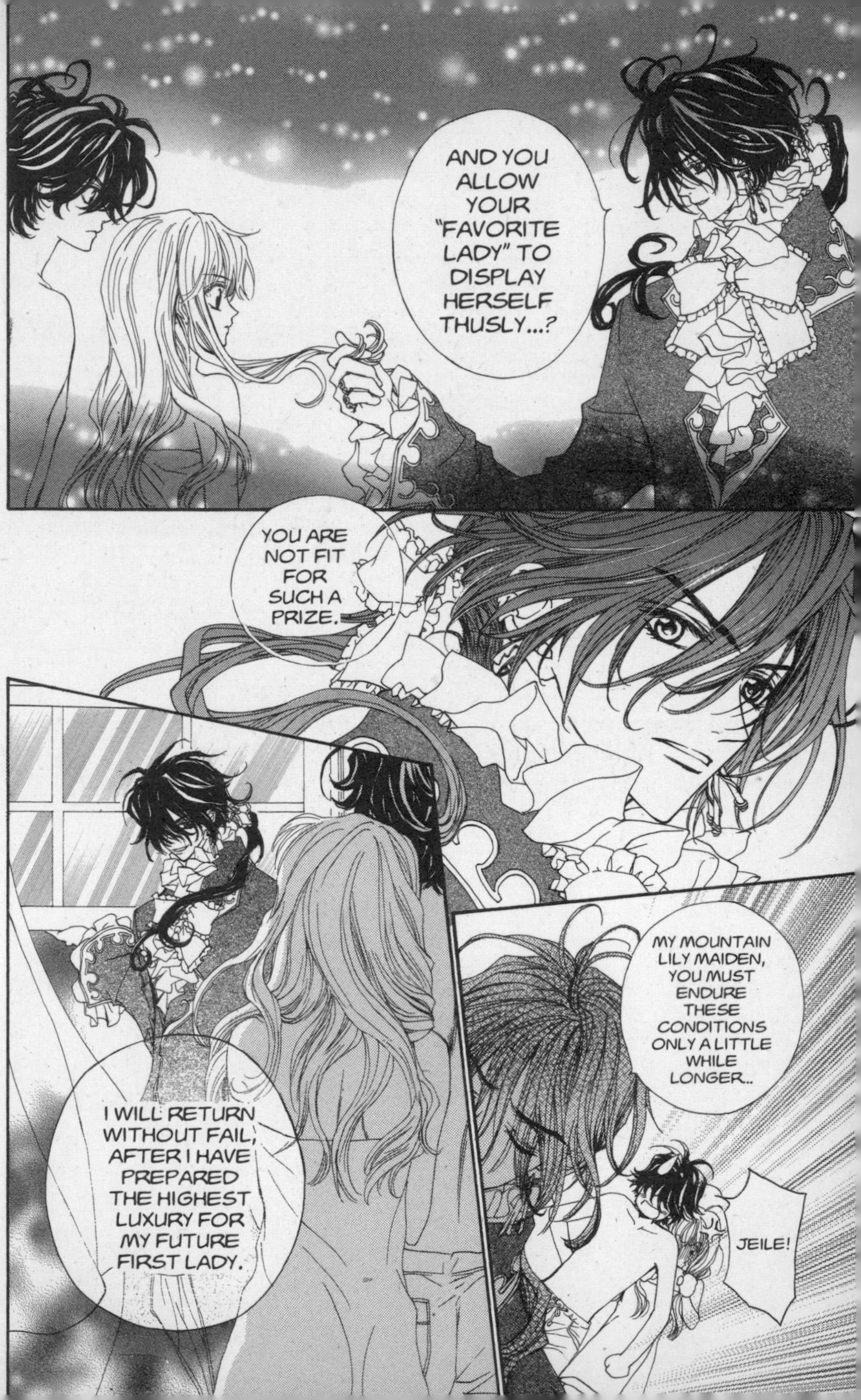
AND YOU ALLOW YOUR "FAVORITE LADY" TO DISPLAY HERSELF THUSLY...?
YOU ARE NOT FIT FOR SUCH A PRIZE.
I WILL RETURN WITHOUT FAIL, AFTER I HAVE PREPARED THE HIGHEST LUXURY FOR MY FUTURE FIRST LADY.
MY MOUNTAIN LILY MAIDEN, YOU MUST ENDURE THESE CONDITIONS ONLY A LITTLE WHILE LONGER...
JEILE!

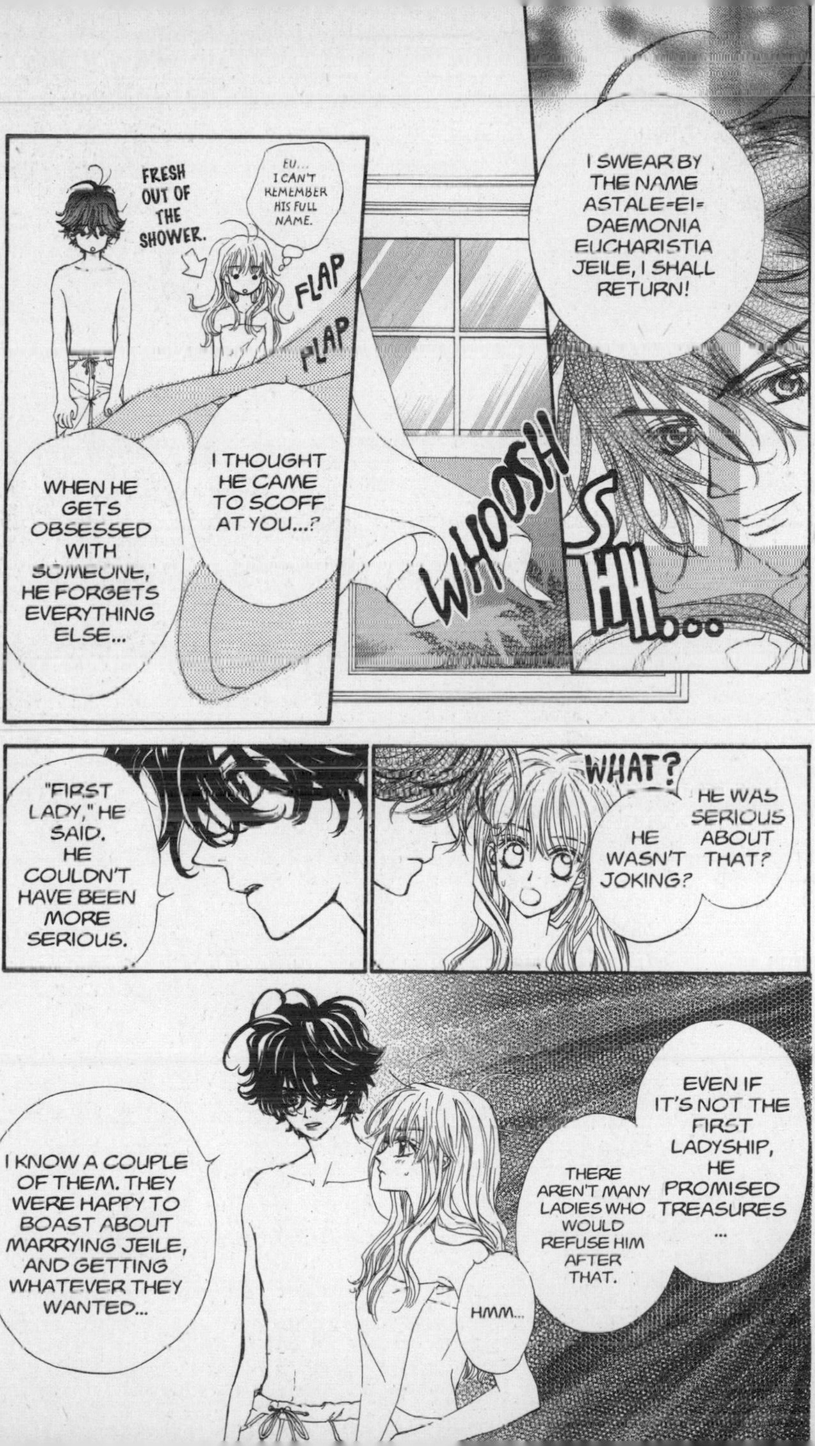
I SWEAR BY THE NAME ASTALE=EI= DAEMONIA EUCHARISTIA JEILE, I SHALL RETURN!
WHOOSH
SHHooo
FRESH OUT OF THE SHOWER.
EU... I CAN'T REMEMBER HIS FULL NAME.
FLAP
FLAP
I THOUGHT HE CAME TO SCOFF AT YOU...?
WHEN HE GETS OBSESSED WITH SOMEONE, HE FORGETS EVERYTHING ELSE...
WHAT?
HE WAS SERIOUS ABOUT THAT?
HE WASN'T JOKING?
"FIRST LADY," HE SAID. HE COULDN'T HAVE BEEN MORE SERIOUS.
EVEN IF IT'S NOT THE FIRST LADYSHIP, HE PROMISED TREASURES ...
THERE AREN'T MANY LADIES WHO WOULD REFUSE HIM AFTER THAT.
HMM...
I KNOW A COUPLE OF THEM. THEY WERE HAPPY TO BOAST ABOUT MARRYING JEILE, AND GETTING WHATEVER THEY WANTED...

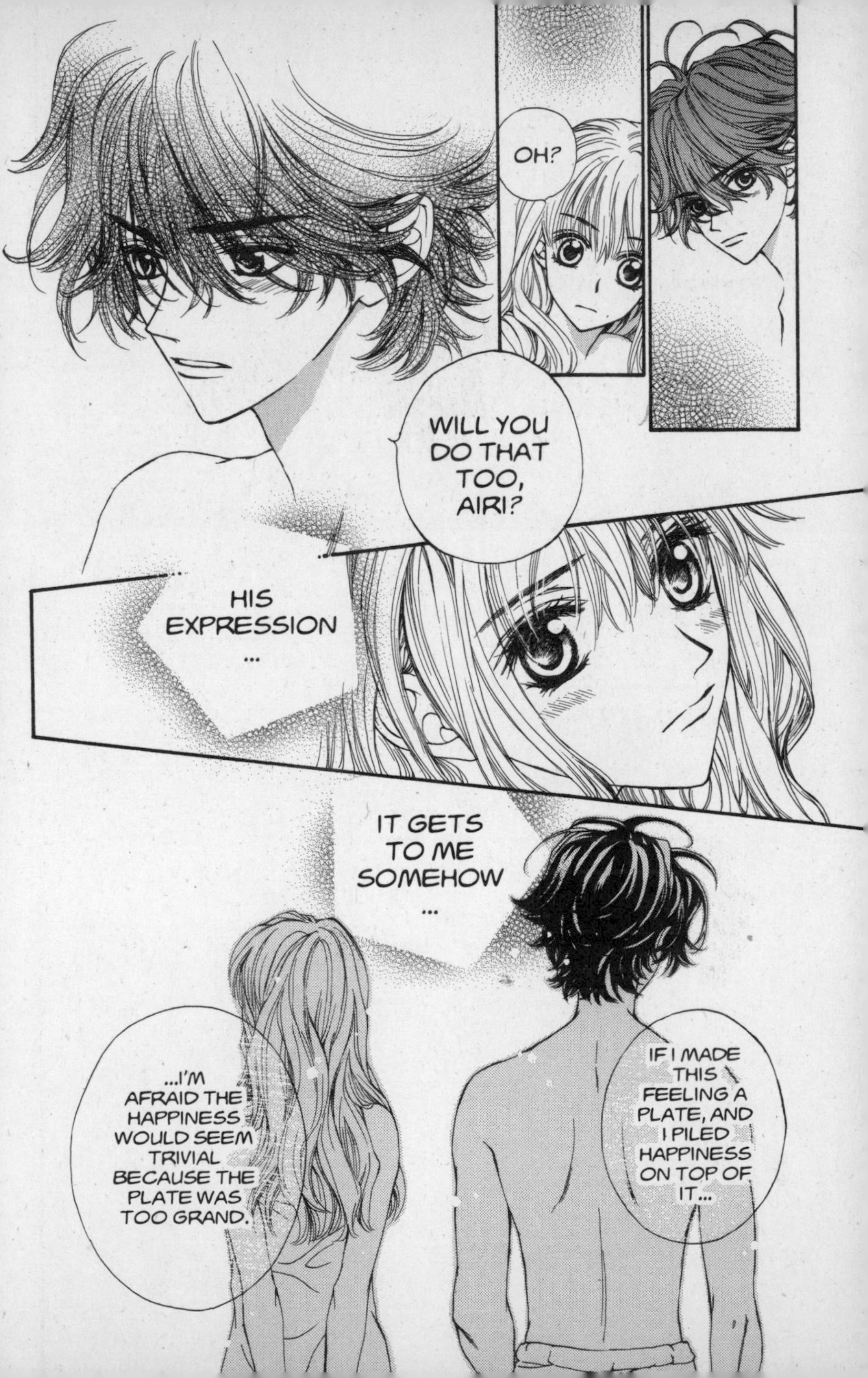
OH?
WILL YOU DO THAT TOO, AIRI?
HIS EXPRESSION ...
IT GETS TO ME SOMEHOW ...
IF I MADE THIS FEELING A PLATE, AND I PILED HAPPINESS ON TOP OF IT...
...I'M AFRAID THE HAPPINESS WOULD SEEM TRIVIAL BECAUSE THE PLATE WAS TOO GRAND.

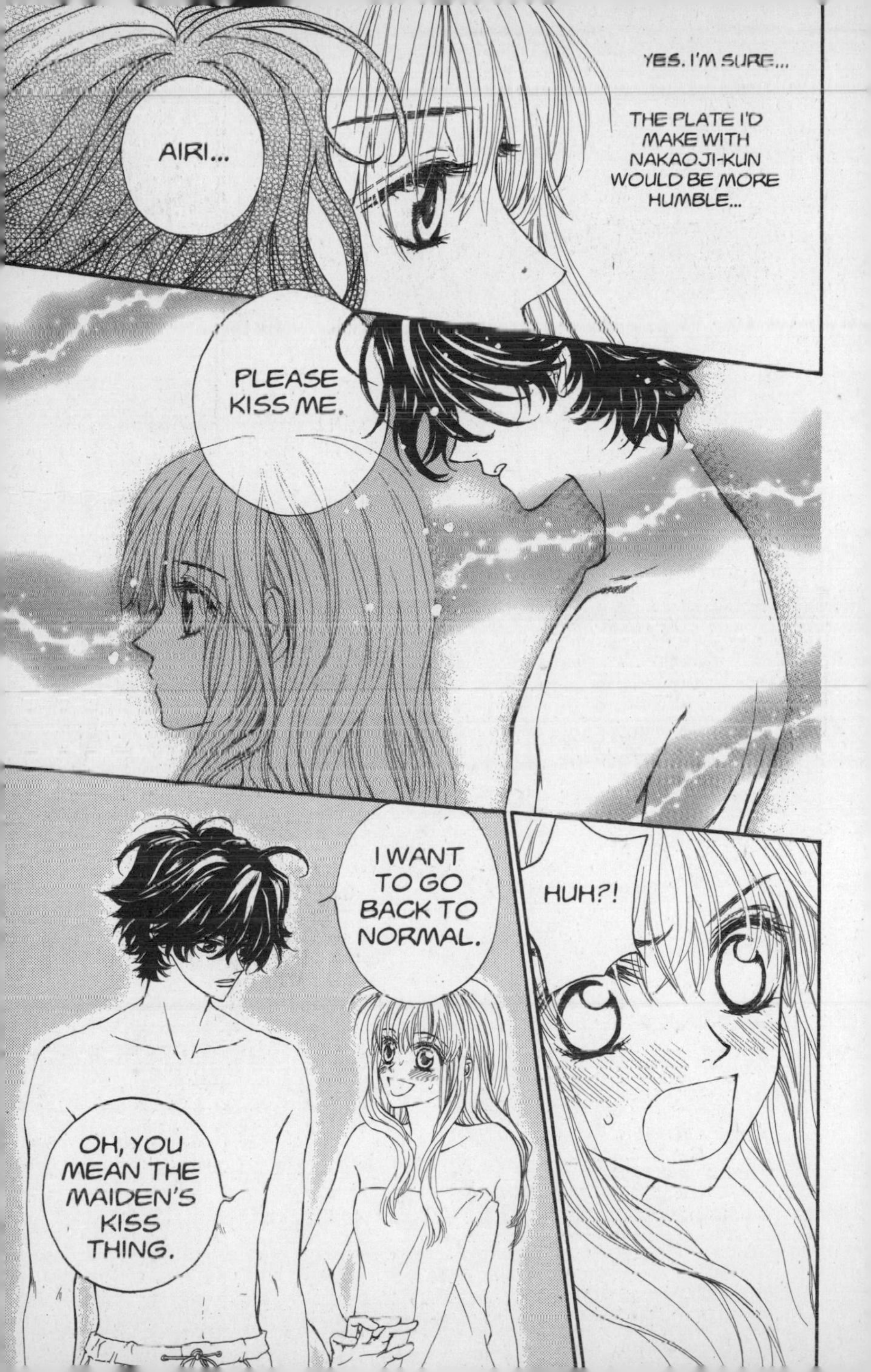
YES. I'M SURE...
THE PLATE I'D MAKE WITH NAKAOJI-KUN WOULD BE MORE HUMBLE...
AIRI...
PLEASE KISS ME.
HUH?!
I WANT TO GO BACK TO NORMAL.
OH, YOU MEAN THE MAIDEN'S KISS THING.

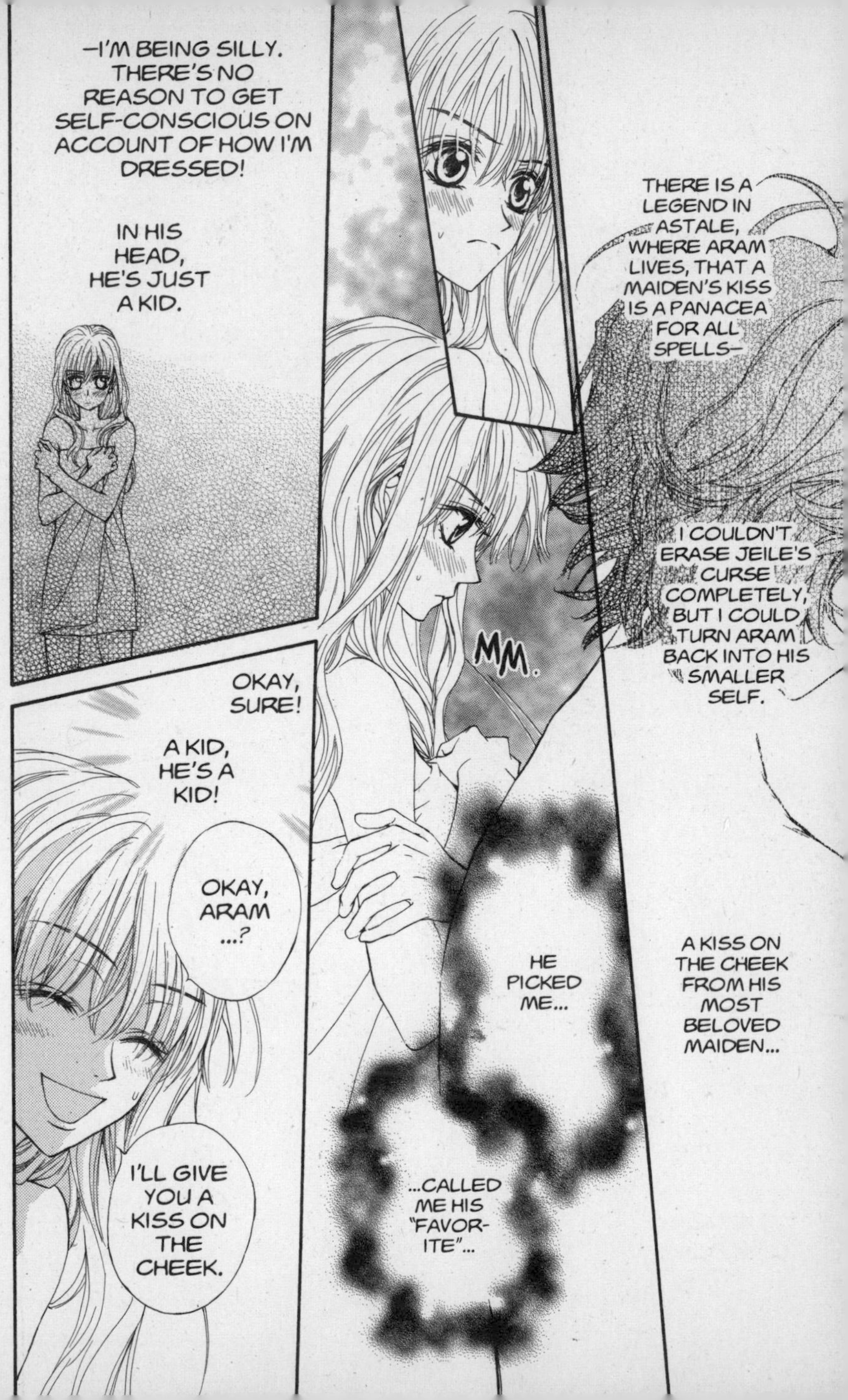
THERE IS A LEGEND IN ASTALE, WHERE ARAM LIVES, THAT A MAIDEN'S KISS IS A PANACEA FOR ALL SPELLS—
I COULDN'T ERASE JEILE'S CURSE COMPLETELY, BUT I COULD TURN ARAM BACK INTO HIS SMALLER SELF.
MM.
A KISS ON THE CHEEK FROM HIS MOST BELOVED MAIDEN...
HE PICKED ME...
...CALLED ME HIS "FAVOR-ITE"...
—I'M BEING SILLY. THERE'S NO REASON TO GET SELF-CONSCIOUS ON ACCOUNT OF HOW I'M DRESSED!
IN HIS HEAD, HE'S JUST A KID.
OKAY, SURE!
A KID, HE'S A KID!
OKAY, ARAM ...?
I'LL GIVE YOU A KISS ON THE CHEEK.

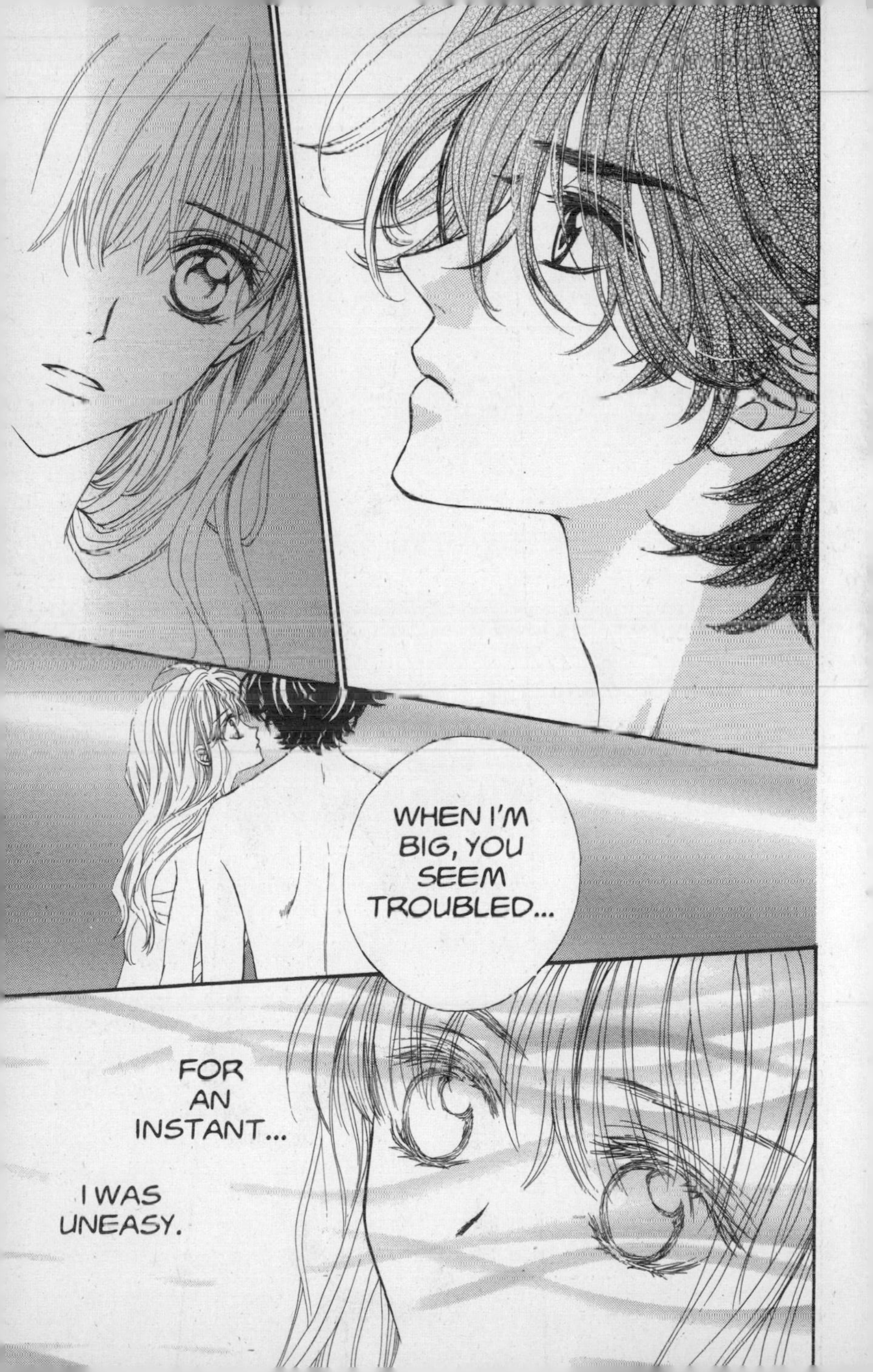
WHEN I'M BIG, YOU SEEM TROUBLED...
FOR AN INSTANT...
I WAS UNEASY.

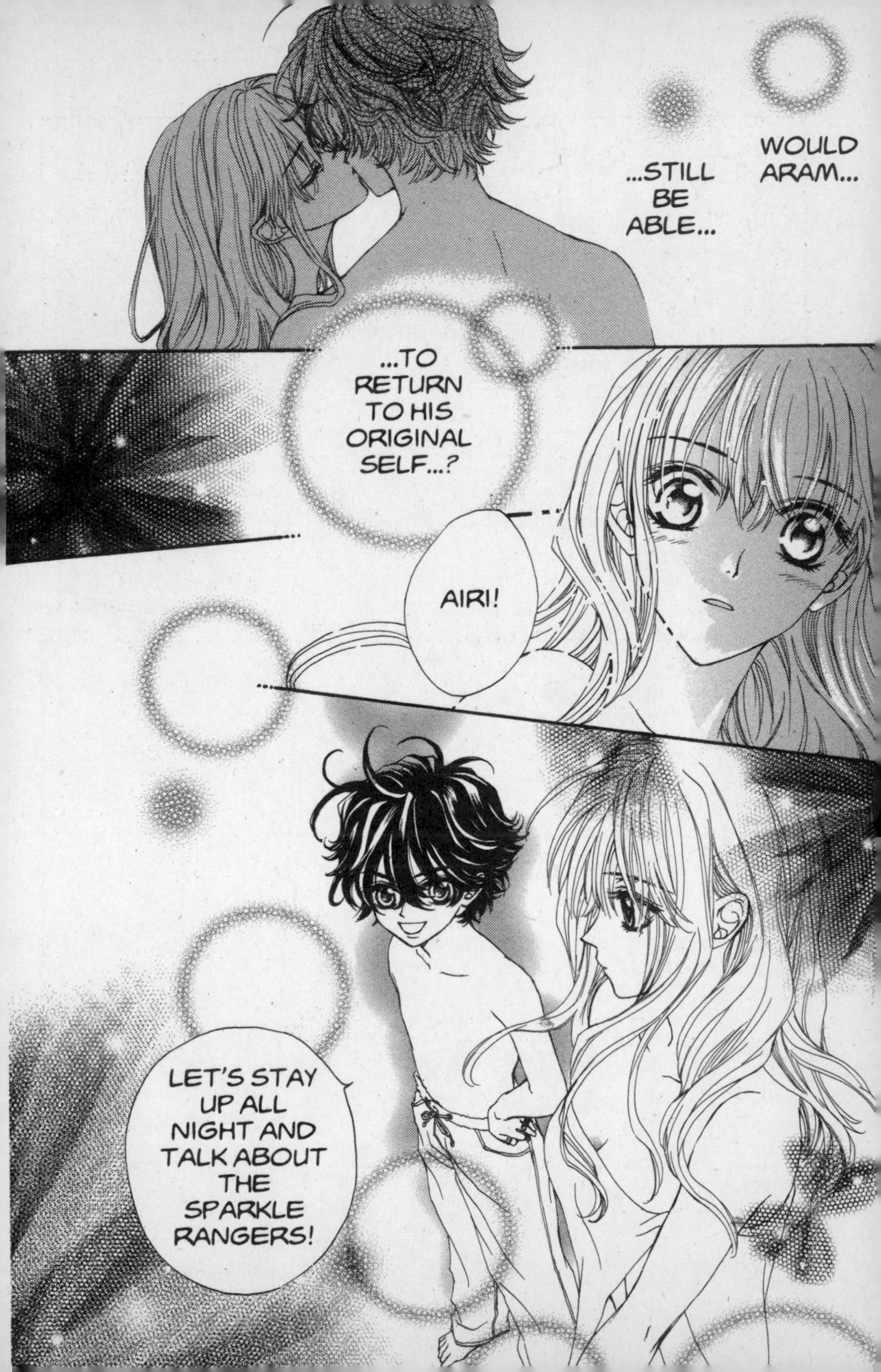
WOULD ARAM...
...STILL BE ABLE...
...TO RETURN TO HIS ORIGINAL SELF...?
AIRI!
LET'S STAY UP ALL NIGHT AND TALK ABOUT THE SPARKLE RANGERS!

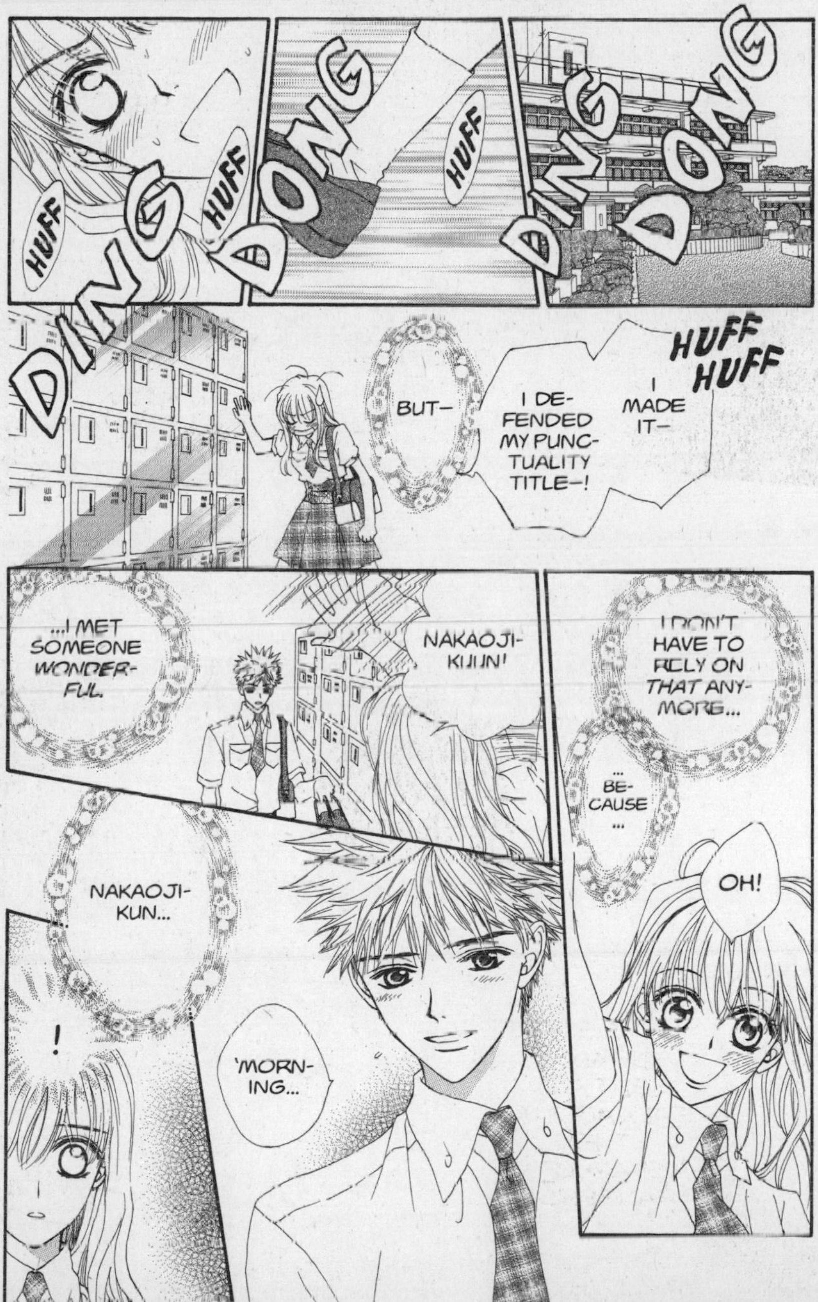
DING DONG
HUFF
DONG
HUFF HUFF
HUFF
DING
HUFF HUFF
I MADE IT—
I DE-FENDED MY PUNC-TUALITY TITLE—!
BUT—
DING
I DON'T HAVE TO RELY ON THAT ANY-MORE...
...BE-CAUSE...
NAKAOJI-KUN!
...I MET SOMEONE WONDER-FUL.
OH!
'MORN-ING...
NAKAOJI-KUN...
!

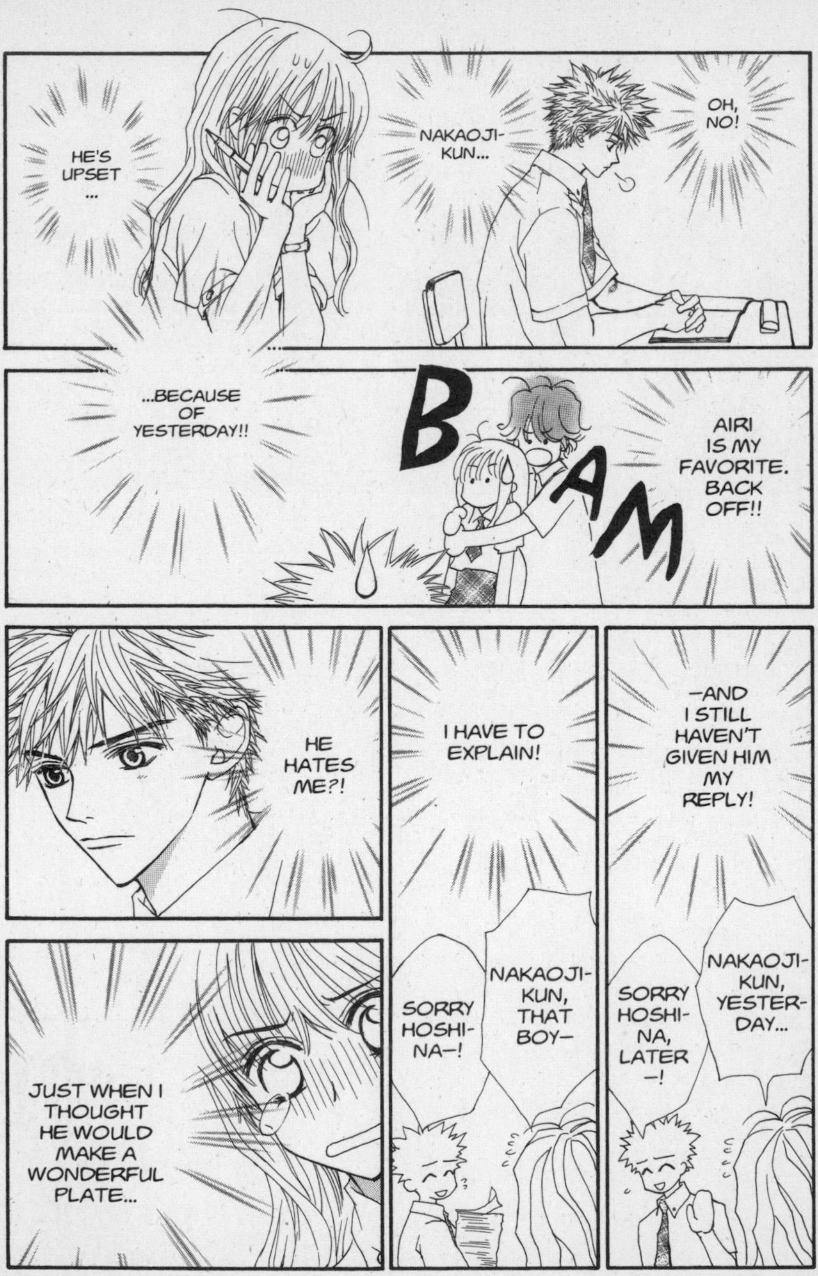
OH, NO!
NAKAOJI-KUN...
HE'S UPSET ...
...BECAUSE OF YESTERDAY!!
AIRI IS MY FAVORITE. BACK OFF!!
BAM
—AND I STILL HAVEN'T GIVEN HIM MY REPLY!
NAKAOJI-KUN, YESTER-DAY...
SORRY HOSHI-NA, LATER —!
I HAVE TO EXPLAIN!
NAKAOJI-KUN, THAT BOY—
SORRY HOSHI-NA—!
HE HATES ME?!
JUST WHEN I THOUGHT HE WOULD MAKE A WONDERFUL PLATE...

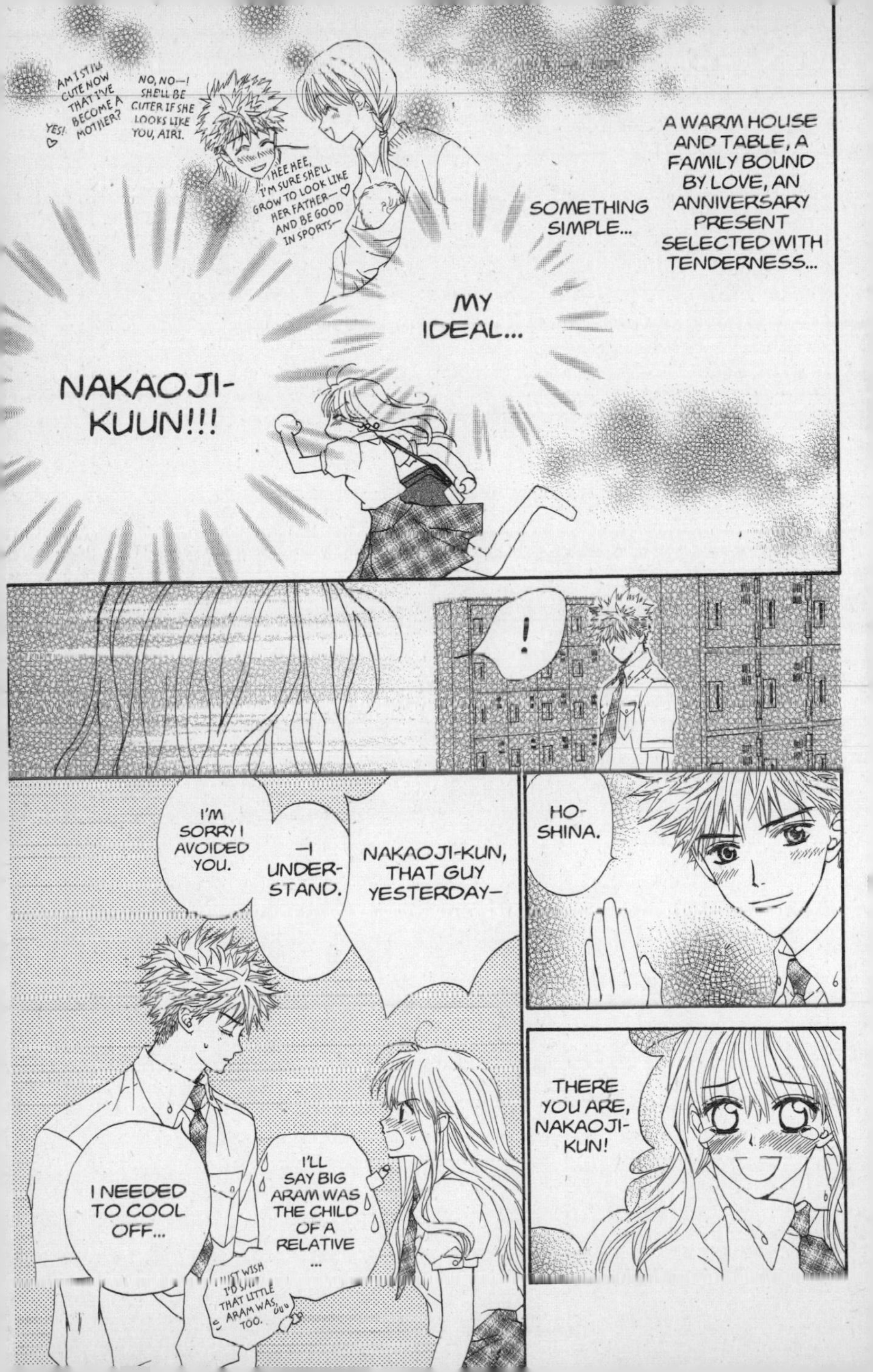
A WARM HOUSE AND TABLE, A FAMILY BOUND BY LOVE, AN ANNIVERSARY PRESENT SELECTED WITH TENDERNESS...
SOMETHING SIMPLE...
NO, NO—! SHE'LL BE CUTER IF SHE LOOKS LIKE YOU, AIRI.
AM I STILL CUTE NOW THAT I'VE BECOME A MOTHER?
YES! ♡
HEE HEE, I'M SURE SHE'LL GROW TO LOOK LIKE HER FATHER— ♡ AND BE GOOD IN SPORTS—
MY IDEAL...
NAKAOJI-KUUN!!!
!
HO-SHINA.
THERE YOU ARE, NAKAOJI-KUN!
NAKAOJI-KUN, THAT GUY YESTERDAY—
—I UNDERSTAND.
I'M SORRY I AVOIDED YOU.
I'LL SAY BIG ARAM WAS THE CHILD OF A RELATIVE ...
I NEEDED TO COOL OFF...
...JUST WISH I'D S... THAT LITTLE ARAM WAS, TOO. UUU

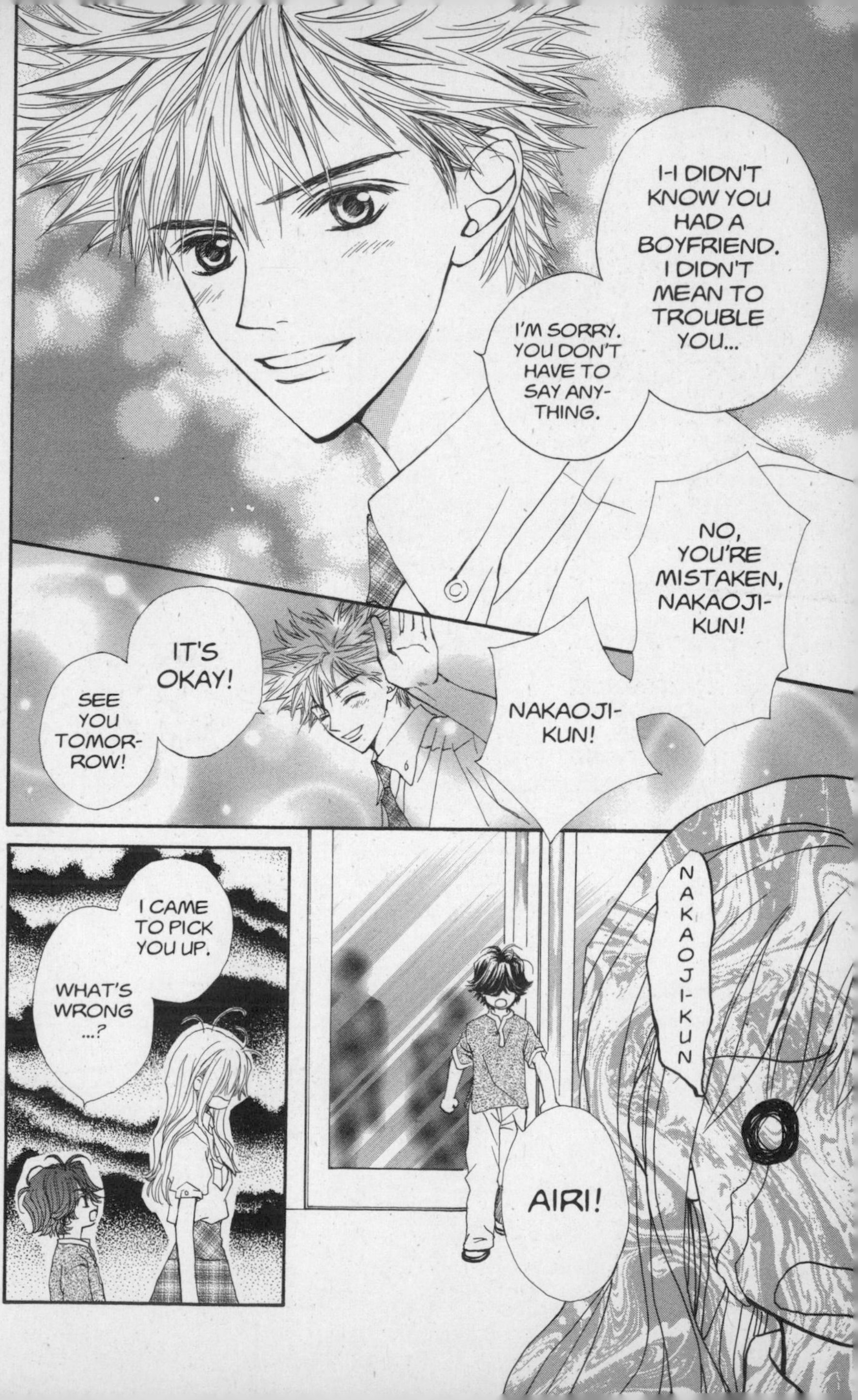
I-I DIDN'T KNOW YOU HAD A BOYFRIEND. I DIDN'T MEAN TO TROUBLE YOU...
I'M SORRY. YOU DON'T HAVE TO SAY ANY-THING.
NO, YOU'RE MISTAKEN, NAKAOJI-KUN!
NAKAOJI-KUN!
IT'S OKAY!
SEE YOU TOMOR-ROW!
NAKAOJI-KUN
AIRI!
I CAME TO PICK YOU UP.
WHAT'S WRONG ...?

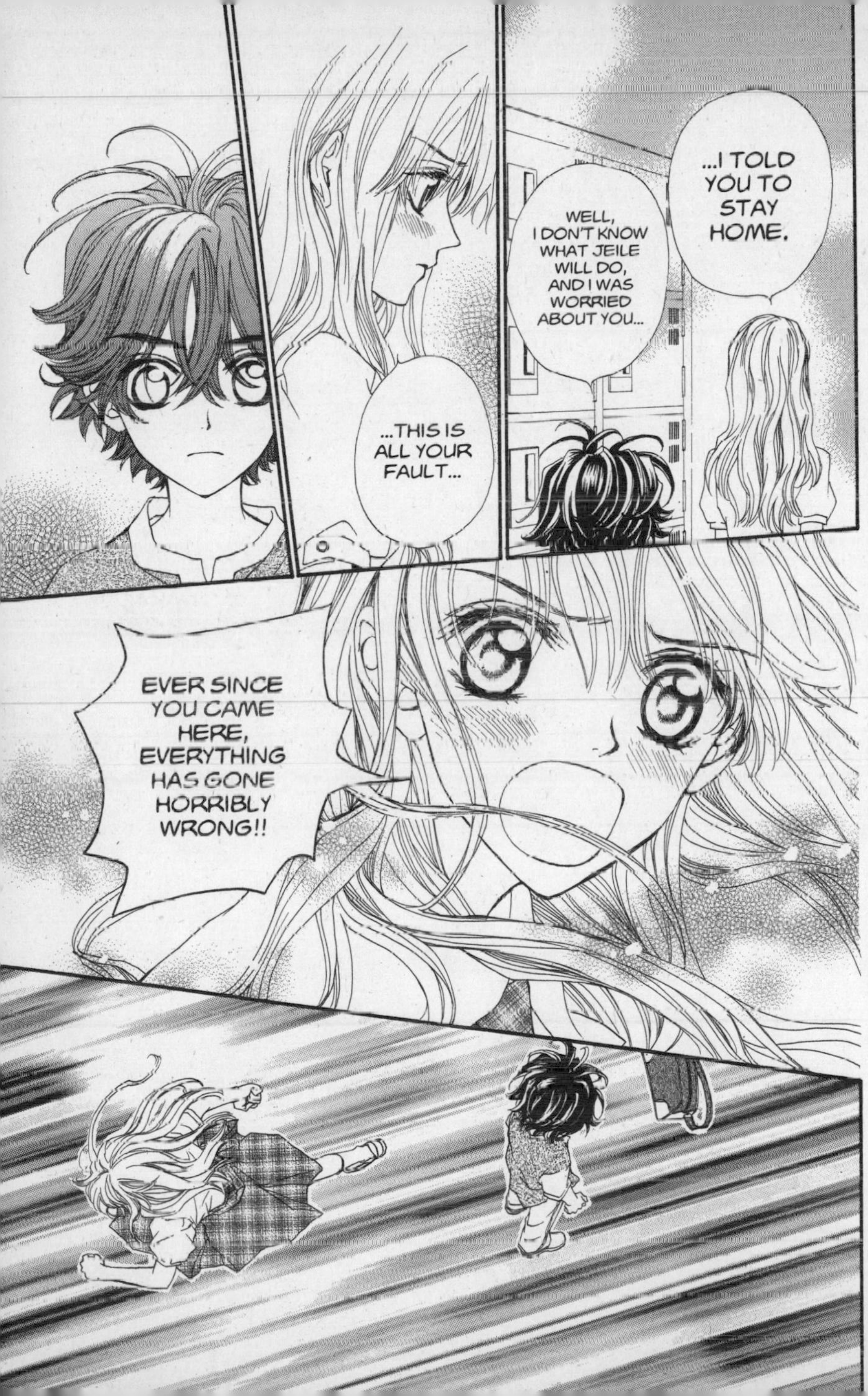
...I TOLD YOU TO STAY HOME.
WELL, I DON'T KNOW WHAT JEILE WILL DO, AND I WAS WORRIED ABOUT YOU...
...THIS IS ALL YOUR FAULT...
EVER SINCE YOU CAME HERE, EVERYTHING HAS GONE HORRIBLY WRONG!!

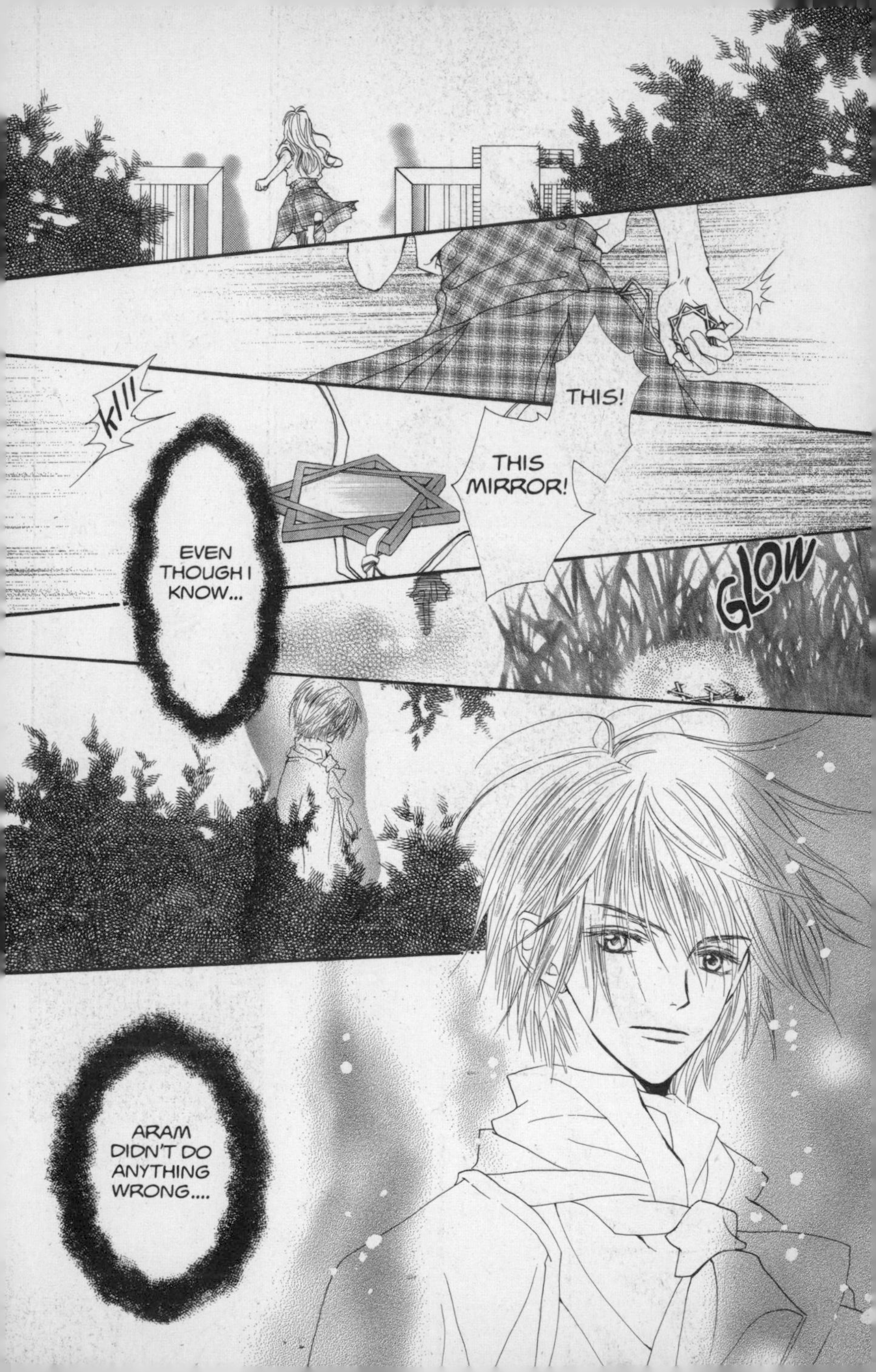
THIS!
THIS MIRROR!
KL!!!
GLOW
EVEN THOUGH I KNOW...
ARAM DIDN'T DO ANYTHING WRONG....

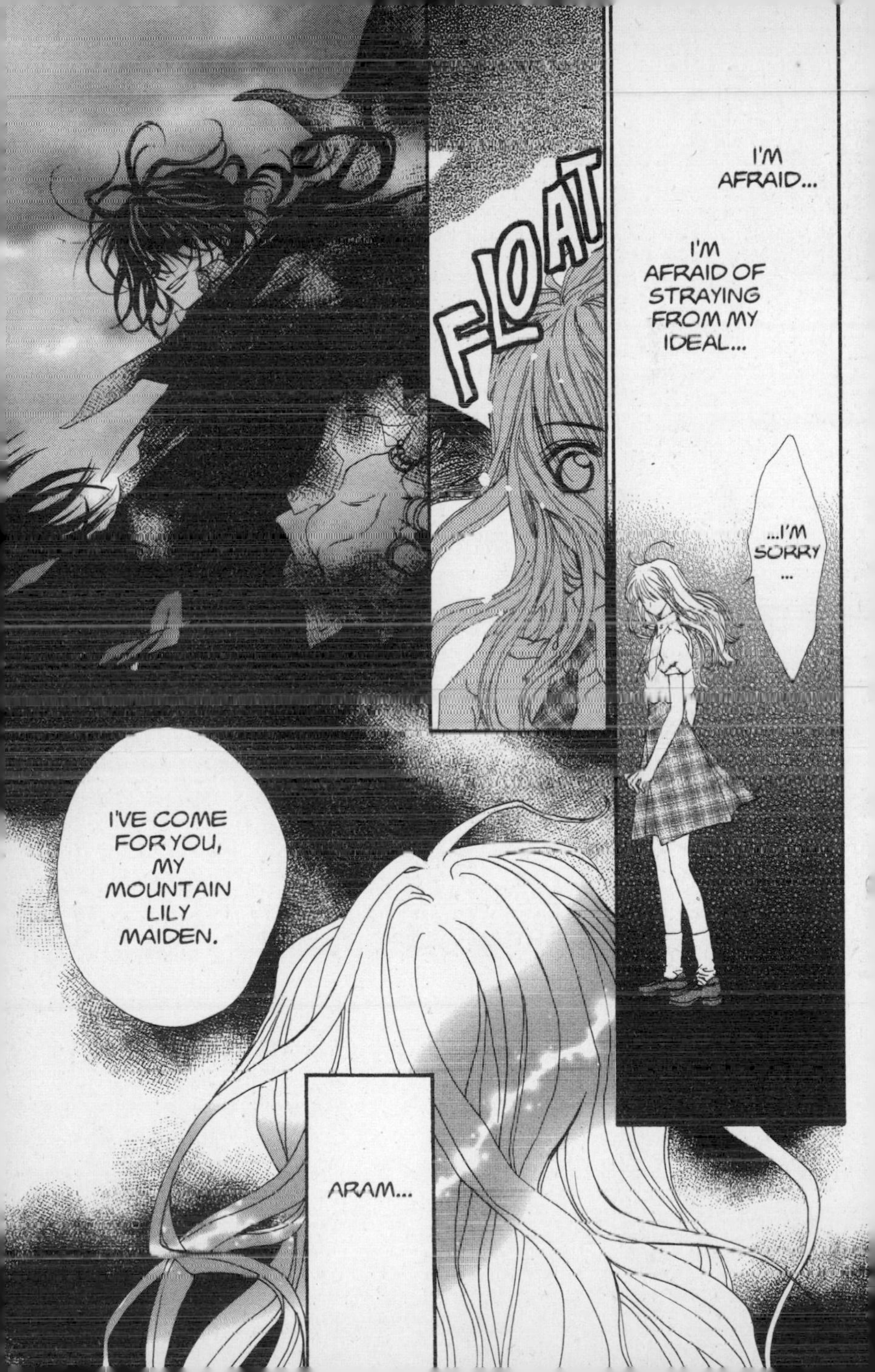
I'M AFRAID...
I'M AFRAID OF STRAYING FROM MY IDEAL...
...I'M SORRY ...
FLOAT
I'VE COME FOR YOU, MY MOUNTAIN LILY MAIDEN.
ARAM...

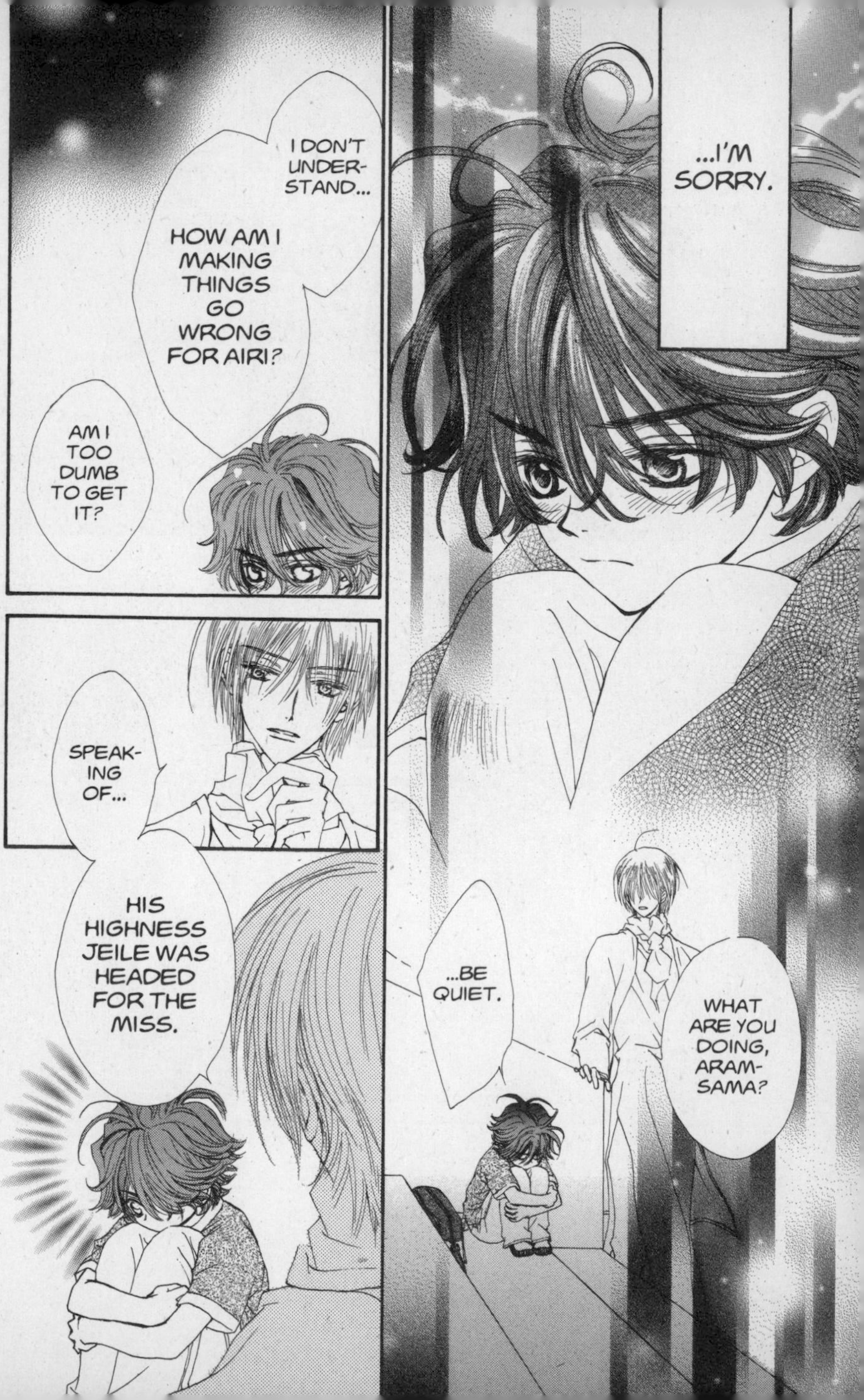
...I'M SORRY.
WHAT ARE YOU DOING, ARAM-SAMA?
...BE QUIET.
I DON'T UNDER-STAND...
HOW AM I MAKING THINGS GO WRONG FOR AIRI?
AM I TOO DUMB TO GET IT?
SPEAK-ING OF...
HIS HIGHNESS JEILE WAS HEADED FOR THE MISS.

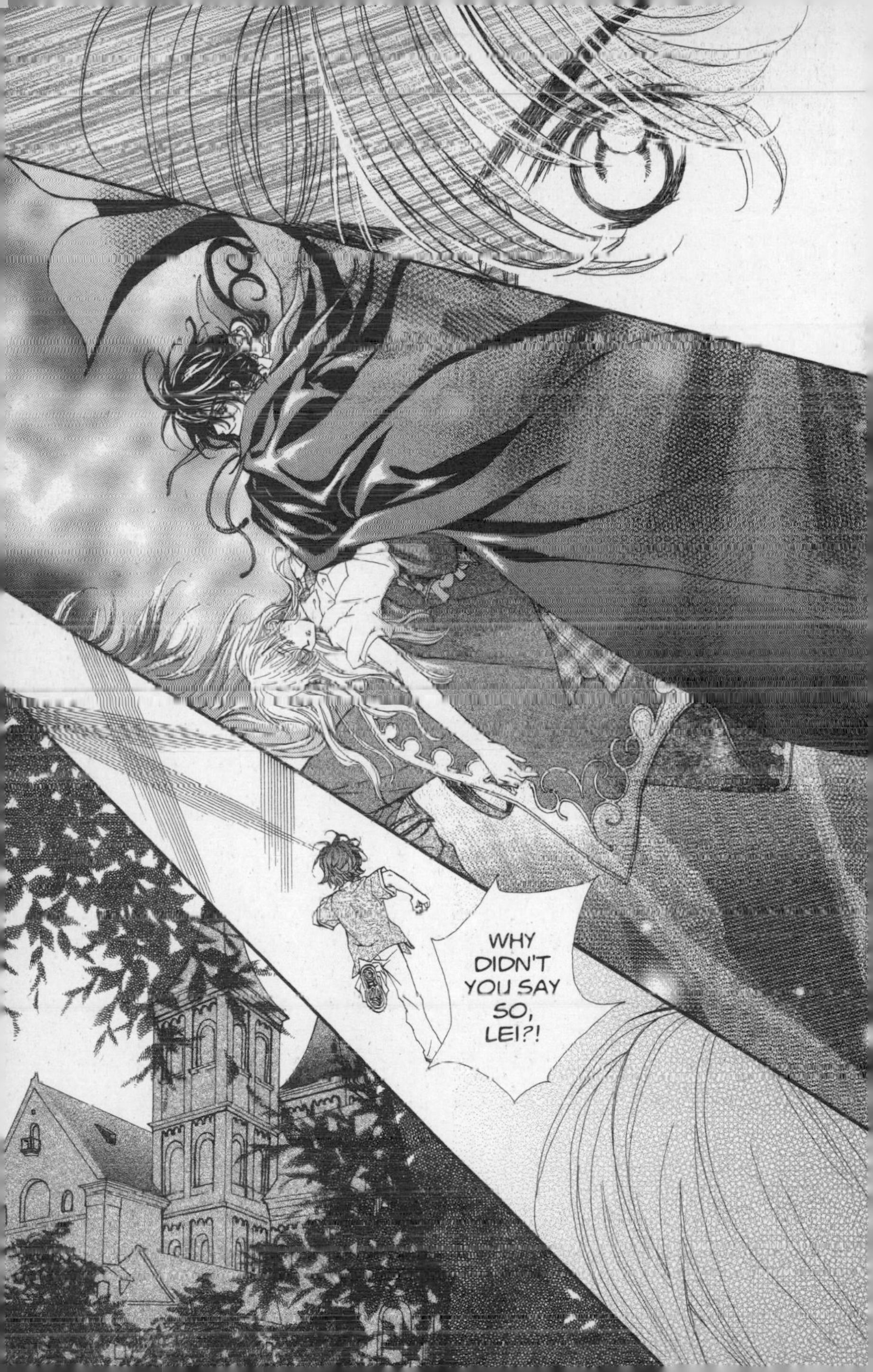
WHY DIDN'T YOU SAY SO, LEI?!

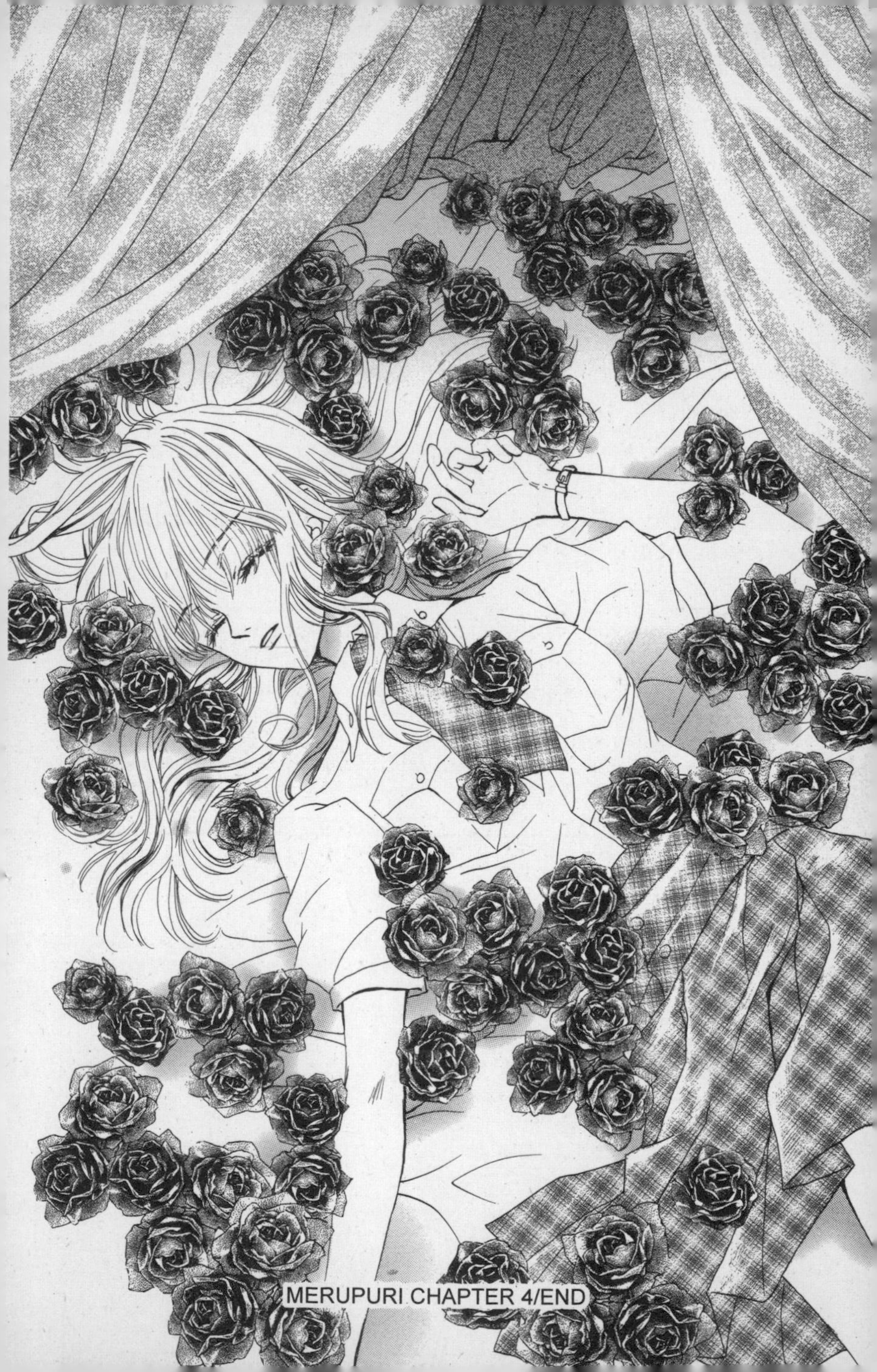
MERUPURI CHAPTER 4/END

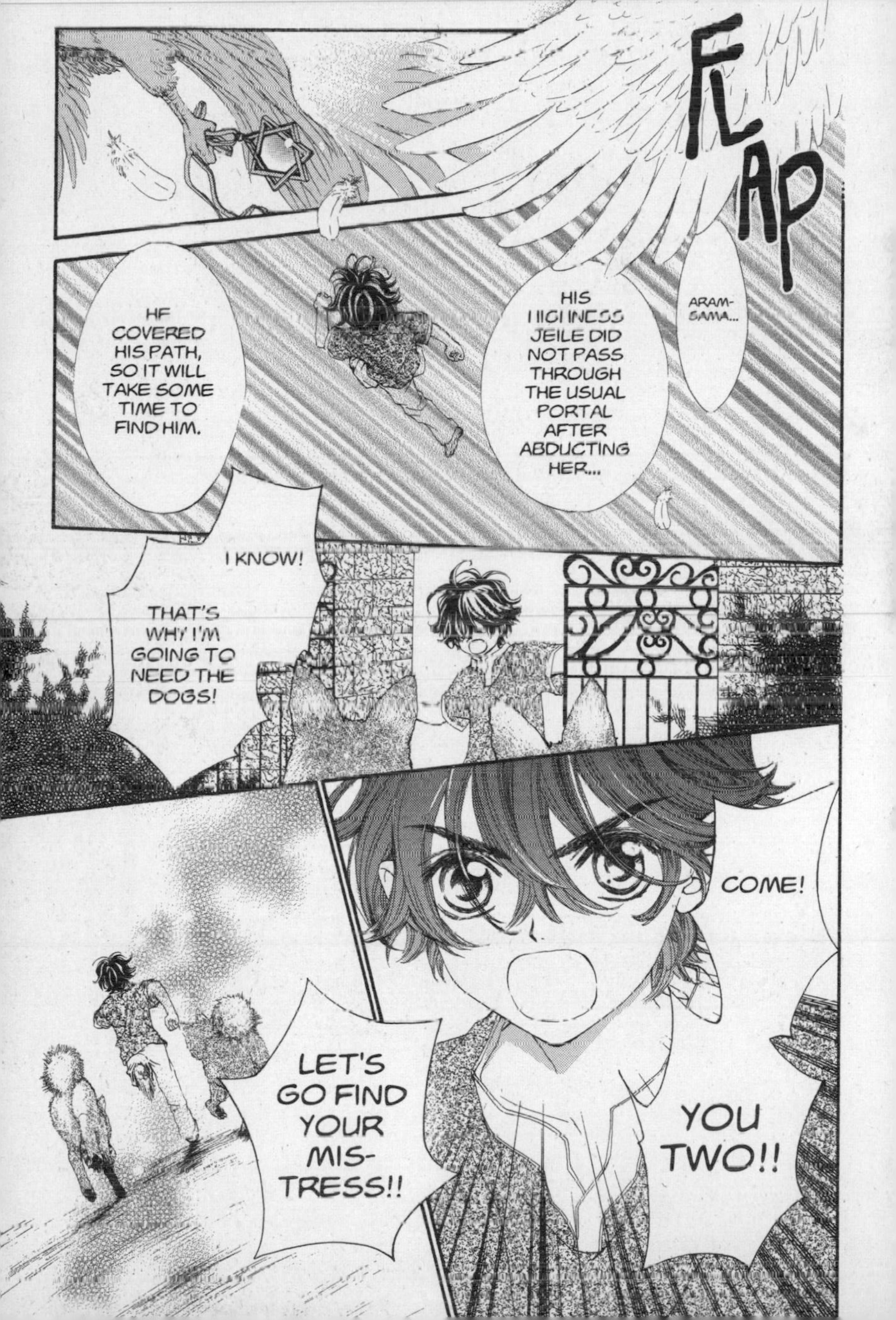
FLAP
ARAM-SAMA...
HIS HIGHNESS JEILE DID NOT PASS THROUGH THE USUAL PORTAL AFTER ABDUCTING HER...
HE COVERED HIS PATH, SO IT WILL TAKE SOME TIME TO FIND HIM.
I KNOW!
THAT'S WHY I'M GOING TO NEED THE DOGS!
COME!
YOU TWO!!
LET'S GO FIND YOUR MIS-TRESS!!

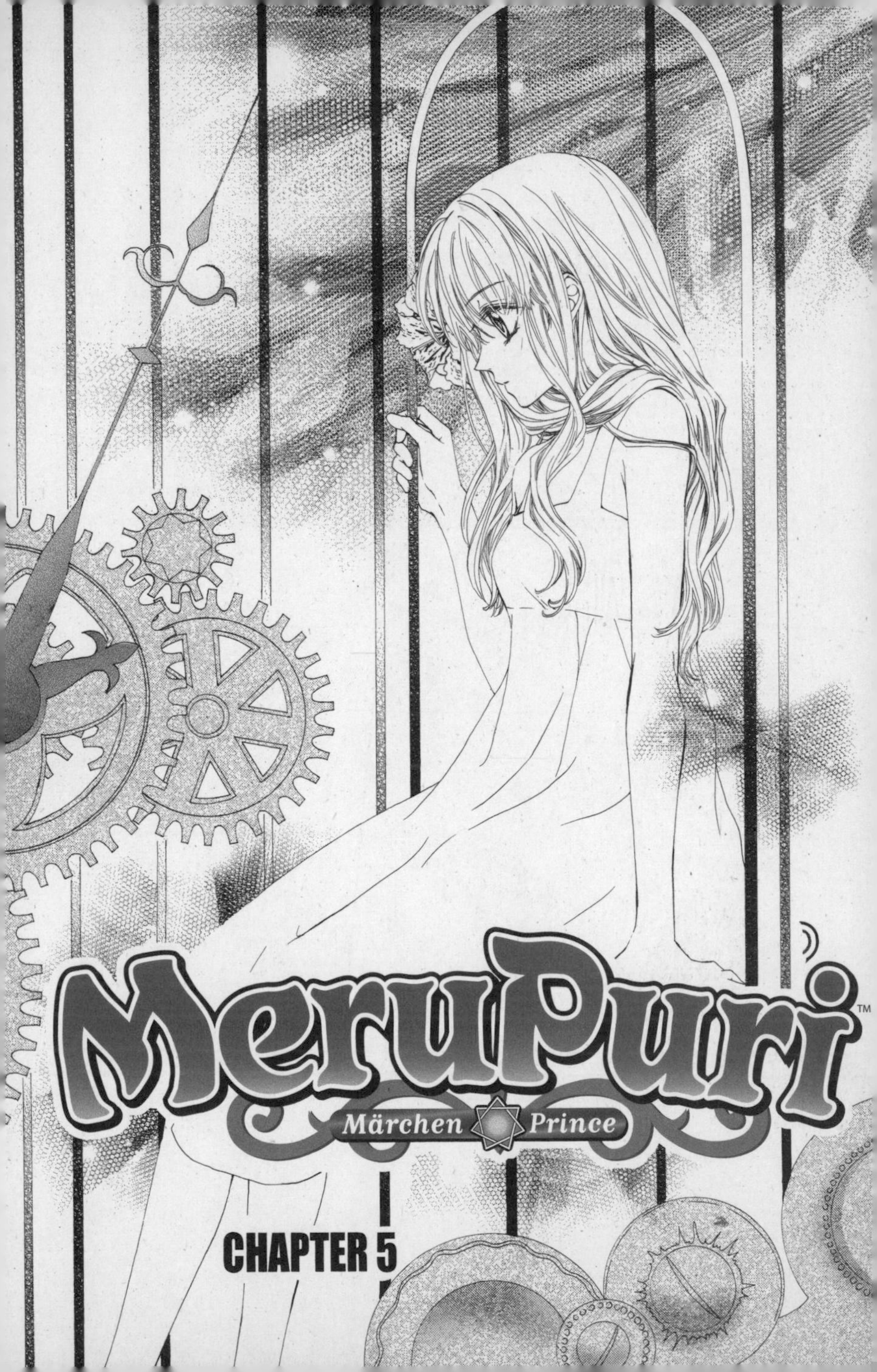
MeruPuri™
Märchen Prince
CHAPTER 5

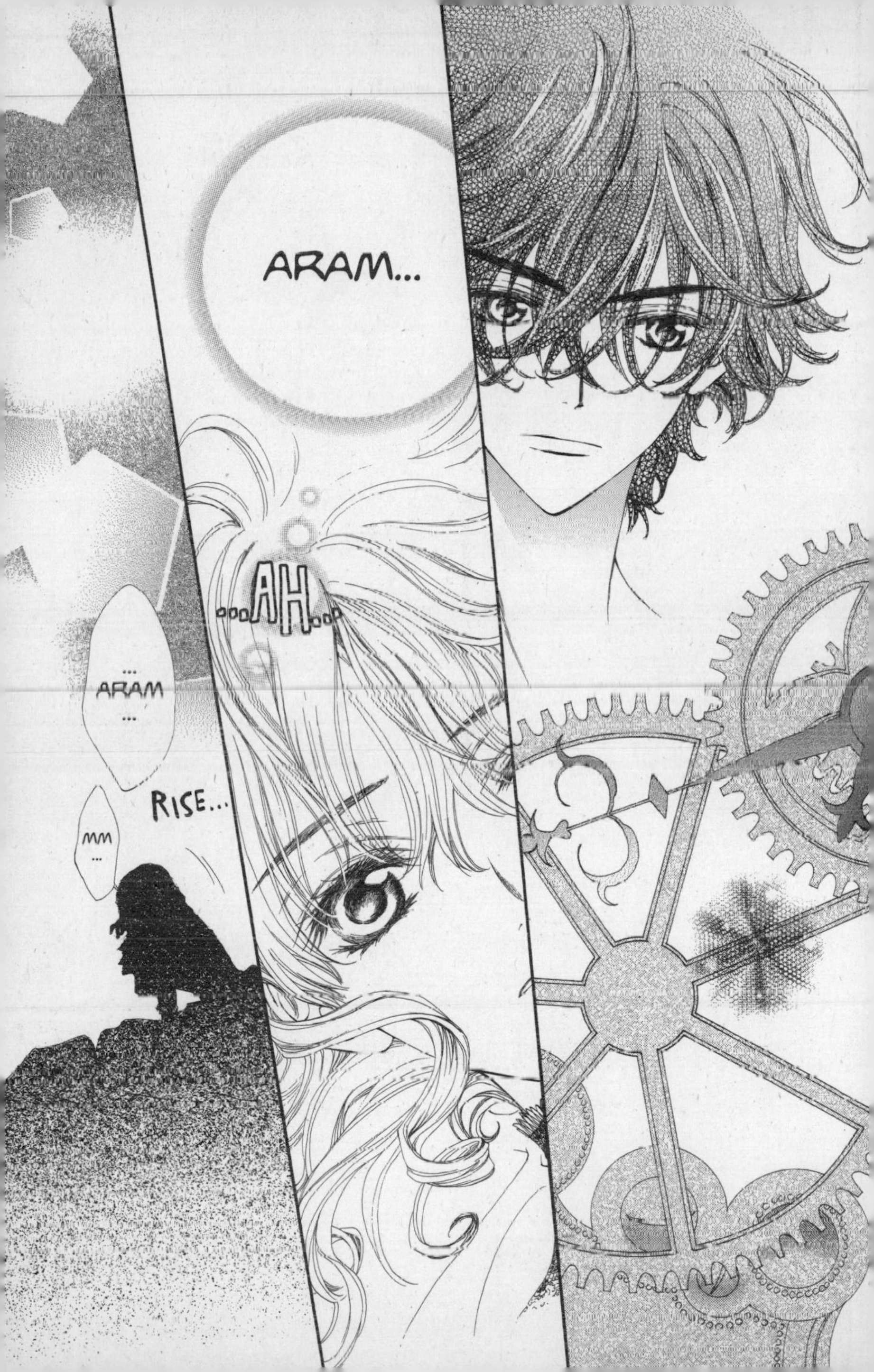
ARAM...
...AH...
...ARAM...
RISE...
MM...

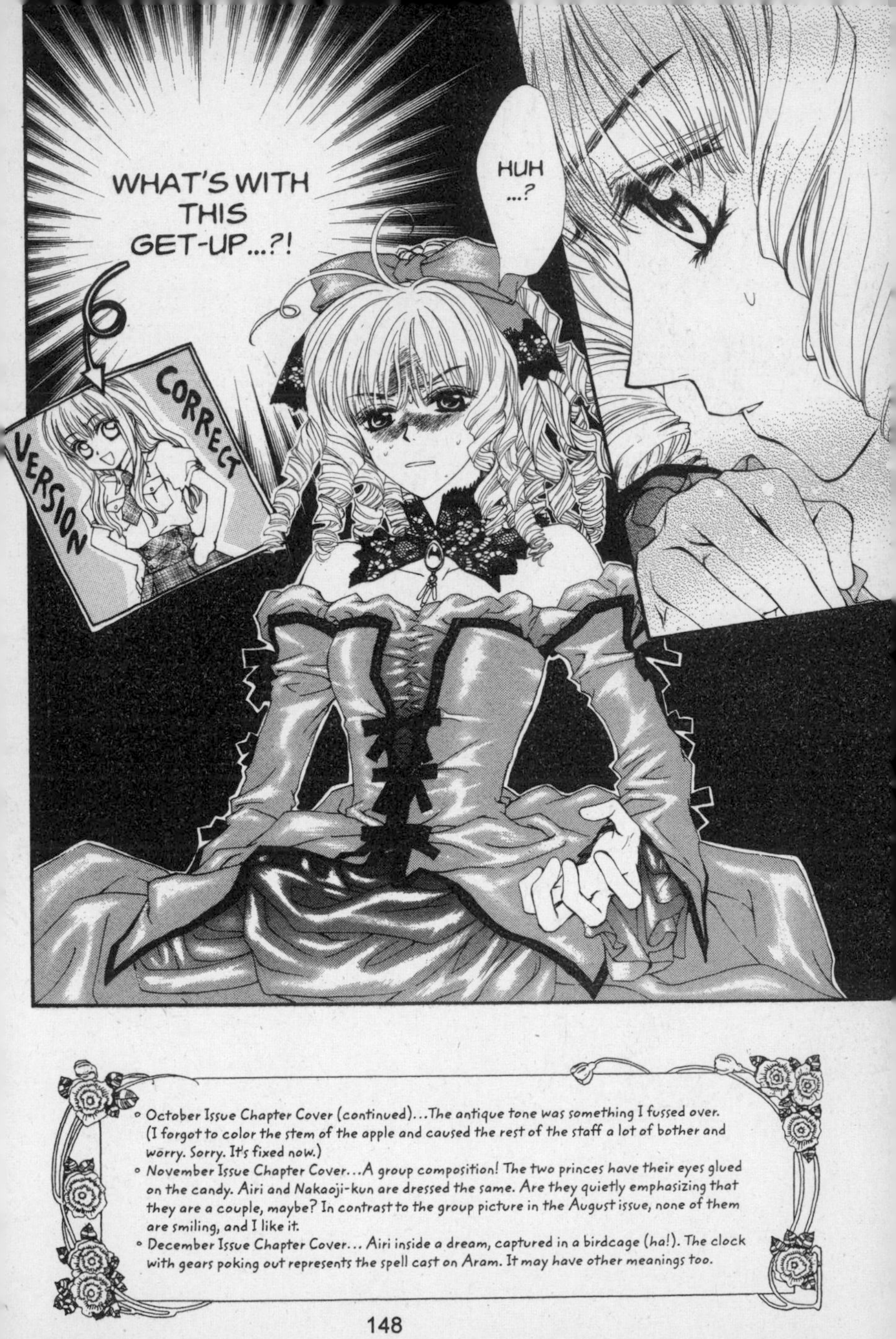
HUH ...?
WHAT'S WITH THIS GET-UP...?!
CORRECT VERSION

- October Issue Chapter Cover (continued)...The antique tone was something I fussed over. (I forgot to color the stem of the apple and caused the rest of the staff a lot of bother and worry. Sorry. It's fixed now.)
- November Issue Chapter Cover...A group composition! The two princes have their eyes glued on the candy. Airi and Nakaoji-kun are dressed the same. Are they quietly emphasizing that they are a couple, maybe? In contrast to the group picture in the August issue, none of them are smiling, and I like it.
- December Issue Chapter Cover... Airi inside a dream, captured in a birdcage (ha!). The clock with gears poking out represents the spell cast on Aram. It may have other meanings too.

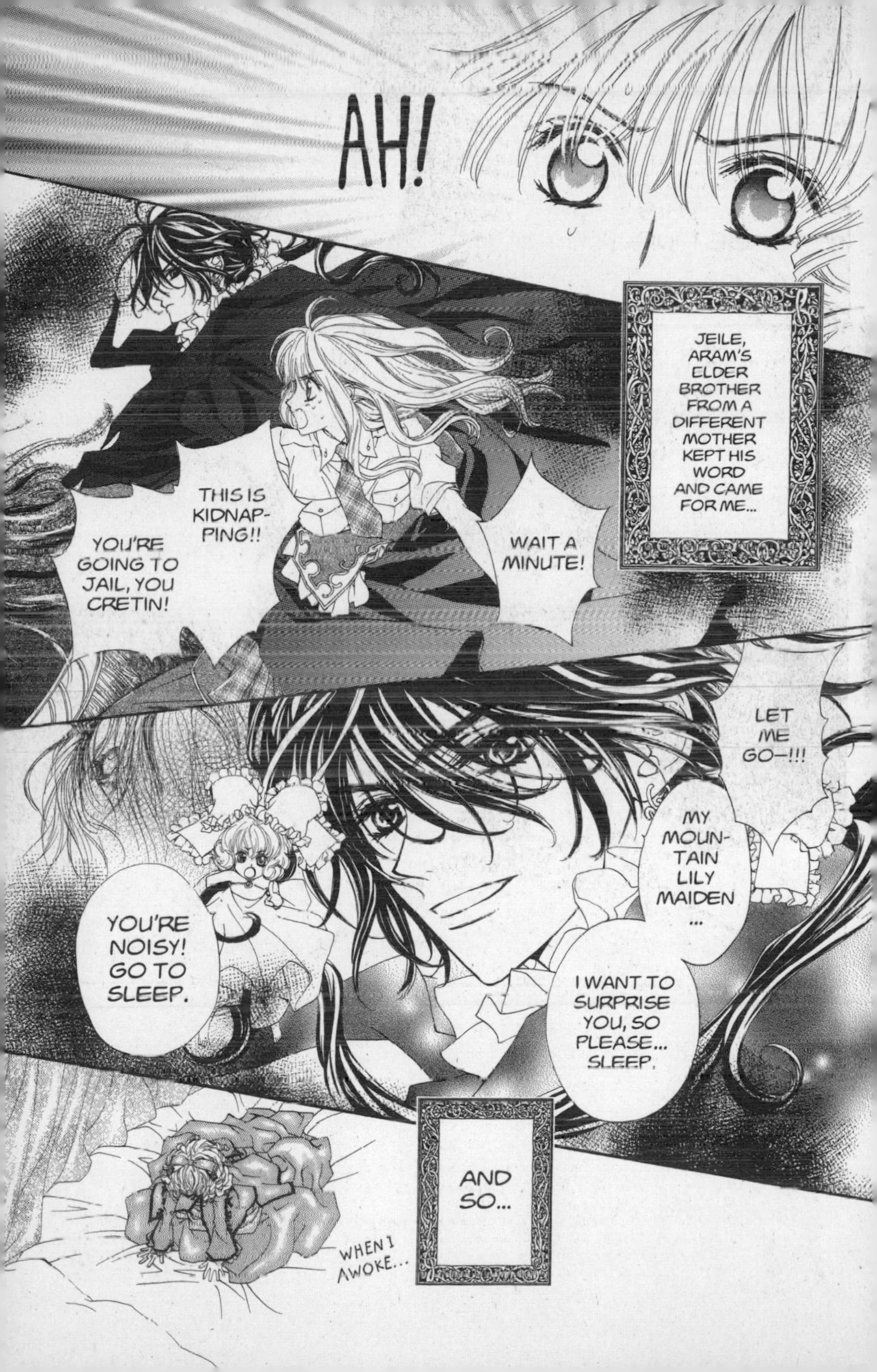
AH!
JEILE, ARAM'S ELDER BROTHER FROM A DIFFERENT MOTHER KEPT HIS WORD AND CAME FOR ME...
WAIT A MINUTE!
THIS IS KIDNAPPING!!
YOU'RE GOING TO JAIL, YOU CRETIN!
LET ME GO—!!!
MY MOUNTAIN LILY MAIDEN...
I WANT TO SURPRISE YOU, SO PLEASE... SLEEP.
YOU'RE NOISY! GO TO SLEEP.
AND SO...
WHEN I AWOKE...

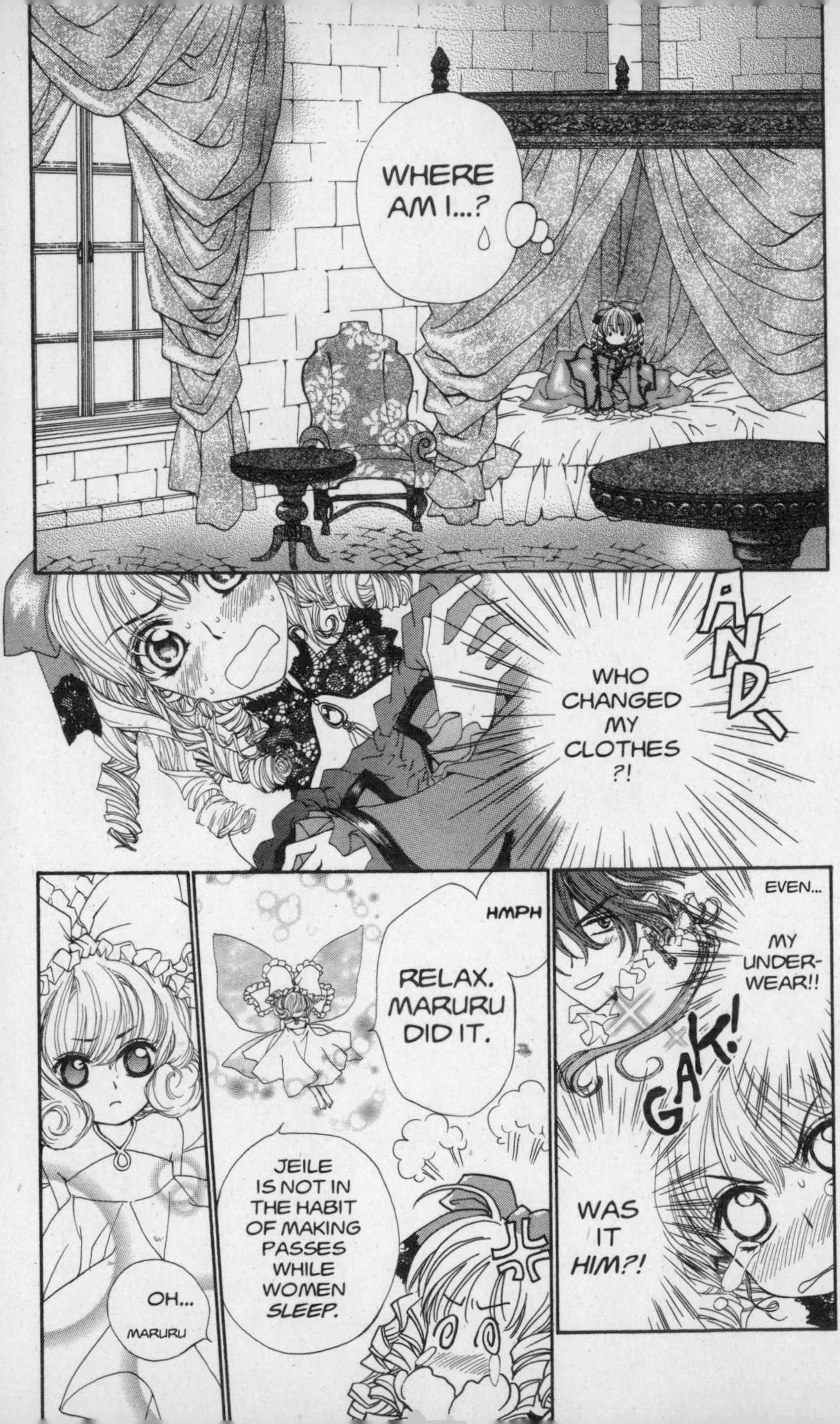
WHERE AM I...?
AND,
WHO CHANGED MY CLOTHES ?!
EVEN...
MY UNDERWEAR!!
GAK!
WAS IT HIM?!
HMPH
RELAX. MARURU DID IT.
JEILE IS NOT IN THE HABIT OF MAKING PASSES WHILE WOMEN SLEEP.
OH...
MARURU

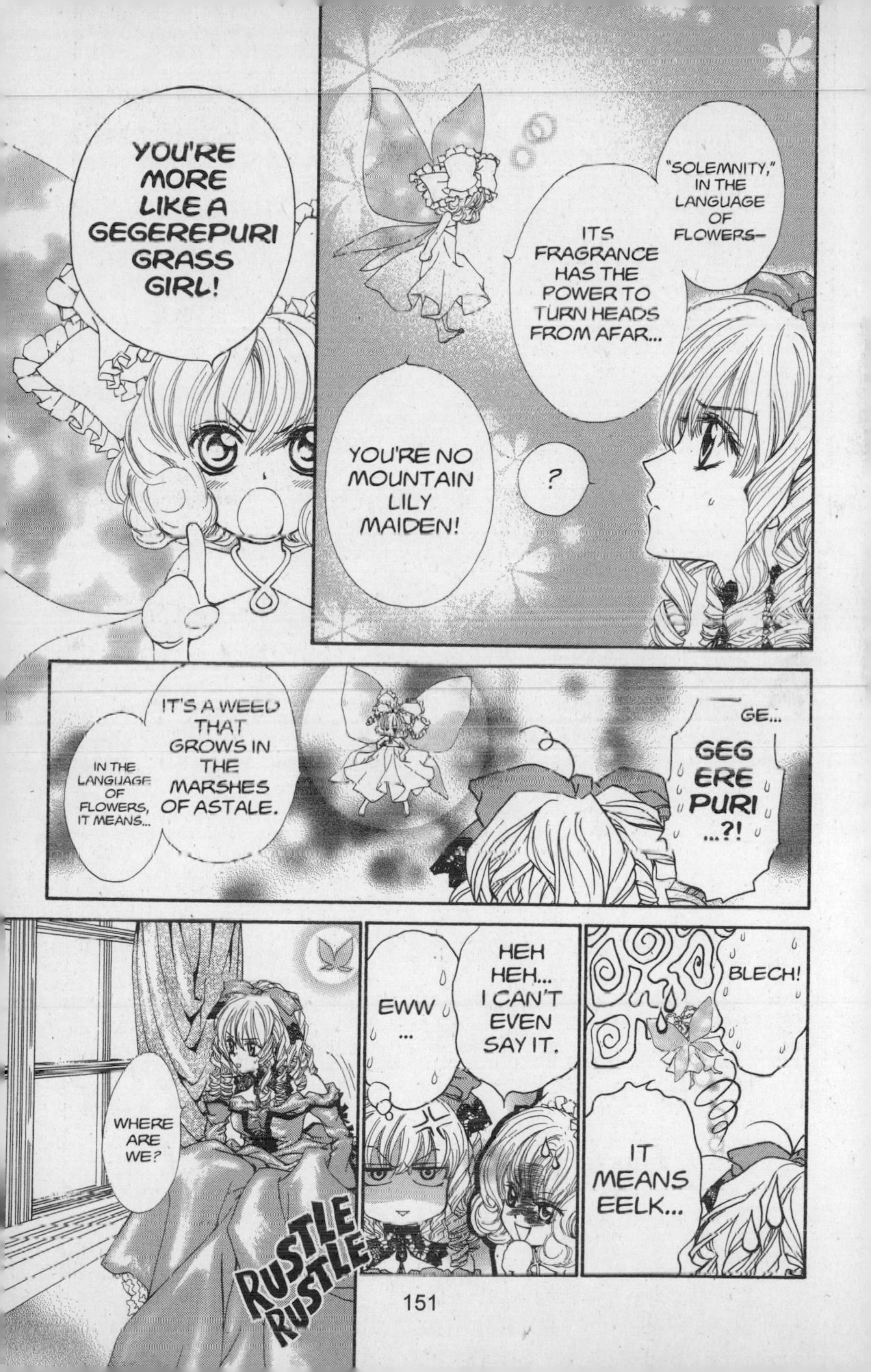
"SOLEMNITY," IN THE LANGUAGE OF FLOWERS—
ITS FRAGRANCE HAS THE POWER TO TURN HEADS FROM AFAR...
?
YOU'RE NO MOUNTAIN LILY MAIDEN!
YOU'RE MORE LIKE A GEGEREPURI GRASS GIRL!
GE... GEG ERE PURI ...?!
IT'S A WEED THAT GROWS IN THE MARSHES OF ASTALE.
IN THE LANGUAGE OF FLOWERS, IT MEANS...
BLECH!
IT MEANS EELK...
HEH HEH... I CAN'T EVEN SAY IT.
EWW ...
WHERE ARE WE?
RUSTLE RUSTLE

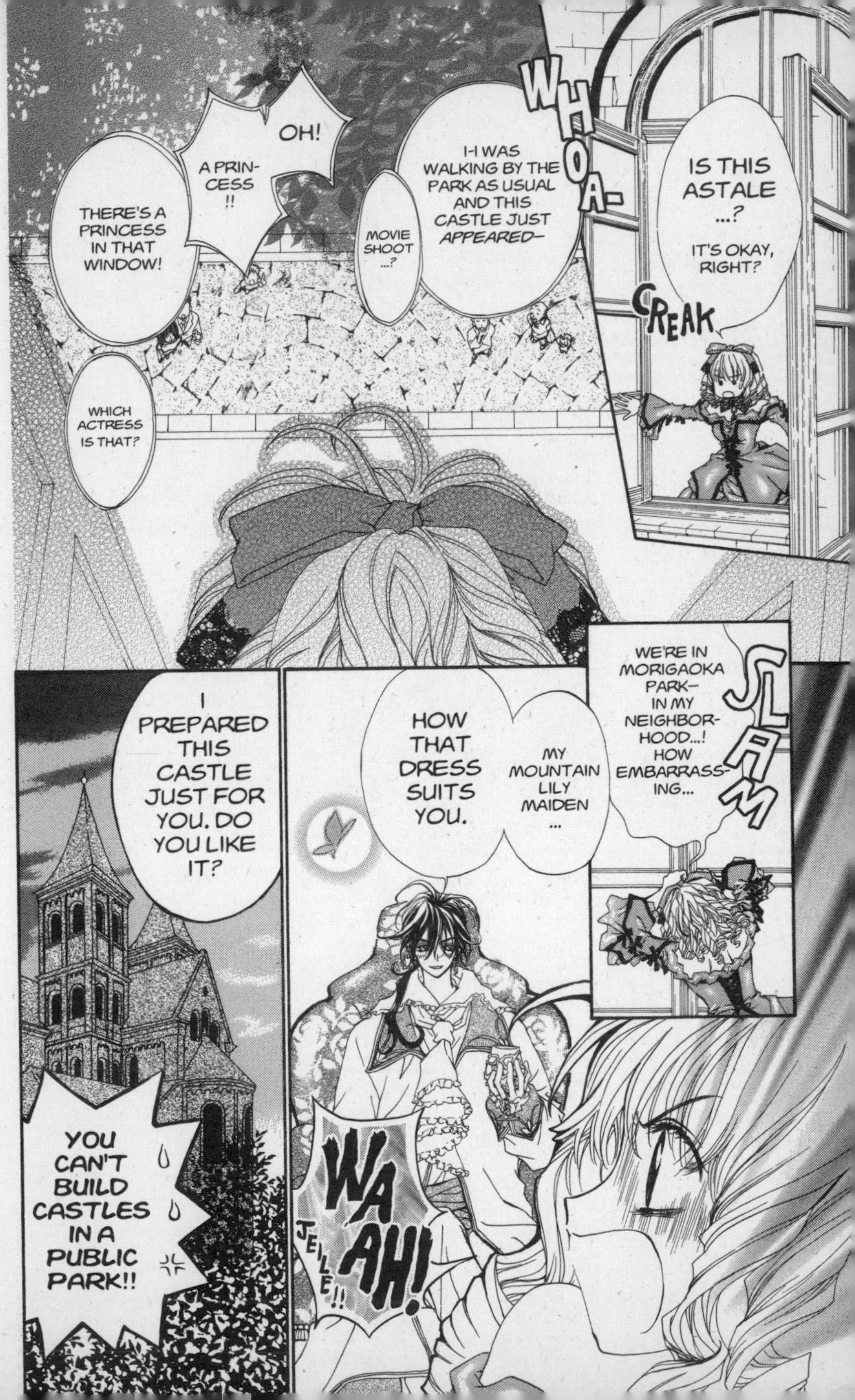
WHOA-
IS THIS ASTALE ...?
IT'S OKAY, RIGHT?
CREAK
I-I WAS WALKING BY THE PARK AS USUAL AND THIS CASTLE JUST APPEARED—
MOVIE SHOOT ...?
OH!
A PRIN-CESS !!
THERE'S A PRINCESS IN THAT WINDOW!
WHICH ACTRESS IS THAT?
WE'RE IN MORIGAOKA PARK— IN MY NEIGHBOR-HOOD...! HOW EMBARRASS-ING...
SLAM
MY MOUNTAIN LILY MAIDEN ...
HOW THAT DRESS SUITS YOU.
WAAH!
JEILE!!
I PREPARED THIS CASTLE JUST FOR YOU. DO YOU LIKE IT?
YOU CAN'T BUILD CASTLES IN A PUBLIC PARK!!

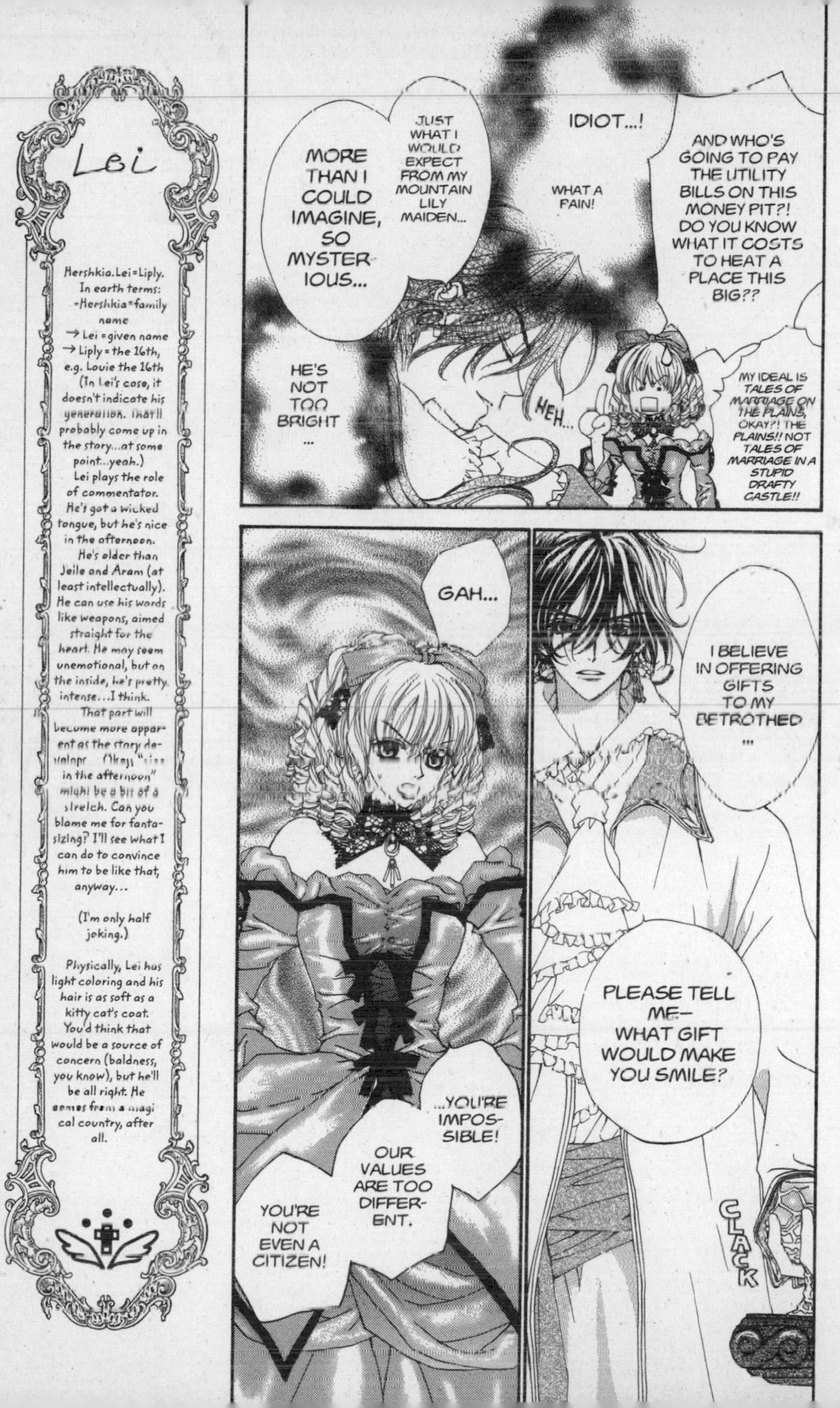
AND WHO'S GOING TO PAY THE UTILITY BILLS ON THIS MONEY PIT?! DO YOU KNOW WHAT IT COSTS TO HEAT A PLACE THIS BIG??
IDIOT...!
JUST WHAT I WOULD EXPECT FROM MY MOUNTAIN LILY MAIDEN...
WHAT A PAIN!
MORE THAN I COULD IMAGINE, SO MYSTERIOUS...
MY IDEAL IS TALES OF MARRIAGE ON THE PLAINS, OKAY?! THE PLAINS!! NOT TALES OF MARRIAGE IN A STUPID DRAFTY CASTLE!!
HEH...
HE'S NOT TOO BRIGHT...
I BELIEVE IN OFFERING GIFTS TO MY BETROTHED...
PLEASE TELL ME— WHAT GIFT WOULD MAKE YOU SMILE?
CLACK
GAH...
...YOU'RE IMPOSSIBLE!
OUR VALUES ARE TOO DIFFERENT.
YOU'RE NOT EVEN A CITIZEN!

Lei

Hershkia.Lei=Liply. In earth terms:
-Hershkia=family name
→ Lei=given name
→ Liply=the 16th, e.g. Louie the 16th (In Lei's case, it doesn't indicate his generation. That'll probably come up in the story...at some point...yeah.)

Lei plays the role of commentator. He's got a wicked tongue, but he's nice in the afternoon. He's older than Jeile and Aram (at least intellectually). He can use his words like weapons, aimed straight for the heart. He may seem unemotional, but on the inside, he's pretty intense...I think. That part will become more apparent as the story developes. Okay, "nice in the afternoon" might be a bit of a stretch. Can you blame me for fantasizing? I'll see what I can do to convince him to be like that, anyway...

(I'm only half joking.)

Physically, Lei has light coloring and his hair is as soft as a kitty cat's coat. You'd think that would be a source of concern (baldness, you know), but he'll be all right. He comes from a magical country, after all.

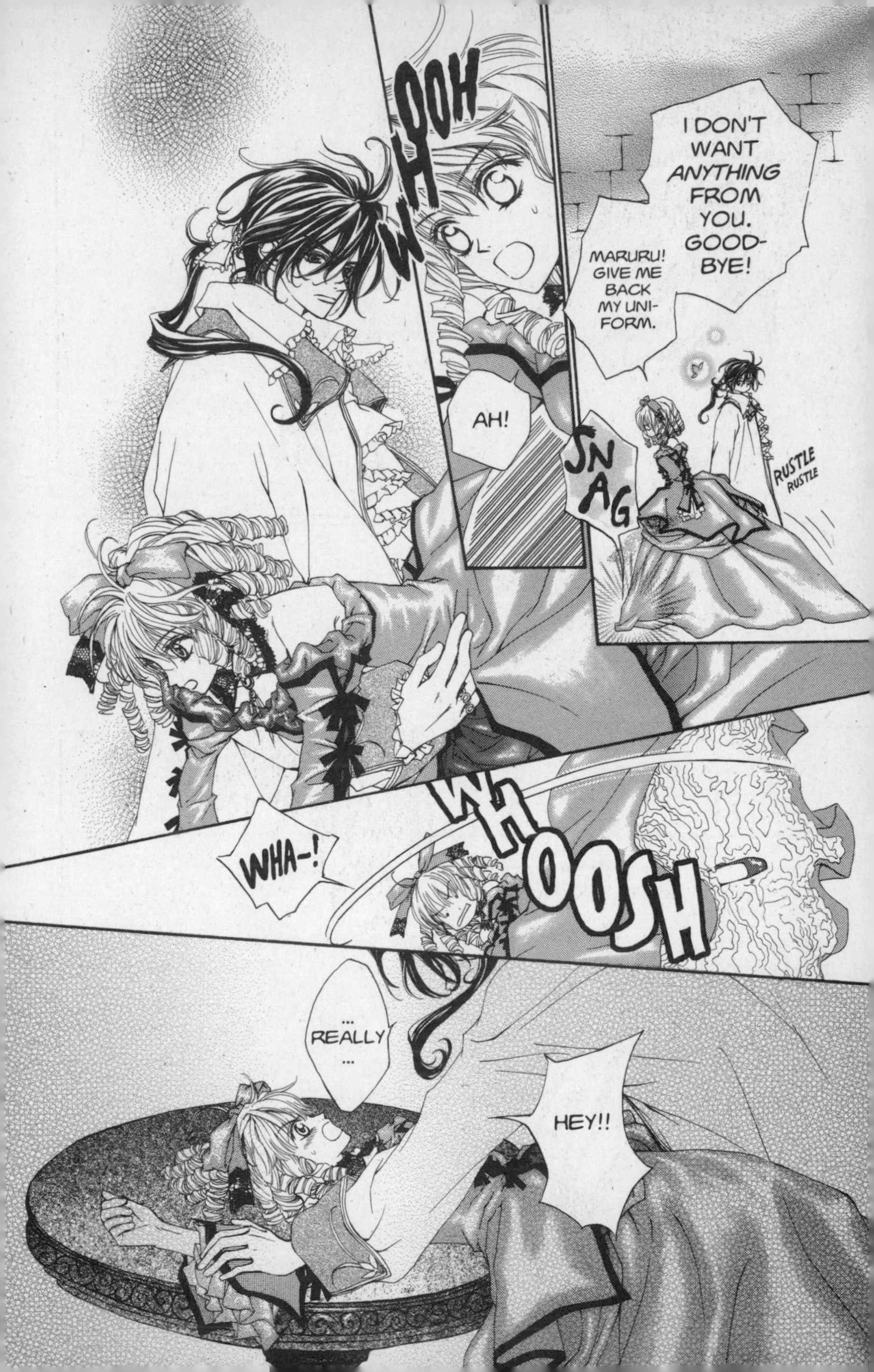
I DON'T WANT ANYTHING FROM YOU. GOOD-BYE!
MARURU! GIVE ME BACK MY UNI-FORM.
RUSTLE RUSTLE
SNAG
WHOOSH
AH!
WHOOSH
WHA-!
HEY!!
... REALLY ...

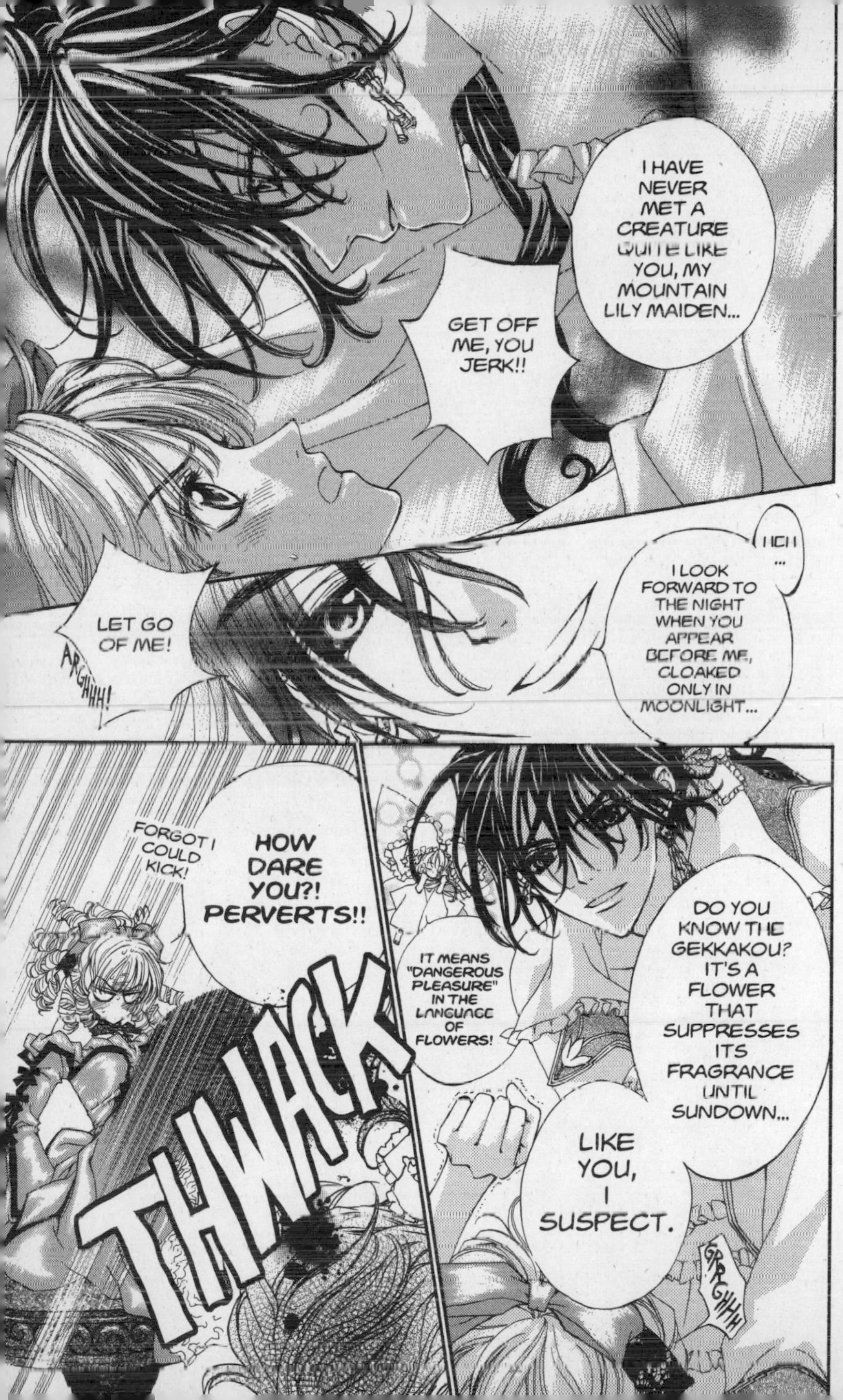
I HAVE NEVER MET A CREATURE QUITE LIKE YOU, MY MOUNTAIN LILY MAIDEN...
GET OFF ME, YOU JERK!!
HEH...
I LOOK FORWARD TO THE NIGHT WHEN YOU APPEAR BEFORE ME, CLOAKED ONLY IN MOONLIGHT...
LET GO OF ME!
ARGHHH!
DO YOU KNOW THE GEKKAKOU? IT'S A FLOWER THAT SUPPRESSES ITS FRAGRANCE UNTIL SUNDOWN...
LIKE YOU, I SUSPECT.
GRRGHHH
IT MEANS "DANGEROUS PLEASURE" IN THE LANGUAGE OF FLOWERS!
HOW DARE YOU?! PERVERTS!!
FORGOT I COULD KICK!
THWACK

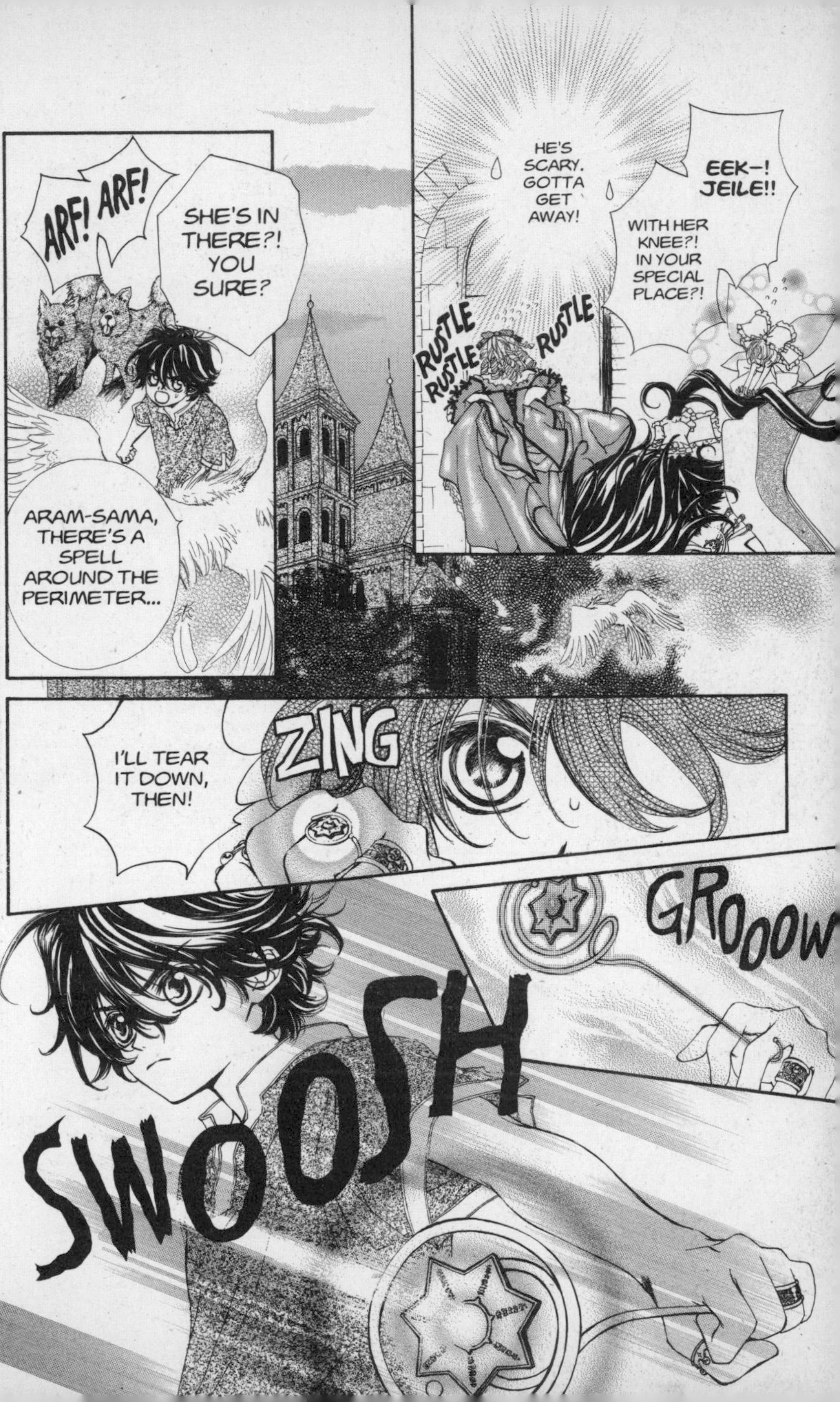
EEK—! JEILE!!
WITH HER KNEE?! IN YOUR SPECIAL PLACE?!
HE'S SCARY. GOTTA GET AWAY!
RUSTLE
RUSTLE
RUSTLE
RUSTLE
SHE'S IN THERE?! YOU SURE?
ARF! ARF!
ARAM-SAMA, THERE'S A SPELL AROUND THE PERIMETER...
ZING
I'LL TEAR IT DOWN, THEN!
GROOOW
SWOOSH

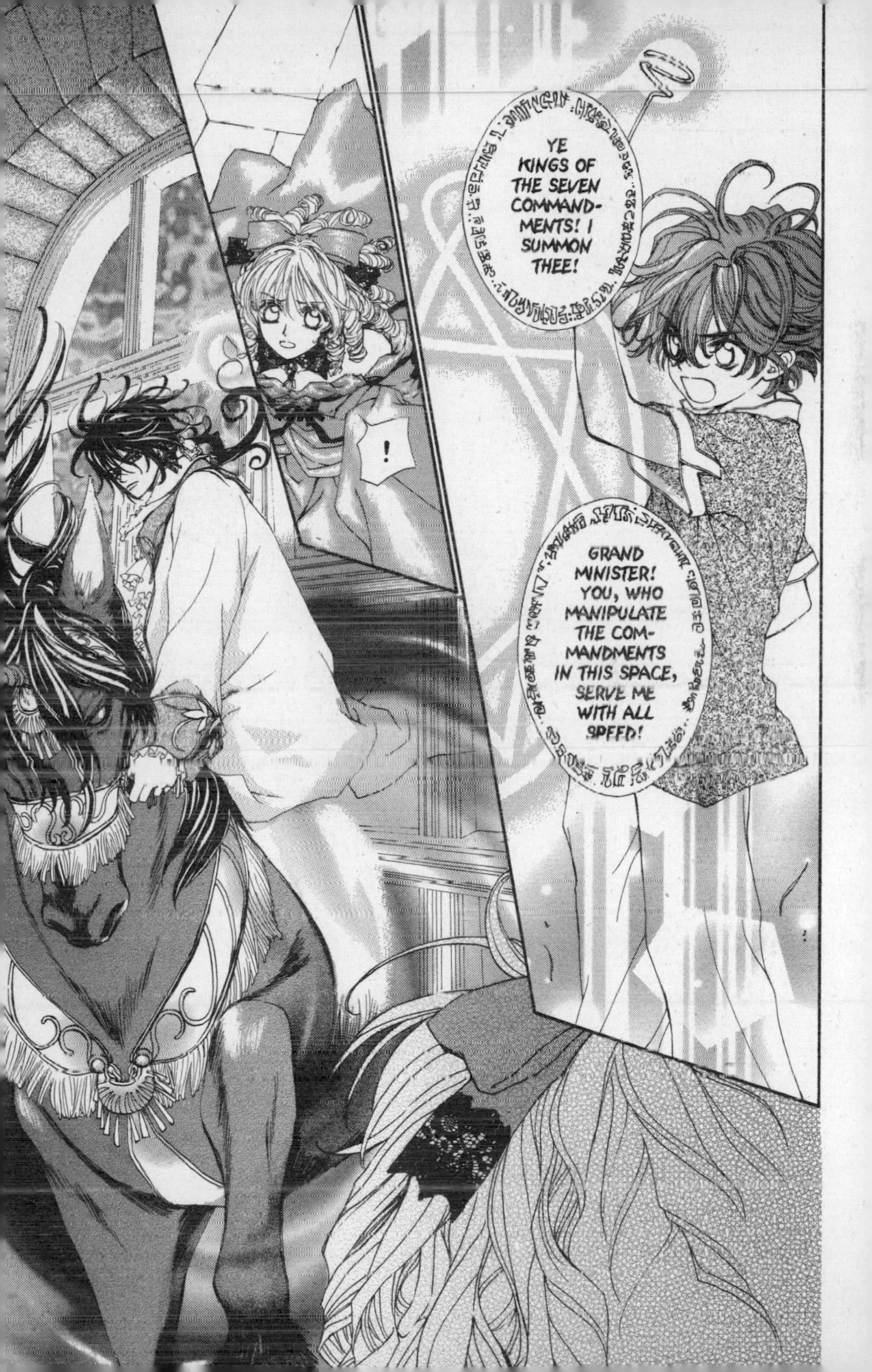
YE KINGS OF THE SEVEN COMMANDMENTS! I SUMMON THEE!
GRAND MINISTER! YOU, WHO MANIPULATE THE COMMANDMENTS IN THIS SPACE, SERVE ME WITH ALL SPEED!
!

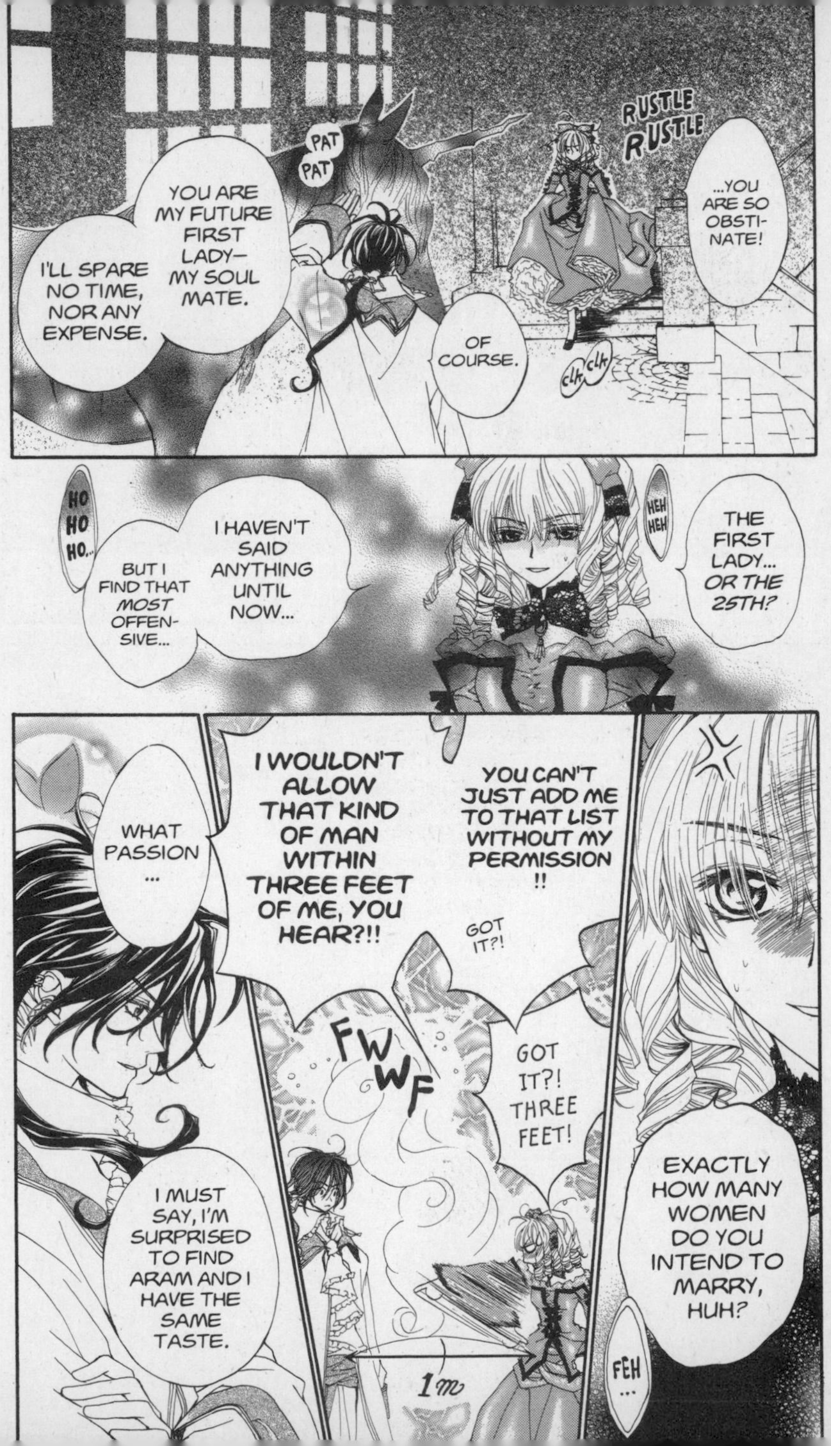
RUSTLE RUSTLE
...YOU ARE SO OBSTINATE!
CLK CLK
OF COURSE.
PAT PAT
YOU ARE MY FUTURE FIRST LADY— MY SOUL MATE.
I'LL SPARE NO TIME, NOR ANY EXPENSE.
HEH HEH
THE FIRST LADY... OR THE 25TH?
I HAVEN'T SAID ANYTHING UNTIL NOW...
BUT I FIND THAT *MOST* OFFENSIVE...
HO HO HO...
EXACTLY HOW MANY WOMEN DO YOU INTEND TO MARRY, HUH?
FEH...
YOU CAN'T JUST ADD ME TO THAT LIST WITHOUT MY PERMISSION!!
I WOULDN'T ALLOW THAT KIND OF MAN WITHIN THREE FEET OF ME, YOU HEAR?!!
GOT IT?!
FWWF
GOT IT?! THREE FEET!
1m
WHAT PASSION...
I MUST SAY, I'M SURPRISED TO FIND ARAM AND I HAVE THE SAME TASTE.

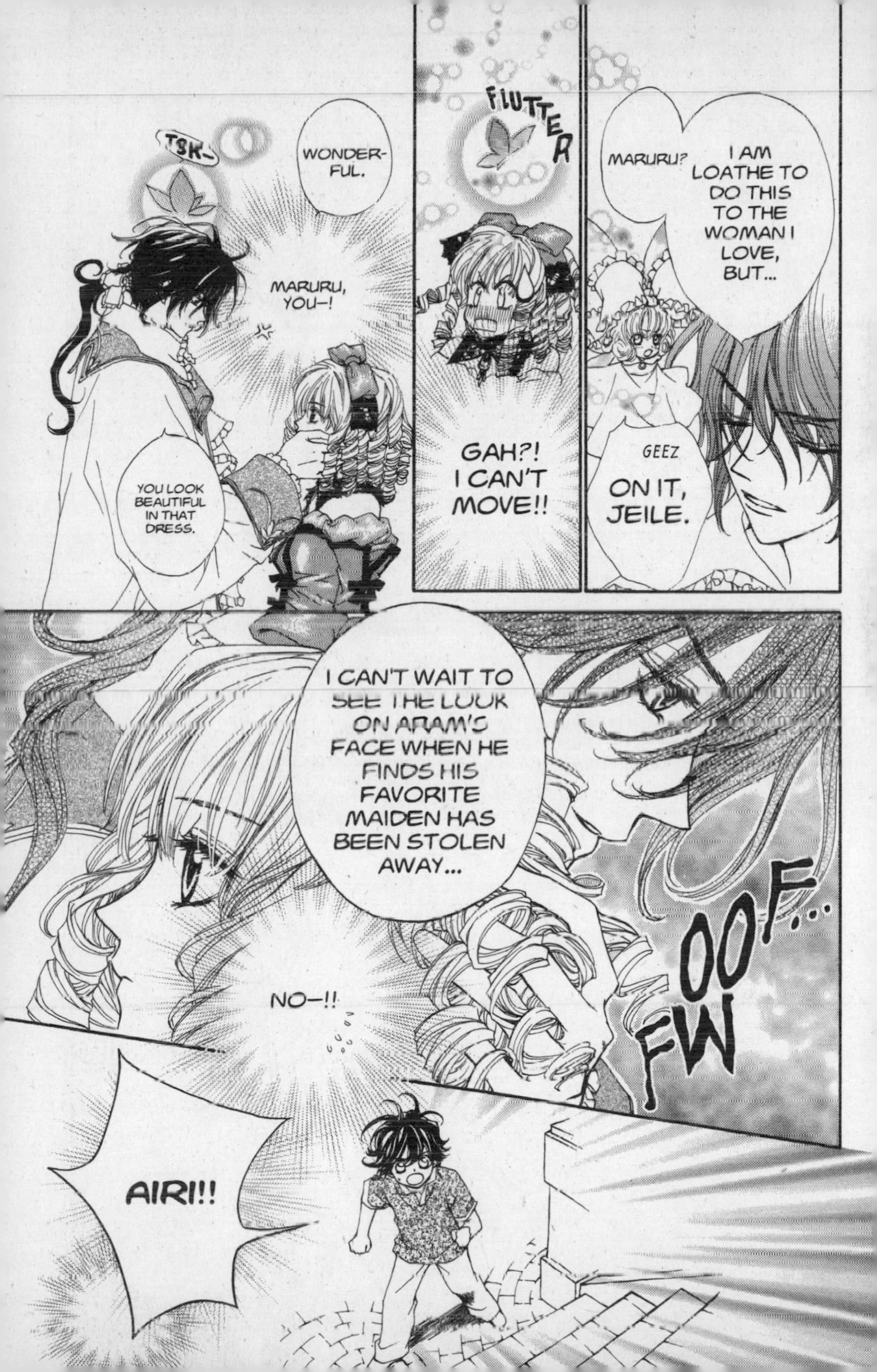
I AM LOATHE TO DO THIS TO THE WOMAN I LOVE, BUT...
MARURU?
GEEZ
ON IT, JEILE.
FLUTTER
GAH?! I CAN'T MOVE!!
WONDERFUL.
TSK-
MARURU, YOU-!
YOU LOOK BEAUTIFUL IN THAT DRESS.
I CAN'T WAIT TO SEE THE LOOK ON ARAM'S FACE WHEN HE FINDS HIS FAVORITE MAIDEN HAS BEEN STOLEN AWAY...
FWOOF...
NO-!!
AIRI!!

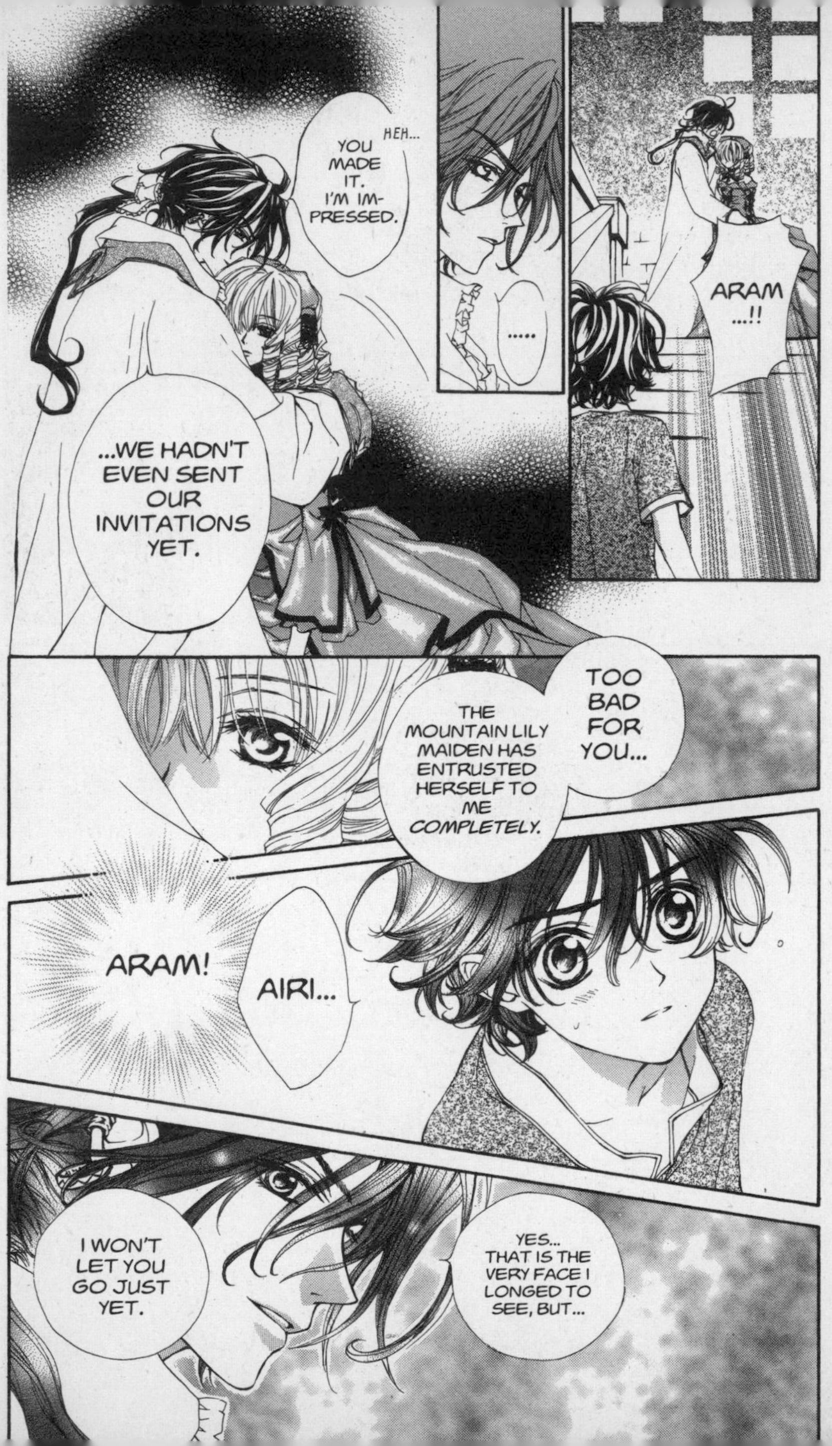
ARAM ...!!
.....
HEH... YOU MADE IT. I'M IM-PRESSED.
...WE HADN'T EVEN SENT OUR INVITATIONS YET.
TOO BAD FOR YOU...
THE MOUNTAIN LILY MAIDEN HAS ENTRUSTED HERSELF TO ME COMPLETELY.
AIRI...
ARAM!
YES... THAT IS THE VERY FACE I LONGED TO SEE, BUT...
I WON'T LET YOU GO JUST YET.

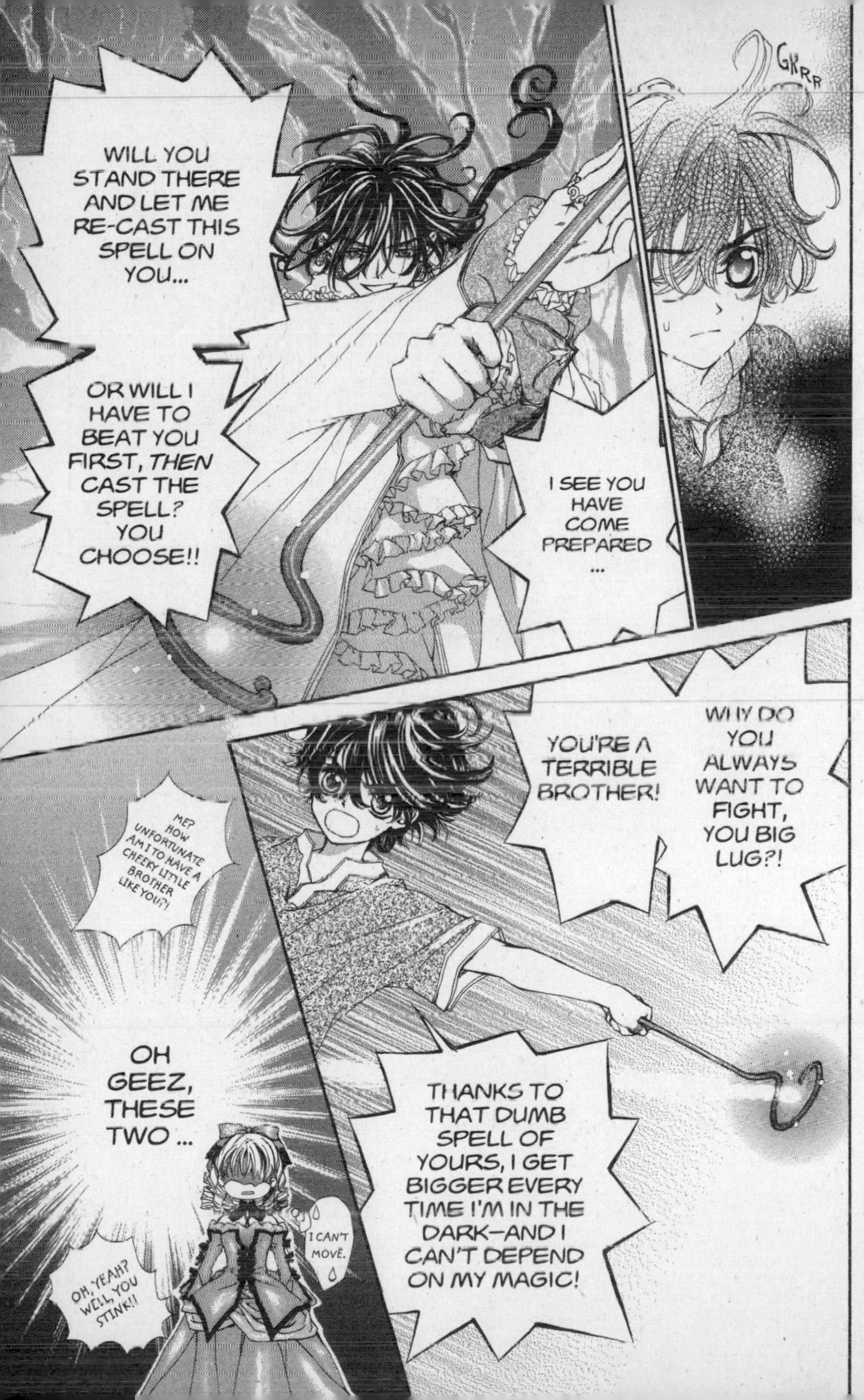
GKRRR
I SEE YOU HAVE COME PREPARED ...
WILL YOU STAND THERE AND LET ME RE-CAST THIS SPELL ON YOU...
OR WILL I HAVE TO BEAT YOU FIRST, *THEN* CAST THE SPELL? YOU CHOOSE!!
WHY DO YOU ALWAYS WANT TO FIGHT, YOU BIG LUG?!
YOU'RE A TERRIBLE BROTHER!
THANKS TO THAT DUMB SPELL OF YOURS, I GET BIGGER EVERY TIME I'M IN THE DARK—AND I CAN'T DEPEND ON MY MAGIC!
ME? HOW UNFORTUNATE AM I TO HAVE A CHEEKY LITTLE BROTHER LIKE YOU?!
OH GEEZ, THESE TWO ...
I CAN'T MOVE.
OH, YEAH? WELL, YOU STINK!!

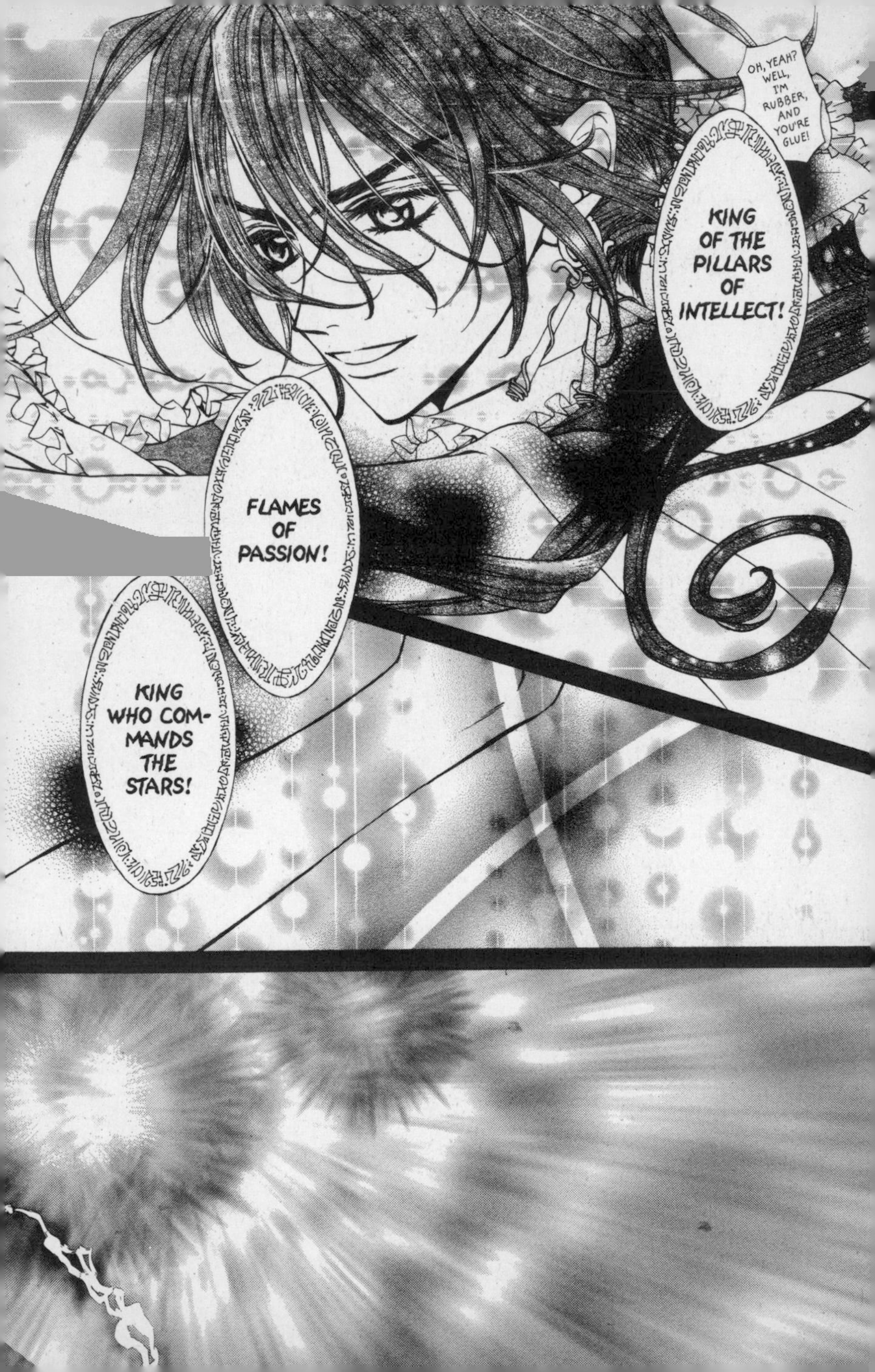
OH, YEAH? WELL, I'M RUBBER, AND YOU'RE GLUE!
KING OF THE PILLARS OF INTELLECT!
FLAMES OF PASSION!
KING WHO COMMANDS THE STARS!

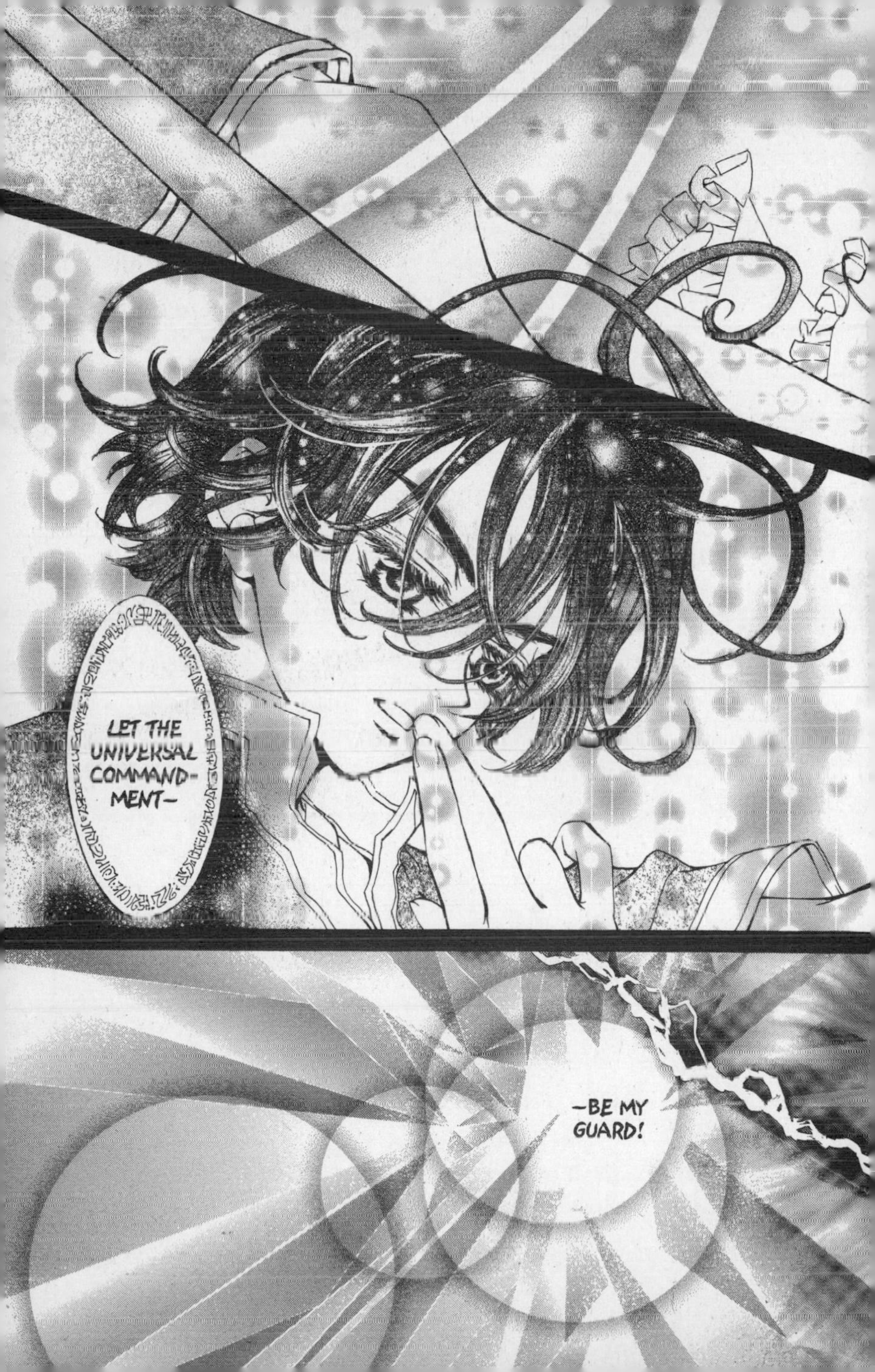
LET THE UNIVERSAL COMMAND-MENT–
–BE MY GUARD!

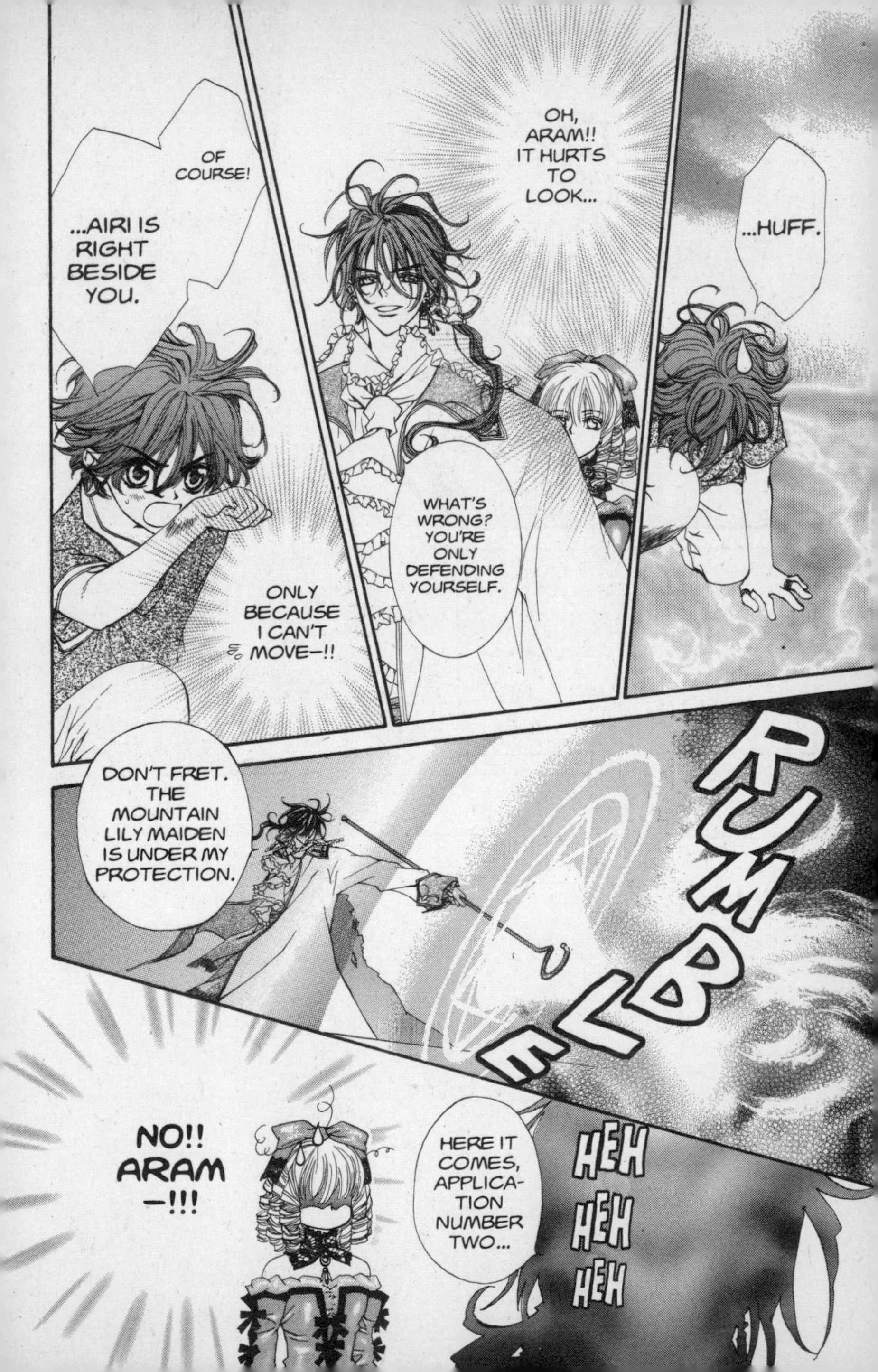
...HUFF.
OH, ARAM!! IT HURTS TO LOOK...
WHAT'S WRONG? YOU'RE ONLY DEFENDING YOURSELF.
OF COURSE!
...AIRI IS RIGHT BESIDE YOU.
ONLY BECAUSE I CAN'T MOVE—!!
RUMBLE
DON'T FRET. THE MOUNTAIN LILY MAIDEN IS UNDER MY PROTECTION.
HEH HEH HEH
HERE IT COMES, APPLICATION NUMBER TWO...
NO!! ARAM—!!!

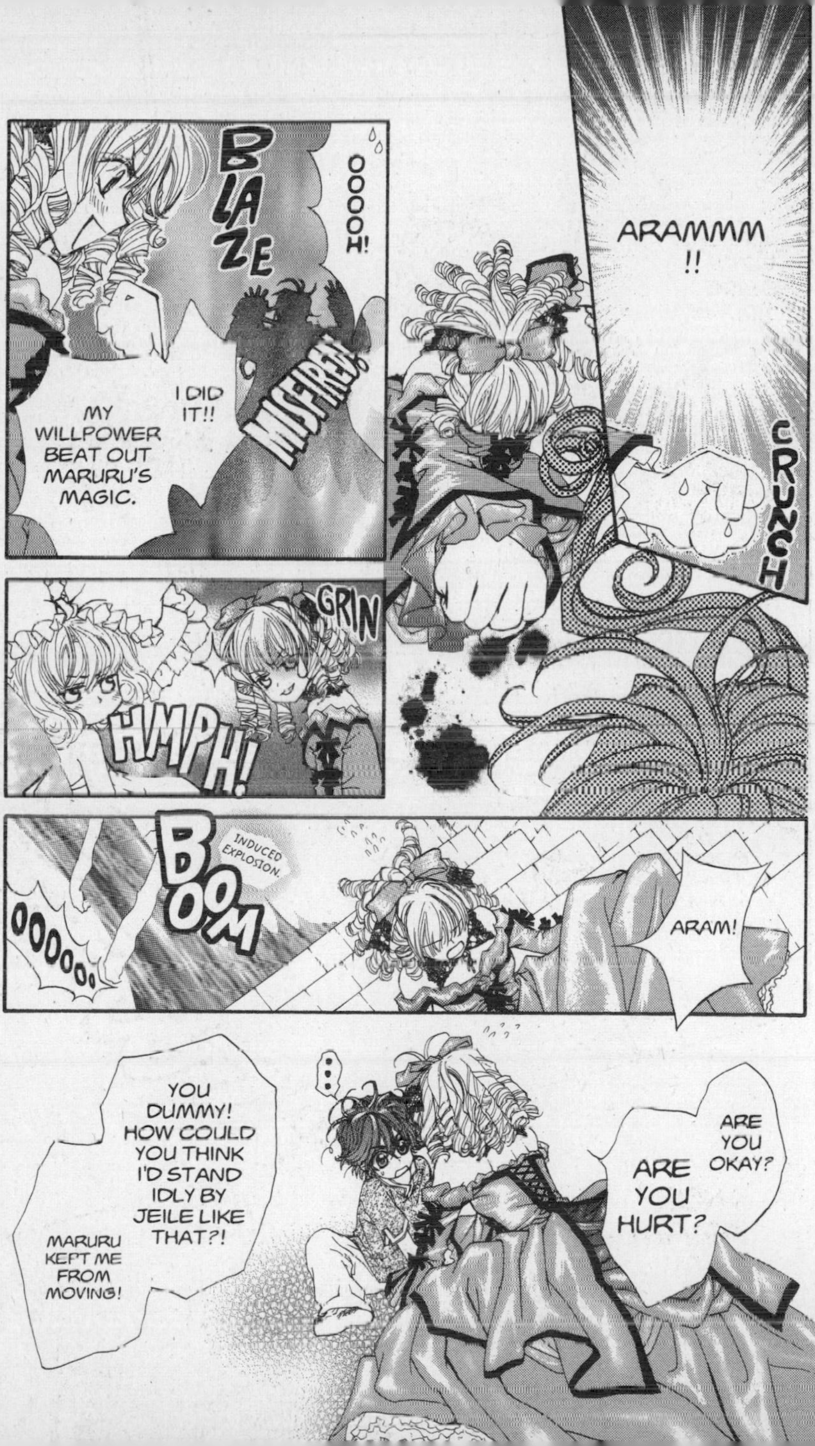
ARAMMM !!
CRUNCH
OOOOH!
BLAZE
I DID IT!!
MY WILLPOWER BEAT OUT MARURU'S MAGIC.
MISFIRED
GRIN
HMPH!
ARAM!
BOOM
INDUCED EXPLOSION.
OOOOOo
ARE YOU OKAY?
ARE YOU HURT?
...
YOU DUMMY! HOW COULD YOU THINK I'D STAND IDLY BY JEILE LIKE THAT?!
MARURU KEPT ME FROM MOVING!

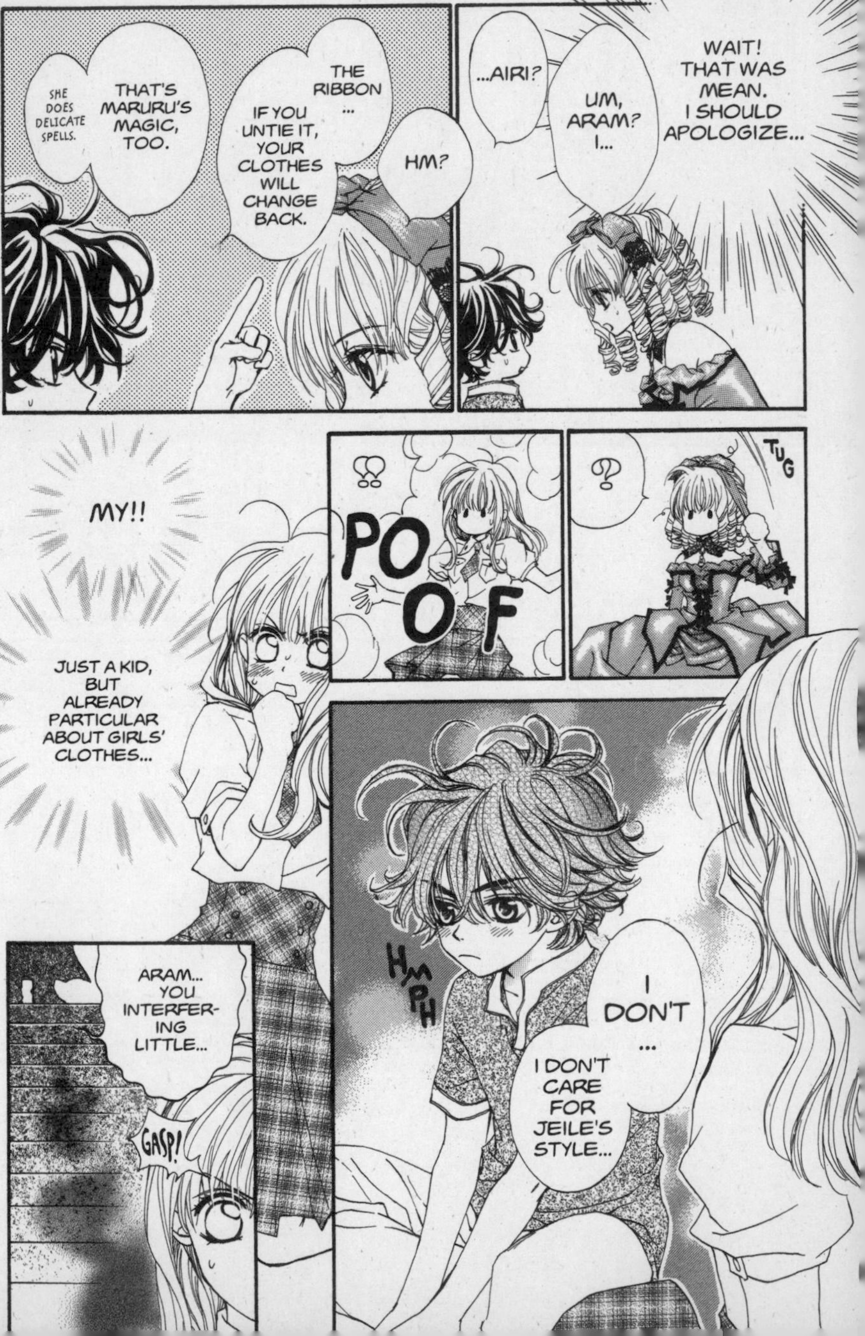
WAIT! THAT WAS MEAN. I SHOULD APOLOGIZE...
UM, ARAM? I...
...AIRI?
HM?
THE RIBBON ... IF YOU UNTIE IT, YOUR CLOTHES WILL CHANGE BACK.
THAT'S MARURU'S MAGIC, TOO.
SHE DOES DELICATE SPELLS.
TUG
POOF
HMPH
I DON'T ...
I DON'T CARE FOR JEILE'S STYLE...
MY!!
JUST A KID, BUT ALREADY PARTICULAR ABOUT GIRLS' CLOTHES...
ARAM... YOU INTERFER-ING LITTLE...
GASP!

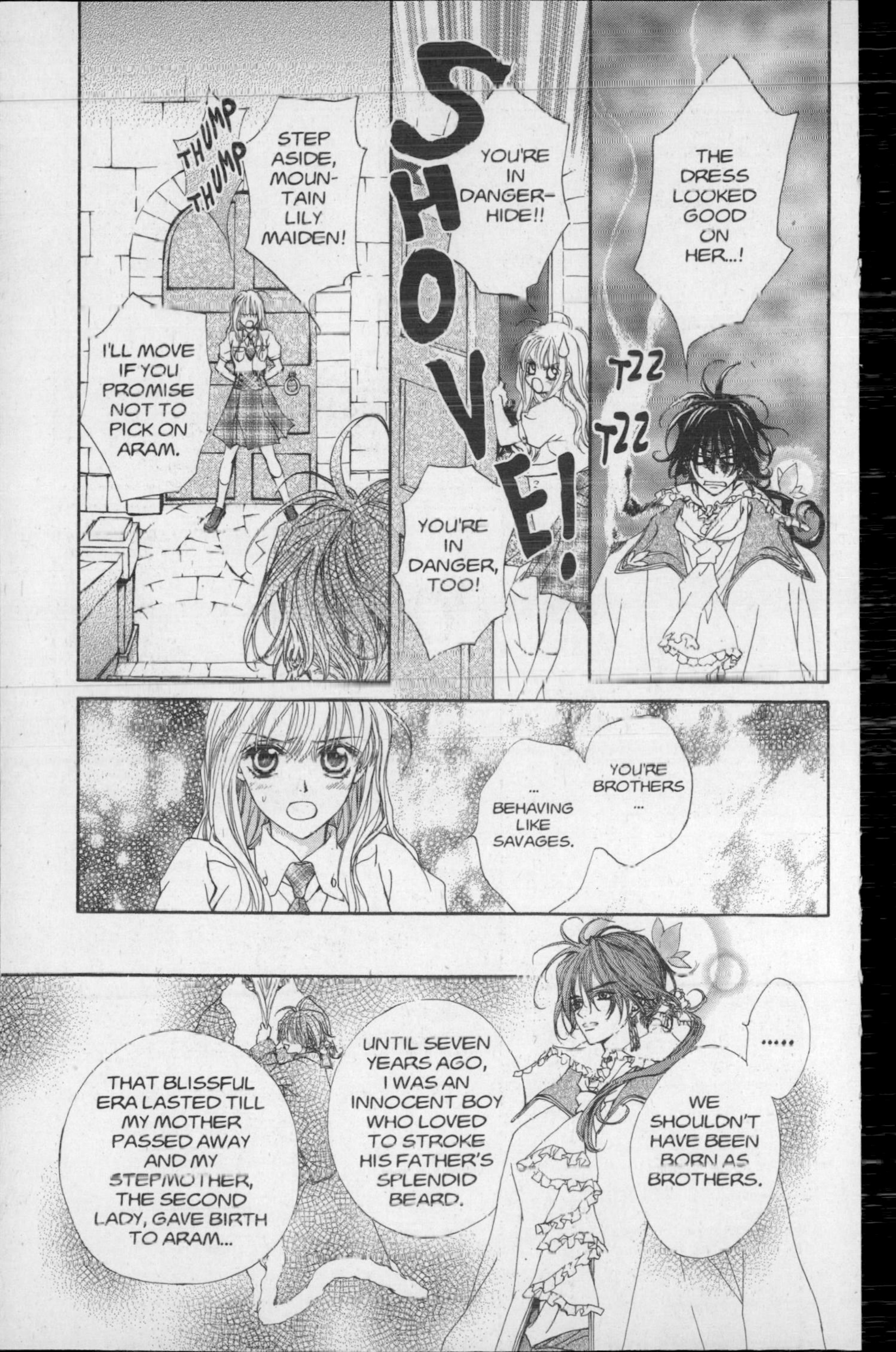
THE DRESS LOOKED GOOD ON HER...!
TZZ TZZ
SHOVE!
YOU'RE IN DANGER-HIDE!!
YOU'RE IN DANGER, TOO!
THUMP THUMP
STEP ASIDE, MOUNTAIN LILY MAIDEN!
I'LL MOVE IF YOU PROMISE NOT TO PICK ON ARAM.
YOU'RE BROTHERS ...
... BEHAVING LIKE SAVAGES.
......
WE SHOULDN'T HAVE BEEN BORN AS BROTHERS.
UNTIL SEVEN YEARS AGO, I WAS AN INNOCENT BOY WHO LOVED TO STROKE HIS FATHER'S SPLENDID BEARD.
THAT BLISSFUL ERA LASTED TILL MY MOTHER PASSED AWAY AND MY STEPMOTHER, THE SECOND LADY, GAVE BIRTH TO ARAM...

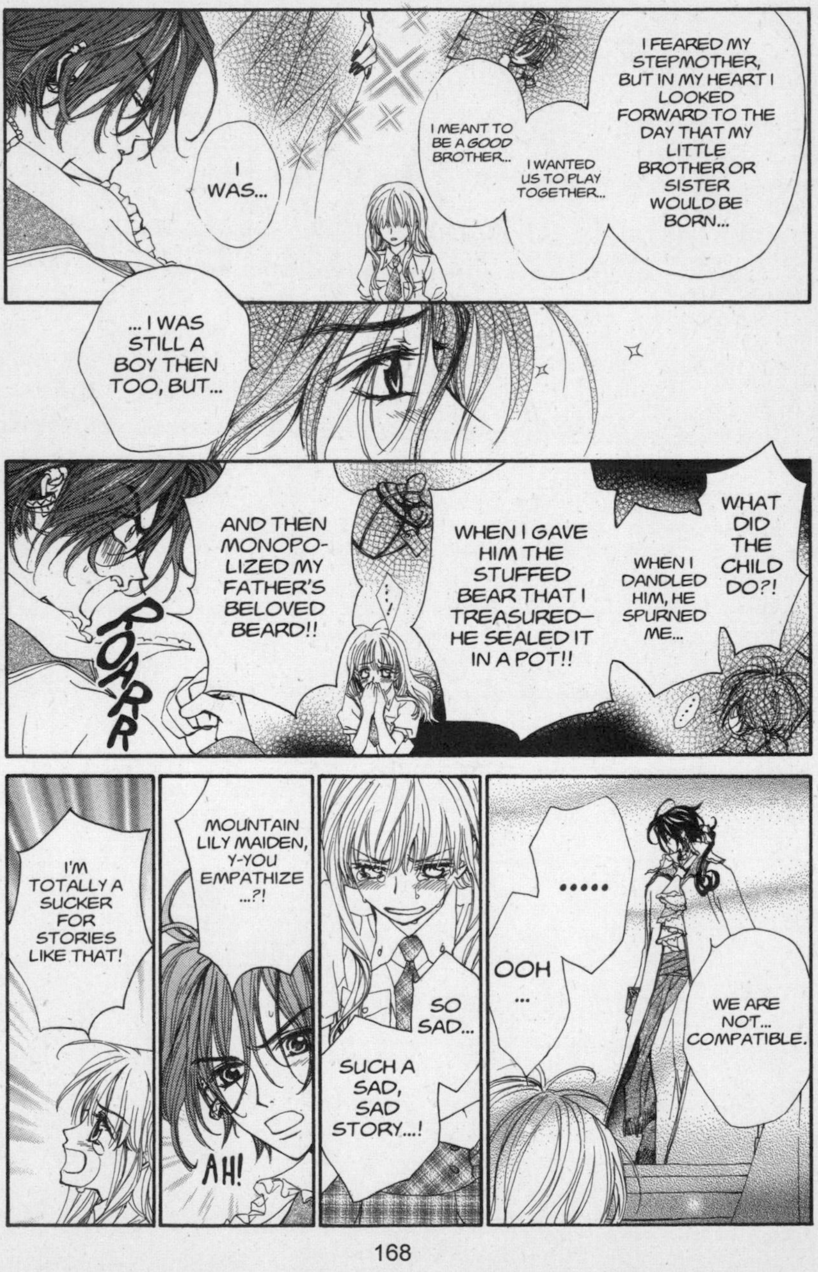
I FEARED MY STEPMOTHER, BUT IN MY HEART I LOOKED FORWARD TO THE DAY THAT MY LITTLE BROTHER OR SISTER WOULD BE BORN...
I WANTED US TO PLAY TOGETHER...
I MEANT TO BE A GOOD BROTHER...
I WAS...
... I WAS STILL A BOY THEN TOO, BUT...
WHAT DID THE CHILD DO?!
WHEN I DANDLED HIM, HE SPURNED ME...
WHEN I GAVE HIM THE STUFFED BEAR THAT I TREASURED— HE SEALED IT IN A POT!!
AND THEN MONOPOLIZED MY FATHER'S BELOVED BEARD!!
ROARR
.....
WE ARE NOT... COMPATIBLE.
OOH ...
SO SAD...
SUCH A SAD, SAD STORY...!
MOUNTAIN LILY MAIDEN, Y-YOU EMPATHIZE ...?!
AH!
I'M TOTALLY A SUCKER FOR STORIES LIKE THAT!

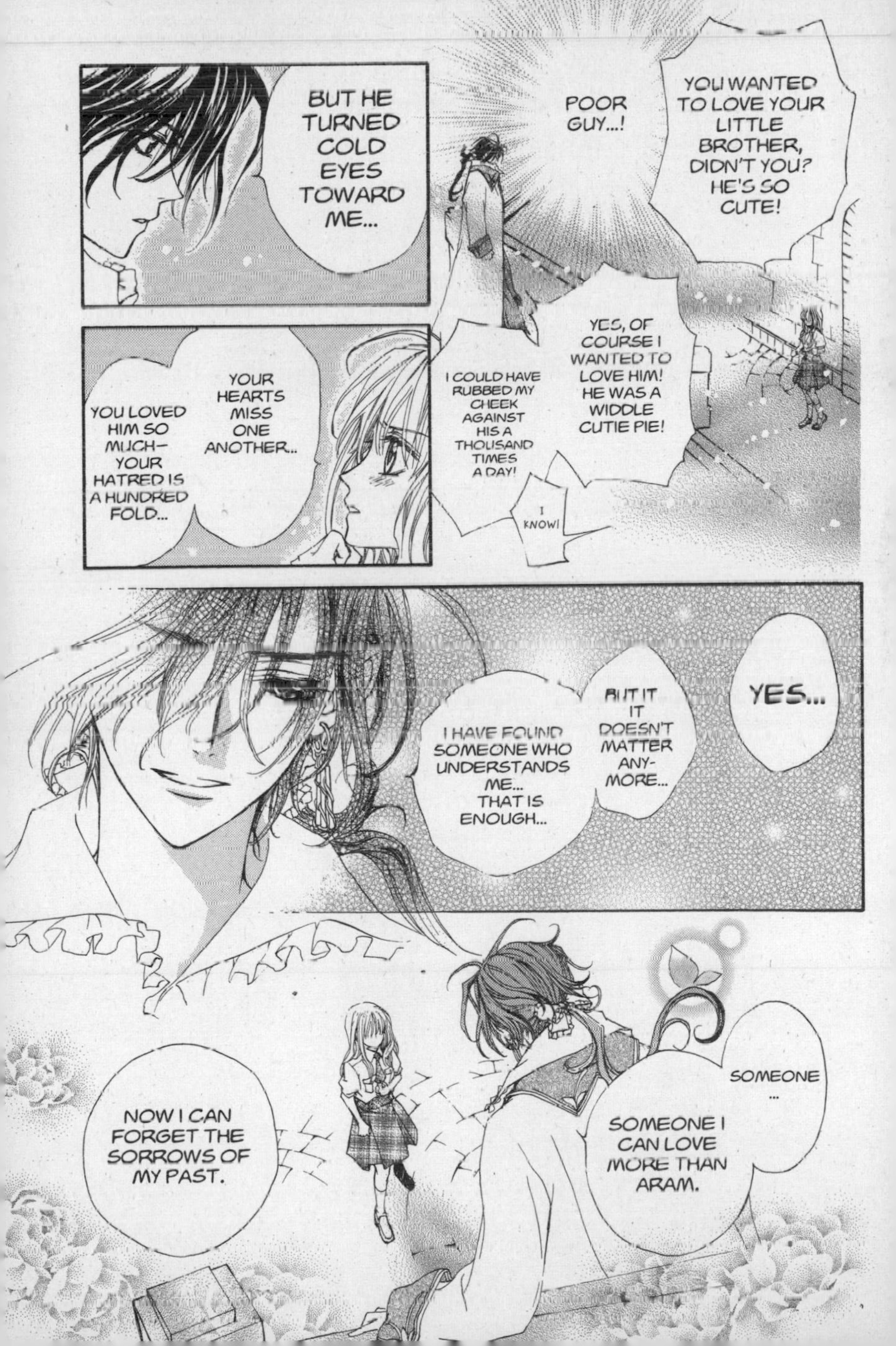
YOU WANTED TO LOVE YOUR LITTLE BROTHER, DIDN'T YOU? HE'S SO CUTE!
POOR GUY...!
YES, OF COURSE I WANTED TO LOVE HIM! HE WAS A WIDDLE CUTIE PIE!
I COULD HAVE RUBBED MY CHEEK AGAINST HIS A THOUSAND TIMES A DAY!
I KNOW!
BUT HE TURNED COLD EYES TOWARD ME...
YOUR HEARTS MISS ONE ANOTHER...
YOU LOVED HIM SO MUCH—YOUR HATRED IS A HUNDRED FOLD...
YES...
BUT IT IT DOESN'T MATTER ANY-MORE...
I HAVE FOUND SOMEONE WHO UNDERSTANDS ME... THAT IS ENOUGH...
SOMEONE ...
SOMEONE I CAN LOVE MORE THAN ARAM.
NOW I CAN FORGET THE SORROWS OF MY PAST.

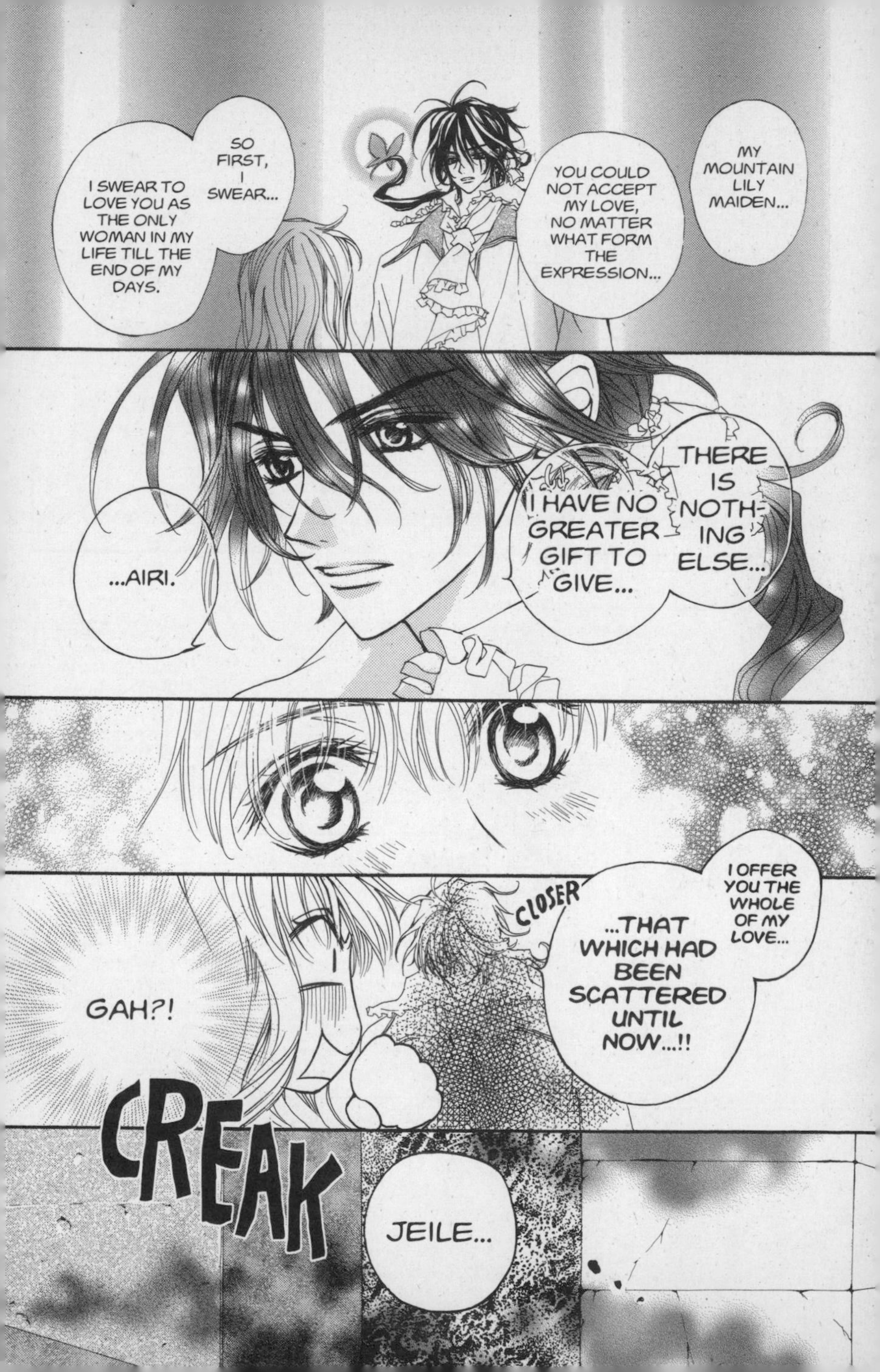
MY MOUNTAIN LILY MAIDEN...
YOU COULD NOT ACCEPT MY LOVE, NO MATTER WHAT FORM THE EXPRESSION...
SO FIRST, I SWEAR...
I SWEAR TO LOVE YOU AS THE ONLY WOMAN IN MY LIFE TILL THE END OF MY DAYS.
THERE IS NOTH-ING ELSE...
I HAVE NO GREATER GIFT TO GIVE...
...AIRI.
I OFFER YOU THE WHOLE OF MY LOVE...
...THAT WHICH HAD BEEN SCATTERED UNTIL NOW...!!
CLOSER
GAH?!
CREAK
JEILE...

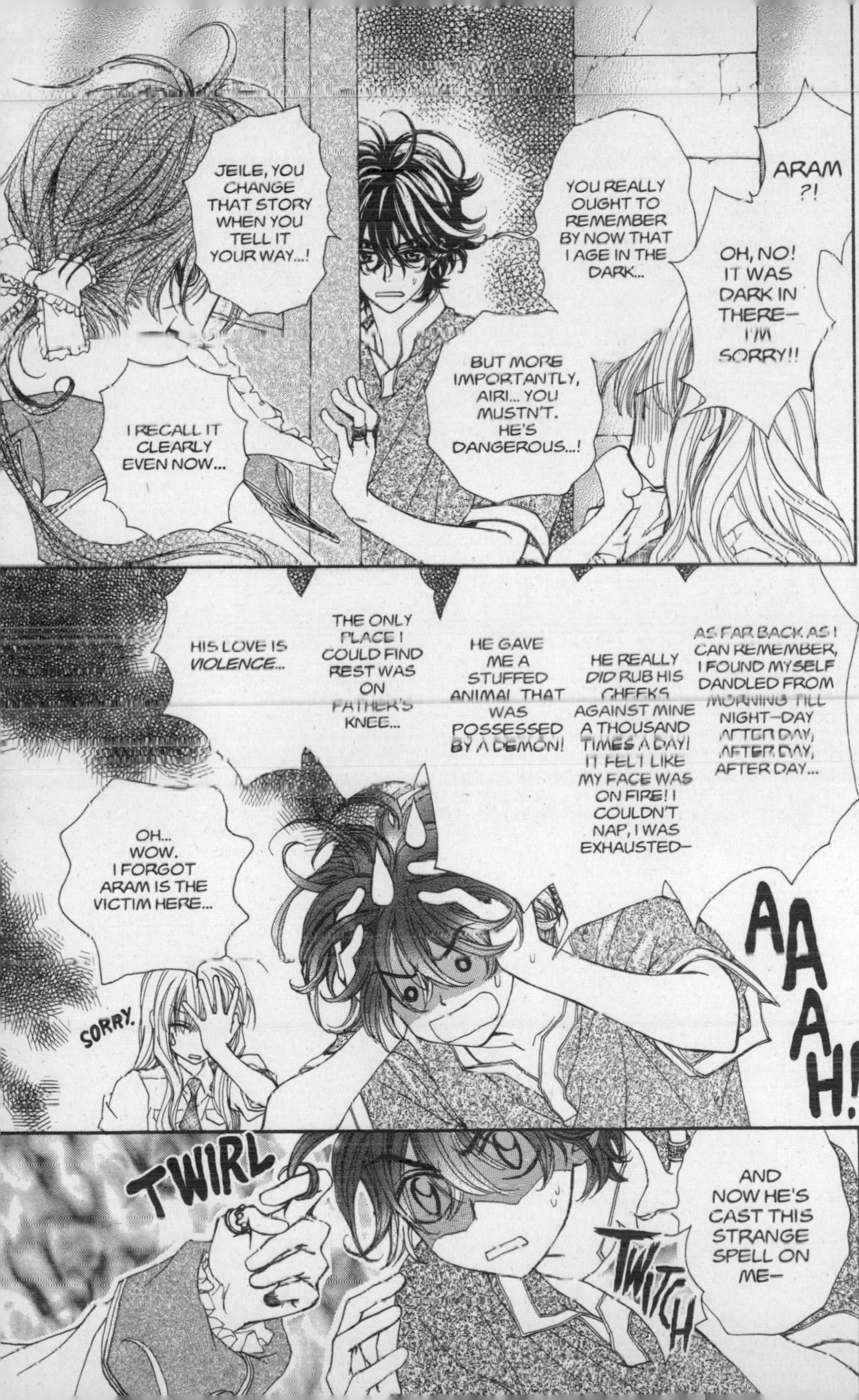
ARAM ?!
OH, NO! IT WAS DARK IN THERE— I'M SORRY!!
YOU REALLY OUGHT TO REMEMBER BY NOW THAT I AGE IN THE DARK...
BUT MORE IMPORTANTLY, AIRI... YOU MUSTN'T. HE'S DANGEROUS...!
JEILE, YOU CHANGE THAT STORY WHEN YOU TELL IT YOUR WAY...!
I RECALL IT CLEARLY EVEN NOW...
AS FAR BACK AS I CAN REMEMBER, I FOUND MYSELF DANDLED FROM MORNING TILL NIGHT—DAY AFTER DAY, AFTER DAY, AFTER DAY...
HE REALLY *DID* RUB HIS CHEEKS AGAINST MINE A THOUSAND TIMES A DAY! IT FELT LIKE MY FACE WAS ON FIRE! I COULDN'T NAP, I WAS EXHAUSTED—
HE GAVE ME A STUFFED ANIMAL THAT WAS POSSESSED BY A DEMON!
THE ONLY PLACE I COULD FIND REST WAS ON FATHER'S KNEE...
HIS LOVE IS *VIOLENCE*...
AAAAH!
OH... WOW. I FORGOT ARAM IS THE VICTIM HERE...
SORRY.
AND NOW HE'S CAST THIS STRANGE SPELL ON ME—
TWITCH
TWIRL

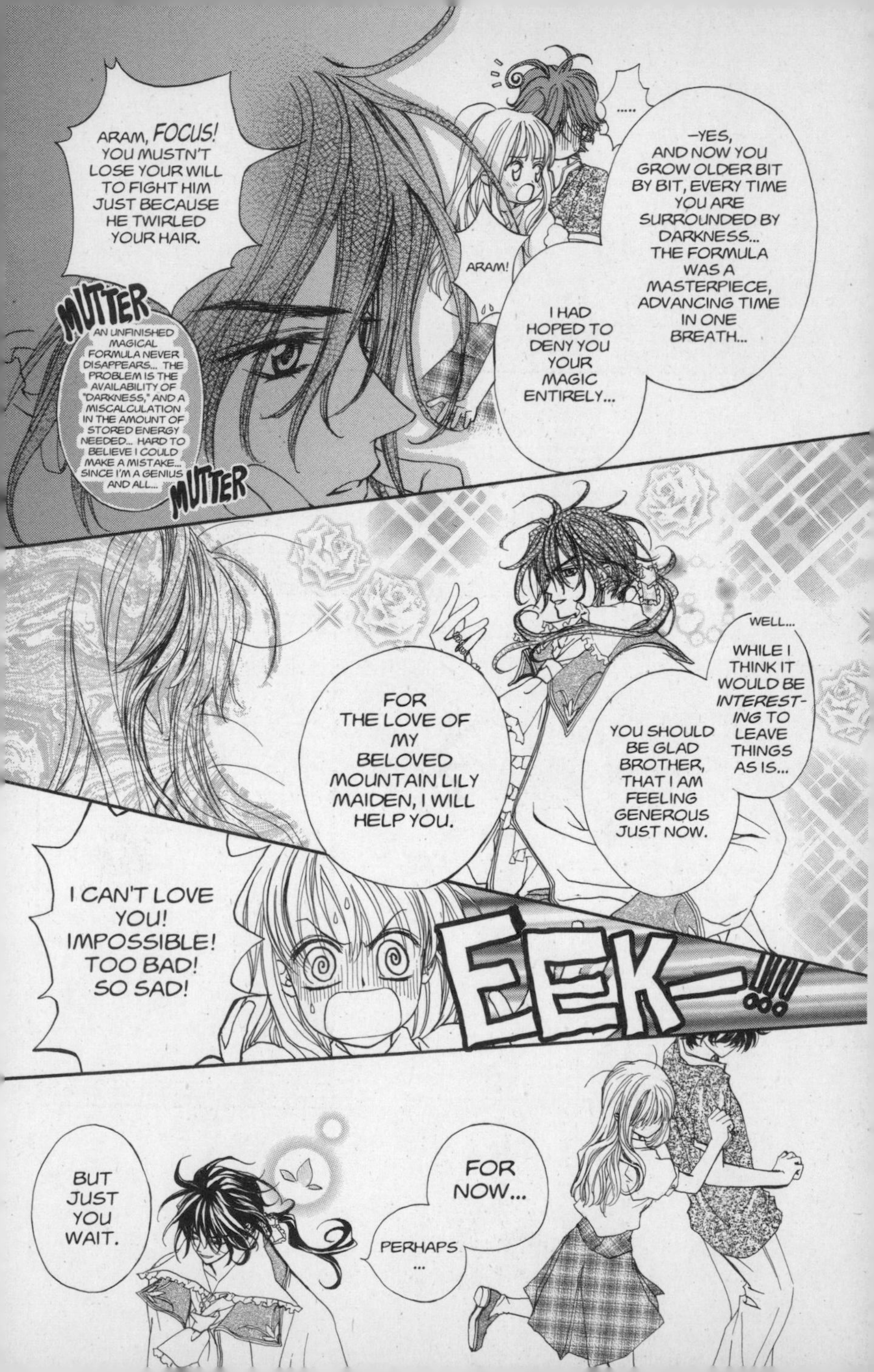
.....
—YES, AND NOW YOU GROW OLDER BIT BY BIT, EVERY TIME YOU ARE SURROUNDED BY DARKNESS... THE FORMULA WAS A MASTERPIECE, ADVANCING TIME IN ONE BREATH...
ARAM!
I HAD HOPED TO DENY YOU YOUR MAGIC ENTIRELY...
ARAM, FOCUS! YOU MUSTN'T LOSE YOUR WILL TO FIGHT HIM JUST BECAUSE HE TWIRLED YOUR HAIR.
MUTTER
AN UNFINISHED MAGICAL FORMULA NEVER DISAPPEARS... THE PROBLEM IS THE AVAILABILITY OF "DARKNESS," AND A MISCALCULATION IN THE AMOUNT OF STORED ENERGY NEEDED... HARD TO BELIEVE I COULD MAKE A MISTAKE... SINCE I'M A GENIUS AND ALL...
MUTTER
WELL...
WHILE I THINK IT WOULD BE INTERESTING TO LEAVE THINGS AS IS...
YOU SHOULD BE GLAD BROTHER, THAT I AM FEELING GENEROUS JUST NOW.
FOR THE LOVE OF MY BELOVED MOUNTAIN LILY MAIDEN, I WILL HELP YOU.
EEK—!!!!
I CAN'T LOVE YOU! IMPOSSIBLE! TOO BAD! SO SAD!
FOR NOW...
PERHAPS...
BUT JUST YOU WAIT.

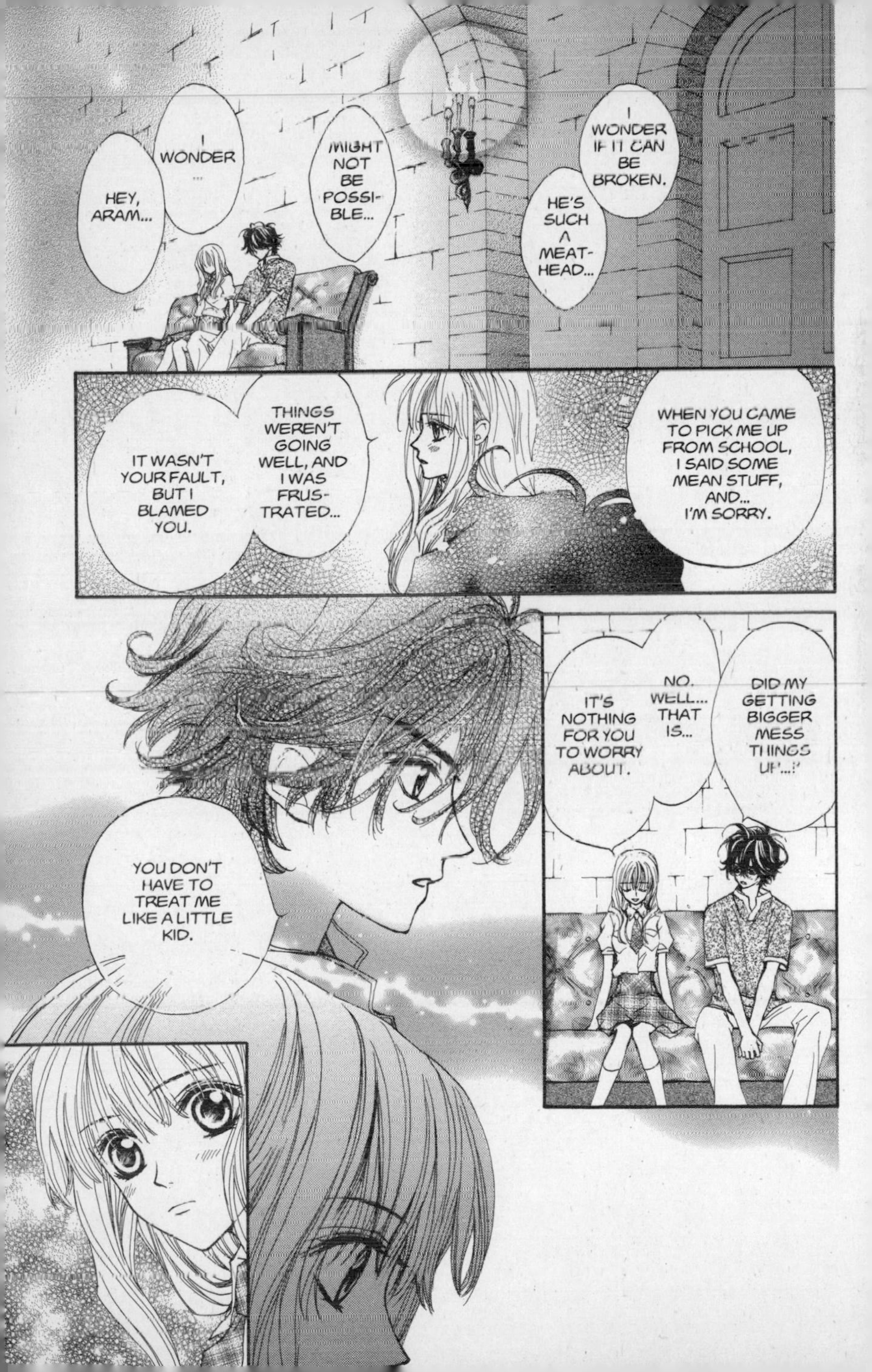
I WONDER IF IT CAN BE BROKEN.
HE'S SUCH A MEAT-HEAD...
MIGHT NOT BE POSSIBLE...
I WONDER...
HEY, ARAM...
WHEN YOU CAME TO PICK ME UP FROM SCHOOL, I SAID SOME MEAN STUFF, AND... I'M SORRY.
THINGS WEREN'T GOING WELL, AND I WAS FRUSTRATED...
IT WASN'T YOUR FAULT, BUT I BLAMED YOU.
DID MY GETTING BIGGER MESS THINGS UP...?
NO. WELL... THAT IS...
IT'S NOTHING FOR YOU TO WORRY ABOUT.
YOU DON'T HAVE TO TREAT ME LIKE A LITTLE KID.

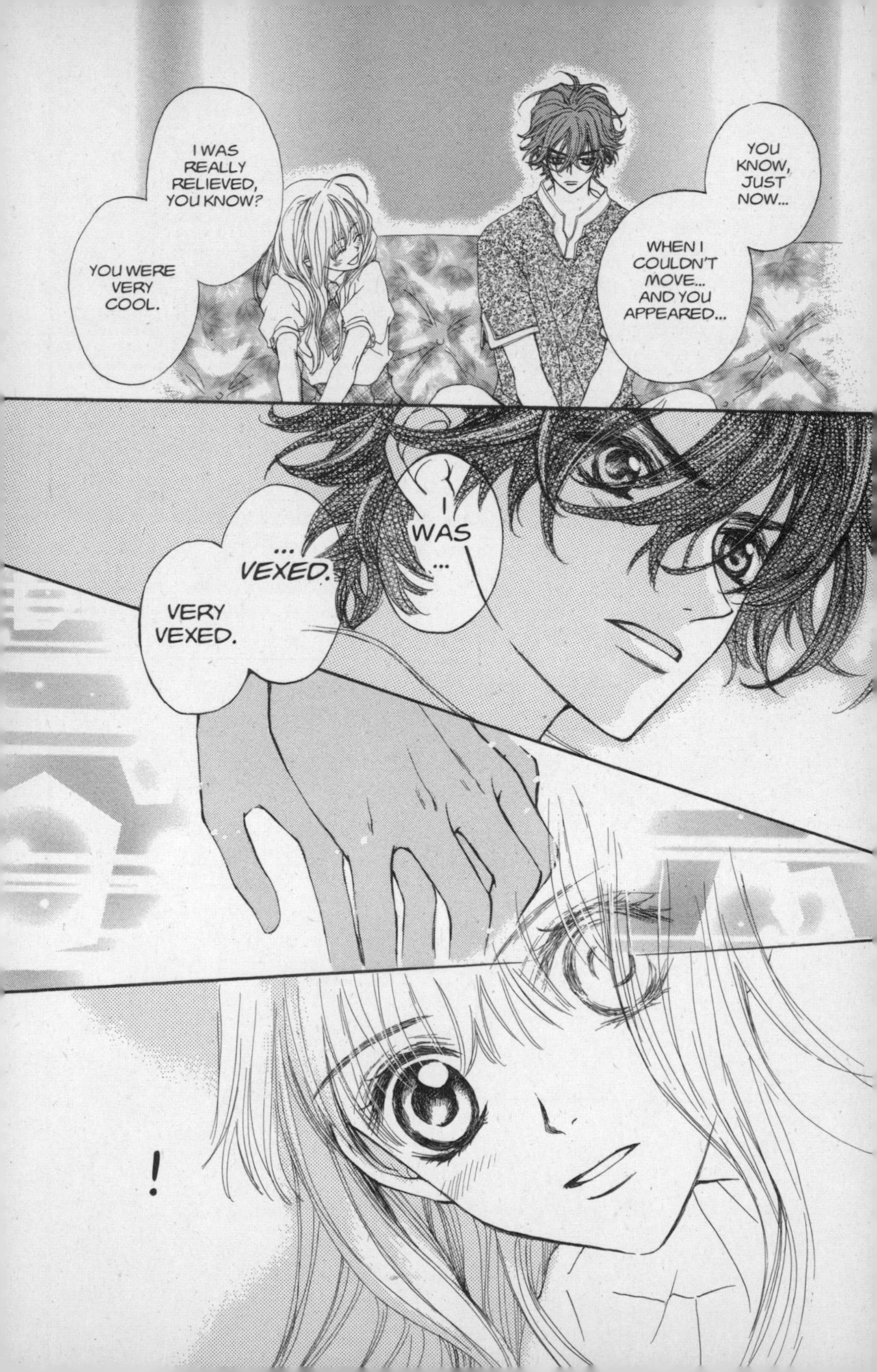
YOU KNOW, JUST NOW...
WHEN I COULDN'T MOVE... AND YOU APPEARED...
I WAS REALLY RELIEVED, YOU KNOW?
YOU WERE VERY COOL.
I WAS...
...VEXED.
VERY VEXED.
!

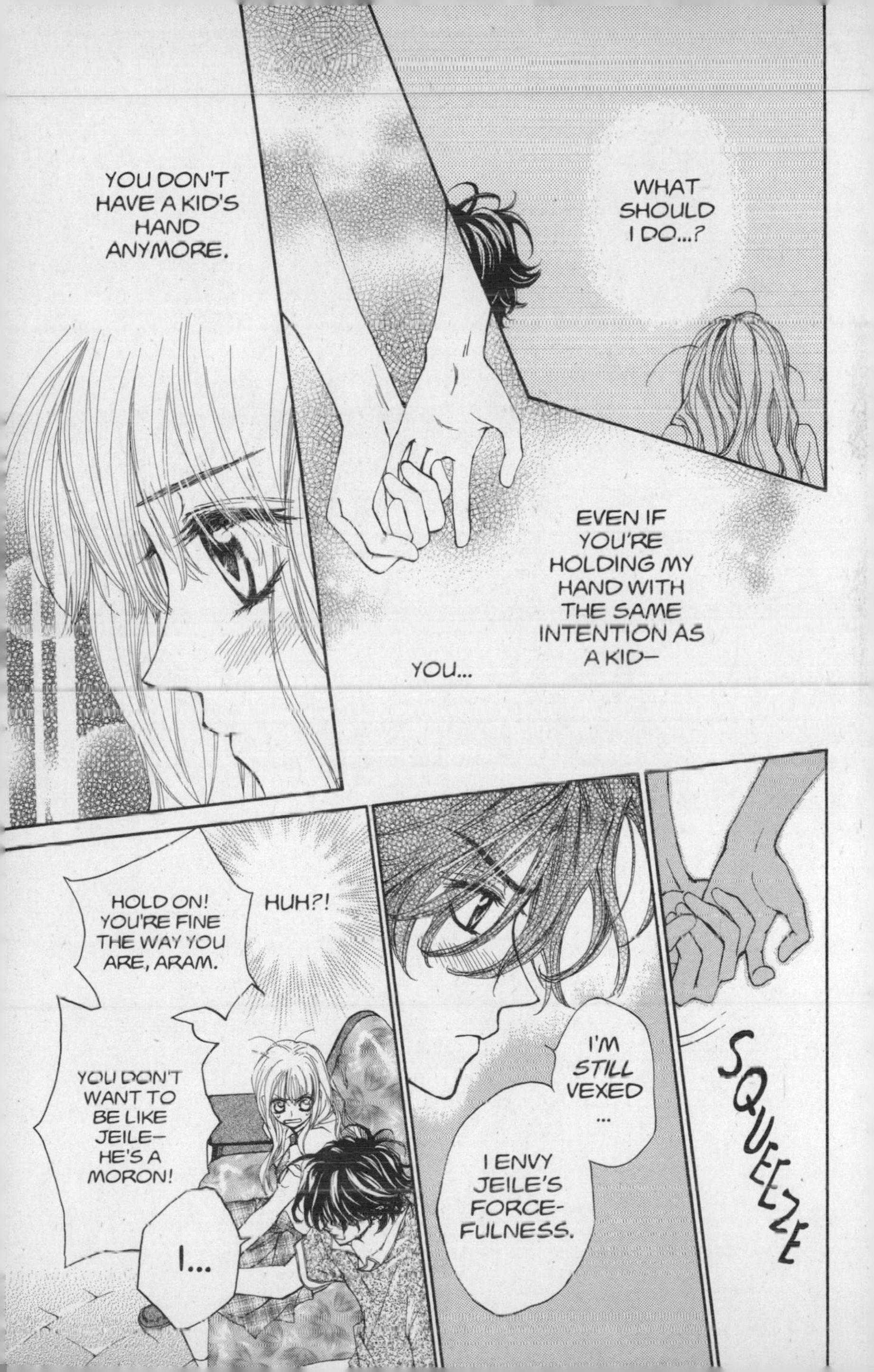
WHAT SHOULD I DO...?
EVEN IF YOU'RE HOLDING MY HAND WITH THE SAME INTENTION AS A KID—
YOU...
YOU DON'T HAVE A KID'S HAND ANYMORE.
SQUEEZE
I'M STILL VEXED ...
I ENVY JEILE'S FORCE-FULNESS.
HUH?!
HOLD ON! YOU'RE FINE THE WAY YOU ARE, ARAM.
YOU DON'T WANT TO BE LIKE JEILE— HE'S A MORON!
I...

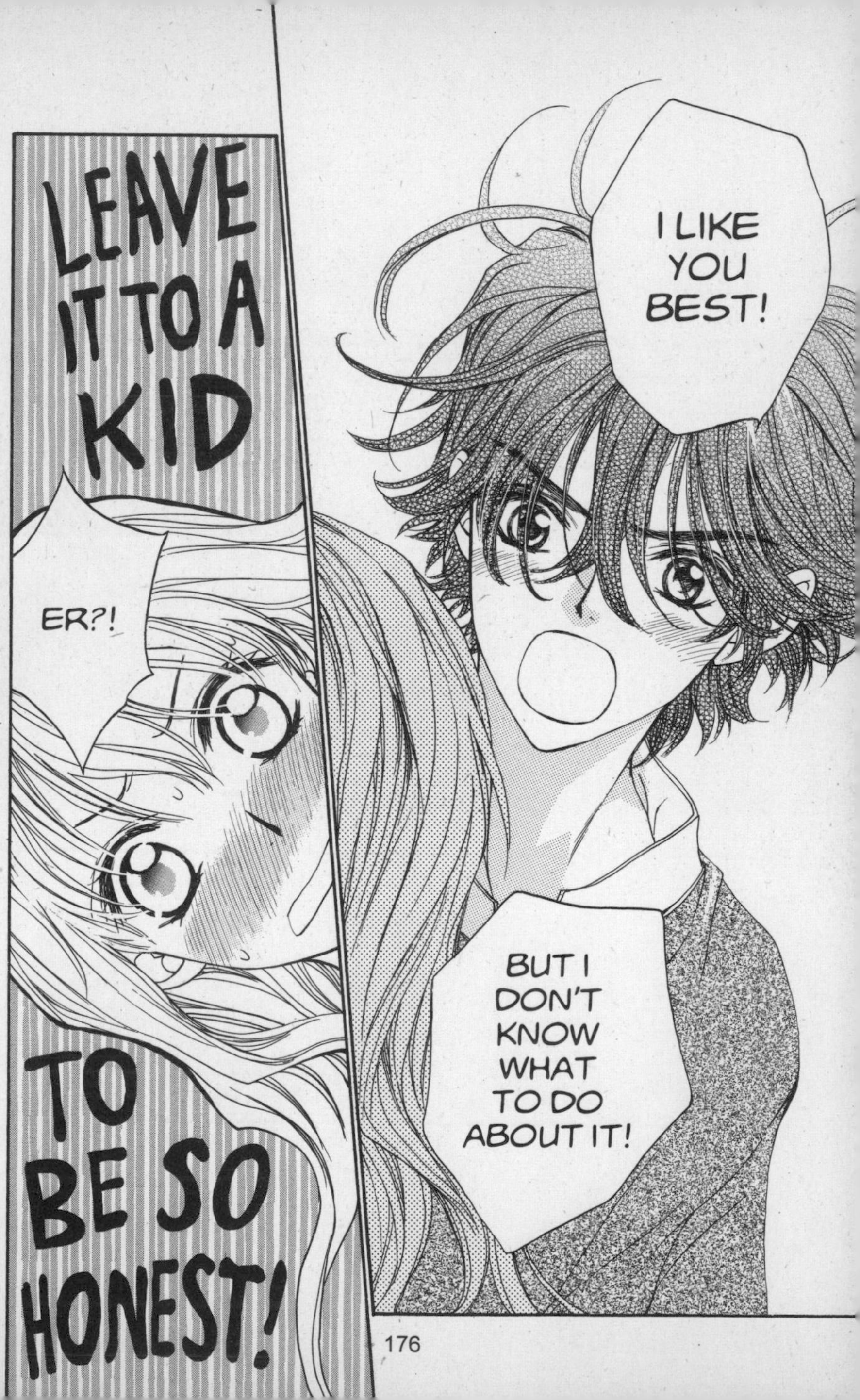
I LIKE YOU BEST!
BUT I DON'T KNOW WHAT TO DO ABOUT IT!
LEAVE IT TO A KID
ER?!
TO BE SO HONEST!

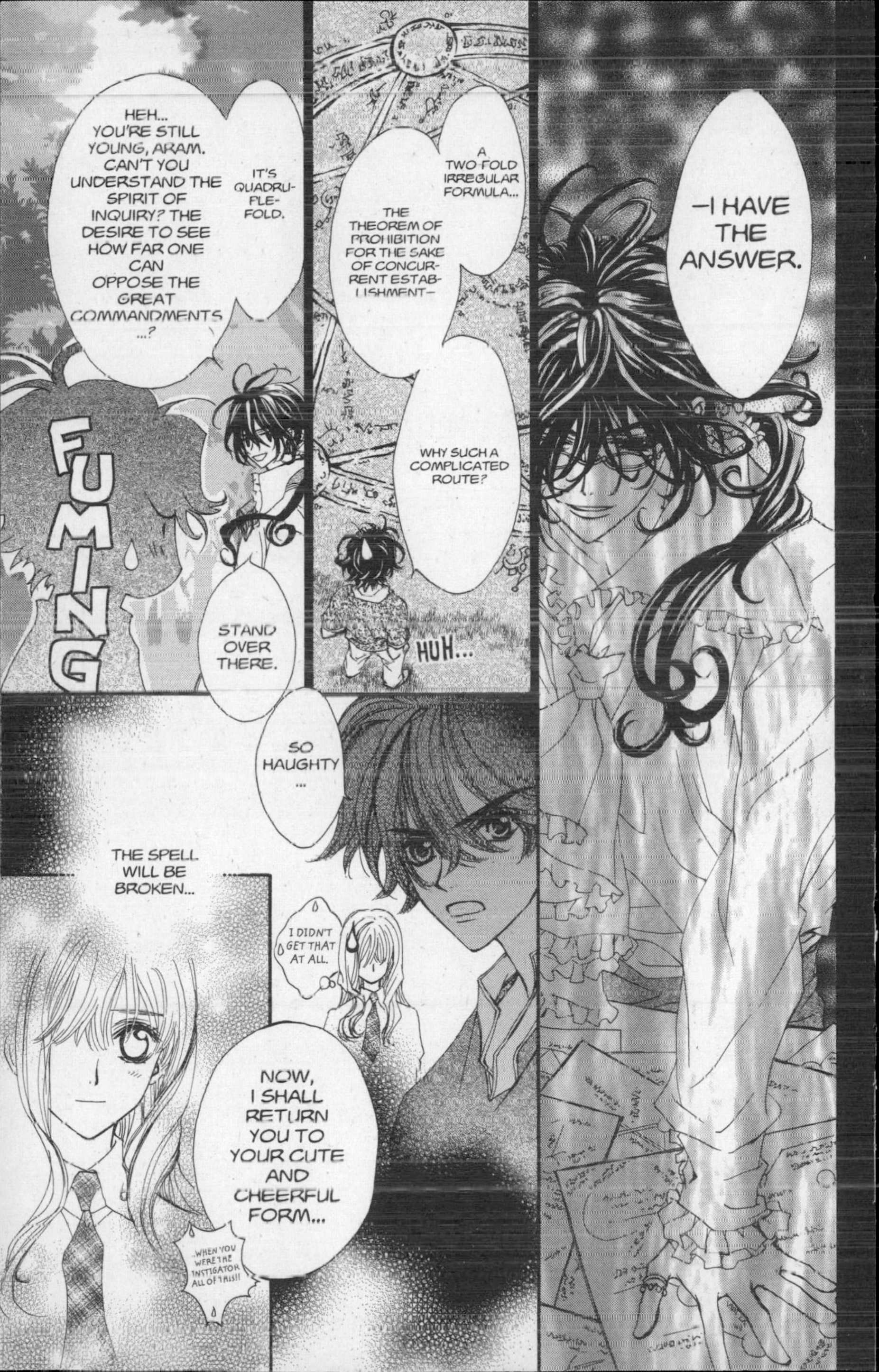
—I HAVE THE ANSWER.
A TWO-FOLD IRREGULAR FORMULA...
THE THEOREM OF PROHIBITION FOR THE SAKE OF CONCURRENT ESTABLISHMENT—
WHY SUCH A COMPLICATED ROUTE?
HUH...
IT'S QUADRUPLE-FOLD.
HEH... YOU'RE STILL YOUNG, ARAM. CAN'T YOU UNDERSTAND THE SPIRIT OF INQUIRY? THE DESIRE TO SEE HOW FAR ONE CAN OPPOSE THE GREAT COMMANDMENTS ...?
FUMING
STAND OVER THERE.
SO HAUGHTY ...
I DIDN'T GET THAT AT ALL.
THE SPELL WILL BE BROKEN...
NOW, I SHALL RETURN YOU TO YOUR CUTE AND CHEERFUL FORM...
..WHEN YOU WERE THE INSTIGATOR ALL OF THIS!!

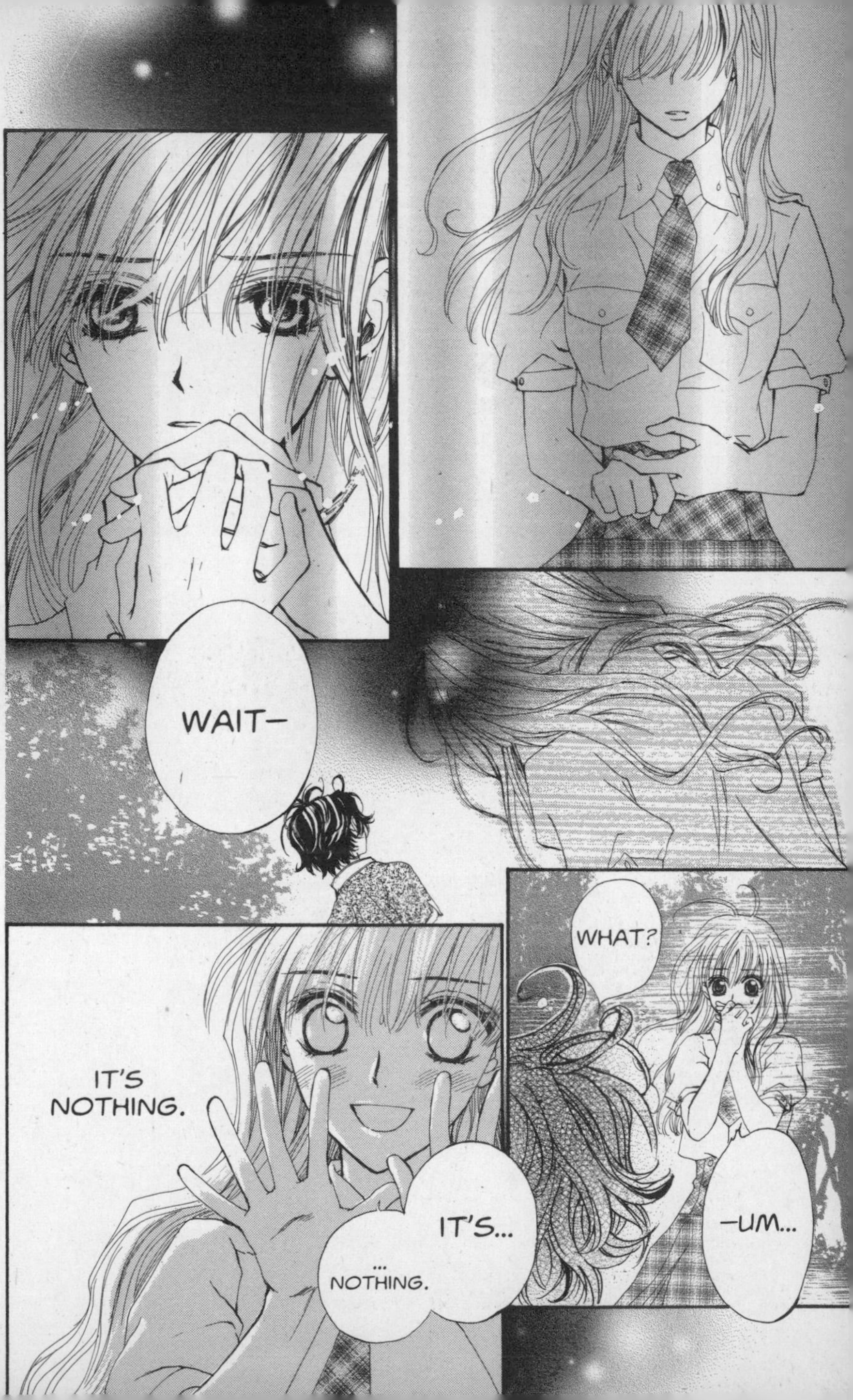
WAIT—
WHAT?
—UM...
IT'S...
...NOTHING.
IT'S NOTHING.

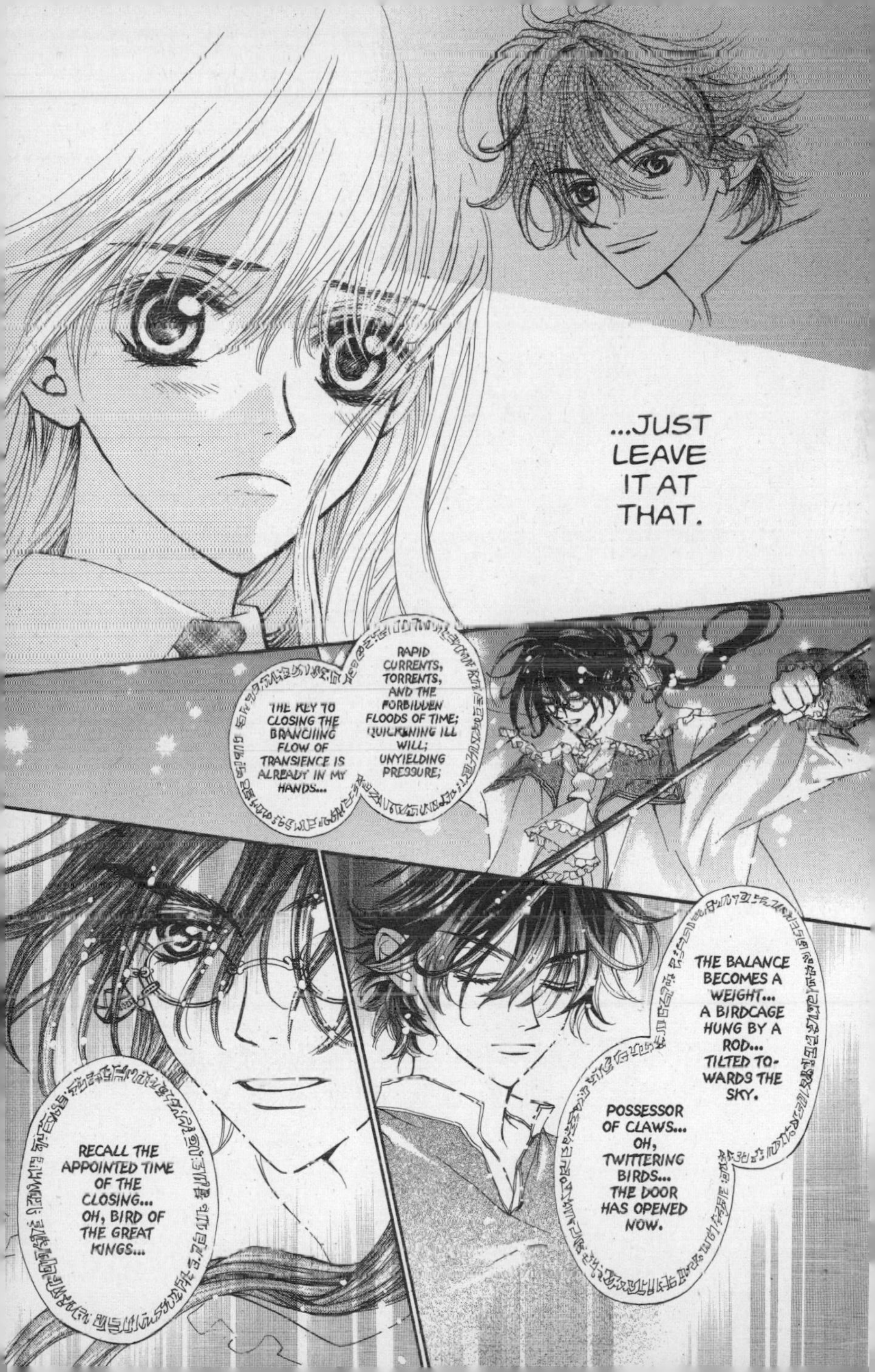
...JUST LEAVE IT AT THAT.
RAPID CURRENTS, TORRENTS, AND THE FORBIDDEN FLOODS OF TIME; QUICKENING ILL WILL; UNYIELDING PRESSURE;
THE KEY TO CLOSING THE BRANCHING FLOW OF TRANSIENCE IS ALREADY IN MY HANDS...
THE BALANCE BECOMES A WEIGHT... A BIRDCAGE HUNG BY A ROD... TILTED TO-WARDS THE SKY.
POSSESSOR OF CLAWS... OH, TWITTERING BIRDS... THE DOOR HAS OPENED NOW.
RECALL THE APPOINTED TIME OF THE CLOSING... OH, BIRD OF THE GREAT KINGS...

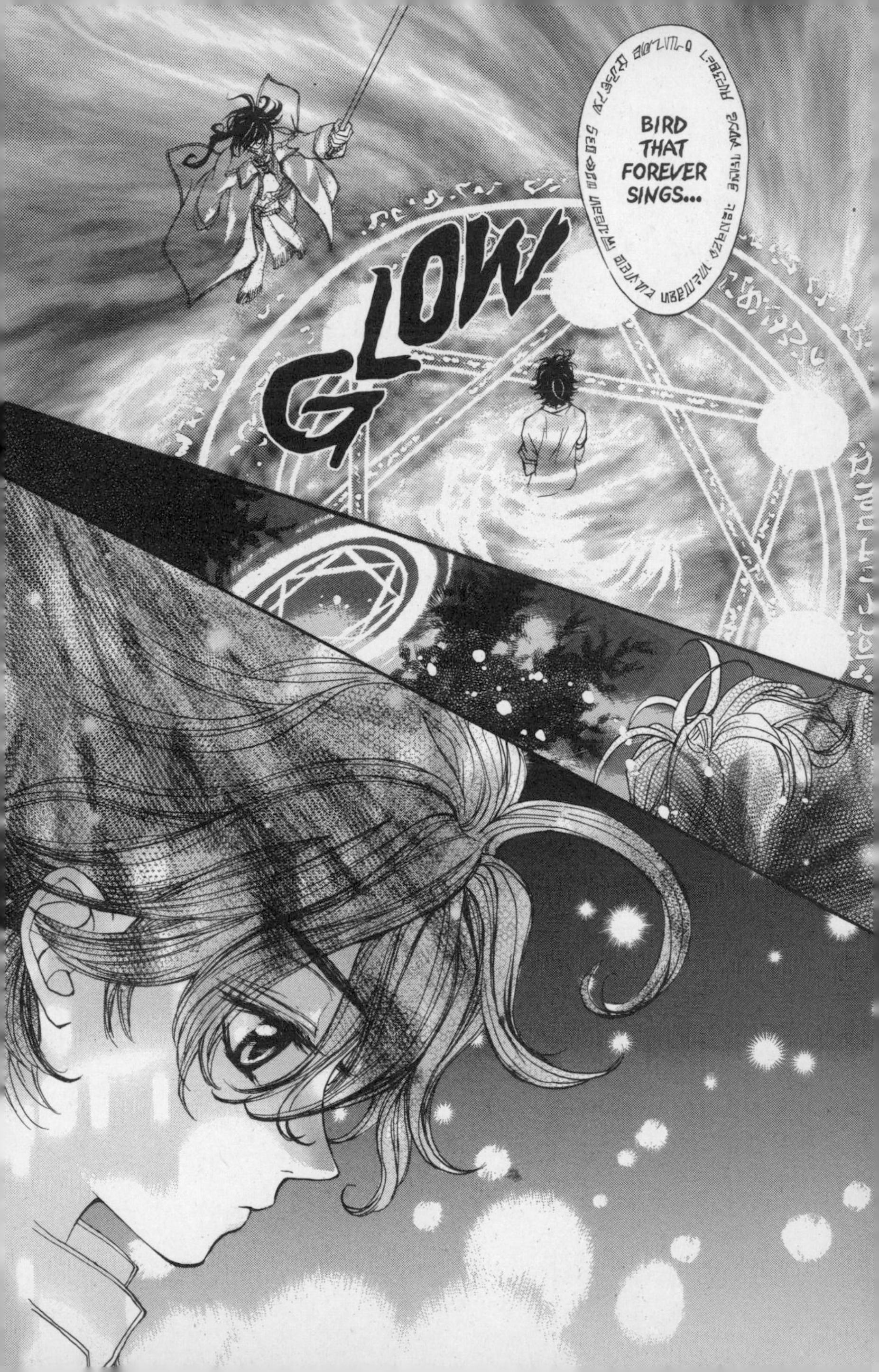
BIRD THAT FOREVER SINGS...
GLOW

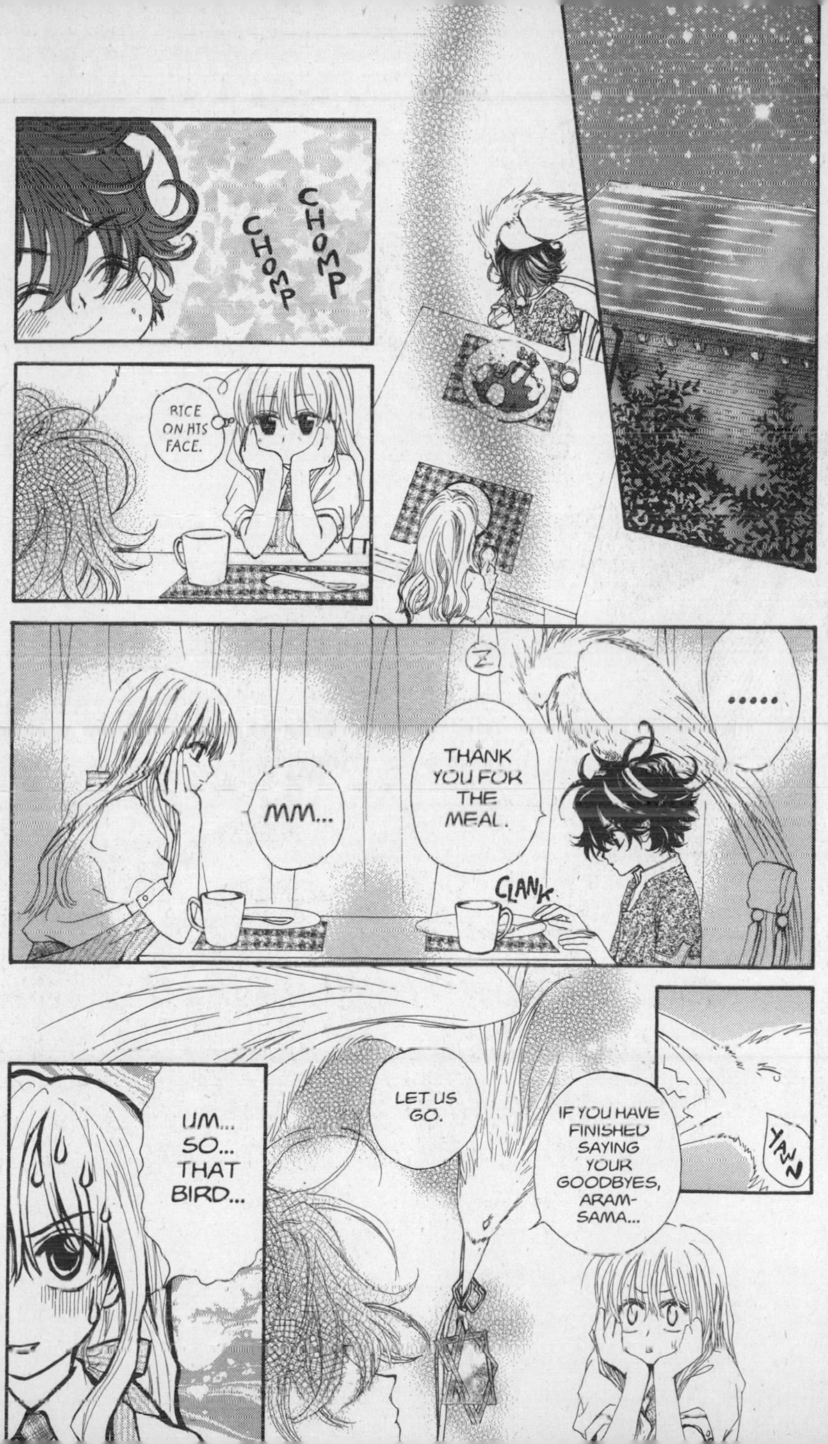
CHOMP CHOMP
RICE ON HIS FACE.
Z
.....
THANK YOU FOR THE MEAL.
CLANK
MM...
YAWN
IF YOU HAVE FINISHED SAYING YOUR GOODBYES, ARAM-SAMA...
LET US GO.
UM... SO... THAT BIRD...

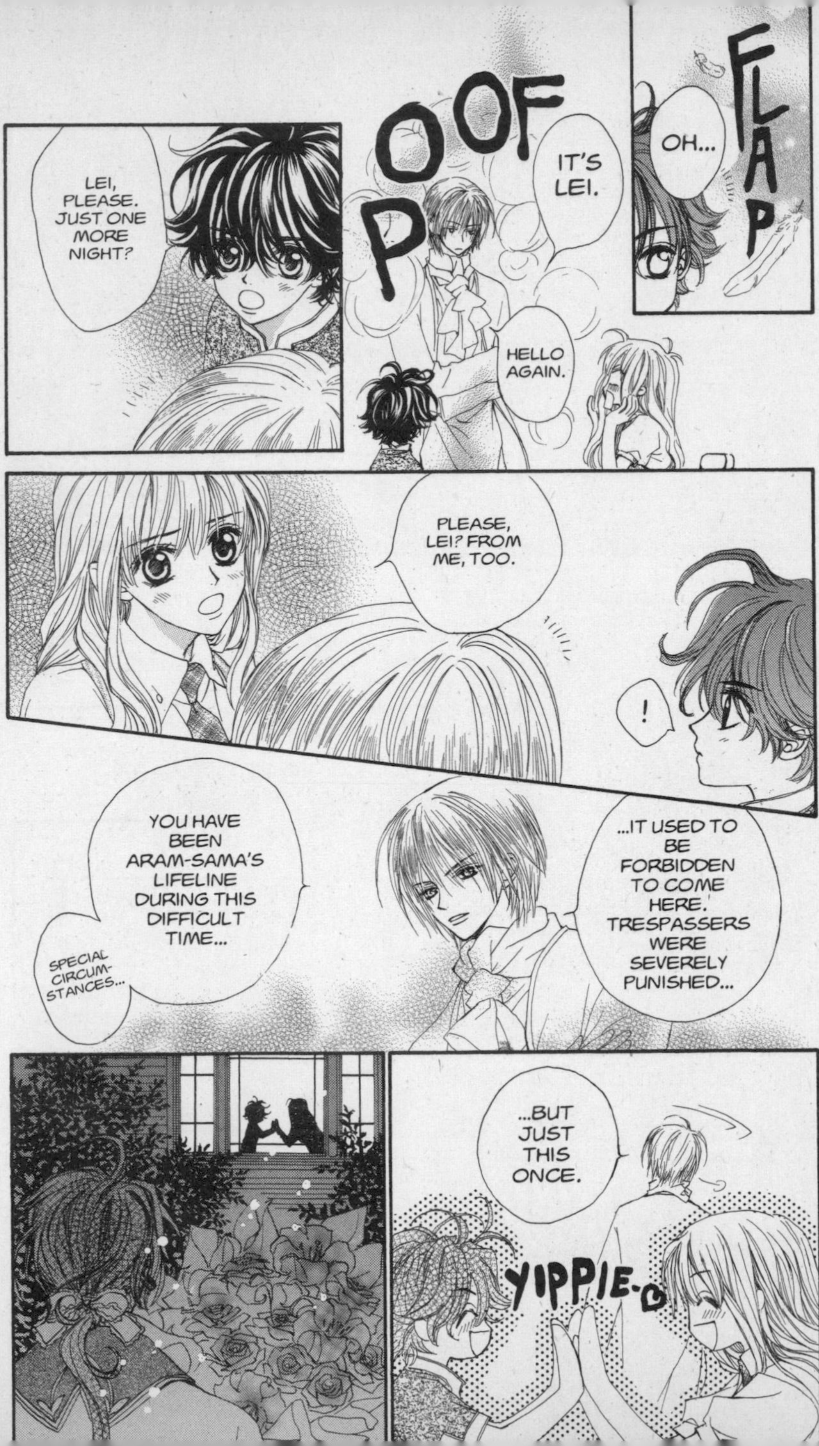
FLAP
OH...
POOF
IT'S LEI.
HELLO AGAIN.
LEI, PLEASE. JUST ONE MORE NIGHT?
PLEASE, LEI? FROM ME, TOO.
!
...IT USED TO BE FORBIDDEN TO COME HERE. TRESPASSERS WERE SEVERELY PUNISHED...
YOU HAVE BEEN ARAM-SAMA'S LIFELINE DURING THIS DIFFICULT TIME...
SPECIAL CIRCUM-STANCES...
...BUT JUST THIS ONCE.
YIPPIE-♡

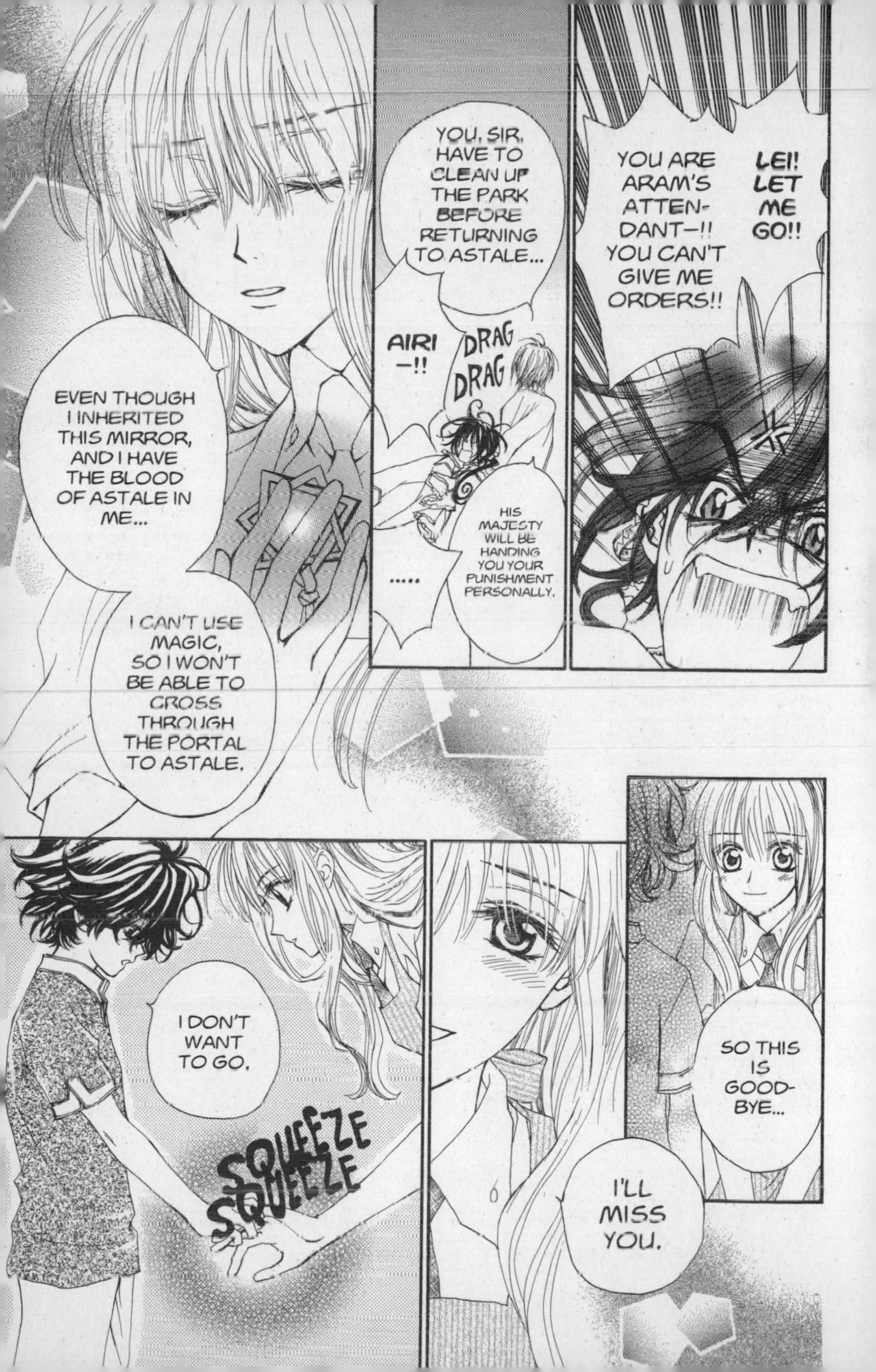
LEI! LET ME GO!!
YOU ARE ARAM'S ATTEN-DANT—!! YOU CAN'T GIVE ME ORDERS!!
YOU, SIR, HAVE TO CLEAN UP THE PARK BEFORE RETURNING TO ASTALE...
DRAG DRAG
AIRI—!!
HIS MAJESTY WILL BE HANDING YOU YOUR PUNISHMENT PERSONALLY.
.....
EVEN THOUGH I INHERITED THIS MIRROR, AND I HAVE THE BLOOD OF ASTALE IN ME...
I CAN'T USE MAGIC, SO I WON'T BE ABLE TO CROSS THROUGH THE PORTAL TO ASTALE.
SO THIS IS GOOD-BYE...
I'LL MISS YOU.
I DON'T WANT TO GO.
SQUEEZE SQUEEZE

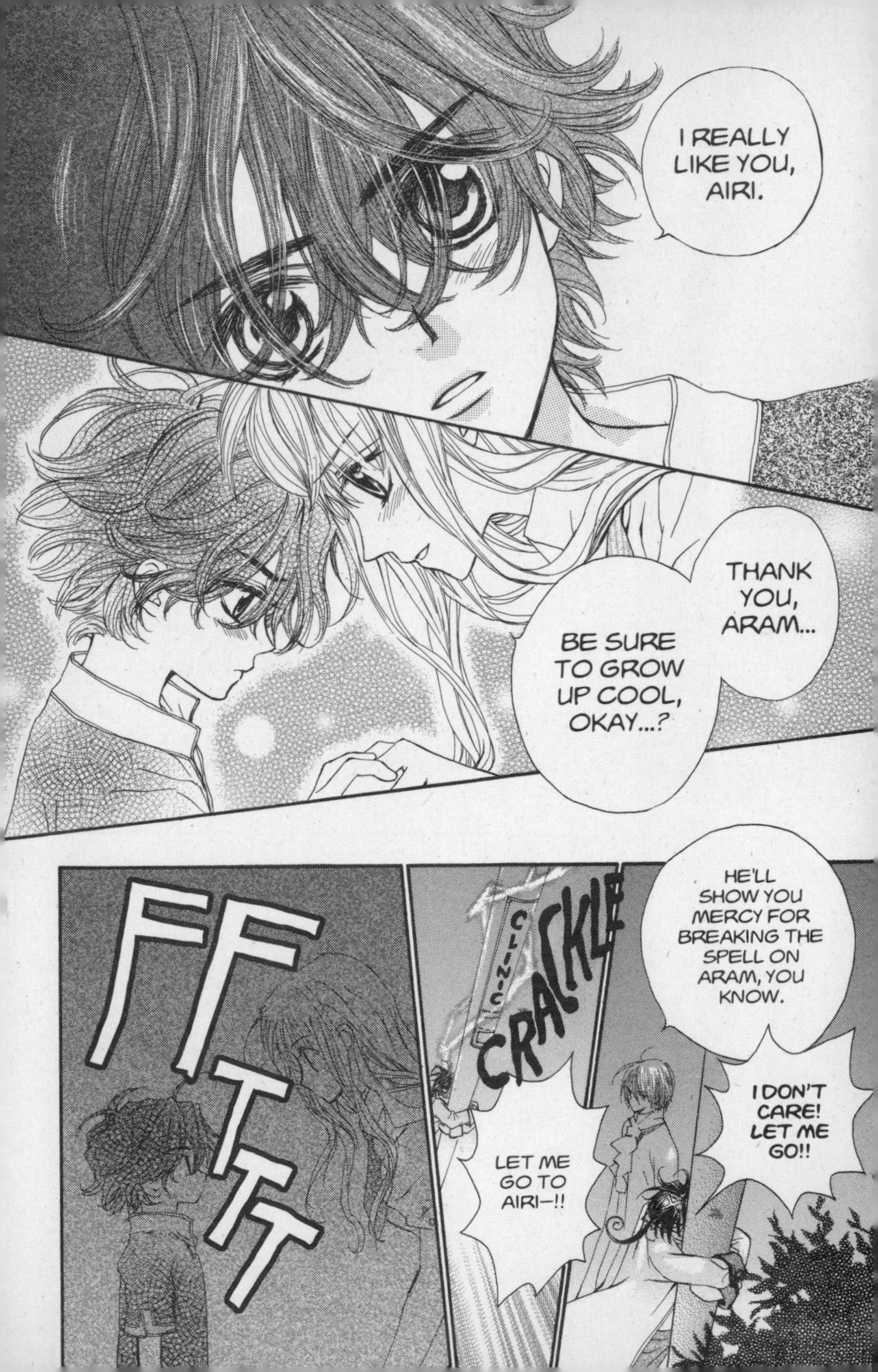
I REALLY LIKE YOU, AIRI.
THANK YOU, ARAM...
BE SURE TO GROW UP COOL, OKAY...?
HE'LL SHOW YOU MERCY FOR BREAKING THE SPELL ON ARAM, YOU KNOW.
I DON'T CARE! LET ME GO!!
LET ME GO TO AIRI—!!
CLINIC
CRACKLE
FFTTTT

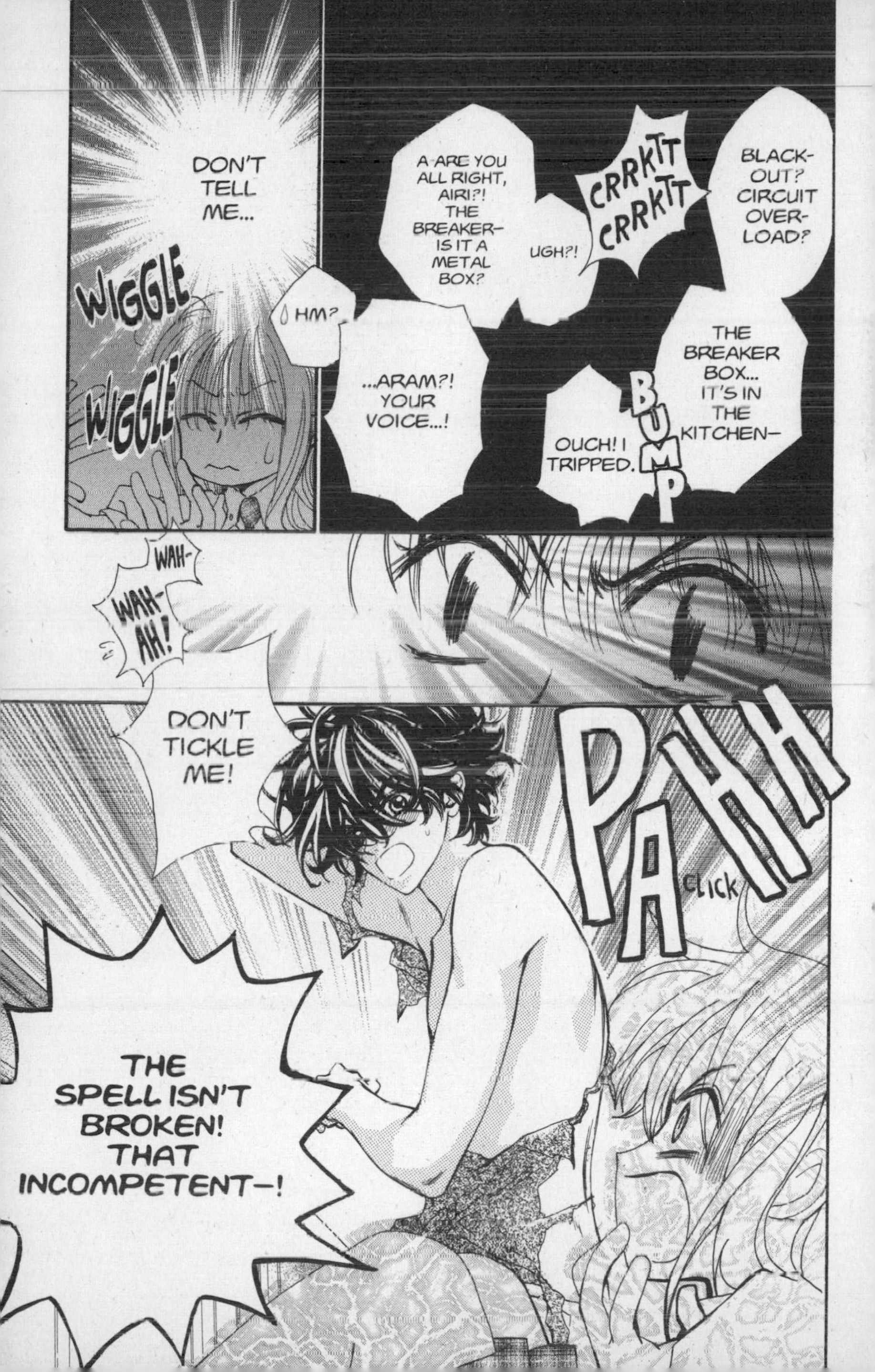
BLACK-OUT? CIRCUIT OVER-LOAD?
CRRKTT CRRKTT
UGH?!
A-ARE YOU ALL RIGHT, AIRI?! THE BREAKER-IS IT A METAL BOX?
THE BREAKER BOX... IT'S IN THE KITCHEN–
BUMP
OUCH! I TRIPPED.
...ARAM?! YOUR VOICE...!
HM?
DON'T TELL ME...
WIGGLE
WIGGLE
WAH-WAH-AH!
PAHH
CLICK
DON'T TICKLE ME!
THE SPELL ISN'T BROKEN! THAT INCOMPETENT–!

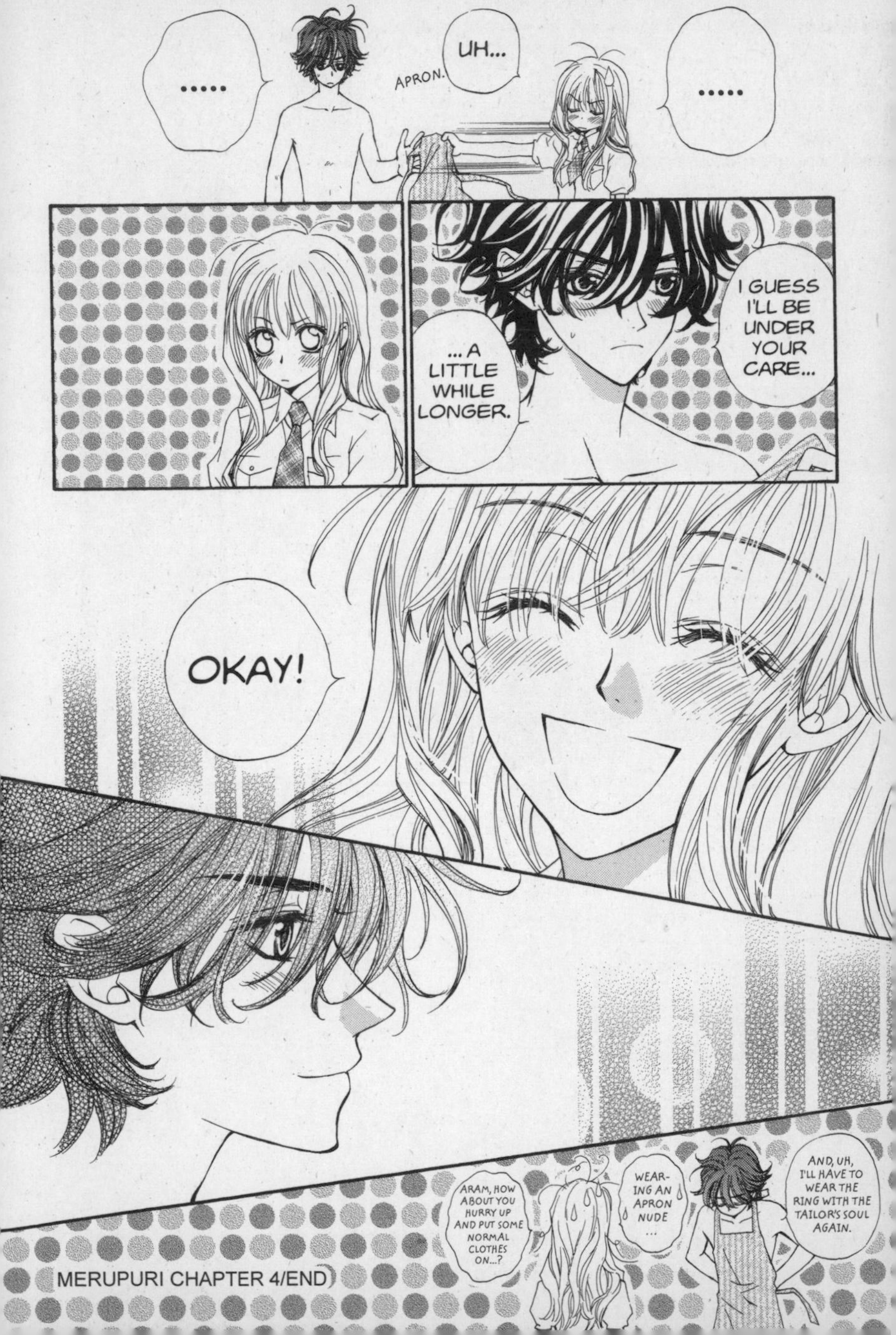
.....
UH...
APRON.
.....
I GUESS I'LL BE UNDER YOUR CARE...
...A LITTLE WHILE LONGER.
OKAY!
AND, UH, I'LL HAVE TO WEAR THE RING WITH THE TAILOR'S SOUL AGAIN.
WEAR-ING AN APRON NUDE ...
ARAM, HOW ABOUT YOU HURRY UP AND PUT SOME NORMAL CLOTHES ON...?
MERUPURI CHAPTER 4/END

(Continued...)
It seems like these days most titles are abbreviated right from the start. If that's the case, I'd like this book to be called "MeruPuri." It might be a little strange for me to say so myself, but I reeeeeeally like this title. Don't you think it's cute? It just rolls off the tongue. I did something I rarely do and pushed for this one. It is hard to read the meaning in it, I know, so we wrote "MeruPuri" with "Märchen Prince" stuck on it like furigana (a pronunciation guide)...and that's how the series was started.

I haven't given up, though, and I look forward to the day when it will be okay just to use "MeruPuri" all by itself.

There was one more A4-size sheet that I faxed to my editor: possible names for Aram, Jeile, Lei and Airi's great-great-great-(?)grandmother Chrisnele-san.

Airi and Nakaoji-kun's names were decided rather quickly, but the foreign names...I was clueless. I wrote down everything I could think of—names of herbs, gems, dishes...and in the end, none of them stuck. Completely at a loss, I stared at a page in the dictionary. Once the first name hit me, the rest came quickly. If I hadn't picked up that reference book, Aram might have been "Bazil" or "Adam." Jeile might have been "Carlo" or...(ha ha!)

FYI, Aram is from "alarm," Jeile is from "jewel" and "gyro," Lei is from "laser beam" ...and so on! That's all there was to it! What do they have in common? Maybe that they're all somewhat mechanical...?

Things like motives and histories, they weren't taken too seriously—but a big development is coming soon, as well as some new characters! I'm also looking forward to doing a side story or two.

I'd be most pleased if you continued to read!!

December, 2002. Hino Matsuri

P.S. "MeruPuri" will be made into a dramatic CD intended as a give-away. Want to try guessing who the voice actors and actresses will be? They'll be limited editions, so act fast once they're released.

P.P.S. The seven-pointed star was done by a special designer. Thank you very much! ♭

A former bookstore shopkeeper, **Matsuri Hino** burst onto the manga scene with her title *Kono Yume ga Sametara* (When This Dream Is Over), which was published in *LaLa DX* magazine. Hino was a manga artist a mere nine months after she decided to become one.

With the success of her popular series *Toraware no Minoue (Captive Hearts)*, and *MeruPuri*, Hino has established herself as a major player in the world of shojo manga. Her new title, *Vampire Knight*, currently runs in monthly *LaLa* magazine.

Hino enjoys creative activities and has commented that she would have been either an architect or an apprentice to traditional Japanese craft masters if she did not become a manga artist.

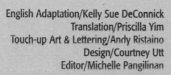

MERUPURI: MÄRCHEN PRINCE, VOLUME 1
The Shojo Beat Manga Edition

STORY AND ART BY
MATSURI HINO

English Adaptation/Kelly Sue DeConnick
Translation/Priscilla Yim
Touch-up Art & Lettering/Andy Ristaino
Design/Courtney Utt
Editor/Michelle Pangilinan

VP, Production/Alvin Lu
VP, Publishing Licensing/Rika Inouye
VP, Sales & Product Marketing/Gonzalo Ferreyra
VP, Creative/Linda Espinosa
Publisher/Hyoe Narita

Printed in the U.S.A.

Published by VIZ Media, LLC
P.O. Box 77010
San Francisco, CA 94107

Shojo Beat Manga Edition
10 9 8 7 6 5
First printing, June 2005
Fifth printing, May 2009

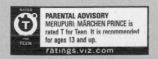

store.viz.com

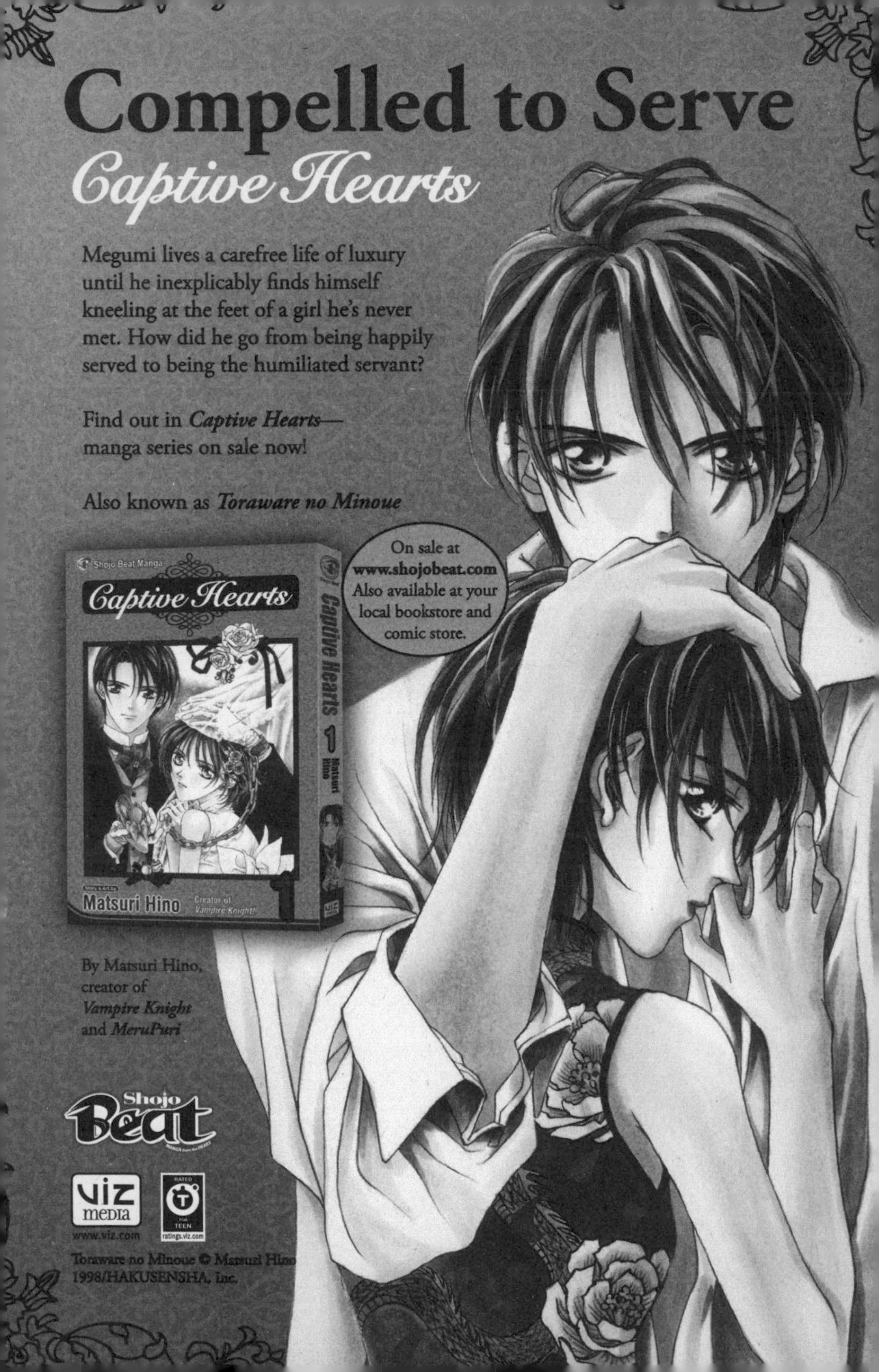

Compelled to Serve
Captive Hearts
Megumi lives a carefree life of luxury until he inexplicably finds himself kneeling at the feet of a girl he's never met. How did he go from being happily served to being the humiliated servant?
Find out in Captive Hearts—manga series on sale now!
Also known as Toraware no Minoue
On sale at www.shojobeat.com Also available at your local bookstore and comic store.
Shojo Beat Manga
Captive Hearts
Matsuri Hino
Captive Hearts 1
By Matsuri Hino, creator of Vampire Knight and MeruPuri
Shojo Beat
viz media
www.viz.com
RATED T TEEN
ratings.viz.com
Toraware no Minoue © Matsuri Hino 1998/HAKUSENSHA, Inc.

High Seas Hostage!

WANTED

BY MATSURI HINO, CREATOR OF
MERUPURI AND *VAMPIRE KNIGHT*

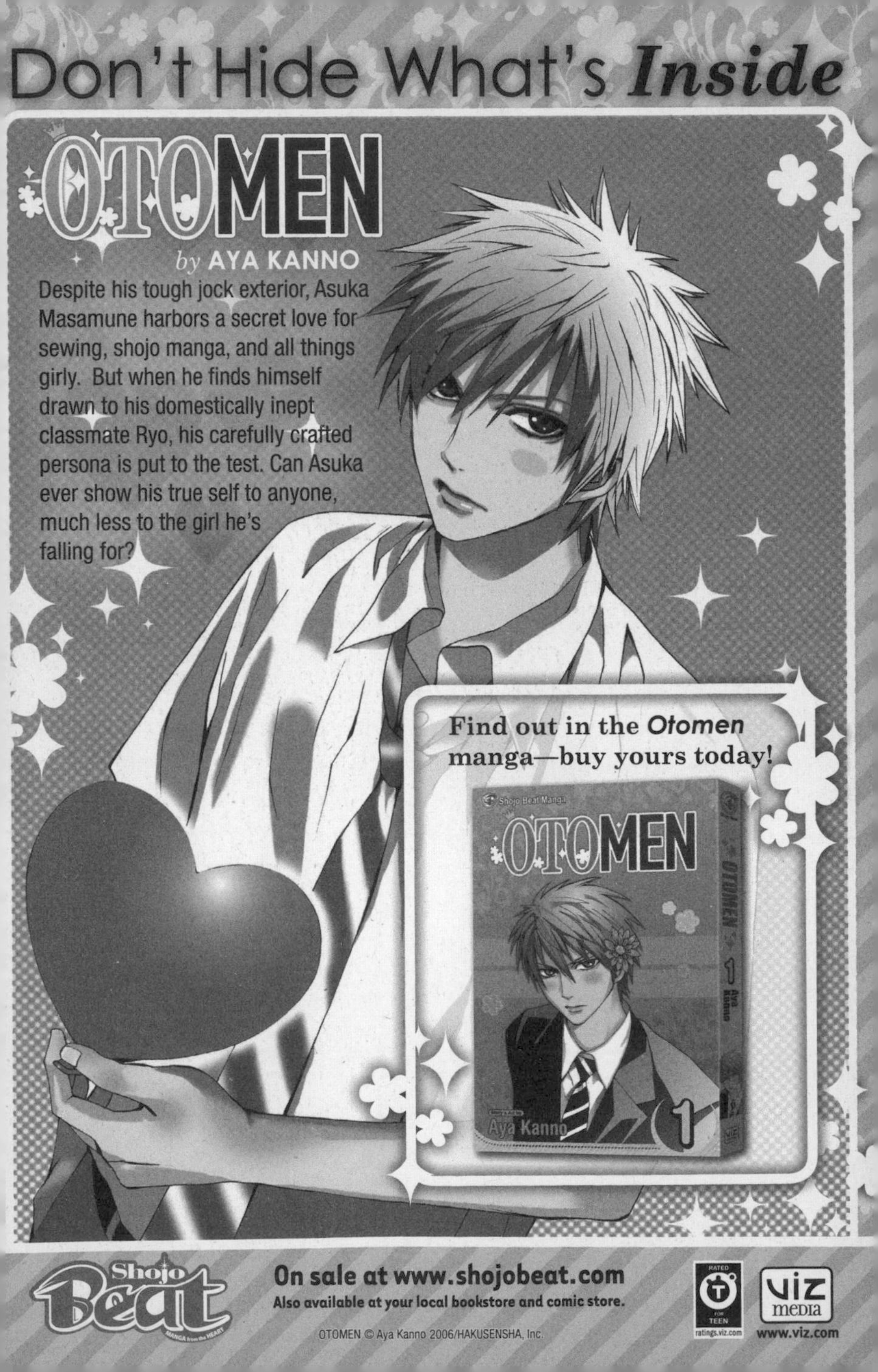
Don't Hide What's Inside
OTOMEN
by AYA KANNO
Despite his tough jock exterior, Asuka Masamune harbors a secret love for sewing, shojo manga, and all things girly. But when he finds himself drawn to his domestically inept classmate Ryo, his carefully crafted persona is put to the test. Can Asuka ever show his true self to anyone, much less to the girl he's falling for?
Find out in the Otomen manga—buy yours today!
Shojo Beat Manga
OTOMEN
Aya Kanno
1
Shojo Beat
On sale at www.shojobeat.com
Also available at your local bookstore and comic store.
OTOMEN © Aya Kanno 2006/HAKUSENSHA, Inc.
RATED T FOR TEEN
ratings.viz.com
VIZ media
www.viz.com

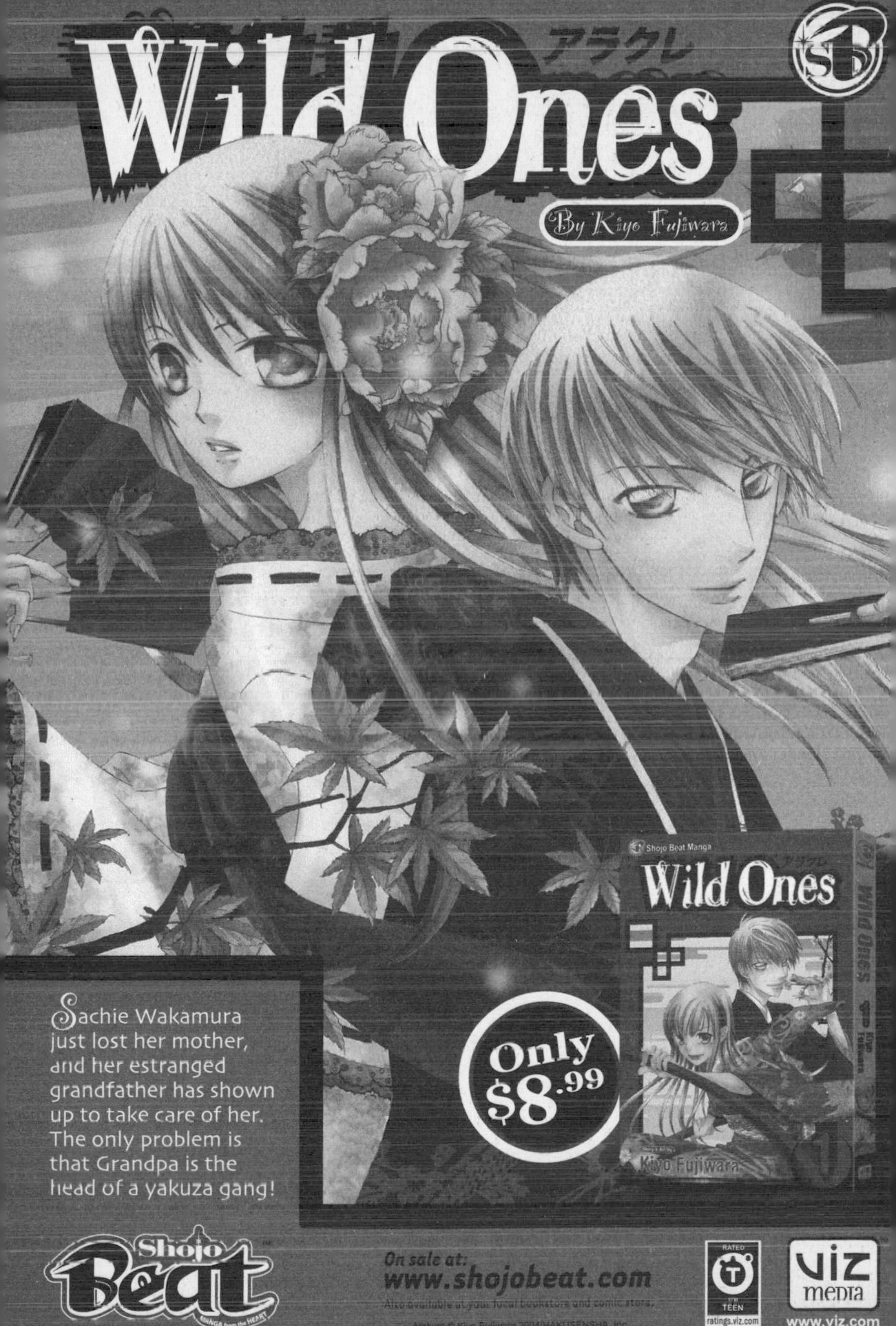
Wild Ones
アラクレ
By Kiyo Fujiwara
Shojo Beat Manga
Wild Ones
Kiyo Fujiwara
Only $8.99
Sachie Wakamura just lost her mother, and her estranged grandfather has shown up to take care of her. The only problem is that Grandpa is the head of a yakuza gang!
Shojo Beat
MANGA from the HEART
On sale at:
www.shojobeat.com
Also available at your local bookstore and comic store.
Arakure © Kiyo Fujiwara 2004/HAKUSENSHA, Inc.
RATED T TEEN
ratings.viz.com
viz media
www.viz.com

LAND OF *Fantasy*

MIAKA YÛKI IS AN ORDINARY JUNIOR-HIGH STUDENT WHO IS SUDDENLY WHISKED AWAY INTO THE WORLD OF A BOOK, *THE UNIVERSE OF THE FOUR GODS*. WILL THE BEAUTIFUL CELESTIAL BEINGS SHE ENCOUNTERS AND THE CHANCE TO BECOME A PRIESTESS DIVERT MIAKA FROM EVER RETURNING HOME?

THREE VOLUMES OF THE ORIGINAL *FUSHIGI YÛGI* SERIES COMBINED INTO A LARGER FORMAT WITH AN EXCLUSIVE COVER DESIGN AND BONUS CONTENT

EXPERIENCE THE BEAUTY OF *FUSHIGI YÛGI* WITH THE HARDCOVER ART BOOK

ALSO AVAILABLE: THE *FUSHIGI YÛGI: GENBU KAIDEN* MANGA, THE EIGHT VOLUME PREQUEL TO THIS BEST-SELLING FANTASY SERIES

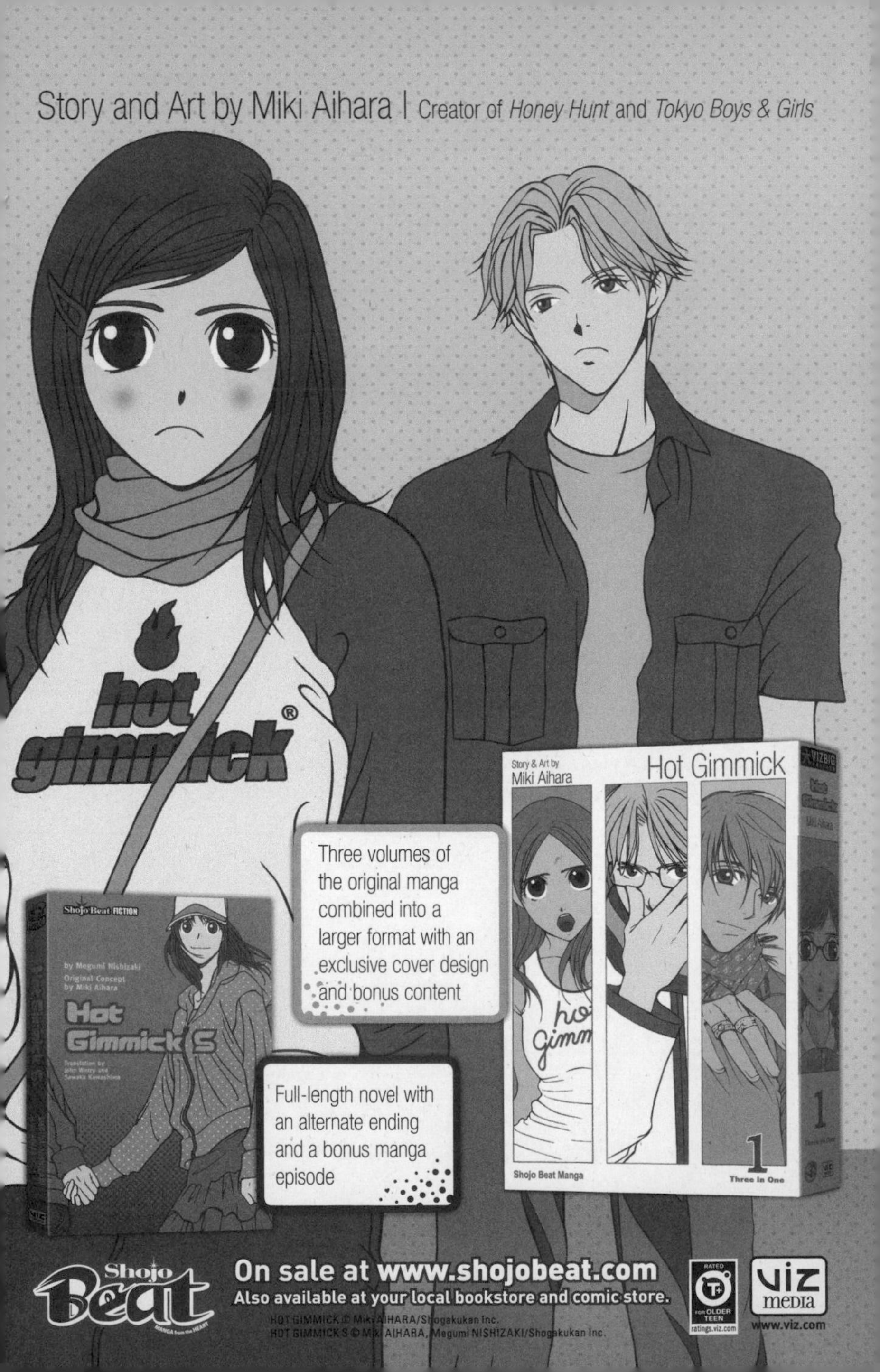
Story and Art by Miki Aihara | Creator of Honey Hunt and Tokyo Boys & Girls
hot gimmick®
Three volumes of the original manga combined into a larger format with an exclusive cover design and bonus content
Story & Art by Miki Aihara
Hot Gimmick
1
Three in One
Shojo Beat Manga
Shojo Beat FICTION
by Megumi Nishizaki
Original Concept by Miki Aihara
Hot Gimmick S
Full-length novel with an alternate ending and a bonus manga episode
Shojo Beat
On sale at www.shojobeat.com
Also available at your local bookstore and comic store.
HOT GIMMICK © Miki AIHARA/Shogakukan Inc.
HOT GIMMICK S © Miki AIHARA, Megumi NISHIZAKI/Shogakukan Inc.
RATED T+ FOR OLDER TEEN
ratings.viz.com
VIZ media
www.viz.com

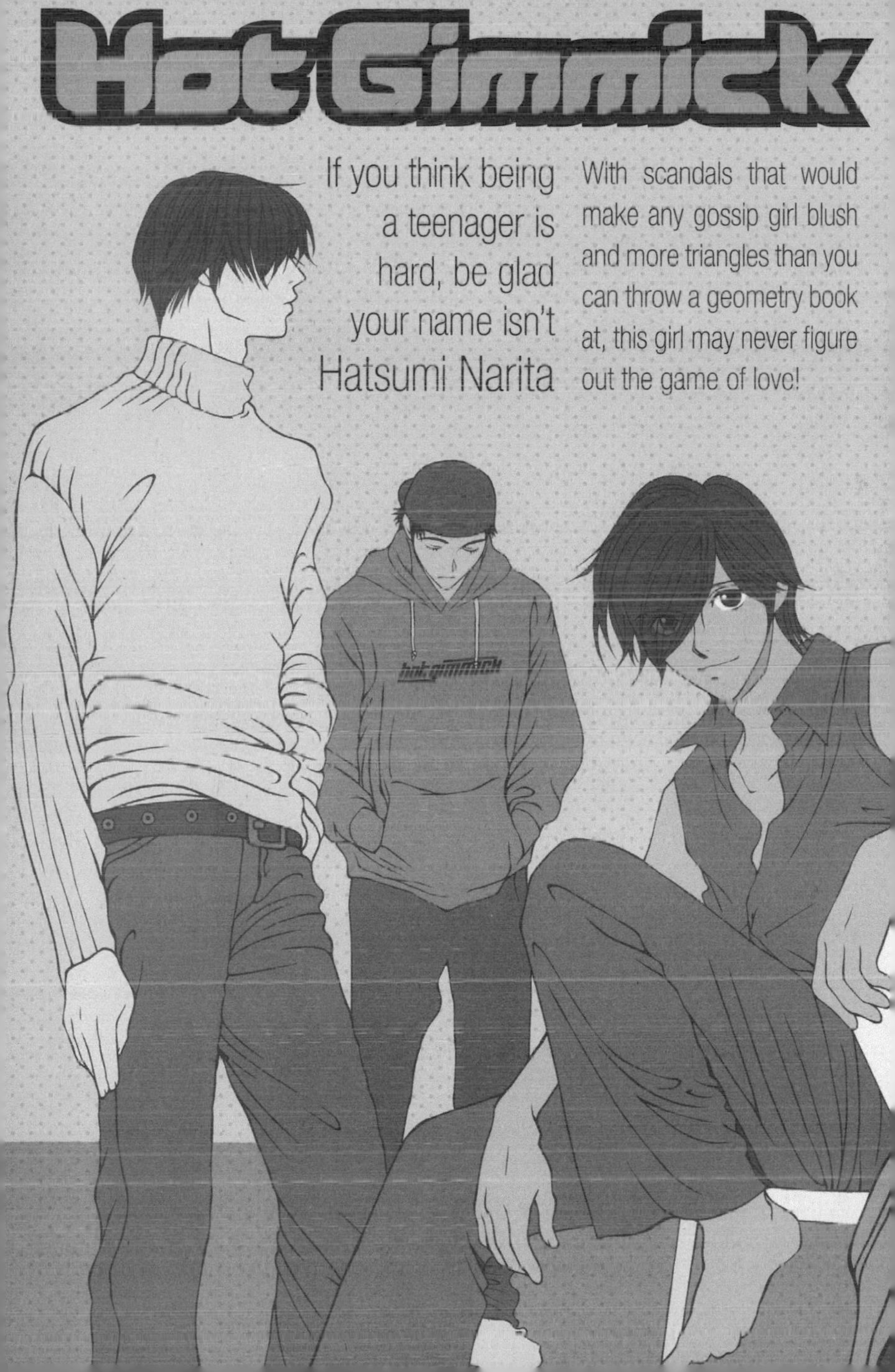
Hot Gimmick
If you think being a teenager is hard, be glad your name isn't Hatsumi Narita
With scandals that would make any gossip girl blush and more triangles than you can throw a geometry book at, this girl may never figure out the game of love!
hot gimmick

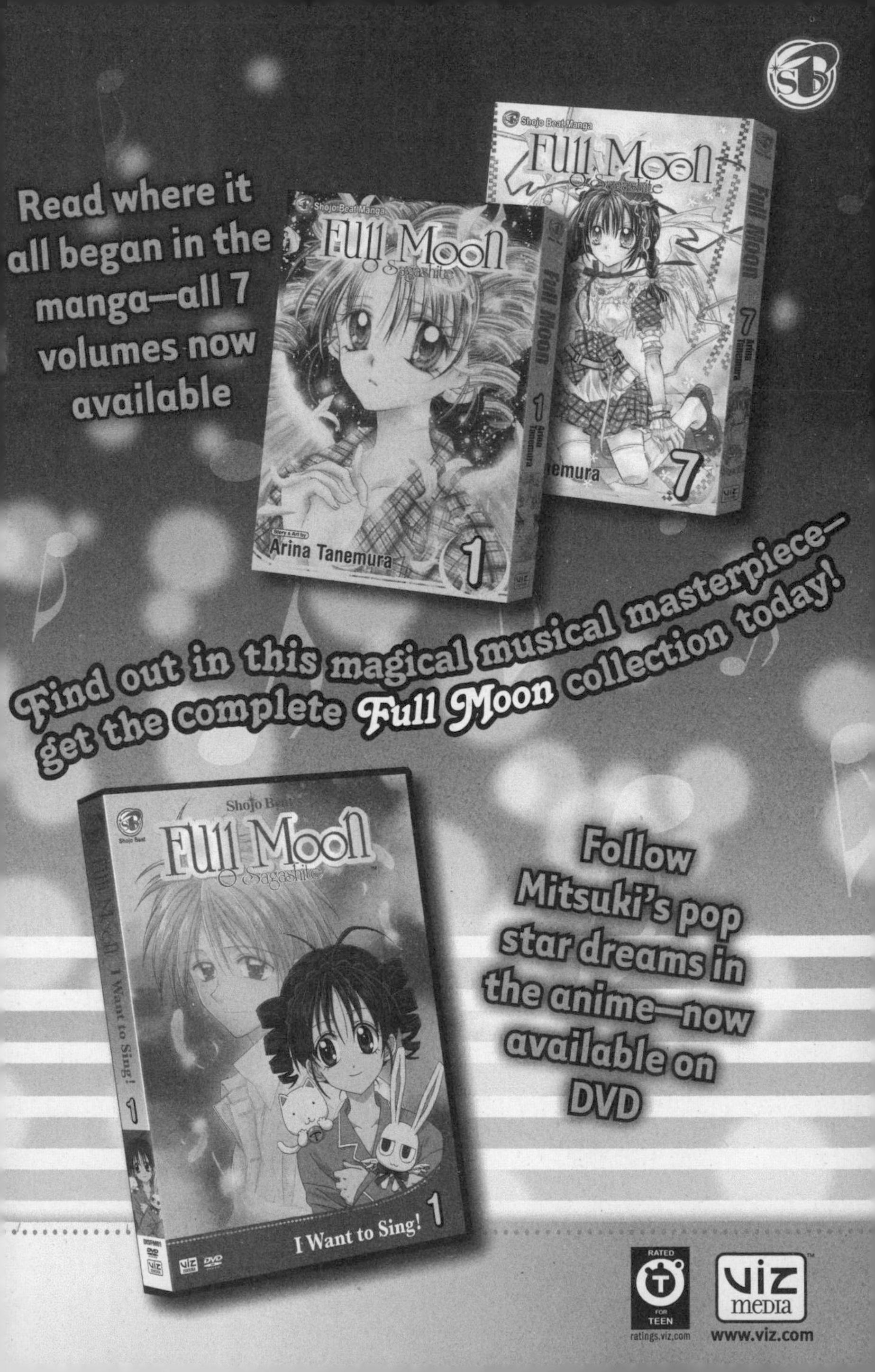
Read where it all began in the manga—all 7 volumes now available
Shojo Beat Manga
Full Moon o Sagashite
Story & Art by Arina Tanemura
1
7
Find out in this magical musical masterpiece—get the complete Full Moon collection today!
Shojo Beat
Full Moon o Sagashite
I Want to Sing! 1
Follow Mitsuki's pop star dreams in the anime—now available on DVD
RATED T FOR TEEN
ratings.viz.com
VIZ media
www.viz.com

FULL MOON
O Sagashite

By Arina Tanemura

creator of *The Gentlemen's Alliance †*

Mitsuki loves singing, but a malignant throat tumor prevents her from pursuing her passion.

Can two fun-loving Shinigami give her singing career a magical jump-start?

Tell us what you think about Shojo Beat Manga!

Our survey is now available online. Go to:

shojobeat.com/mangasurvey

Help us make our product offerings better!

THE REAL DRAMA BEGINS IN...